Claiming the City

Claiming the City

Protest, Crime, and Scandals in Colonial Calcutta, c. 1860–1920

ANINDITA GHOSH

OXFORD
UNIVERSITY PRESS

OXFORD
UNIVERSITY PRESS

Oxford University Press is a department of the University of Oxford. It furthers the University's objective of excellence in research, scholarship, and education by publishing worldwide. Oxford is a registered trademark of Oxford University Press in the UK and in certain other countries.

Published in India by
Oxford University Press
YMCA Library Building, 1 Jai Singh Road, New Delhi 110 001, India

First Edition published in 2016

ISBN-13: 978-0-19-946479-1
ISBN-10: 0-19-946479-0

Typeset in Scala Pro 10.5/13
by Tranistics Data Technologies, New Delhi 110 044
Printed in India by Rakmo Press, New Delhi 110 020

Contents

List of Figures vii
List of Tables viii
Acknowledgements ix

Introduction 1

1 Urban Space, Technology, and Community 37

2 Songs, the City, and the Everyday 86

3 Sexuality, Scandals, and the Urban Order 123

4 Battle for the Streets: Contesting Municipal Regimes 163

5 Criminality, Class, and Moral Anxieties 207

6 Collective Protest and Riots 248

Conclusion 292

Bibliography 299
Index 319
About the Author 329

Figures

I.1	A Police Map of Calcutta Showing the Various Administrative Districts Together with Population Figures at the End of the Nineteenth Century	11
1.1	Mud and Bamboo *Bustees* in the Foreground with 'Streetless Better-Class Property' at the Back	45
1.2	*Ghaut* [*sic*] and Temples on the Banks of the Hooghly, 1851 (Hand-Coloured Photographic Print by Frederick Fiebig)	59
1.3	Advertisement for the Original Edition of Harisadhan Mukhopadhyay, *Kolikata Sekaler O Ekaler* (Calcutta, 1915), Showing the Town Hall and Factories on the Right and Bengali Temples and Villages on the Left	60
2.1	Ships Were Actually Thrown Up on the Shore by the 1864 Cyclone	108
2.2	The Pontoon Bridge on the Hooghly, Calcutta; Johnston and Hoffman, Postcard from the 1890s	116
3.1	Courtroom Scene of the Elokeshi Murder Case, Kalighat Painting, c. 1875	129
4.1	Mid-day Traffic on Canning Street in Calcutta's Premium Business District, 1914	172
4.2	Chitpore Road with Trams Running in 1914. Narrow Footpaths Compound the Difficulty of the Pedestrians	177

Tables

4.1 Injury and Death Rates in Traffic Accidents in Calcutta in 1914 178
4.2 Convictions and Fines for Municipal Conservancy Offences by Year 185

Acknowledgements

This book started as what I thought was a controlled research project until it acquired a life of its own, holding me captive to its whims and wishes; stretching me as an author trying to write a book and not a magnum opus as I constantly reminded myself; and getting derailed twice—when my two children were born—enough, one would think, to make me give up. Strangely though, this proved a virtue. As I mulled and toyed with my ideas over the years, I was increasingly certain that this was to be as it was to be. The sprawling scope of the monograph was definitely a challenge, as was the subject matter. I had to retell a very familiar story from an unfamiliar angle, while risking the wrath of middle-class Bengalis to whom the city of Calcutta has traditionally signified a collective self-representation. To suggest that the city could be as much claimed by scavengers, prostitutes, and criminals as intellectual giants like Rabindranath Tagore and Rammohun Roy was to invite a hail of recrimination from those who are fiercely proud of its outstanding cultural heritage. What I offer here, however, is another perspective, a parallel one—of a city that was built as much by the labour, imaginations, and aspirations of the lower social rungs as the elites and aristocrats like the Roys and the Tagores. This book is, in part, dedicated to the city of Calcutta where I grew up, a place I have loved and hated over the years, and that I have come to rediscover through my archives.

As with all long projects, the list of people and institutions to thank have piled up over the years. I am, first, grateful to my home institution, the University of Manchester, for allowing me time off to research during my two sabbatical leaves. A faculty research grant gave me the initial opportunity to conduct preliminary researches into British and Indian archives. A major grant (British Academy Research Development Award) from the British Academy and a two-year leave period later helped me to get the project off the ground. I am grateful to the staff of the British Library (London), the National Library, Calcutta Centre for Studies in Social Sciences, and the West Bengal State Archives (all in Kolkata) for their kind help and co-operation throughout the duration of this project. Permissions granted by some of these libraries have enabled me to include invaluable images of nineteenth- and twentieth-century Calcutta in this book. A shorter and different version of Chapter 2, 'Singing in a New World: Street Songs and Urban Experience in Colonial Calcutta', was published in the *History Workshop Journal*, issue 76, Autumn 2013, pp. 111–36. The editorial team at Oxford University Press were extremely supportive. My thanks are due to them for their superb efforts and understanding throughout.

I am indebted to colleagues and friends who at various stages heard my ideas, read drafts, acted as priceless sounding boards, and fed back their comments. Thanks to Sumanta Banerjee, C.A. Bayly (who had immense trust in this work but sadly could not see it completed), Tanika Sarkar, Crispin Bates, Sunil Amrith, Clare Anderson, Tilman Frasch, David Arnold, Peter Robb, Deana Heath, Riho Isaka, and Chandak Sengoopta for their generous time.

Friends at Manchester strengthened me with their friendship, laughter, and support. Anastasia Valassopoulos, Natalie Zacek, Peter Gatrell, Patrick Joyce, Laurence Brown, Steven Pierce, and Yangwen Zheng were faithful and believed in me.

Finally, this book would not have been done without the staunch and loving support of the family back in India—especially my parents—and the more demanding but steadfastly loyal family inhabiting my world here in Manchester. Gayatri and Dhiman arrived to turn my life upside down in the most pleasant ways possible. Thanks are also due to Partha for his patience, constant encouragement, and understanding that kept me going. There was another book project that ran alongside mine when I was finishing this monograph, as Dhiman feverishly put together a 'book of facts and stories' with all the indomitable energies of a five year old and that Gayatri promptly undertook to publish on a Mac. To these young authors and publishers in the family I dedicate this book.

Anindita Ghosh

Introduction

As the administrative and commercial capital of British India and the earliest experiment in modern urbanization in the sub-continent, Calcutta posed an enormous challenge to both its residents and its architects. This book is structured around a set of key questions concerning space, popular culture, and everyday practices in colonial Calcutta in the nineteenth and early twentieth centuries. It investigates the role of the city in fundamentally reconfiguring the social, cultural, and moral landscapes of its diverse inhabitants, while itself being constituted of their complex practices, negotiations, and imaginations. Emerging discourses on sexuality, gender, crime, and community are analysed to reveal tensions and anxieties, exacerbated by the entry of new social actors—migrants, women, and subalterns—in the dense urban milieu. The work makes use of some specific entry points to unpack these sensibilities: a series of sensational scandals erupting in the city; the streets as arenas of social and political protest; the impact of technology on the new urban order and shifting definitions of crime and the new municipal and urban laws. Materially this is situated in the midst of actual physical changes to the city's everyday spaces—in the layout of bridges, drains, tramways, parks, and streetlights.

Scholars have routinely used Calcutta as a backdrop for tracing historical processes, but the city itself has rarely been the focus of their attention. Calcutta in extant historical literature floats between two dated approaches, one which views the city as a sum of aggregates, trade and population data,[1] and another which sees

[1] See, for example, Pradip Sinha (ed.), *The Urban Experience: Calcutta* (Calcutta: Riddhi-India, 1987).

it as the product of Western education, modern civic institutions, and a cultural regeneration[2]—both uncritical assimilations from colonial records. The overwhelming image still is that of an otherwise orderly city with a chaotic native quarter spilling over its boundaries.[3] The present work breaks this impasse by passing such representations through the lens of the city's indigenous population to offer competing ideas and self-images.

An unqualified assumption of Calcutta as a British creation produces problematic narratives of glorified British agency on the one hand and Bengali passivity on the other. As in the case of other colonial cities too, an inordinate emphasis in architectural and planning studies on static buildings and landscapes as self-evident histories of a city, and therefore, its people, perpetuates such notions.[4] Additionally, the inclination to examine colonial cities as caught in the web of imperial, global capitalism limits indigenous initiative in colonial territories.[5]

[2] See David Kopf, *British Orientalism and the Bengal Renaissance* (Berkeley and Los Angeles: University of California Press, 1969); V.C. Joshi (ed.), *Rammohun Roy and the Process of Modernization in India* (Delhi: Vikas Publishing House, 1975).

[3] Most recently, Sumanta Banerjee, *The Parlour and the Streets: Elite and Popular Culture in Nineteenth Century Calcutta* (Calcutta: Seagull Books, 1989).

[4] See, for example, Thomas Metcalf, *An Imperial Vision: Indian Architecture and Britain's Raj* (Berkeley and Los Angeles: University of California Press, 1989); Veena Talwar Oldenburg, *The Making of Colonial Lucknow, 1857–1877* (Princeton, NJ: Princeton University Press, 1984); Mariam Dossal, *Imperial Designs and Indian Realities: The Planning of Bombay City, 1845–1875* (New York: Oxford University Press, 1991). The more recent work by Glover on Lahore combines both social and built spaces within its ambit, but ultimately adopts the same approach. See William Glover, *Making Lahore Modern: Constructing and Imagining a Colonial City* (Minneapolis: University of Minnesota Press, 2007).

[5] Parimal Ghosh, *Colonialism, Class and a History of the Calcutta Jute Millhands, 1880–1930* (Chennai: Orient Longman, 2000); Sandip Hazareesingh, *The Colonial City and the Challenge of Modernity: Urban Hegemonies and Civic Contestations in Bombay City, 1900–1925* (Hyderabad: Orient Longman, 2007).

Modernization in the colonial context did not represent the inexorable unfolding of industrial capitalism or 'Westernization'.[6] Rather, it was a contested and contingent process that was born out of the market, state and politics, urbanization, and rapid technological change on the one hand and differential urban experiences, social and moral anxieties, and a 'shock of the new' on the other.[7] In particular, the book highlights the manner in which the turbulent changes unleashed by European modernity were negotiated, appropriated, or resisted by the colonized at every turn.[8]

Calcutta in the nineteenth century was the product as much of British as of Indian imagination. The dominant colonial image of an otherwise orderly city being constantly threatened by an unruly and disease-ridden Indian section is sufficiently compromised when placed alongside Bengali understandings and expectations of public space and property, communal living, bodily practices, and social hierarchies. In contemporary nationalist imagination, the city, for instance, represented exploitation, corruption, and decadence, while the ancestral rural home was a haven of peace. Parallel representations proliferating in popular culture—as a city sporting awesome modern bridges and streetlights and offering sizzling night-time entertainment—further complicate the picture. To this end, while making use of the rather overused but important colonial archive, my study also embraces

[6] An excellent example of this being evidenced in the introduction of science and technology to colonial India is shown by Gyan Prakash, *Another Reason: Science and the Imagination of Modern India* (Princeton, NJ: Princeton University Press, 1999). Janaki Nair has applied this paradigm to the specific study of modern Indian cities such as Bangalore. See her *The Promise of the Metropolis: Bangalore's Twentieth Century* (New Delhi: Oxford University Press, 2005).

[7] This is a play on the title of David Edgerton's recent work, *Shock of the Old: Technology and Global History since 1900* (London: Profile Books Limited, 2006), where he highlights the uses of technology in a globalized world, putting innovations in the context of their usages.

[8] Brenda Yeoh's engaging study of colonial Singapore offers an excellent example of these contested processes in another context. See Brenda S.A. Yeoh, *Contesting Space in Colonial Singapore: Power Relations and the Urban Built Environment* (Singapore: Singapore University Press, 2003).

a range of indigenous primary sources such as vernacular writings, scandal and topical literature, popular paintings, and songs.

The present study is deliberately strung lower to take into account not just the responses of the educated bhadralok (literally, gentlefolk) groups, but also various other layers of city life—equally representative, but not so strongly visible in historical literature—such as subalterns and the lower middling orders, women, and migrant communities. Popular culture airing scandals (for example, the Elokeshi–Mohunta case of 1874 where a wife was beheaded by her husband for straying) and topical themes (for example, the Contagious Diseases Act and the cyclone of 1864) with serious social and political concerns, and the coming of technology to the city (for example, songs on the Howrah Bridge), the work demonstrates, brought together such lower and middling social groups in shared constituencies for reflection, critique, and contestation of the contemporary urban experience.

Calcutta: The City and Its History

Calcutta in cultural and social history of the nineteenth and twentieth centuries remains by and large polarized between its depiction as a crucible of liberalism, enlightenment, and nationalism on the one hand and a hell-hole of mass squalor, exploitative capitalism, and radical labour movements on the other. Even Swati Chattopadhyay's otherwise thought-provoking study of colonial Calcutta, while highlighting reception theory, limits itself by examining educated middle-class responses to the city.[9] While the urban poor have not been entirely neglected within this larger story of industrialization and modernity, as evident in detailed studies of labour historians, it would be fair to say that the obvious concern has rarely been Calcutta except as a location for their studies.[10]

[9] Swati Chattopadyay, *Representing Calcutta: Modernity, Nationalism and the Colonial Uncanny* (London and New York: Routledge, 2005).

[10] Dipesh Chakrabarty, *Rethinking Working Class History, Bengal 1890–1940* (Princeton: Princeton University Press, 1989); Parimal Ghosh, *History of the Calcutta Jute Millhands*; Subho Basu, *Does Class Matter? Colonial Capital and Workers' Resistance in Bengal, 1890–1937* (New Delhi: Oxford University Press, 2004).

The social history of the city has also been explored in another context—that of the play of forces of capital, urban planning, trade, and migration. From the politics of municipal bodies to the vested interests of business groups, Calcutta seems caught up in inexorable economic forces that shape its destiny.[11] The changing nature of the city's population is explained in terms of land acquisition patterns and the shifting exigencies of planners.[12] Despite some recent attempts to view the emergent metropolis as made up of certain social imaginations and community cultures, sustained inroads into the cultural history of urban collectivities and the ways in which they animated the urban public sphere are lacking in the context of Calcutta.[13]

Sumanta Banerjee's scholarship has perhaps been the only notable and consistent exception to this trend. From his pathbreaking work on popular culture in the city to his study of prostitutes and most recent explorations of crime and punishment in colonial Calcutta, Banerjee presents the picture of a

[11] Rajat K. Ray, *Urban Roots of Indian Nationalism: Pressure Groups and Conflict of Interests in Calcutta City Politics, 1875–1939* (New Delhi: Vikas, 1979); T. Stewart Gordon, *Jute and Empire: The Calcutta Jute Wallahs and the Landscapes of Empire* (Manchester: Manchester University Press, 1998); Stephen J. Hornsby, 'Discovering the Mercantile City in South Asia: The Example of Early Nineteenth Century Calcutta', *Journal of Historical Geography* 23, no. 2 (1997): 135–50.

[12] Pradip Sinha, *Calcutta in Urban History* (Calcutta: Firma K.L. Mukhopadhyay, 1978); Norma Evenson, *The Indian Metropolis: A View Towards the West* (New Haven and London: Yale University Press, 1989); Samita Gupta, 'Theory and Practice of Town Planning in Calcutta 1817–1912: An Appraisal', *Indian Economic and Social History Review* 30, no. 1 (1993): 29–55.

[13] Sumit Sarkar, 'The City Imagined' in *Writing Social History* (New Delhi: Oxford University Press, 1999); Anne Hardgrove, *Community and Public Culture: The Marwaris in Calcutta, c. 1897–1997* (New Delhi: Oxford University Press, 2004); Suchetana Chattopadhyay, 'War, Migration and Alienation in Colonial Calcutta: The Remaking of Muzaffar Ahmad', *History Workshop Journal* 64, no. 1 (2007): 212–39.

vibrant and vocal subaltern world in the colonial metropolis.[14] The profiles of prostitutes, criminals, and street artistes reveal how the city offered multifarious opportunities for its less prosperous residents to engage with and participate in the thriving urban cultural economy. Their activities and presence in the city, however, Banerjee shows, were a cause of tension to the local administration who acted purposefully, therefore, to limit their influence.

While useful, such a narrative bypasses the important contributions to the urban world made by these subaltern actors. In their social, cultural, and political contributions, this book shows, the streets and social margins of the city had a vital role to play in shaping the urban public sphere. Thus, scandal stories circulating in popular culture fixed social imaginaries on domesticity and sexuality, everyday violation of civic rules curbed municipal expectations, and collective protest against the police harnessed anti-government sentiments in significant ways.

Two other works have pushed this book in the direction it has taken. Tanika Sarkar's deeply insightful essay on the Elokeshi–Mohunta scandal involving adultery and murder showed the ways in which, from the 1870s onwards, the urban public sphere was reaching much further down the social levels to draw in an increasing community of readers and participants who were evidently deeply animated by the social and conjugal concerns thrown up by the incident.[15] Arguably while not directly concerned with either subalterns or urban cultures, Sumit Sarkar's monumental study of the Swadeshi Movement of 1905 offered an astounding narrative of the transformation of ordered, authoritarian urban spaces during mass nationalist demonstrations.[16]

[14] Sumanta Banerjee, *The Parlour and the Streets*; *Dangerous Outcast: The Prostitute in Nineteenth Century Bengal* (Calcutta: Seagull Books, 1998); *The Wicked City: Crime and Punishment in Colonial Calcutta* (New Delhi: Orient Blackswan, 2009).

[15] Tanika Sarkar, 'Talking about Scandals: Religion, Law and Love in Late Nineteenth Century Bengal', *Studies in History* 13, no. 1 (1997): 63–95.

[16] Sumit Sarkar, *The Swadeshi Movement in Bengal* (New Delhi: Oxford University Press, 2011; original edition 1973).

Methodologically, it suggested the possibility of reading a city not just in its built-up environment but in the actions of its residents. The teeming swadeshi shops that sprang up alongside the European establishments, passionate meetings in the hitherto rather exclusive spaces of the Town Hall and Maidan, and the vast crowds of flag-waving and singing students who marched in processions down Calcutta's streets had a dramatic impact on the city's self-imagination. As the twentieth century progressed, it was clear that mass protests on streets had come to stay in urban India.

Calcutta's importance for British India in the nineteenth century cannot be overstated. The city was the hub of commerce and trade. The principal organs of the government—the army, judiciary, and bureaucracy—all had their headquarters in Calcutta. Originally starting out as a small trading outpost in the late seventeenth century, the city grew in size and impact after the East India Company captured power in the region following the deposition of the nawab of Bengal in 1757. With its spacious European classical-style villas lining the eastern and southern reaches, and official buildings along the Esplanade marking the nerve-centre of British trade and administration, it was a city that evoked a sense of grandeur and elegance, giving rise to the expression 'City of Palaces' in the eighteenth century. Its rapid growth, stretching longitudinally along the banks of the Hooghly, also saw segregation in the residential settlement pattern—with a White Town of largely European inhabitants populating the area surrounding the fort, and a teeming Black Town peopled by Indians squeezed into the northern part of the city.[17] Although the areas were not strictly speaking hermetic, yet, the segregated city provided a conceptual template for colonial

[17] It should be said, however, that the distinction did not ultimately survive as strongly as perhaps intended. The areas ran into each other in the east, where, as Pradip Sinha describes it, an 'intermediate' zone thrived, peopled by mixed race and diverse mercantile populations such as Armenians and Greeks, as well as those offering menial labour like servants, milkmen, and washermen. See his *Calcutta in Urban History*, pp. 7–8.

urbanism that structured the organization of space as we shall see in this book.[18]

Pradip Sinha describes the state of the city in the beginning of the eighteenth century as a conglomeration of different functionalities:

> In the embryonic state of its development ... Calcutta consisted of a European Calcutta (part of *Dihi Kalikata*), a residential village with some sacred traits (Gobindapur), a traditional Indian Bazar settlement (later Burrabazar), and a riverine mart (Sutanati). These were surrounded by peripheral hamlets (*dihis*), forming a varied range of agricultural and fishing settlements, sacred spots, trading halts or nodal points and jungles of various densities.[19]

As the urban areas began to grow and spread, the various component units mutated and interpenetrated each other while retaining some of the older features. Over time, the fort declined in importance as an organizational nucleus while the central bazaar or Burrabazar took that position.

Attracting a great deal of trade from both the hinterland and overseas, Calcutta gained increasing prominence in the late eighteenth and early nineteenth centuries. Cosmopolitan trade drew a cosmopolitan population and Portuguese, Persians, Jews, Greeks, Armenians, and racially mixed groups lived in impoverished neighbourhoods between the Black and White Towns. Functionality replaced the traditional caste-ordered layout as did the land and property market. Hectic building activity and land purchase in Calcutta from the mid-eighteenth to the early nineteenth century, and the housing of tenants in such property, remarks Sinha, added to the cosmopolitanism.[20] Slums also grew alongside the White settlements, filled with service providers, servants, and manual labourers.

[18] For studies that have questioned the 'Black–White' divide, see R.M. Brown, 'The Cemeteries and the Suburbs', *Journal of Urban History* 29, no. 2 (2003): 151–72; Swati Chattopadyay, *Representing Calcutta*, pp. 126–32; and J. Heitzman, *The City in South Asia* (London and New York: Routledge, 2008), pp. 118–23.

[19] P. Sinha, *Calcutta in Urban History*, p. 7.

[20] P. Sinha, *Calcutta in Urban History*, pp. 15, 16–17.

Comparing maps of the city devised for census and survey purposes between 1850 and 1901, it is possible to see how Calcutta had grown at a breathtaking speed within a span of just fifty years, with the total acreage increasing from about 5,000 to 13,000 during the period.[21] Population figures show a commensurate increase, from over 200,000 in 1837 to nearly 900,000 in 1911.[22] Following the pioneering attempts of the governor-general, Lord Wellesley, and the use of lottery funds to improve Calcutta in 1817, the revenues of the Municipal Corporation rose considerably, and these could be ploughed back into the city's infrastructure.[23] Metal roads, water supply, oil lighting, and drainage works initiated the process.[24]

The city up until the 1870s developed in fits and starts. But from the 1870s onwards more dramatic and visible improvements took place. The Howrah (pontoon) Bridge was constructed across the River Hooghly in 1874; sewers and underground drains were extended from the 1870s onwards; the Strand Bank was widened to accommodate warehouses towards the north of the city; new open squares were built to ensure open spaces in crowded areas; horse-drawn trams (and omnibuses) were introduced from the 1880s; and finally, electric lighting and trams arrived from 1900 onwards, as did motor cars, telephones, and bicycles.[25] These innovations not only radically altered the everyday sensory and material landscape of the city, but also had a fundamental impact on people's lifestyles, social imaginaries, and occupations.[26]

[21] A.K. Roy, 'Short History of Calcutta: Town and Suburbs', *1901 Census*, vol. 7, part I, pp. 52–3.

[22] See A.K. Roy, 'Short History of Calcutta', p. 63; *Census of the Town of Calcutta* (1911), p. 2.

[23] Income thus rose from Rs 419,167 in 1850 to Rs 5,786,580 in 1901; A.K. Roy, 'Short History of Calcutta', p. 64.

[24] The first metalled roads were being built 1820 onwards, while lighting was introduced under the Lottery Committee. Drainage works started in 1859, and clean water supply arrived the following year. See A.K. Roy, 'Short History of Calcutta', pp. 74, 77–9.

[25] A.K. Roy, 'Short History of Calcutta', pp. 80–2, 86.

[26] Generally neglected in the modernity narratives of the subcontinent, except as tools of control and exploitation (for example, Daniel

Technology as a theme threads through many of the chapters in this book, highlighting its mobilizations, contestations, and accommodations.

The built-up area of the city too grew enormously during this period with newer architectural glories such as the High Court, Writers' Building, Imperial Secretariat, and Treasury buildings, joining older ones such as the Bank of Bengal, the Mint, and the Town Hall, dotting the business and administrative quarters, the central area of the city dominated by Europeans. Together with the British-owned jute mills lining the banks of the River Hooghly to the west and the hub of business houses, banks, and government buildings, Calcutta represented the heart of British interests in trade and capital in the sub-continent and eastwards, and the symbol of its resounding success.

The northern and western parts of Calcutta formed the Black Town inhabited by the Indian population. In European official and travel literature, it comprised narrow lanes and overcrowded living quarters with filth accumulating at the sides of streets, and drains 'mere excavations by the roadside' (see Figure I.1).[27] The accounts deliberately overlook the thriving marts, religious centres, popular festivals, and communalities that animated life in these parts. In this study (Chapter 1), however, they become useful filters for understanding the experiences of the Indian inhabitants.

Headrick, *Tentacles of Progress: Technology Transfer in the Age of Imperialism, 1850–1940* [New York: Oxford University Press, 1988]; Deep Kanta Lahiri-Choudhury, *Telegraphic Imperialism: Crisis and Panic in the Indian Empire, c. 1830–1920* [Basingstoke: Palgrave Macmillan, 2010]), technology has been put on the centre stage of the history of urbanity and modernity in recent works. See David Arnold, *Everyday Technology: Machines and the Making of India's Modernity* (Chicago: University of Chicago Press, 2013). As excellent studies of technology at the intersections of political, cultural, and social power networks in modern cities, see Thomas P. Hughes, *Networks of Power* (Baltimore and London: Johns Hopkins University Press, 1983); Mark Rose, *Cities of Light and Heat* (University Park, PA: Penn State University Press, 1995).

27 A.K. Roy, 'Short History of Calcutta', p. 100.

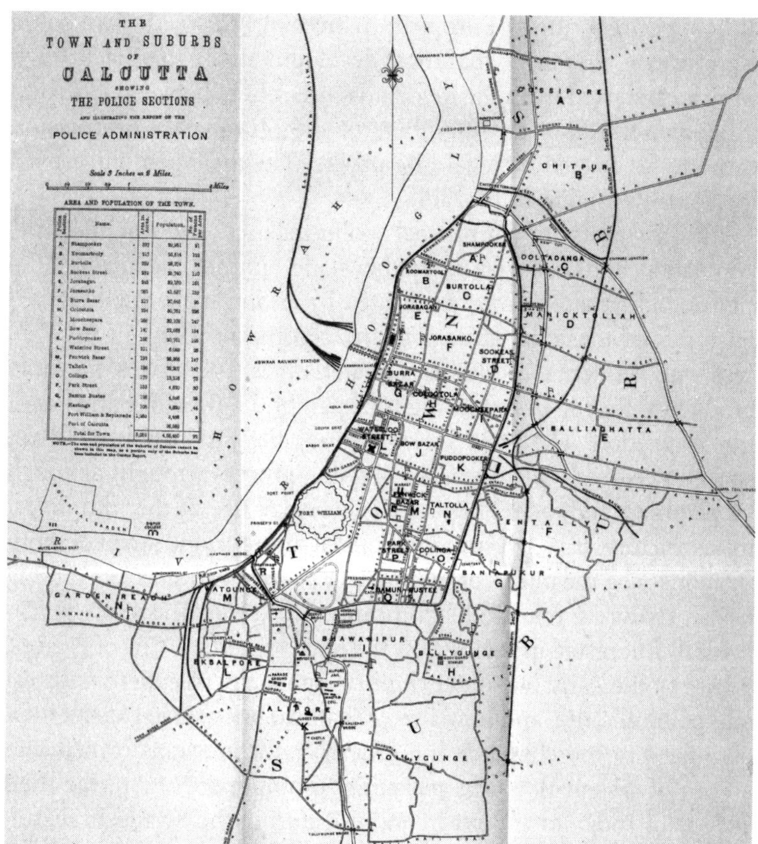

FIGURE I.1 A Police Map of Calcutta Showing the Various Administrative Districts Together with Population Figures at the End of the Nineteenth Century

Source: Annual Police Report, 1896. IOR/V/24/3215 © The British Library Board. Courtesy of the British Library, London.

Over time, the two areas became less distinctive, but the informal racialized division of the city, as we shall see in Chapter 4, did guide the layout of the city's infrastructure, with the amenities taking a much longer time to migrate to the Indian quarters once they had been introduced in the White Town. The Municipal Corporation from 1856 onwards and its earlier incarnations were almost entirely run by European Justices of Peace.[28] It is of some significance, therefore, that most developments in the Black Town were kick-started from the 1870s onwards when, between 1876 and 1899, two-thirds of the members of the Municipal Commission came to be elected by local rate payers. The arrangement proved too controversial to last for long.

But accounts of municipal policymaking and architecture, population, and trade give us a rather static, enumerable image of the city unfolding along lines predicated by an inevitable modernity.[29] Histories of tensions, struggles, and accommodations in the process with resident communities, materialities, and spaces are more productive for me in rendering transparent the fraught narrative of modernization. The book seeks to study the production of urban space in colonial Calcutta as an ongoing process wrought as much by planning and technology as the everyday use of this municipal infrastructure, through rumour, scandal, murder, and street demonstrations. The meanings of the spaces I study shift with their varying usage, changing role, and significance over time. The study is particularly interested in seeing how the once proverbial 'City of Palaces' turns, by the early twentieth century, into a city of endemic unrest and political strife, and how streets that had once served as the thoroughfares of merchandise and orderly traffic are transformed into arenas of violent riots and picketing, prompting Curzon, the then viceroy of India, to cry out in anguish during the Swadeshi disturbances of 1905 that he did not recognize Calcutta any more.

Cities, Communities, and the Colonial Urban Order

Moving outside the Bengal context, urban histories of colonial India have traditionally been considered within the rigid framework of

[28] An elected Indian element was introduced in 1848 in a new Commission for the Improvement of Calcutta, but did not last very long, being superseded in 1863 by an entirely government-nominated body of Justices of Peace. Ranjit Sen, *A Stagnating City: Calcutta in the Eighteenth Century* (Calcutta: Institute of Historical Studies, 2000), pp. 26–7, 65–6.

[29] Even Partho Datta's recent and meticulous study, while offering an excellent account of urban planning in Calcutta, highlights the relentless

political economy[30] or dominant colonial ideologies.[31] A selection of studies in the 1970s focused on the urban origins of modern politics and Indian nationalism in the subcontinent, but in this they were concerned with the larger processes at work rather than the specific local contexts of the cities themselves.[32] A much later approach that is closer to my interest emerged a few decades later when scholars started to explore the public culture of Indian cities in the colonial period, analysing the dynamics of collective mobilization, symbolical culture, and power politics—a point explored in further detail below.[33]

The last decade has witnessed a renewed and reinvigorated interest in South Asian cities resulting in some interesting scholarship. Studies of both colonial and post-colonial cities

---

ascendancy of colonial authority in the city. See Partho Datta, *Planning the City: Urbanisation and Reform in Calcutta, c. 1800–c. 1940* (New Delhi: Tulika Books, 2012).

30 Morris D. Morris, *The Emergence of an Indian Labour Force: A Study of the Bombay Cotton Mills, 1854–1947* (Berkeley: University of California Press, 1965); R. Sen, *A Stagnating City*; P. Sinha, *The Urban Experience*.

31 Metcalf, *An Imperial Vision*; Dossal, *Imperial Designs and Indian Realities*; Susan Nield, 'Colonial Urbanism: The Development of Madras City in the Eighteenth and Nineteenth Centuries', *Modern Asian Studies* 13, no. 2 (1979): 217–46; Oldenburg, *The Making of Colonial Lucknow*; Narayani Gupta, *Delhi between Two Empires, 1803–1931: Society, Government and Urban Growth* (Delhi: Oxford University Press, 1981).

32 For example, Christine Dobbin, *Urban Leadership in Western India: Politics and Communities in Bombay City, 1840–85* (Oxford: Oxford University Press, 1972); C.A. Bayly, *The Local Roots of Indian Politics: Allahabad, 1870–1920* (Oxford: Oxford University Press, 1975); R.K. Ray, *Urban Roots of Indian Nationalism.*

33 See Sandria Freitag, *Collective Action and Community: Public Arenas and the Emergence of Communalism in North India* (New Delhi: Oxford University Press, 1990); Sandria Feitag (ed.), *Culture and Power in Banaras* (Berkeley, Los Angeles, and Oxford: University of California Press, 1989); Douglas Haynes, *Rhetoric and Ritual in Colonial India: The Shaping of a Public Culture in Surat City, 1852–1928* (Berkeley, Los Angeles, and Oxford: University of California Press, 1991).

have emerged, reflecting concerns varying from colonial governmentality[34] and labour/poor politics[35] to the churning of the multiple urban constituencies of the post-colonial state.[36] The abiding concern, however, in even most of the recent studies has been the state as an architect of 'modernity'—if not as a distinct structural form, then at least as an 'idea'—that in turn prompted responses of a certain kind from the various urban groups being studied, whether in the form of associational cultures such as in Prashant Kidambi's study of colonial Bombay, or local activism as in Janaki Nair's analysis of post-colonial Bangalore. Moving the focus beyond the structures of governance, this book argues, helps us locate the social history of a city that happened to be 'modern' and 'colonial'.

Communities, more specifically urban communities, are an important organizational category for me. Far from being finite entities with manageable borders, these appear in the study as dynamic collectivities that readily change orientations, limits, and loyalties, or hold ambiguous positions on seemingly closed issues and even defy the leadership. Social histories of the nineteenth and early twentieth centuries have predominantly worked with quantifiably and ideologically recognizable social constructs defined by caste, religion, nation, gender, and class, each seemingly transparent in purpose and action.

Nandini Gooptu's study of the urban poor in north India in the early twentieth century offers a robust challenge to such sociological paradigms.[37] In her meticulous analysis of four towns in north India during the interwar period, Gooptu presents the 'politics of

[34] Stephen Legg, *Spaces of Colonialism: Delhi's Urban Governmentalities* (Oxford: Blackwell Publishing, 2004); Prashant Kidambi, *The Making of an Indian Metropolis: Colonial Governance and Public Culture in Bombay, 1890–1920* (Aldershot: Ashgate Publications, 2007).

[35] Nandini Gooptu, *The Politics of the Urban Poor in Early Twentieth Century India* (Cambridge: Cambridge University Press, 2001); Chitra Joshi, *Lost Worlds: Indian Labour and Its Forgotten Histories* (New Delhi: Permanent Black, 2003).

[36] J. Nair, *The Promise of the Metropolis.*

[37] Gooptu, *Politics of the Urban Poor.*

the poor' as being shaped by both their immediate local environment and all-India movements and party politics. The 'poor' here emerge as not any given class category but a product of urban policies, elite rehabilitation programmes, populist caste and communal ideologies, and nationalist overtures. With its close focus on the radicalization and politicization of the urban poor, however, the work presents only a partial picture of the urban identity of these groups. In the current study, I bring the 'urban' firmly back in by fundamentally underlining the role of the city in shaping the perspectives and aspirations of its residents—political and otherwise.[38] Such an approach will help us appreciate the sea-change that was taking place in Indian towns and cities from the late nineteenth century onwards in terms of social structuring, discursive practices, and cultural imagining that helped embed the popular politics of caste, nation, and religion.

There have been emerging some provocative pointers within the work of labour historians which show that multiple registers for opening up given social constructs offer really instructive inroads into understanding collective consciousness.[39] Leela Fernandes and Samita Sen have shown how political processes are at work in shaping the struggles between managers and workers in the factory and how prevailing gender ideologies amongst trade union leaders limit the definitions of 'class' and devalue women's labour.[40] Elsewhere, Dipesh Chakrabarty's seminal

[38] For an excellent account of an activist and an intellectual being specifically transformed by his urban experiences of poverty, alienation (as a Muslim migrant), and police repression in Calcutta during the period of the First World War, see Suchetana Chattopadhyay, 'War, Migration and Alienation in Colonial Calcutta'.

[39] In wider literature too, class, in its limited sense, has come to be understood as only one of the many ways in which the social order is understood and interpreted. See, for example, Patrick Joyce (ed.), *Class: Oxford Reader* (Oxford: Oxford University Press, 1995).

[40] Leela Fernandes, *Producing Workers: The Politics of Gender, Class and Culture in the Calcutta Jute Mills* (Philadelphia: University of Pennsylvania Press, 1997); Samita Sen, *Women and Labour in Late Colonial India: The Bengal Jute Industry* (Cambridge: Cambridge University Press, 1999).

treatise on labour politics in the Bengal jute industry highlighted the importance of caste, religion, and region in informing working class consciousness in order to highlight its 'peculiarities'. Workers were thus also migrants with strong regional identities, as much as they were defined by their experience on the factory floor. Indeed, the labouring population often included occupational groups who were not permanently engaged in wage labour, but involved in petty trade, service occupations, and part-time farming. Caste and religion were other dimensions of the worker experience that came across during festivities, conflict, and leisure activities.[41]

This study forefronts urban experiences and urban identities in terms of lived lives of communities in the city through the forging of particular relationships with their material, social, and cultural environments. As the book shows, pressures engendered by city living impacted acutely on discourses surrounding gender and sexuality (Chapter 3), while apparent class and communal riots on the streets were a direct outcome of restriction of civic rights and privileges (Chapter 6). Crime too could not be just explained away any more by criminal typologies—of caste and class—spawned by the colonial regime. The lure of material wealth in Calcutta bred newer groups of sophisticated and educated law breakers from the end of the nineteenth century onwards (Chapter 5), prompting a rethinking of the sociology of crime.

Categories of class, caste, and religion too were configured in tandem with the urban experience, which gave such identities new contextual significance and immediacy. Competing for scarce resources while limited by colonial governance led to a sharpening of class tensions which often reinforced and even precipitated caste or religious differences. Equally, solidarities of class could be undercut by strong communitarian ties of region and religion of migrants in a harsh urban setting, as we shall

[41] D. Chakrabarty, *Rethinking Working Class History*. Subho Basu has challenged Chakrabarty's thesis more recently by showcasing a more dynamic presence of class categories in labour and nationalist politics during the end of the nineteenth and early decades of the twentieth century. See S. Basu, *Does Class Matter?*

see in the case of the 1891 and 1897 riots discussed in Chapter 6.[42] Communal loyalties on other occasions could be thrown aside just as easily as in the case of the anti-Marwari disturbances of 1918, where Hindus and Muslims joined hands against what was viewed as a corrupt business regime in the commercial capital of wartime British India. Even the educated bhadralok emerge in this study as not the usual nationalists or subaltern intelligentsia of postcolonial studies, but as ordinary tax-paying residents and landlords complaining about the inadequacies of the municipal regime, concerned witnesses of the rising levels of criminality and waywardness in the city, and the racist and unequal nature of urban policing.

Clearly then multiple identities and interests interacted with one another, cross-cutting other solidarities to make for shifting configurations of urban socialities—as tax payers, road users, plague victims, protesting students, and prostitutes. And yet, the thread that ties this all together is the city. Being in the city and shaped by its inescapable materiality, governance, social instability, and relative anonymity was an overwhelming experience for Calcutta's residents. It fundamentally changed the ways in which they viewed themselves and their world, and fed into their social, cultural, and political mindsets. Viewing urban communities as defined by class, caste, and religion alone, thus, seriously limits our understanding of their emerging political consciousness during our period, even though they emerge as a stronger presence in studies based in India of the 1920s and 1930s.

Being structurally constrained by one given set of sociological categories also considerably limits the opportunities of looking into another. In the case of Calcutta, there are two important aspects of its urban composition that I would like to mention

[42] See Arjan De Haan, 'Unsettled Settlers: Migrant Workers and Industrial Capitalism in Calcutta', *Modern Asian Studies* 31, no. 4 (1997): 919–49, for an excellent account of how caste, region, and religion informed social networks in Calcutta and the mill towns among the migrant population, which points to clear segmentations within class categories. The fact that they came from only certain districts in Bihar, Uttar Pradesh (UP), and Orissa helps explain the tighter cohesion. See *Census of the Town and Suburbs of Calcutta, 1881*, p. 41.

here. One is the predominant presence of immigrants in the city. Migrants had always populated this cosmopolitan city but the inflows increased considerably from the end of the nineteenth century onwards. While there was a significant presence of Bengalis born outside the city, 13.2 per cent of the total population came from Bihar, Uttar Pradesh (UP), and Orissa in 1881.[43] By 1921 this figure had risen to 50 per cent.[44] Hindi and Urdu spoken by the up-country migrants were therefore returned as the most commonly spoken languages in the city after Bengali in the census figures of the early twentieth century.[45] Their presence in urban spaces was heightened by the tendency to concentrate in certain areas. Wards such as Kalutola, Muchipara, Entally, Jorabagan, and Burrabazar, thus, registered a heavy presence of immigrants.

Migration radically altered the demographic profile of the city, with a large expansion of the ranks of the underprivileged, and their consequent emergence as a crucial social force. Also populating the mill-towns along the Hooghly and employed as factory labour, these uprooted poor urban groups repeatedly proved volatile and restive, quick to seize opportunities for redressing their grievances against the government or joining in targeted class and communal riots from the end of the nineteenth century onwards. But migrant men were also employed as traders, domestic servants, day-labourers, and clerks, with the higher castes dominating the government and clerical services, as well as the municipal police constabulary.[46] For Calcutta's Bengali residents, these populations represented additional claimants to an already pressurized world of job opportunities, leading to social tensions.

43 *Census of the Town and Suburbs of Calcutta, 1881*, p. 41.

44 *Census of India, 1921*, vol. 6, no. 1, p. 18. This figure included migrants from other regions as well.

45 By 1901, 36.3 per cent of the city's residents spoke Hindustani, while native Bengali speakers constituted barely more than half the population. *Census of India, 1901*, vol. 7, no. 4, p. 72. Also see *Census of the Town and Suburbs of Calcutta, 1911*, pp. 47–8.

46 *Census of the Town and Suburbs of Calcutta, 1911*, p. 17.

Besides, there was a huge migrant day population of workers—mostly clerks—who travelled daily to the city, taking advantage of newer rail and road connections. While existing river traffic was augmented by ferry steamer services along the Hooghly, the suburban railways opened up convenient routes into the city. The considerable increase in the sale of season tickets on the services connecting Calcutta with the suburbs and the surrounding districts is an evident indicator of this booming traffic.[47] Living on meagre salaries and exposed to the enslaving rigours of work life on the one hand and yet educated and articulate on the other, these groups formed some of the most sensitive chroniclers of city life for us as we shall see later.

The second point I would like to make is regarding the remarkably low number of women in the city. A defining characteristic of the urban population in Calcutta was its unequal sex ratio. In the 1881 census, men were returned twice as numerous as females and this continued to be the pattern for the next two decades.[48] The imbalance was higher amongst the immigrant population who preferred to leave their womenfolk behind in the villages while they travelled to the city in search of livelihood. By 1911—if women of child-bearing age are taken into consideration (15–40) —there were three men to every woman among the immigrants in Calcutta.[49] Women worked mostly as

[47] Between 1901 and 1910, the number of season tickets issued by the East Indian Railway to and from Howrah rose from 31,543 to 54,187 (an increase of 60 per cent); monthly ticket holders travelling on the Howrah–Amta and Howrah–Salkia Light Railway rose from 1,038 to 7,522; while on the Eastern Bengal State Railway the number of season tickets issued to and from Sealdah was 31,766. *Census of the Town and Suburbs of Calcutta, 1911*, p. 4.

[48] Women comprised 33 per cent of the total population of Calcutta in 1881. See *Census of the Town and Suburbs of Calcutta, 1881*, pp. 21, 25. Roughly the same results are available for 1891 (see *Census 1891*, p. 21) and 1911, with the proportion of women of child bearing age (15–40) constituting only 15 per cent of the total population that year. *Census 1911*, p. 2.

[49] *Census of the Town and Suburbs of Calcutta, 1911*, p. 17. These were the figures for the immigrant population.

domestic servants, prostitutes, workers in the hotel/food business, labourers, and shopkeepers/hawkers.[50] Prostitutes alone constituted 21 per cent of the female work force, and 4.5 per cent of the total women in the city.[51] Their small numbers made for a heightened presence in the city, therefore, as evident in contemporary print and popular literature and accounts of crime and scandals in the city.

Re-producing the City: Beyond Lefebvrian Constructs

Arguably, cities in the South Asian context were not just sites of disciplining and governance as a spate of recent studies would have us believe.[52] They also witnessed the ambivalence of late colonial power, the increasing role of the colonized in negotiating the political order, and the emergence of anti-colonial movements from the late nineteenth century onwards. The gradual and fitful process of the colonial devolution of institutional power at the municipal level during this period reinvented the South Asian city as a space of political negotiation. Initiated by the Riponian reforms of 1882 and continued with the Government of India Acts, Indians could populate municipal bodies, although within considerably restricted terms. As noted in the previous section, municipal boards and government units at the local and district levels served as crucial venues for the elaboration of nationalist political demands. As spheres for Indian political participation expanded, the urban arena remained crucial as a subject of anti-colonial struggles rather than merely their location.

Increasing politicization of the public sphere in a climate of rising nationalism also played a due role. Against a backdrop

[50] *Census of the Town and Suburbs of Calcutta, 1881*, p. 46. Of these trades, domestic service claimed 42 per cent of the immigrant female work force, and prostitution, 25 per cent. *Census of the Town and Suburbs of Calcutta, 1911*, p. 17.

[51] *Census of the Town and Suburbs of Calcutta, 1911*, p. 64.

[52] Most notably Legg, *Spaces of Colonialism*; Datta, *Planning the City*.

of the colonial city as space for socio-spatial control, Sandip Hazareesingh's work examines confrontations over urban policies that shaped Bombay from the First World War through decolonization.[53] Hazareesingh argues that participants saw the struggle for the city as integral to the fight for the nation-state, as the critiques of the urban colonial regime—emanating from the press and activist groups—represented visions of self-rule and robust alternatives. Other studies have begun to suggest that informal arenas of urban power—and not formal political spaces alone—were also crucial domains of struggles. While primarily highlighting it as a landscape of imperial control, Legg's work only very briefly casts Delhi as a negotiated space, of which the municipal domain was one arena.[54] Negotiations over the colonial city also flourished beneath the level of formal politics, rarely visible interventions in the form of informal engagements of city-dwellers with the state and urban practices.

Henri Lefebvre's theoretical analysis of the processes of production of space has gone a long way in unravelling any conception of it as a given, uncontested category.[55] Through a focus on the ways in which conceived and perceived spaces are articulated, the framework allows for an understanding of space that is at once physical and material on the one hand and ideological and social on the other, thereby throwing meaningful light on a range of urban spatial phenomena and practices—from social movements

[53] Hazareesingh, *The Colonial City and the Challenge of Modernity*. Hazareesingh, however, is concerned mostly with the press and radical political groups in Bombay.

[54] The competing interests of the partly Indianized Old Delhi Municipal Corporation (DMC) and imperially dominated New Delhi body (NDMC) provided a framework for the playing out of competing visions of the city. See, for example, Legg, *Spaces of Colonialism*, pp. 66–70, 74–5. In this Legg follows in the footsteps of Narayani Gupta's earlier foundational work, *Delhi Between Two Empires, 1803–1931*.

[55] Henri Lefebvre, *The Production of Space*, translated by Donald Nicholson Smith (Oxford: Blackwell Publishing, 1991) and *Writings on Cities*, selected, translated, and introduced by E. Kofman and E. Lebas (Oxford: Blackwell Publishing, 1996).

to use of symbolic spaces—and the exacerbation of inequalities and hierarchies in capitalist urban models.[56] The Lefebvrian model is important for this book. It shows the city crafted in the practices of its people. Their interlocution of urban planning and municipal governance as well as their social imagination and aspirations constituted fundamental interventions in the ways Calcutta was received and ultimately reshaped.

This work goes beyond Lefebvrian concerns as it traces the emergence of a wider public sphere specifically springing from the urban experience in colonial India from the closing decades of the nineteenth century onwards. The turmoil engendered by the traditional social order in a city like Calcutta, it argues, opened up critical and deeply animated discursive spaces about sexuality, community, religion, and ritual authority that signalled a sea-change in the social imagination of urban groups, prising open closed questions and allowing room for realigning of interests and opinions. In addition, the insecurities of a highly competitive labour market, rising prices, and racial marginalization in Calcutta shaped urban collectivities that came to be forged in the face of an authoritarian municipal government that was increasingly unhesitant to use its police force for the enforcement of colonial laws. In this study, the city emerges primarily as a collection of political communities with an agenda of rights-claims that address city living as its substance; and the materiality of the city comes to be reshaped (even marginalized) through conflicts over the terms and aspirations of urban life. Over time the patterns of mass protest that were spawned by these groups in the conflict ridden urban milieu proved enduring enough to feed into the later communal, caste, and nationalist struggles of the interwar period, often precipitating urban violence.[57]

[56] See, for example, Jane Jacobs, *The Death and Life of Great American Cities* (New York: Random House, 1992).

[57] Apart from Gooptu, *Politics of the Urban Poor*, also see David Arnold, 'The Armed Police and Colonial Rule in South India, 1914–1947', *Modern Asian Studies* 11, no. 1 (1977): 101–25; C.A. Bayly, 'Local Control in Indian Towns: The Case of Allahabad, 1880–1920', *Modern Asian Studies* 5, no. 4 (1971): 289–311; Jim Masselos, 'Audiences, Actors and Congress Dramas: Crowd Events in Bombay City in 1930', *South Asia: Journal of South Asian*

Calcutta in the archives appears to have been a city resolutely in the clutches of its labouring populations. Carters, hackney carriage drivers, scavengers, butchers, and dairyfolk repeatedly brought the municipal administration to its knees, prompting the vice chairman of the Suburban Municipality, Sterndale, to comment:

> It is to be greatly deplored that nearly every sanitary ... improvement scheme which has been initiated in the Calcutta suburbs has to a certain extent assumed the aspect of a class battle, a struggle for life as it were between a certain class of men and the municipality: it was so with the butchers and slaughter-house owners, with the *tolah mehters* [night-soil workers or scavengers], and now again with the *Gowallas* [milkmen] ...[58]

Perhaps the most formidable was the opposition of the scavengers or *methars*, as evident in municipal records, such as Sterndale's own account in a memorandum:

> These men have become so exorbitant in their charges and so care less in performing their duties that very serious inconvenience and annoyance is felt by many persons.... If a sweeper neglects his duty, the householder is liable to summons and fine in the Municipal Court; he on the other hand has no remedy. If he remonstrates with the *mehter*, or detains his pay on account of services not rendered, or attempts to discharge the man and engage another, he subjects himself to endless annoyance and persecution. The *mehter* strikes work, becomes abusive and sometime revenges himself by surreptitiously conveying soil collected from other privies and depositing it in the remonstrating householder's privy (this is a common occurrence).[59]

Studies 8, nos. 1–2 (1985): 71–86; D. Chakrabarty, *Rethinking Working Class History: Bengal, 1890–1940*; Freitag, *Collective Action and Community*; Sumit Sarkar, 'The Conditions and Nature of Subaltern Militancy: Bengal from Swadeshi to Non-Cooperation, c. 1905–22', in *Subaltern Studies III: Writings on South Asian History and Society*, edited by Ranajit Guha (Delhi: Oxford University Press, 1984), pp. 271–320.

58 *Administrative Report of the Calcutta Suburbs for 1879–80*, pp. 56–7, italics mine.

59 *Administrative Report of the Calcutta Suburbs for 1873–74*. I have retained the term *mehter*, the English rendering of the original Bengali *methar*, in all quotations from official sources.

Strikes in the unorganized sector, especially in occupations serving the everyday city, form the subject matter of Chapter 4. The defiance of the labouring population is matched by another development from the late nineteenth century onwards—unrest and riots on the streets in response to municipal decisions—long before the more coordinated Swadeshi Movement of 1905. The disturbances following the adoption of harsh plague control measures in 1898, and the demolition of a temporary mosque in 1897 showcased public mistrust of governmental policies.

Both, the everyday and moments of crisis, are equally important for me. While the study recognizes that the city reacted in specific ways during extraordinary events such as natural calamities and disease, protest and riots, it demonstrates how the everyday also presents equally prescient sites for understanding urban political and social imaginaries. Even though difficult to account for in a systematic fashion, this domain of urban political engagement and practice is analytically indispensable. It provides a basis for thinking beyond the powerful ordering impulse of colonial urbanist technologies of control. Further, focus on everyday practices reveals non-elite interventions in the late colonial city, parallel to the formal political domain of elites who entered into, and later inherited, the institutions of colonial urbanism. Violation of traffic rules and defying sanitation regimes were thus endemic features of daily urban strife in Calcutta, leading to a proliferation of laws and their abuse alike. The streets in Chapter 4 of this book emerge as veritable battlefields between Calcutta's residents and its municipal government in the fight over urban legislation.

The importance of low-scale symbolic protest by the urban poor has been pointed out by Sudipta Kaviraj in a study of Calcutta's more recent history of economic inequality and public behaviour. As he comments: 'To look for an economic rationality behind this kind of act [despoliation] is futile, but to deny its political significance as an act is foolish.'[60] I find such a paradigm for understanding protest in the public spaces of colonial Calcutta extremely useful. Calcutta's population apparently took no civic pride in its

60 Sudipta Kaviraj, 'Filth and the Public Sphere: Concepts and Practices about Space in Calcutta', *Public Culture* 10, no. 1 (1997): 83–113, 112.

urban assets. Wanton damage to public property—such as fouling water of public tanks,[61] injuring public lamps,[62] the spoiling of Beadon Park by tearing up the flower garden,[63] attacks on shrubberies and flower beds in Dalhousie and Wellesley squares[64]—is reported repeatedly in official documents. What are we to make of such attitudes? As the book shows, interpretations of such acts may range from a registration of protest to alternative understandings of civic public spaces. Chapter 1 of the book thus charts other spaces that Calcutta's Indian residents were more attached to and which held much more symbolic value for them, such as temples and bathing ghats, mosques, and open fair grounds, which could double up as sites for communal and political action, or even street entertainment.

In recent times, the concept of citizenship has been used in urban studies to analyse a variety of specific cases of conflict over urban spaces and resources. In one of the first attempts to develop the idea of the contemporary city as a key site of citizenship, James Holston and Arjun Appadurai pointed to the particularities of cities—as spaces concentrating diversity, difference, opportunity, and conflict.[65] Over the past decade, the body of scholarship on

[61] *Annual Report on the State of Police of the Town of Calcutta during the Year* [henceforth *ARPC*], *1862–3*, p. 20. One hundred and four cases were reported that year.

[62] *ARPC, 1863–4*, p. 12. Fifty-five cases were reported that year.

[63] *Administrative Report of the Calcutta Municipality, 1872* (hereafter *ARCM*), p. 20.

[64] *ARCM for 1867*, p. 13; *ARCM for 1876*, p. 54.

[65] James Holston and A. Appadurai, 'Cities and Citizenship', in *Cities and Citizenship*, edited by James Holston (Durham and London: Duke University Press, 1999), pp. 1–20; J. Nair, *The Promise of the Metropolis*; Renu Desai and Romola Sanyal, *Urbanizing Citizenship: Contested Spaces in Indian Cities* (Thousand Oaks: Sage, 2011); Ananya Roy, 'Slumdog Cities: Rethinking Subaltern Urbanism', *International Journal of Urban and Regional Research* 35, no. 2 (2011): 223–38; M. Purcell,'Citizenship and the Right to the Global City: Reimagining the Capitalist World Order', *International Journal of Urban and Regional Research* 27, no. 3 (2003): 564–90; U. Ramanathan, 'Illegality and the Urban Poor', *Economic and Political Weekly* 41, no. 29 (2006): 3193–7.

urban citizenship has steadily expanded as scholars have examined citizenship in relation to diverse urban processes in the context of globalization and its discontents. Stimulated by this approach, this book examines practices of protest, claims-making, and even violence, through which various groups in colonial Calcutta asserted their regional and communal identities, demanded the protection of workers in the city, and negotiated access to urban resources. By examining the strategies and outcomes of these practices, the book interrogates how urban groups, particularly those who were marginalized in formal structures of governance, claimed a right to the city, and uncovers the implications of this for their politics in the city.

Subaltern Cultures, Everyday Spaces, and the Urban Public Sphere

In print and popular culture, the city stands out as a defining framework of contemporary lives. Accounts of work regimes regulated by the relentless chiming of bells from clock towers and cannon fires; the daily inundation of the city by an army of weary clerks pouring in by road, rail, and water to serve the numerous government and mercantile firms that kept Calcutta ticking; the awe inspired by gigantic bridges and underground drains, steamships, and railway; the crushing prices; the upsetting of traditional rituals and practices; and the intimidating presence of baton-wielding municipal police—all sum up the novelties as well as the trials and tribulations of the new urban experience.

As we shall see in the book—more particularly in Chapter 2—residents of the city wrote, sang, and talked about these experiences in ways that offer significant glimpses of their perspectives on the city. A vigorous printing and publishing industry based in Calcutta carried such viewpoints into the discursive spaces of households, neighbourhoods, and communities. Serialized police tales challenged and reconfigured the boundaries of good and evil in society. Relative culpabilities in sensational city scandals were assessed, the moral economy of crime discussed, and vigorous debates staged about the politics of rival markets in accessible formats of dramas and songs. In the nineteenth century, such songs were also performed on the streets, adding a whole new layer of listeners to the audience of the printed texts. In all of this, the study argues, we can see an energetic and loquacious public sphere in operation that seemed deeply invested in the urban society it represented. Weighty, if not eloquent, they offered reasoned opinion in discussions on gender, family, morality, and governance, as well as nation, which drew on their experiences of living in the city.

The shift from society being organized around local community to one in which individuals identified with the nation, Jürgen Habermas poses in his influential theory, happened with the emergence of the public sphere that mediated collective participation in the emerging European nation-states of the eighteenth century.[66] In the Habermasian structure, liberal-minded private citizens came together in a 'public' capacity to discuss matters of common concern to act as a counter-balance to the state. Over time, and with the growth of literacy and print-culture, the borders of the 'public' widened to acquire a broader democratic resonance, and that of the 'nation'. Eventually the state and the public sphere came to draw on the same collective values and behavioural models in a common frame of reference.

Notwithstanding its critics, the model has remained important enough worldwide for scholars to engage with, even if to refute.[67] South Asian scholars have questioned its holding power without doing away with it altogether. In all these studies, however, it is the middle classes who are seen as the distinct architects of public spheres, while pointing to other popular customary caste and communal realms that are seen as contributing to the discussion of

[66] Jürgen Habermas, *The Structural Transformation of the Public Sphere* (Cambridge: Cambridge University Press, 1989).

[67] See, for example, Geoff Eley, 'Nations, Publics, and Political Cultures' in *Habermas and the Public Sphere*, edited by Craig Calhoun (Cambridge, Massachusetts: MIT Press, 1992), pp. 289–339; Joan Landes, *Women and the Public Sphere on the Age of the French Revolution* (Ithaca: Cornell University Press, 1988). Also see Nick Crossley and John Michael Roberts (eds), *After Habermas: New Perspectives on the Public Sphere* (Oxford and Malden, MA: Blackwell, 2004), for more recent debates.

the 'public'.[68] An alternative term that has been coined and gained currency in the colonial Indian context from the 1990s onwards is 'public arena' or a space for collective articulation of identity that is tied closely to immediate social and political contexts. The world of ritual public performances in towns and cities in north India in the late nineteenth and early twentieth centuries as theatres of self-representation and constitution of community identities for both elite and subaltern groups has been outlined in a rich literature by anthropologists and historians of colonial India.[69] Sandria Freitag has shown how community could be 'witnessed and experienced through collective activities in public arenas ...' or 'ritual enactments of polity' in shared public spaces.[70]

In taking the public sphere beyond the highly educated and self-conscious layers, I am encouraged by the above approaches. This study, however, is more interested in gaining deeper insights on the underlying urban experiences that shaped these identities, while also bringing other trajectories of cultural, social, and emotional understandings to the drawing-board. In fact, as scholars have estab-

[68] See Francesca Orsini, *The Hindi Public Sphere, 1920–1940* (New Delhi: Oxford University Press, 2006); Charu Gupta, *Sexuality, Obscenity, Community: Women, Muslims and the Hindu Public in Colonial India* (New Delhi: Permanent Black, 2001); Sanjay Joshi, *Fractured Modernity: Making of a Middle Class in Colonial North India* (New Delhi: Oxford University Press, 2001).

[69] Douglas E. Haynes, *Rhetoric and Ritual in Colonial India*; Philip Lutgendorf, *The Life of a Text: Performing the Ramcaritmanas of Tulsidas* (Berkeley and Los Angeles: University of California Press, 1991); Kathryn Hansen, *Grounds for Play: The Nautanki Theatre of North India* (Berkeley and Los Angeles: University of California Press, 1992); Raminder Kaur, *Performative Politics and the Cultures of Hinduism: Public Uses of Religion in Western India* (London: Anthem Press, 2005).

[70] Freitag, *Collective Action and Community*, pp. 218, 192. For similar studies on articulations of community identities and opinions see Majid Hayat Siddiqui, 'History and Society in a Popular Rebellion: Mewat, 1920–33', *Comparative Studies in Society and History* 28, no. 3 (1986): 442–67; Rosalind O' Hanlon, *Caste, Conflict and Ideology: Mahatma Jotirao Phule and Low Caste Protest in Nineteenth-Century Western India* (Cambridge: Cambridge University Press, 1985).

lished, the same kind of community mobilizations could alternate between civic and communal protest.[71] There is a lot of currency in this method as it helps us bounce off architecture and technologies, health and tax regimes, jobs and migration from standpoints other than those based on religion, caste, or nation. Nita Kumar's work, for instance, has shown how the perspectives on work and leisure of artisans in Benares are shaped more firmly than anything else by the sacred geography of Hinduism.[72] This book addresses public concerns in both everyday realms and public spaces, and not spectacular public performances (riots, festivals) or public opinion (voluntary associations, newspapers)—the classic subjects of subaltern and public sphere approaches, respectively—alone. It is both about discursive spheres and public arenas, discourses, and actions.

A small caveat is in order here. While the book most evidently is concerned with violence and protest in Calcutta, it stops short of including the revolutionary activities of the many anticolonial political cells that had sprung up in and around Calcutta in the early decades of the twentieth century. The reason for this is twofold. One, the revolutionary movement has its own trajectory of political action which cannot be restricted to the context of the urban arena alone, and as such deserves to be treated as a separate study in its own right. Second, my concern here is with collective action and the relatively isolated doings of these cells, while no doubt having a great impact on the general political climate of the times, do not qualify as the subject matter of my current study.

The book, while being inspired by subaltern history, is not about simply rendering visible the lower urban orders and their dialectical relationship with the educated middle classes.[73] Neither

[71] As seen in the religious riot of 1809 and the collective House Tax protests of the following year in Banaras. Freitag, *Collective Action and Community*, pp. 19–52.

[72] Nita Kumar, *Artisans of Benares: Popular Culture and Identity, 1880–1986* (Princeton: Princeton University Press, 1989).

[73] Admirable historical ethnographies of that kind exist, however, in other contexts. For an outstanding account of rickshaw pullers in colonial Singapore, see James Francis Warren, *Rickshaw Coolie: A People's History of Singapore, 1880–1940* (Singapore: Singapore University Press, 2003).

is it an account delineating how they were caught up in the larger all-India waves of nationalism and communalism.[74] More unconventionally, it does not follow the familiar tradition of labour history of which there is a surfeit of studies for Calcutta and its surrounding mill towns. Instead, it attempts to trace back to colonial India a phenomenon that has been identified in recent times to more contemporary developments.

Partha Chatterjee has argued how the urban poor have sought to advance their own claims on the city by forging a new domain of 'political society' whose values are antithetical to the norms of middle-class 'civil society'. Many of their practices are 'founded on violations of law' and hence, very different from constitutionally sanctioned relations between the state and citizens within civil society.[75] Equally, it has been argued, collective rituals of 'public protest, violence, and local mobilisations' have been integral to their sense of politics. Such 'political spectacles' in public arenas are increasingly regarded as having played a key role in fashioning new forms of chauvinistic and particularistic identities among the plebeian classes of contemporary Indian cities.[76]

In addition, the ever-growing authority of the colonial municipal administration acutely impacted on everyday lives and over time provoked political and social action against it. From repeated strikes of workers in the city to serious anti-police riots from the end of the nineteenth century onwards, collective disturbances and protests came to form an abiding feature of the human urban landscape. The spectacular upsurges in Calcutta's streets in the early decades of the twentieth century, prompting Curzon's comments about his beloved city changing beyond recognition, cannot be explained by political dissent stemming from mass

[74] As such has been done by Nandini Gooptu, *Politics of the Urban Poor* and Sandip Hazareesingh, *Colonial City and the Challenge of Modernity*.

[75] Partha Chatterjee, 'On Civil and Political Society in Post-colonial Democracies', in *Civil Society: History and Possibilities*, edited by Sudipta Kaviraj and Sunil Khilnani (Cambridge: Cambridge University Press, 2001), pp. 165–78.

[76] See Thomas Blom Hansen, *Violence in Urban India: Identity Politics, 'Mumbai' and the Postcolonial City* (New Delhi: Orient Blackswan, 2001).

nationalism alone. The imperfect configuration of 'civil society' in colonial India, I would like to argue, led to such 'political societies' being born whose agitational agendas formed the only means of reaching out to the colonial state.

The civil society model that has been traced in colonial India's modern urban public cultures does not offer an answer to the 'aberrations'—riots and unrest—in the public spaces of the cities.[77] Scholars have shown how Calcutta, like Bombay (present day Mumbai), became the site of a vigorous associational culture and 'modernizing' social activism that infused civil society with a new dynamism.[78] But there also arose new forms of collective action in public arenas such as demonstrations and protests. Importantly, these developments were a product of the urban context. It was in the city that Indians encountered and came to terms with new definitions of the 'public' and the 'private' and it was here too that they began to recognize the potential for novel modes of collective protest.

Thomas Blom Hansen's rich insights into the nature of urban violence in contemporary Mumbai have shown how the metropolis has been fundamentally constitutive of the emergence of right wing politics in the city following independence. The Shiv Sena's rise to power can thus be understood as an 'assertive, often violent, mode of being urban', a full-blooded plebeian engagement with the modern city.[79] Other more recent works have also shown how urban identities in the semi-industrial settings mobilize ethnicity and gender for asserting citizenship and social privileges.[80]

Perhaps the most important aspect of this book is to trace the antecedents of the kind of 'ground level' political society that later populist ideologies, such as Indian nationalism and religious fundamentalism, were able to tap into. It therefore stops just

77 On the limited utility of the Habermasian 'public' in colonial India, see Joshi, *Fractured Modernity*, Introduction.

78 Rajat Sanyal, *Voluntary Associations and the Urban Public Life in Bengal, (1815–1876): An Aspect of Social History* (Calcutta: Riddhi-India, 1980).

79 T.B. Hansen, *Violence in Urban India.*

80 Atreyee Sen, *Shiv Sena Women: Violence and Communalism in a Bombay Slum* (London: C. Hurst & Co., 2007).

before the launch of a series of Gandhian mass movements, from 1919–20 onwards. The work studies how the 'colonial urban' was not just born out of the ordered institutional and structural spaces inscribed by public parks, libraries and courtrooms, sewers and water supplies, roads and tramways, but also the more plebeian imprint of their circumvention by the city's inhabitants. Various social groups thus attempted to appropriate the built environment for their own purposes and in accordance with their own social, economic, and political aspirations. Their acts revealed a political city much lower down the better-known educated layers who were capable of consciously engaging with the urban environment and expressing their legitimate dissatisfaction in action that was transparent and expressive.

Chapters, Methodologies, and Archives

This study is by nature suggestive. Providing a solid account of informal negotiations and contestations within the urban scene is difficult, owing to the scattered and limited evidence available of this kind of engagement. Drawing on popular vernacular material, the work departs from approaches that see the city as the unproblematic product of British initiative (with some Indian co-option) to present the urban processes shaping Calcutta as contested and partially indigenous. Visual imagery in the form of photographs, maps, and illustrations are also examined to evaluate competing use of city spaces and everyday practices framing its material culture. Court records and police reports are indispensable for tracing infringements of the modern civic order.[81] Placed alongside the official rhetoric of city planning, they constitute powerful interventions in the civic framing of Calcutta's urban world.

[81] For an exemplary use of colonial records to recover political participation of labourers in early colonial Madras, see A. Balachandran, 'Of Corporations and Caste Heads: Urban Rule in Company Madras, 1640–1720', *Journal of Colonialism and Colonial History* 9, no. 2 (2008), at https://muse.jhu.edu/.

In this, I write more within the framework of social and cultural rather than urban history. In interpreting literature as source material I use the methodological tools of cultural history, reading the cultural meanings of literary texts, and the related representations of social order. But then, this work refrains from interpreting the construction of identities as entirely in terms of discursive practices or the 'social imaginary' based on 'self-constitution, randomness and the reflexivity of subjects'. Society is still the external referent and the social context relevant for me, insofar as events and ideas emerge out of reciprocity between conceptual systems and social relations in a given historical moment.[82]

The first chapter lays the foundation of the book by investigating the nature of the relationship between space and material culture in colonial Calcutta. It outlines the changes in spatial layout engendered by the creation of modern streets and esplanades, tramways and bridges, parks and drains. How and why urban space underwent several dramatic reorganizations during the period and its significance for the social, cultural, and political life in Calcutta is central to it. The chaos and uncertainty instituted in city spaces, the chapter underlines, prompted Bengalis to rethink their body social in new ways, a topic that constitutes the subject matter of the next few chapters.

The second chapter is an investigation of urban experiences in the colonial metropolis as articulated in its street song cultures. In all of the songs, as we shall see, the city is the fundamental

[82] For an excellent recent debate on the methodologies employed by cultural and social historians, see Peter Mandler, 'The Problem with Cultural History', *Social and Cultural History* 1, no. 1 (2004): 94–117; C. Hesse 'The New Empiricism', *Social and Cultural History* 1, no. 2 (2004): 201–7; C. *Jones*, 'Peter Mandler's "Problem with Cultural History", or, Is Playtime Over?', *Social and Cultural History* 1, no. 2 (2004): 209–15; and C. Watts, 'Thinking about the X Factor, or, What's the Cultural History of Cultural History?' *Social and Cultural History* 1, no. 2 (2004): 217–24. Also see Patrick Joyce, 'The End of Social History?', *Social History* 20, no. 1 (1995): 73–91, and 'What is the Social in Social History?', *Past and Present*, 206 (Feb 2010): 213–48.

organizing category of the subject matter, and in their presentation the producers draw on shared interests between the listener, performer, and writer. Moving on, the book draws attention to the ways in which a series of scandalous events in the city played a significant role in shaking up and reshaping sexual and moral beliefs of its residents in Chapter 3. They stimulated debate in the popular press about the sexual pathologies that were seen to be generated by contemporary urban life.

An organized network of urban thoroughfares, open squares and gardens, civic buildings, ports, and markets announced a new regime of the modern metropolitan city. A new conceptualization of the streets was a formative element in the creation not merely of colonial power but of a new sense of the public. In Chapter 4, thus, we find a wide range of the city's residents—pedestrians, householders, and low paid occupational groups such as hackney carriage drivers, scavengers, and milkmen—clashing over municipal laws which were affecting the ways in which they moved, lived and earned a wage in the city's streets. The chapter considers these contending claims to the city and outlines newer formations of the body social through these activities.

Chapter 5 continues to discover the moral economy of the city by exploring how criminal activities both defined and challenged the normative urban civic, familial, political, and moral order and offered a choice of lifestyle to the city's residents. Printed police diaries and crime stories unleashed social and moral anxieties for the upwardly mobile and established classes. They would have also to a certain extent acted as a counterweight to the self-representations of the respectable and middling groups. While the tales can be read simply as meaningful stories about danger in the city, other narrative registers suggest that they functioned as key interpretative devices for analysing and sharing reflections on the changing nature of social relationships caused by the strains of urban living.

The last chapter of the book looks at Calcutta during moments of crises and transgressions—communal riots, labour unrest, and nationalist mass movements. As the chapter demonstrates, the symbolical and physical violation of neatly ordered spaces—especially by marginal groups as seen during street protests and mass violence—was both new and shocking to the municipal administration. A series of anti-police riots in the city, the tension generated by the civic and secular ordering of urban space, mobilization of groups on the basis of community and region, strikes and the rise of mass nationalist protest as witnessed in the Swadeshi Movement—all challenged and tested the administration of the city to its limits.

Audacious and astounding inversions of the colonial symbolical order was witnessed in the public gatherings in the Town Hall, College Square, and even the Maidan—once the exclusive reserve of the white population of the city. It altered, in significant ways, the relationship of the people to the city spaces. In tracing how the public spaces of the city—its parks, squares, streets, and public halls—came to be irreversibly changed by the building up of such protest action around the turn of the century, this book unpicks the actual events as they occurred, trying to trace their local roots and local impact as they unfolded in the city. Why were certain spaces more symbolic than others as sites of protest, and what led to collective defiance of the administration on such a mass scale?

European civic mores and the concept of a bourgeois civil society itself, scholars have suggested, are historically imperfect for smooth grafting on to India. This is not to claim any problematic essentialism for the subcontinent but to recognize the different trajectories of modernity across the world. As Sudipta Kaviraj has argued,

> ... it is not surprising that traditional cities did not have a conception of the *civic* in the European sense, since the cities performed very different historic functions. They were not distinguished conceptually and materially from the countryside. They had no corporate life of their own to shelter and encompass the lives of the private families living inside them.... They were not seen as a separate juridical 'body social', with which and about which things could be done, which could be in some cases a proper legal subject. In the modern European conceptualisation of the public, there is an unmistakable strand of control, of order and discipline, which is altogether absent in the indigenous Indian one. Instead there is a sense that the 'outside' is not amenable to control—not by the

> individual or the restricted resources of a small family, nor by any organised authority. The exterior is abandoned to an intrinsic disorderliness. No order, rules, restraints can be expected there.[83]

While the administration resorted to more and more draconian measures in an attempt to restore order, regularity, and authority, disgruntled populations resorted to wanton damage, riots, and unrest. Ideas and actions interacted with municipal ideologies to produce the Calcutta we know during this period.

83 Kaviraj, 'Filth and the Public Sphere', pp. 98–9.

1

Urban Space, Technology, and Community

This foundational chapter investigates the nature of the relationship between space and material culture in colonial Calcutta. It outlines the changes in spatial layout engendered by the creation of modern streets and esplanades, tramways and bridges, parks and drains. How and why urban space underwent several dramatic reorganizations during the period and its significance for the social, cultural, and political life in Calcutta is central to it. While for the colonial government it was a carefully crafted act of civilizational dispensation and orderly rule, the chapter argues that for the indigenous population it signalled disruption and turmoil. Temporary living in the city, the influx of migrants, and the uncertainties of urban existence additionally signalled the breakdown of a familiar world and ritual social hierarchies, encouraging both the tendencies of communal solidarity and disruptive violence.

First, Western conceptions of urban planning militated against Bengali notions of residence and sociability. With their intrinsic interest in land, both physically and emotionally, the bhadralok had the village sitting at the heart of their urban imagination. They conceived of the city as a sum total of many highly localized spatial settings, communities in part organized by patron–client ties, religion, and caste, despite colonial efforts to constantly organize the city into rigid grids. Close examination of parallel norms apparent in contemporary English and Bengali cartography, street planning, landscape, and architecture all provide crucial inroads into the resultant fractures endemic in the urban imagination. Second, the role of technology in fundamentally reconfiguring understandings of community and social space is underlined. Technology homogenized ritual and communal spaces, upset traditional practices, and announced the arrival of an alien modern world. The bhadralok were prompt in critiquing these transformations, but the lower orders were more ambiguous in their response—a point that will be explored in further detail in the next chapter—hailing the technological marvels as remarkable, life-changing experiences.

The City in Its Early Days: Settlements and Layout

Calcutta grew as a longitudinal settlement along the Hooghly, stretching 3.5 miles along the curve of the river and 1.5 miles inland from it in 1742.[1] The physical expansion led in turn to growing internal differentiation and functionally distinct areas. Expansion of the European town took place east and west of the old Fort William, while the building of a new fort further south made way for additional European settlements. Spacious garden houses were built overlooking the river in the Garden Reach area. Chowringhee and Alipore developed into elite suburbs, the line of palatial detached houses arranged on Chowringhee at right angles to the Esplanade, earning the city the epithet, 'A City of Palaces'.[2] Broad roads and avenues, esplanades, and grand buildings dominated the European part of the city. The political and administrative

[1] Pradip Sinha, *Calcutta in Urban History* (Calcutta: Firma K.L.M. Private Limited, 1978), p. 5. The estimate is based on a map by Scrafton, reprinted in Plate XII, C.R. Wilson, *Old Fort William in Bengal* (Calcutta, 1906), vol. 2.

[2] Stephen J. Hornsby, 'Discovering the Mercantile City in South Asia: The Example of Early Nineteenth Century Calcutta', *Journal of Historical Geography* 23, no. 2 (1997): 135–50, 141.

heart of the capital lay in the area framed by the Government House (residence of the governor general), the Supreme Court, the Council Chamber, Treasury, Mint, and Town Hall, located at the centre of the city.

The articulation of exclusiveness and a distinct European urbanity in the organizational layout of the mercantile, bureaucratic, and residential quarters of the White Town 'sharply underscored the dualism of urban space in a colonial city', even as mixed populations, urban practices, and intermediate zones complicated strict segregation.[3] The chronological and spatial discrepancies in the unfolding of Calcutta's civic infrastructure in the form of drains and street lamps further highlighted the divide in the nineteenth century as we shall see in the following section.

Towards the north of the longitudinal settlement, beyond the Bowbazar Street, lay what was known as the Native Town or the section of the city where the indigenous population resided. It comprised densely settled trade and residential clusters organized in tight blocks around the main streets. Markets, religious structures, bathing ghats, and educational institutions, in addition, determined the flow and settlement of population in these parts. The principles behind the arrangement of space were functionality and custom, with traditional norms of living and working operational.

As the new Fort William was being built, the original village of Gobindapur was pulled down and the rich indigenous mercantile community of the Seths, Basaks, and Debs relocated to the Chitpore region in the north of the city.[4] The big merchants acted as patrons—drawing in a large cluster of relatives and

[3] P. Sinha, *Calcutta in Urban History*, p. 8. Recent scholarship on the eighteenth and nineteenth centuries, for instance, has highlighted knowledge exchanges between Europeans and Indians within the city, which show some exceptions to this model. See Peter Marshall, 'The White Town of Calcutta under the Rule of the East India Company', *Modern Asian Studies* 34, no. 2 (2000): 307–31; Kapil Raj, 'The Historical Anatomy of a Contact Zone: Calcutta in the Eighteenth Century', *Indian Economic and Social History Review* 48, no. 1 (2011): 55–82.

[4] See James Long, *Selections from Unpublished Records of the Government* (Calcutta, 1869), pp. 12–13.

dependents in and around the family residence—and developed their respective spheres of influence via *dals* or rival factions. They invested heavily in land and property in the area and housed numerous tenants.[5] The aristocratic mansions of the prominent landed and mercantile families and more modest brick-built residences aside, there were the numerous tenements made up of ill-ventilated clusters of huts known as *bustees*, which became the targets of the city's health and sanitary administration.

Caste or occupational settlements developed in the margins of these clusters organized along strict ritual lines. Migrants who came from other parts of India to the burgeoning city tended to live in distinct regional quarters such as Urepara (housing those from Orissa, Ure being a derogatory Bengali distortion of Oriya, indicating a resident of Orissa). The growth of urban rentiership among the merchant classes and the spurt in house-letting over time accelerated the formation of residential areas around the nuclei of the big mercantile family homes.

The next stage that followed was marked by a proliferation of masonry (*pucca*) houses of middle-class service people—office assistants, doctors, lawyers—of different sizes denoting varying status, alongside the explosion of tiled huts serving as shops, cafes, and hotels, tied in relationships of service to the bigger houses. Even in 1850, Calcutta—a city extending over 7 square miles—was basically a city of hutments (with 13,130 masonry and 49,445 hutments).[6] The situation had not changed very much by 1891.[7]

5 Thus Sobharam Basak had 37 such houses. Ramdulal De died in 1825 leaving behind property worth five lakhs, while the Sinha family of Jorasanko had property worth more than eight lakhs (with one lakh being equivalent to one hundred thousand rupees). P. Sinha, *Calcutta in Urban History*, pp. 27–8.

6 P. Sinha, *Calcutta in Urban History*, pp. 28, 30, 60.

7 In 1881 there was nearly double the number of people living in tiled huts as compared to masonry houses. See H.F.J.T. Maguire, *Census of the Town and Suburbs of Calcutta, 1891*, p. 20.

The population of the city in 1837 was recorded at 229,714.[8] By 1891, it had risen to 681,560,[9] and then again to 847,796 in 1901 and 895,067 in 1911.[10] Between 1821 and 1901, while the population increased by 233 per cent, available pucca buildings had only increased by 178 per cent, leaving a shortfall of 55 per cent.[11] The high density of population sharpened the crisis: three of the northern wards of Kalutola, Jorasanko, and Jorabagan had the highest densities of 255, 227, and 214 (population per acre) respectively. By contrast, the southern wards like Alipore, inhabited by Europeans, had densities as low as 16.[12] The architectural glory of the city applied arguably to the lofty public buildings—administrative and commercial—shops, and offices while a house famine raged in the rest of the city.

Metropolitan Visions, Colonial Spaces, and Lived Experience

A corporation, consisting of a mayor and nine aldermen, invested with powers of civil and criminal jurisdiction in the form of a Mayor's Court, existed in the eighteenth century, but did little to improve the city. Public lotteries were formed to raise money for improving the town in 1793–4, as the English East India Company continued spending its revenues in wars. The earliest plans for the improvement of Calcutta were set afloat by Wellesley, under whose aegis a Town Improvement Committee was set up in 1803.[13] In 1817, a Lottery Committee was set up to run in conjunction with the Town Improvement Committee and operated between

[8] A.K. Roy, 'Short History of Calcutta: Calcutta Town and Suburbs', *Census of the Town and Suburbs of Calcutta, 1901*, p. 63.

[9] *Census of the Town and Suburbs of Calcutta, 1891*, p. 18

[10] *Census of the Town and Suburbs of Calcutta, 1911*, p. 2.

[11] A.K. Roy, 'Short History of Calcutta', p. 65

[12] *Census of the Town and Suburbs of Calcutta, 1911*, pp. 9–10. The average density for London around that time was 60 per acre.

[13] E.P. Richards, *Report by Request of the Trust on the Condition, Improvement and Town Planning of the City of Calcutta and Contiguous Areas* (Calcutta: Calcutta Improvement Trust, 1914), p. 16.

1817 and 1836.[14] It was not until twenty years later that a Municipal Corporation was set up in 1856.[15] In addition, and finally, a Calcutta Improvement Trust (CIT) was set up in 1911 to overhaul the city's streets, housing, and sanitation.

Wellesley's vision was manifold. He envisaged an improvement plan along strictly European lines, with the building of drains, roads, streets, and buildings on the one hand and public markets, slaughterhouses, and burial grounds on the other. He urged the immediate need to develop sewers and watercourses, forbade the indiscriminate location of bazaars and residential buildings, and condemned the open slaughter of cattle and performance of death rituals. The Town Improvement Committee was pressed into service to push through his ideas and resulted in many spectacular enhancements. Roads began to be metalled. The first metalled road came into existence in 1799, running along the Maratha ditch or the Lower Circular Canal.[16] The watering of the dusty streets was ensured by the installation of a 20-horsepower engine at Chandpal Ghat. Tanks, squares, and open spaces were built at regular intervals along the street grids, and oil lamps maintained along major roads and avenues.[17]

The objective of the earliest plans funded by the Lottery Committee was the symmetrical and organized development of the city along a central highway. To this end, a north–south highway was built parallel to Chitpore Road, with adjacent functional districts.[18] The Strand Road running along the river was another major artery that was built connecting the wharfs, warehouses, and administration. Initial roads were *kutcha* or unpaved because of the scarcity of stones and gravel. Bricks were so expensive that, until 1837, there were hardly any proper roads.

[14] C.H. Bompass, cited in Richards, *Report on the Condition, Improvement and Town Planning of Calcutta*, pp. 15–16.

[15] In 1871, the Corporation of Justices was established by a special Act. See A.K. Roy, 'Short History of Calcutta', p. 100.

[16] Nisith Ranjan Ray, *Calcutta: The Profile of a City* (Calcutta: K.P. Bagchi, 1986), p. 58.

[17] A.K. Roy, 'Short History of Calcutta', p. 76.

[18] A.K. Roy, 'Short History of Calcutta', p. 73.

Straight roads were needed for defence and commerce reasons, to enable the movement of big guns and heavy traffic. Roads could cut through dense habitation, create air passages, and enable policing as well. The initial plan was to cut up the northern part of the city by a series of cross streets, which would have created blocks at rectangular intervals. While useful for surveillance, this arrangement would have been disruptive for tightly structured and dependent businesses running adjacent to each other. The plan did not eventually materialize for want of funds.

The state of roads and difficulties of access continued, however, to bother the municipal fathers. The CIT was concerned enough to commission E.P. Richards as Chief Engineer in 1912 to recommend measures for improved town planning. Richards submitted his report in 1914, the first ever planning document for the whole of Calcutta. The report brought out the sharp contrast between the northern and more southern parts of the city. Imagining a straight line that ran between the Howrah Bridge and Park Street cutting across the heart of Calcutta, Richards presented a picture in contrast:

> All that lies north and east of the line is of intense density, is almost streetless, and is served by an abnormally sparse set of right angle main roads, which bound some nineteen huge blocks of property ... [of 2500 acres] arranged anyhow. This slum-like city mass ... houses the bulk of the population of Calcutta and contains both the best and the worst of the Indian residential quarters. In this section lie also the chief Indian markets, shops, bazaars, and places of business.[19]

However,

> South-west of the same line ... we have in general quite different conditions. All around Dalhousie Square, and arranged in moderately good street system, are built the chief British business houses, the Banks, the Exchange, the seats of Government, and the Public Offices. Following along the line, we find just south-west of it, the leading hotels and more European business premises, bringing us via Old Court House Street and Esplanade East, to Chowringhee—the combined Oxford Street, Piccadilly and Park Lane of Calcutta; this development along the Maidan edge continues southwards in

[19] Richards, *Report on the Condition, Improvement and Town Planning of Calcutta*, p. 10.

> a thin band along Chowringhee front and brings one to the Park Street area, the only section of all Calcutta that has a really decent street system. It is almost purely residential, chiefly European, with a sprinkling of Indian.[20]

The perceived contrast between the desirable and the undesirable in the mind of the planner could not be more starkly put. The morass of lanes and bylanes had to be straightened out and widened, squares, parks, and avenues opened up, and arterial networks of roads for the smooth flow of traffic arranged. The main focus for Richards was the commercial district adjacent to the river—extending in a horseshoe shape from the Sealdah railway station to the Ahiritollah Ghat, via Cossipore Bridge, along the northern limits of Calcutta—but this did not preclude the extension of his general model for the road layout and housing for other areas.

Two years earlier, Bompass, the Chairman of the CIT, had commented that Calcutta lacked a system of interconnected roads, and that it was especially in need of radial arteries for traffic running from the centre of the town to the outskirts. There was another problem. The existing gridiron structure of roads enclosed square meshes that were much bigger than any other 'average great city', leaving an 'abnormally low proportion of real roads and streets per square mile'. Half-mile rectangles bounded by narrow streets with irregular lanes, alleys, and passages offering pathways within them were hardly ideal. Streets should be widened to form proper main roads, while alleys and passages should be opened up to form regular street networks.[21]

Richards built on the guidelines provided by Bompass with special attention to the flow of commercial vehicular traffic. His maps showed up an inverse relationship between the traffic capacity and traffic load in the main commercial districts, covering the Circular Road, Cornwallis Street, Chitpore Road, and Strand-Dharmahata Streets. He also suggested the widening up

[20] Richards, *Report on the Condition, Improvement and Town Planning of Calcutta*, p. 11.

[21] Cited extracts from paper by Bompass in Richards, *Report on the Condition, Improvement and Town Planning of Calcutta*, pp. 17–19.

FIGURE 1.1 Mud and Bamboo *Bustees* in the Foreground with 'Streetless Better-Class Property' at the Back
Source: From E.P. Richards, *Report by Request of the Trust on the Condition, Improvement and Town Planning of the City of Calcutta and Contiguous Areas* (Calcutta: Calcutta Improvement Trust, 1914); X775 © The British Library Board. Courtesy of the British Library, London.

of the Howrah Bridge and the opening up of a second bridge at Ahiritollah. Richards was plagued by Calcutta's *streetless* state, referring to it over and over again in his report, maps, and images (see Figure 1.1).[22]

Apart from the roads, Richards was troubled by the bustees. Built-up Calcutta, Richards claimed, contained slum areas of 'an extent and a density undreamt of in European cities', with 2,500 acres of streetless property in the city. Out of this he ranked 800 acres as 'rank slum'. He dealt with the subject in six of his chapters of the report in great detail. Just under a million people lived

[22] Richards, *Report on the Condition, Improvement and Town Planning of Calcutta*, p. 21.

inside the city boundaries in 1914. The most thickly populated wards in the northern-most parts of the city had 130 to 227 people to the acre.[23] What compounded the lack of ventilation in the slum areas was that the buildings were twice the height of those found in London, Birmingham, and Liverpool. The urgency in Richards' tone is evident. Slums were being made 'higher and higher', alleys and gullies 'deeper and deeper', with buildings crammed tighter than ever before. In fact, Richards thought that if the Kennigton slum were transferred to Calcutta, it would constitute 'very decent property'.[24]

Richards laments the lack of effective bye-laws in the city over the last fifty years that could have prevented the construction of 'bad' buildings and organization of 'bad' spaces. Encroachments on to, and 'robberies' of street width, he complained, had gone almost unchecked for a long time. Building and street bye-laws, he held, would have *enforced* the production of a decent street mesh and the spreading out of tightly huddled houses over twice the present area.[25] He suggested the remedy of some slums and demolition of 'hopeless' and 'obstructive' ones, linking up and opening out of lanes and streets, and the formation of many little open spaces. Predictably, parks and squares were also on the agenda for opening up spaces, particularly in the northern parts which had only 9 to 12 per cent open space.[26]

Perhaps the most interesting and most controversial aspect of the Richards report was its sociological map of the city, with populations ostensibly categorized according to their professions, but really driven by class. 'Coolies and the poorer classes' were deemed best living in close proximity of industrial areas where they would mostly work. Working-class suburbs were planned for

[23] Richards, *Report on the Condition, Improvement and Town Planning of Calcutta*, pp. 30–2.

[24] Richards, *Report on the Condition, Improvement and Town Planning of Calcutta*, pp. 230, 233, 235.

[25] Richards, *Report on the Condition, Improvement and Town Planning of Calcutta*, p. 237. The italics are present in the original report.

[26] Richards, *Report on the Condition, Improvement and Town Planning of Calcutta*, pp. 22–3, 230, 301.

the Manicktola and southern and eastern parts of the Cossipore–Chitpore area, northeast near the Sealdah and Beliaghata Canal, Kidderpore, and Howrah, among others. Residential suburbs for 'skilled artisans, clerks, shopkeepers and better-off classes' were to be located in Ballygunge and Bhowanipore, and land south of Ballygunge, Alipore, and Kidderpore. European and Indian 'well-to-do' classes should inhabit parts of Ballygunge and Tollygunge, with potential for extending southwards via the Diamond Harbour Road.[27] Richards' certainty and optimistic spirit regarding his neat racially and class-bound arrangements sound bizarre for 1914:

> Eastern cities that are divided in separate areas for the various races appear to give the most orderly, peaceful and happy results; and even the best architectural results. There seem no good reasons why the working class and second class suburbs should not be this sub-divided. On the other hand there are many sound reasons pointing that this arrangement would be well liked, and would be a social advance on present Calcutta conditions.[28]

Richards also suggests a sliding scale of street meshes, with smaller ones recommended for the poorest dwelling areas and the largest for the richest. Street mesh size indicated the mileage of available streets per square mile of living area, so that dwellings could be spread out, well ventilated, and lower in height. The idea was for intermediary roads to cut across the residential blocks and break up built space. More such roads were recommended for poorer areas and less for well-off ones. In the Richards report, 34 miles to every square mile was recommended for the poorest working-class districts, 30 for low-rent single family detached houses, and 25 for the second-class suburbs.

It is significant that the CIT chose to go along with the Richards model rather than another alternative submitted by Patrick Geddes, a scholar and town planner, who was more empathetic

[27] Richards, *Report on the Condition, Improvement and Town Planning of Calcutta*, pp. 366–8.

[28] Richards, *Report on the Condition, Improvement and Town Planning of Calcutta*, pp. 368–9.

to local traditions, cultural practices, and environment.[29] Geddes was in India when the CIT was launching its major rebuilding programme in the city and came to be eventually consulted by the Calcutta Corporation towards the end of 1918. But when invited to consider improvements to the Burrabazar business area, Geddes, rather than imposing a universalist model based on the European experience, suggested a more organic approach and involving minimal disruption—including limited demolition of buildings—to existing lifestyles and urban forms.[30] The suggestions did not go down too well with the Trust, which continued to relentlessly pursue its plans of rectilinear street grids, wider avenues, and open spaces.

At the end of the First World War, Calcutta's cityscape presented a variegated picture. To the south and southwest were the upper-class, Westernized Indian and European suburbs of Alipore and Ballygunge with spacious houses and gardens. Humbler middle-class Bengali homes populated the suburb of Bhawanipore. Directly north of this area lay the modern European shopping and commercial districts around Chowringhee, where a façade of glittering shops and arcades extended southwards, facing the green space of the Maidan. Further north of Park Street, stretching in a crescent size shape from the Municipal Market to the Howrah Bridge, were Indian commercial and residential areas with a multitude of small business premises doubling up as living quarters in the upper storeys. Up-country migrants lived in large enclaves in the area, while Marwaris, Biharis, and Punjabis tended

[29] Geddes was in India, touring different cities and princely states and offering consultancy on various projects between 1914 and 1924. See Jaqueline Tyrwhitt (ed.), *Patrick Geddes in India* (London: Lund Humphries, 1947). For an account of his life and work, see Helen Meller, *Patrick Geddes: Social Evolutionist and City Planner* (London: Routledge, 1990).

[30] The report that Geddes submitted was entitled *Barra Bazaar Improvement: A Report to the Corporation of Calcutta* (1919). See Martin Beattie, 'Sir Patrick Geddes and Barra Bazaar: Competing Visions, Ambivalence and Contradiction', *The Journal of Architecture* 9, no. 2 (Summer 2004): 131–50.

to dominate the central Indian commercial district of Burrabazar in the northwest. To the north, and beyond Harrison Road, shabby tenement buildings and slums that existed alongside the decaying Hindu aristocratic residences made up the principal and most densely populated residential districts of the city. Behind the crescent reared a replica of the London skyline, centred on Dalhousie Square, with its offices of the major British mercantile firms, the High Court, and the Writers Building.

Plans of turning Calcutta into the model of London, however, came with its costs to the local populations. An act was passed in 1842 to prohibit the construction of thatched buildings following an explosion at the Old China Bazar.[31] The tremendous impact of such sweeping legislation on the lives of the thousands of migrants in the city who could not afford permanent brick-built accommodation cannot be underestimated. Large-scale demolition of temporary mud-and-thatch houses for the purposes of construction of new buildings, roads, tanks, or squares from the mid-nineteenth century onwards saw their former inhabitants being pushed increasingly to the margins and suburbs of the thriving city, or else being forced to live in densely populated bustees amidst unhygienic living conditions.[32]

Census reports detailed how the need for land and buildings for setting up warehouses, road, and rail connections along the river banks emptied the western wards of populations that had to migrate to the northeastern parts of the city.[33] A contemporary history of the Calcutta Municipality notes that this happened despite Lord Dalhousie's assurance to the Calcutta *pottadar*s (lessee landholders)—who handed over the land in 1852—that people of the town would have unrestricted access to the riverbank in the

[31] *ARPC*, p. 7.

[32] See, for example, *Administrative Report of the Municipality of the Suburbs of Calcutta*, 1869–70, p. 18; H. Beverley, *Census of the Town and Suburbs of Calcutta, 1881*, pp. 19–20. For a rich account of such displacement as a direct result of municipal planning, see Partho Datta, 'How Modern Planning Came to Calcutta', *Planning Perspectives* 28, no. 1 (2013): 139–47.

[33] *Census of the Town and Suburbs of Calcutta, 1881*, p. 50.

northern part of the city. Ten years later, '... four-storeyed buildings [stood] erected like the great Chinese Wall not only on the river bank but over the Strand Bank road, blocking forever the air and light to the denizens of the unfortunate northern city and obstructing the free communication of the Hindu community with their sacred river'.[34]

Kshitindranath Tagore, nephew of the poet Rabindranath Tagore, remembered how the CIT continued to brutally clear bustees (in keeping with the recommendations of E.P. Richards) and demolish old structures to make way for multi-storeyed buildings.[35] Bitter disputes ensued between the bustee owners and the municipality in the process as also with regard to their medical and sanitary inspections.[36] Altogether, seventy-five bustees were obliterated in the decade 1901–11. Land was being acquired also for building of hospitals, colleges, and shopping areas as the corporation extended its civic networks. All along Chowringhee and the adjacent area, residential quarters were being replaced by rows of glittering shops by the twentieth century.[37] Even as traders and others protested the eviction of labourers from the central parts of the city where they were closest to their places of employment and therefore fostering efficiency, the Trust was introducing thoroughly impractical housing schemes and plans to rehouse the homeless.[38]

In comparison with the nineteenth-century post-industrial mindset of Europe that viewed cities as deliverers of material gain, efficient administration, and bourgeois lifestyles, there were other

34 Radhachurn Pal, *A Rapid History of Municipal Government in Calcutta* (Calcutta, 1916), p. 17.

35 Kshitindranath Tagore, *Kolikatay Chalafera: Sekale aar Ekale* (Calcutta: Adi Brahmo Samaj Press, 1930), pp. 121–2. Also see *Census of the Town and Suburbs of Calcutta, 1911*, Chapter I, p. 5. The wards most affected were Bamun Bustee, Collinga, and Park Street. Landlords were keen to demolish kutcha houses and have large masonry houses erected instead for renting out as shops and living quarters.

36 *Calcutta Municipality Quarterly Reports, 31 March, 1886; ARCM for 1870.*

37 *Census of the Town and Suburbs of Calcutta, 1911*, p. 6.

38 See *Annual Report of the Calcutta Improvement Trust, 1913*, pp. 10, 22–9; and *Annual Report of the Calcutta Improvement Trust, 1916*, p. 70.

impulses behind the nomenclature and labelling of areas—more practical in nature and more fundamental to the local organization of the city—traceable in the Bengali urban imagination. Clusters of residence based on caste and occupation such as fishermen's colony (*jelepara*), brazier colony (*knasaripara*), colony of liquor vendors (*suripara*), potter's colony (*kumartuli*), and markets such as Mechhuabazar (fishmarket) and Posta outlined the vocational profile of Calcutta's everyday life.

Calcutta had originally consisted of villages with traditional caste-ordered layouts. Even as Calcutta developed as a city, the idea of 'villages' did not entirely disappear from the organizational and functional mentality of Calcutta's residents. They sat uneasily within the modern layout of the metropolis as *tollahs*, *tulis*, and *paras*, various denominations for occupation-based neighbourhoods. Murgihata, Domtollah, and Ahiritollah thus marked out residential and trading spaces for henkeepers, corpse handlers, and cattle-keepers respectively. Materially too, they were laid out as villages, belonged to different castes, and their social usages impressed their surroundings.[39]

The breaking up of hutments as part of municipal clearance, the broadening of roads, and building of larger structures on the one hand and the proliferation of bustees as cheap accommodation on the other initiated other impulses of locality formation over the nineteenth century. Pradip Sinha believes that hectic building activity and land purchase in Calcutta from the mid-eighteenth to the early nineteenth century contributed to cosmopolitanism and the growth of a non-caste-based heterogeneous population. Thus rental and house prices, migration patterns, and affordability rather than caste groupings came to determine residential profiles, making for more mixed groups in any neighbourhood.[40]

The trend towards urban heterogeneity became stronger mid-nineteenth century onwards, but the impact was being felt even earlier. In 1837, a letter was sent by a group of high-caste Bengali

39 See A.K. Roy, 'Short History of Calcutta', pp. 88–95. The municipality's Annual Administrative Reports as late as the 1880s still referred to tenements and hut clusters or bustees as 'villages'.

40 P. Sinha, *Calcutta in Urban History*, p. 17.

Hindus in the Bowbazar–Dharamtollah intermediate area to a contemporary newspaper, *Samachar Darpan*, highlighting the need for firmer social organization in the locality.[41]

Occupational and caste habitation patterns comforted the Bengali urban imagination. Writing at the start of the twentieth century, Binoykrishna Deb (of the Shobhabazar Deb family) recalled how, in earlier days, different trades and caste groups crystallized around definite urban spaces, in perfect harmony with and in reference to their overall spatial ordering in the city. Regrettably, however, he writes:

> Nowadays ... [people] no longer think of holding congregations of fellow caste men. Thus few of the localities and streets now bear any association with the inhabitants. The houses in the northern part of the town have sprung up in quite an irregular way without any method or consistency ...[42]

For those like Deb, the indiscriminate colonial reordering of the city space was disorientating and discomforting, in spite of the claims of the triumphant city fathers. Even E.P. Richards, writing in 1914, noted 'the enforced mixture of castes, creeds, and races found in every street, and in nearly every dwelling-house or place' in north Calcutta unlike other Indian cities, where there were well demarcated separate Hindu, Brahmin, Mohammedan, Eurasian, and European quarters.[43]

Alternative Imaginings: Locality, Community, and Vernacular Spaces

While the topology of the city in writings by Europeans and in official archives celebrated its civic and economic successes and ornamental built aspects in the southern parts, Bengali literary and cartographic

[41] Letter to the Editor, *Samachar Darpan*, 5 August 1837, in B.N. Bandyopadhyay (ed.), *Samvadpatre Sekaler Katha* vol. 2 (Calcutta: Bangiya Sahitya Parishat, 1970), p. 274.

[42] Raja Binoykrishna Deb, *The Early History and Growth of Calcutta* (Calcutta, 1905), p. 65.

[43] Richards, *Report on the Condition, Improvement and Town Planning of Calcutta*, p. 31. He does note that Bombay was the other exception.

representations focused almost exclusively on the Black Town or northern sector of the city. In contemporary writings, the middle classes and aristocracy conceived of the city's history as a panegyric to important local families, social reformers, and public intellectuals. Creation of ghats (wharfs or bathing steps) and markets, tanks, and temples by prominent benefactors paralleled the creation of public buildings, squares, and monuments in the European quarters in such accounts. Local histories commemorated and celebrated such munificence as those of Huzuri Chand Mal (tanks), Nubkissen Deb (streets), and Govindaram Mitra (the Navaratna or nine-steepled temple, 'the highest point of which was higher than the Ochterloney monument' in Calcutta).[44] Wealthy individuals, of course, also contributed to governmental projects and institutions, and the Bengali accounts proudly report these too. They set up pauper hospitals and educational institutions, opened charity stores, organized food centres in times of famine, and even donated to churches.[45]

The histories trace the rise of various important aristocratic families and their influence in the city—the Shils, Lahas, Debs, Duttas, Mitras, and Mullicks—and the pivotal role played by them in the growth of Calcutta. Nineteenth-century Calcutta was further celebrated in the numerous biographies and eulogies published of notable public figures of the time, commemorating their lives in and contributions to the city—presenting them as foundational to the community's identity in the modern era.[46] Together, the local histories and biographies are seen to showcase the achievements of Bengalis in the eighteenth and nineteenth centuries—both

44 Deb, *The Early History and Growth of Calcutta*, pp. 63, 67. Also see Prankrishna Dutta, *Kolikatar Itibritta* (Calcutta: Pustak Bipani, 1981), especially Chapters 3–5. The chapters in the book were originally published in the journal *Navyabharat* between 1901 and 1903.

45 Nubkissen Deb thus donated a sum of 30,000 rupees towards the building of the St John's Church in Calcutta in 1787. Deb, *The Early History and Growth of Calcutta*, p. 76. The Sikh trader Huzuri Mal gifted the St James' Church and even built the spire of the Armenian Church. Rajendrakumar Mitra, *Gokulchandra Mitra O Sekaler Kolikata*, vol. 1 (Calcutta, 1951), pp.53–4.

46 See, for example, Debendranath Chuckerbutty, *Life of the Late Babu Takoordas Chuckerbutty* (Calcutta, 1917); Hemchandra Sarkar, *Life*

commercial and intellectual—in a spectacular display of architecture, commerce, arts, scholarship, social reform, and philanthropy.

In a fictional–factual account of Calcutta featuring gods who arrive as tourists, entitled *Debganer Martye Agaman*, serialized in a prominent literary journal in 1883, the city is celebrated as a composite of Bengali achievements and British power.[47] While public institutions and buildings like the Bengal and Oriental Banks, High Court, Asiatic Museum, Geological and Trigonometrical Survey Offices, Writers and Bengal Secretariat Buildings, Treasury Building, Town Hall, the Collectorate, Revenue Board, General Post Office (GPO) and parks like the Eden Gardens and Beadon Park are acknowledged,[48] the author establishes with fervent zeal the important contributions of its Bengali residents too—bankers and merchants, scholars and pundits, prominent government officials and social reformers. As a member of the educated middle classes, the anonymous author might well have himself been a beneficiary of the colonial government, but insofar as he chooses to ignore this connection, he makes a political choice.

The names and short biographical accounts—Ramkamal Sen, Dwarkanath Mitra, Rammohan Roy, Iswarchandra Vidyasagar, Mahendralal Sircar, Rajendralal Mullick—read like a 'Who's Who' of contemporary Calcutta, and the description of their involvement in the modern metropolis, that is Calcutta, is endless.[49] Thus, we

---

of Anandamohan Bose (Calcutta, 1910); Sivnath Sastri, *Men I Have Seen* (Calcutta, 1919); M.N. Sircar, *Life of Peary Churn Sircar* (Calcutta, 1914); Kissory Chund Mitter, *Mutty Lal Seal* (Calcutta: Toolat, 1993; original edition Calcutta, 1869).

47 The original contributions in the journal, *Kalpadrum* (editor, Dwarkanath Vidyabhushan), in 1883 were anonymized, while the authorship of the book version of the essays, which was published in 1886, was not entirely clear. A later reprint traced them to a Durgacharan Ray of Jamalpur. See the reprint edition, Durgacharan Ray, *Debganer Martye Agaman* (Calcutta: Deys Publishing, 2001). This is the accepted authorship amongst scholars today.

48 D. Ray, *Debganer Martye Agaman*, pp. 272, 315, 274, 297–8, 313–14, 328–9, 332, 280–1.

49 The lengthiest biographical account is that of the *Kalpadrum* editor, Dwarkanath Vidyabhushan. The only two Europeans with biographic

learn how judges, deputy magistrates, collectors, doctors, educators, scholars, and municipal commissioners enhanced Bengali lives and matched the British in scholarship, skill, and acumen. In the fields of social and religious leadership, philanthropy, and intellectual exchange, the Bengali middle classes and aristocracy alike are held supreme.

Houses of prominent residents were the nerve centres of northern Calcutta and served as informal clusters of patronage and influence by virtue of their intellectual networks, leadership, and public service to the local community. Shivnath Sastri, the Brahmo reformer and intellectual, remembers arriving as a nine-year-old boy at the household of his maternal uncle, Pandit Dwarkanath Vidyabhushan—intellectual, social reformer, and editor of several prominent literary journals and newspapers, including the *Somprakash*—to find it functioning as 'something like a large lodging house where men of different ages, some students and others otherwise employed, lived and messed together'.[50] In times of festivals such as the Durga Puja or moments of crisis such as famines, thousands gathered at the houses of benefactors to be fed, clothed, and resuscitated. Some of the many thousands flocking into the city following the 1865–6 famine were thus provided food by the charitable centres that had sprung up in the houses of Peary Charan Sarkar, Rajendralal Mullick, and Haji Zakaria, where sometimes over a thousand people would flock every day.[51]

We are also informed of the immense wealth of some of the aristocratic residents and traders and their public spirited and substantial contributions to the city.[52] As in the local histories, in this work too, the markets, ghats, temples, hospitals, orphanages, charitable guesthouses, free schools, and feeding centres are lasting public symbols of aristocratic benevolence and the sites where wealthy

---

presence in the book are Warren Hastings and David Hare, both of whom are noted for their empathy and concern for Indians, and particularly their contributions to the field of education.

[50] Sastri, *Men I Have Seen*, p. 1.

[51] M.N. Sircar, *Life of Peary Churun Sircar*, pp. 73–4. In the Sircar household, this continued for three months.

[52] Thus a Parsi merchant, Premchand Raichand, contributed 2 lakh rupees to the Calcutta University; Rajendralal Mullick and Ramdulal Sarkar

Indians invariably leave their mark. Their palatial residences and garden houses, matching British architectural grandeur, inspired awe and captured popular imagination. In local parlance, the mighty residences of the two brothers—Madhusudan and Kalidas Sandel—thus came to be known as 'Indian palace',[53] while the huge mansion of Mathuramohan Sen, a goldsmith by trade, had four gates built around it in the style of the lieutenant governor's residence.

Calcutta in the early nineteenth century was a cosmopolitan city where people from all over the world converged for trade and commerce, and the names of its different localities and streets of the time reflected this.[54] Thus, Kidderpore was named after Colonel Kyd; Tiretta Bazar after an Italian who established the bazaar in 1788, and who was also the superintendent of streets and buildings; Barretto Street after the Portuguese merchant Joseph Barretto; and Loudon Street after the Countess of Loudon.[55] Bengali notables who had contributed to the city too left their mark on street names in the eighteenth and early nineteenth centuries.[56]

---

donated several lakhs during famines—including the Madras famine of 1867; Raja Sukhomoy built the Cuttack Road at the expense of 1.5 lakh rupees for the ease of pilgrims visiting the Puri temple; Raja Baidyanath and Durgacharan La each donated 50,000 rupees to the Hindu College and Baidyanath even gifted 8,000 rupees to the London Geological Society; Dwarkanath Tagore set up the Leper Asylum in Calcutta and donated 1 lakh rupees to the Charitable Infirmary in the Calcutta suburb of 24 Parganas; Ramgobinda Pal paved the street adjoining the Kalighat temple in stone at the cost of 25,000 rupees. The work also inserts a sizeable list of donations made by Rani Swarnakumari, including 10,000 rupees to the Irish Famine Relief Fund and a humble 100 rupees to the author himself for his current publication. D. Ray, *Debganer Martye Agaman*, pp. 348, 385, 394, 387, 399, 411, 398.

53 The annual income of the brothers from indigo and landed property was about 40 lakh rupees. D. Ray, *Debganer Martye Agaman*, p. 382.

54 For a very comprehensive contemporary account of Calcutta streets and their histories, see Harisadhan Mukhopadhyay, *Kolikata Sekaler O Ekaler* (Calcutta: P.M. Bagchi, 1991; original edition Calcutta, 1915), pp. 471–535.

55 Deb, *The Early History and Growth of Calcutta* (Calcutta, 1905), pp. 62–5.

56 A.K. Roy, 'Short History of Calcutta', pp. 103–10.

However, it is possible to see how over time the names of Bengali benefactors and aristocrats, and even East India Company servants and traders, are replaced by those of colonial officials in symbolic erasures of local history and memory. Raja Nabakrishna Deb built a long arterial road connecting the Chitpore and Upper Circular Road and named it initially after himself as Raja Nabakrishna's Lane. By the 1880s this had been renamed as Cornwallis Street.[57] Similarly the street built by Rajchandra Das running from Chowringhee to Babughat, initially named after himself, was later renamed Auckland Road.[58] Yet, another case of local patronage being obliterated was in the naming of Clive Row, the land for which was donated by Brajabandhu Mullick.[59]

Calcutta had become the showcase of metropolitan success in India, and could not be occupied by streets named after its lowly residents, once celebrated as part of the city's multilayered heritage. In fact, since 1877, the Municipal Corporation launched on a renaming programme whereby streets named after servants, masons, scavengers, barbers, and the like were awarded more 'respectable' appellations.[60] References to bustees were also summarily removed—as indeed were the huts themselves—as they came to be replaced at the end of the nineteenth century with grand architecture. The road, previously known as Duncan Bustee-ka Rasta (The Road to Duncan Bustee) was renamed Camac Street after a senior merchant of the East India Company, following the restructuring in the 1890s.[61] Signifiers of pre-industrial urban spatial indices, featuring prominent physical landmarks such as 'a pair of lakes' or Joda talao, or collective memory such as that of

[57] D. Ray, *Debganer Martye Agaman*, p. 408.

[58] Radharaman Mitra, *Kolikata Darpan* (Calcutta: Subarnarekha, 1988), p. 311.

[59] D. Ray, *Debganer Martye Agaman*, p. 382; P. Dutta, *Kolikatar Itibritta*, p. 71.

[60] A.K. Roy, 'Short History of Calcutta', p. 111; H. Mukhopadhyay, *Kolikata Sekaler O Ekaler*, p. 477. Similar municipal impositions on street names under colonial rule have also been pointed out for Singapore. See Brenda Yeoh, *Contesting Space: Power Relations and the Urban Built Environment in Colonial Singapore* (Singapore: Singapore University Press, 2003), pp. 219–42.

[61] H. Mukhopadhyay, *Kolikata Sekaler O Ekaler*, p. 476.

boats washed up and destroyed during the 1737 cyclone (enshrined in street names such as Dinga Bhanga or 'broken boats') gradually disappeared along principal and showcase thoroughfares. They came to be replaced instead by the inscribing of the East India Company's more recent and triumphant successes, as evident in the renaming of Dinga Bhanga as Wellington Square.[62]

An intrinsic vernacular spatial category that could not be captured in street names was that of the *para* or neighbourhood or locality. The para represented a contained area comprising a few streets—usually residential but also sometimes engaging in trade—which also formed a basic socio-spatial component unit in the city. Thus, people belonged to certain paras by virtue of their social background—by status, trade, or regional origin—but a para could also denote a more heterogeneous settlement tied to a local feature such as a pond (*pukur*) or bazaar, as evident in names such as Jhamapukur and Shyambazar. The limits of the para were neither regular nor fixed, but known to residents and locals and nurtured strong ties of fellow-feeling, locality, and community.

Initially, the basic units of police administration or *thanas* were loosely based on paras. But the wards that replaced the thanas in 1852 for administrative purposes bypassed the idea of paras, coinciding their boundaries with major arterial networks of streets instead. In administrative maps from the mid-nineteenth century onwards, the paras ceased to feature altogether, as official cartographies did away with information unrelated to efficient governance. As cognitive categories, however, the paras continued to inform the Bengali sociocultural sphere as we shall see below, serving as one of the major navigational indices for visitors to the city in the late nineteenth century, as well as meshes of sociability and community.

In Bengali accounts, maps, and travel guides, the layout of the city is repeatedly explained in terms of important markets or bazaars, riverside ghats, religious sites, and homes of important local residents.[63] As thriving centres of business and markers of

[62] This was done by way of commemoration of the military exploits of Arthur Wellesley or the Duke of Wellington in the Deccan wars against Mysore and the Marathas. H. Mukhopadhyay, *Kolikata Sekaler O Ekaler*, pp. 477, 479.

[63] See, for example, Mitra, *Gokulchandra Mitra O Sekaler Kolikata*. The chapters in the book are built around the various ghats, their builders, and

social and intellectual life in Calcutta, these alternate sites inscribed different trajectories of urbanization and community development than usually appreciated. Ghats formed the hubs of riverine commerce and passenger traffic while also doubling as sites for ritual ablution in the holy Ganges.[64] Numerous such ghats lining the Hooghly River—a distributary of the Ganges—were built in the nineteenth century before railways and road traffic took over in the early twentieth century (see Figure 1.2).

FIGURE 1.2 *Ghaut* [*sic*] and Temples on the Banks of the Hooghly, 1851 (Hand-Coloured Photographic Print by Frederick Fiebig)
Source: Photo 247/1(52) © The British Library Board. Courtesy of the British Library, London.

---

histories. Ghats were also built by rich Hindu merchant-traders like Kashinath, Nayan Mullick, Gokul Mitra, Gobindaram Mitra, and Banamali Sircar. Also see Pramathanath, Mullick, *Sachitra Kalikatar Katha* (Calcutta, 1935), vol. 2, p. 20.

64 Most ghats were bathing ghats (comprising steps descending to the waterline), although a sizeable number were reserved for commerce. A few served as cremation grounds. See Mitra, *Kolikata Darpan*, pp. 253–315.

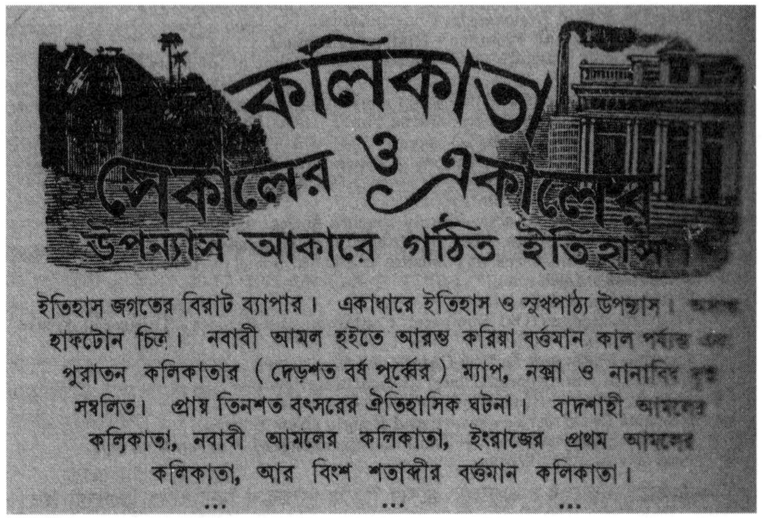

FIGURE 1.3 Advertisement for the Original Edition of Harisadhan Mukhopadhyay, *Kolikata Sekaler O Ekaler* (Calcutta, 1915), Showing the Town Hall and Factories on the Right and Bengali Temples and Villages on the Left

Source: Reproduced from the 1991 edition published by P.M. Bagchi, Calcutta.

An exhaustive, though highly idiosyncratic, compendium on Calcutta, comprising selections from newspapers, government reports, and memoirs, lists twenty-four ghats at the end of the eighteenth century.[65] Temples were invariably open to the public and, in the nineteenth century, were usually grand, renovated structures built on popular sites of worship and veneration.[66] A list of 'important sites in Calcutta' mentions temples, mosques, and *pir* (Muslim holy men) burial grounds alongside government buildings, theatres, gardens, fountains, and public statuettes, underlining the mixed heritage of the city (see Figure 1.3).

In a close study of a Bengali lithographed map and directory by Ramanath Das from the late nineteenth century for 'general use', Keya Dasgupta has shown how it is attentive to paras alongside

[65] H. Mukhopadhyay, *Kolikata Sekaler O Ekaler*, p. 415.

[66] H. Mukhopadhyay, *Kolikata Sekaler O Ekaler*, pp. 574–8

roads; religious institutions alongside educational and commercial; wholesale markets and bazaars alongside European mercantile houses; and residences of prominent Indians—aristocrats and intellectuals—alongside administrative centres such as courts, government offices, and police stations.[67] The presentation of spatial information here is based almost entirely on the social and functional categories of the daily lives of Bengalis in the northern part of the city with exhaustive lists of commodities available at the various bazaars (such as wooden furniture in Baithakkhana and Bowbazar, spices in Raja Sukhomoy's Posta, and cotton in Burrabazar and Chinabazar), and inclusion of intimate local knowledge of the area, which allowed one to navigate through various paras and using markets, ghats, mosques, temples, and residences of local notables as landmarks.[68]

The directory listed such information in great detail with accompanying letters and numerals to correspond with the use of numbered and lettered grids on the map itself. In resorting to the grids, Das could thus present much needed local information to users that had been erased by official maps and that street names alone could not encompass. The alternative method of presenting spatial information relevant for local users through officially produced cartographies of the city was a clever strategy to bypass the problem.[69] The directory and the map thus complemented each other and represented not so much a street map as a specific introduction to the locality and community.

[67] See Keya Dasgupta, 'A City Away from Home: The Mapping of Calcutta' in *Texts of Power: Emerging Disciplines in Colonial Bengal*, edited by Partha Chatterjee (Calcutta: Samya, 1996), pp. 145–66. The map and directory, *Kolikatar Manchitra*, was produced by Ramanath Das in 1884.

[68] Thirty-eight such residences were located in north Calcutta, and eight in the district of the 24 Parganas. K. Dasgupta, 'A City Away from Home, p. 156.

[69] A recent study confirms the irrelevance of house numbers and street names in early twentieth-century India for residents of colonial cities who, it argues, used other methods of navigation. See Richard Hariss and Robert Lewis, 'Numbers Didn't Count: The Streets of Colonial Bombay and Calcutta', *Urban History* 39, no. 2 (2012): 639–58.

Textual accounts like *Debganer Martye Agaman*, discussed previously, present similar navigational grids. Alongside the generic markers—public buildings, parks and squares, European shopping areas and taverns—the gods travel around Calcutta using the houses of Bengali aristocratic and bureaucratic elite as prominent landmarks. Architecturally speaking, these would have been spectacular residences rising above the surrounding homes and naturally providing a focal point in the local urban landscape. But as presented in the book, the stately stature of the buildings is matched by the monumental achievements of their owners. The narrative format induces the travellers to pause at important locations and introduce the inhabitants with brief accounts of their self-made careers in colonial service and boundless charity to the local community, and even beyond.[70] Streets are rarely mentioned while paras and bazaars provide vital signposts.[71] Like Ramanath's map, the work lavishes great details on the bazaars, listing goods and wares available. Thus, Napibazar was renowned for its stock of the koi fish, Tiretta Bazar specialized in birds, and cottage cheese could only be found in Mullick Bazar.[72]

Popular street literature—novels and songs—focussed almost entirely on the northern 'Black Town', with spatial typologies of different parts of the city indexing popular perceptions of these areas. A tract describing leisure activities on a Saturday paints a picture of roving bands of youth indulging in drunken and disorderly behaviour, courting prostitutes, and being generally

[70] D. Ray, *Debganer Martye Agaman*, pp. 377, 381–7, 394–7, 400, 405–6, 408–13.

[71] See D. Ray, *Debganer Martye Agaman*: This work thus mentions Ukilpara surrounding the high court (p. 279), Chunagali (p. 352), Khalasitollah, Sindurepati, Mecchhuabazar (p. 365), Hatkhola (p. 405), and Knasaripati (p. 411) denoting residential and occupational clusters. As for bazaars, we find all the prominent ones listed, such as Burrabazar (p. 283), municipal Hogg Market (p. 291), Janbazar (p. 299), New and old China Bazars (pp. 318–19), Madhab Babu's Bazar (p. 349), Bowbazar (p. 354), Canning Bazar (p. 360), Lalbazar (p. 362).

[72] D. Ray, *Debganer Martye Agaman*, pp. 299, 363, 382–3.

dissolute.[73]. The cartography of the city's entertainment district comes alive—the alcohol shops of Mechhuabazar and Radhabazar, the prostitute quarters of Sonagatchi, the busy streets of Harkata and Siddheswari—in the vivid descriptions. The opening lines thus declare:

> Oh Hail the city of Calcutta! Hail Saturday!
> It looks glorious with the [alcohol] bottles everywhere.
> The festive banners are fluttering over Sonagaji [Sonagatchi],
> The opium is burning with great style,
> Mechhuabazar is immersed in alcohol and merriment.
> Harkata smiles while drinking from a glass,
> And says, 'Oh what fun!'[74]

Throughout the rest of the tract, there is absolutely no reference to the immensely busy and important office and business districts that drove the city's economic engine—except by way of mentioning the welcome release of office workers from it during the weekend—its European leisure quarters in the southern parts, its parks and promenades.[75]

Another much later work also bears the imprint of the same cartography, outlining the centres of addiction in the northern parts of the city but also taking considerable pride in the achievements of this area. The poem commemorates a host of celebrities inhabiting these parts such as Nabin the sweetmaker (widely known for devising the *rasagulla*, a milk based product filled with a sugary syrup); Girish Ghosh, the famous nineteenth-century playwright and social reformer; and the stars of the Bengal Theatre such as Ardhendu Mustafi, Amritalal Basu, and Dharma Das. It also walks the readers through the occupational quarters of the northern city—the brazier, fishermen, and brewer colonies—as well as its landmarks such as the Madan Mohan temple of Chitpore and the Kashi Mitra burning ghats.[76]

[73] Chandrakanta Sikdar, *Ki Mojar Shonibar* (Calcutta, 1863). Another important work mentions the special occasion that the Saturday night was in the city. Kaliprasanna Sinha, *Hutom Pnechar Naksha*, edited by Arun Nag (Calcutta: Subarnarekha, 1991; originally published in 1861), p. 38.

[74] Sikdar, *Ki Mojar Shonibar*, p. 1 (translation mine).

[75] Sikdar, *Ki Mojar Shonibar*, p. 9

[76] Devendra Sharma, *Sahar Chitra* (Calcutta, 1921), p. 56.

Wandering Baul or popular syncretic religious minstrels too rendered a thick indexing of the city in their songs offering allegories of the human body, life, and death. In one such song, the seemingly invincible presence of the British in Calcutta (formidable series of cannons at the riverside fort with rooms guarded by armed personnel, the prison at Alipore, the Medical and Hindu Colleges, the Mint) is summarily demolished when the song triumphantly declares the superiority and beauty (comparable to the *Jadughar*, literally House of Wonders, or museum) of the human body over the impermanent nature of the British material (and power) structures in the city. Instead various indigenous quarters of Calcutta come across as busy, thriving areas—the various bazaars, the temple of Kalighat, the red-light areas, and the occupational quarters of fishermen, butchers, barbers, oilpressers, potters, and shoemakers.[77]

Technology and the Changing Social Imaginary

Technological wonders amazed Calcutta's residents and many were in wondrous rapture of its achievements. Rupchand Pakshi, the progenitor of the hemp-smoking club at Bagbazar, and a fashionable member of Calcutta's early nineteenth-century gentry, was also a songster in his own right. Like Kaliprasanna Sinha (pseud. Hutom), he wrote about the world around him, and although composed in a light satirical vein, they provide rich insights into contemporary perceptions of how technology was changing life in the city:

> Dirty water is being expelled by a drainage machine,
> Another sprinkler machine helps settle the dust [of the streets]
> When fires rage there is the fire hydrant ...
> Making it impossible for houses to be burnt down
> (When you wind it up the water comes roaring and gushing out).
> There is the jute mill, the flour mill ... the cloth mill and the brick grinder
> A machine for lifting water, and another for crushing stones,
> A huge elephant of a machine straightens out the roads in a day.

[77] Sudhir Chakrabarty, *Bangla Dehatattver Gan* (Calcutta: Pustak Bipani, 1990), pp. 206–9.

Now that the world is being filled by machines,
Perhaps there will even be one for making heirs;
So that no one dies without a proper inheritor.[78]

Contemporary newspapers wrote of the considerable crowds visiting one of the earliest steam engines set up in Calcutta. The Strand Mill set up next to the Hooghly for milling grain and oil attracted hundreds of viewers and the *Samachar Darpan* advised its readers to go and see for themselves this remarkable machine that could mill over 740 kilograms of wheat in 24 hours.[79] The printing press at Serampore Mission—the first Bengali printing press—run by Baptist missionaries, had imported from England in 1820 a 12-horsepower steam engine to work its paper mill. It proved a major curiosity, attracting viewers even four years after it had been installed. It was believed to have created as much of a stir as the earliest steam rail and steam boat, records J.C. Marshman of the Mission, and locals came to know it by the name of the 'fire machine' or *aaguner kol*.[80] The biographer of William Carey, the well-known Serampore missionary, notes how the European who worked the machine was repeatedly pelted by questions from inquisitive onlookers.[81]

Technological innovations, it can be argued, had infiltrated multiple social levels and their reception is recorded in a range of cultural artefacts, prints, and memoirs from the times.[82]

[78] Siddhartha Ghosh, 'Purono Kolkatar Kolkobja: Oupanibeshik Shaharer Prajukti Proyash', in *Kolkatar Purakatha*, edited by Debashis Basu (Calcutta: Pustak Bipani, 1990), pp. 222–45, at 222–3.

[79] *Samachar Darpan*, 8 August 1829. The original amount of wheat cited in indigenous units was two thousand *mon* (maund), with one unit being equivalent to 82 lbs (pounds).

[80] John Clark Marshman, *The History of the Serampore Mission Embracing the Life and Times of William Carey, Joshua Marshman and William Ward*, 2 vols. (London, 1859), vol. 2, pp. 224–5.

[81] George Smith, *The Life of William Carey: Shoemaker and Missionary* (London: John Murray, 1887), p. 232.

[82] The next chapter covers in detail how contemporary songs—both oral and printed—offered textual representations of the response to the arrival of modern technology in the city.

Painted Kalighat *pats*, woodcut prints, and even embroidered sarees and carved friezes from terracotta temples provide visual records of the contemporary response.[83] In *Debganer Martye Agaman*, Bengalis appear unable to match the power of colonial technology. Here the British have emerged victorious, and the gods openly praise the wonders of modern science, as evident in the city's gas and electric lights, clean water supply, and gas supply.[84] But the same work also recorded a more troubled conscience that was simultaneously witnessing, for instance, the loss of symbolical status of the mighty Ganges River and the cost of technology with regard to manual jobs.[85]

In a separate example, Sumanta Banerjee has shown how Baradaprasad Roy, a struggling rural poet in the city, offers a woeful assessment of its flourishing infrastructural and technological establishments in a direct address to the British Empress: 'Where are you, mother Victoria?... I don't even get two full meals; what's the use of roads? What's the use of tap water and gas light?.... I don't need news through the wire, mother. Who'll hear our news after some time?'[86]

It would be difficult to contest the idea that over time the Indian middle classes started to mimic European civilizational paradigms. Sudipta Kaviraj, for instance, argues how these groups responded quite positively to the prospects of self-making that the new world of the colonial city offered them. Though still threatening to the sensibilities of a segmented small-scale society, its promise was the large-scale operation of modernity, a world of freedom rather than restriction. The middle-class city represented this new

[83] Ashit Paul (ed.), *Woodcut Prints of Nineteenth Century Calcutta* (Calcutta: Seagull Books, 1983), pp. 90–1; S. Ghosh, 'Purono Kolkatar Kolkobja', p. 227.

[84] D. Ray, *Debganer Martye Agaman*, pp. 281, 361, and 365.

[85] Thus, not only was the Howrah Bridge defiling the river's mythological glory, people were beginning to prefer bathing at home using tap water, rather than taking a ritual dip in the holy river. D. Ray, *Debganer Martye Agaman*, pp. 306–7, 324–5.

[86] See citation from an unpublished diary by Sumanta Banerjee, *Parlour and the Streets: Elite and Popular Culture in Nineteenth Century Calcutta* (Calcutta: Seagull Books, 1998), p. 115. Translation by Sumanta Banerjee.

ideology spatially, where the outside was tamed and governed by a civil order instead of the state of nature ...[87]

But it is important to recognize that middle classes were not so clearly and involuntarily socialized at first. In the writings of the Bengali educated in the nineteenth and early twentieth centuries, there emerges a critique of the urbanization process, and a record of anxiety, contention, and struggles. Nineteenth-century Calcutta had become a vital nerve-centre for the Bengali bhadralok, providing access to liberal education and professions, and later, political action. They wielded their social influence and intellectual prestige by leading movements for reform in caste Hindu society, and using the print media to effect a general moral and intellectual improvement of society. And yet, it is hardly surprising that the bhadralok harboured a deep and uneasy discomfort about Calcutta—at once their source of livelihood, social prestige, and symbol of subjugation.

While the convenience and general benefits flowing from the improvement of the city's infrastructure from about the 1860s onwards is acknowledged in bhadralok writings, the critique is not too far behind.[88] There is a constant dialectic of identity and alienation for the bhadralok within the colonial urban space. Anxiety persisted particularly on the upsetting of Hindu ways of life and codes. Prankrishna Dutta, born into the Hindu aristocracy of Calcutta in 1851 and later editor of *Sulabh Patrika*, reminisced about bygone days and practices in the columns of a Bengali

[87] Sudipta Kaviraj, 'Filth and the Public Sphere: Concepts and Practices about Space in Calcutta', *Public Culture*, 10, no. 1 (1997): 83–113, 94.

[88] Middle-class objections to the technologization of cities from the mid-nineteenth century onwards have been studied by scholars for other locations, although the concerns were very different. Americans thus opposed the introduction of electric trolley cars in the 1890s on grounds of safety, noise, and aesthetics. See Eric Schatzberg, 'Culture and Technology in the City: Opposition to Mechanised Street Transportation in Late-Nineteenth-Century America', in *Technologies of Power: Essays in Honor of Thomas Parke Hughes and Agatha Chipley Hughes*, edited by Michael T. Allen and Gabrielle Hecht (Cambridge, Massachusetts: MIT Press, 2001), pp. 57–94.

monthly at the start of the twentieth century.[89] He talked of the bodily benefits of an early rise and dip in the Ganges, the worship of family deities, and the contribution of traditional games such as wrestling, sword and baton fighting, archery, and swimming towards the making of a healthy constitution.[90] People, it would appear, had simpler palates in earlier days but ate wholesome food. The weak constitution of Bengalis in latter days, Dutta held, should be traced to the lack of milk in their diet and adulteration of food items like oil and ghee. The legendary appetites of yesteryears were presented with a degree of nostalgia and symbol of healthy lives.[91] Kaliprasanna Sinha, in his witty urban sketches of the mid-nineteenth century, noted how those coming into the city from the villages of Bengal invariably suffered from indigestion and dyspepsia.[92]

Calcutta's educated hark back repeatedly to the more salubrious condition of rural Bengal in earlier times in their writings.[93] Born in Calcutta in 1851, Bepin Krishna Bose recalled a visit with his parents to a village in Burdwan as a little boy where they stayed for several months.

> To one who had been brought up amidst the dirt and dust of a large and crowded town like Calcutta, the change to village-life was most agreeable. Bengal villages were not then so many death-traps, as they have since become owing to malaria.... The enforced migration to Calcutta has neither improved the physique of

[89] See P. Dutta, *Kolikatar Itibritta*, pp. 96–132. See also Rajnarayan Bose, *Sekal Ar Ekal* [Those Times and These Times] (Calcutta, 1874) for a similar comparison of pre-colonial and colonial times.

[90] P. Dutta, *Kolikatar Itibritta*, pp. 100–3.

[91] P. Dutta, *Kolikatar Itibritta*, pp. 1–3–7.

[92] Nag (ed.), K. Sinha, *Hutom Pnechar Naksa*, p. 44.

[93] Recent studies have contested any projected separation of the metropolitan city and its surrounding villages and suburbs, making a case instead for more organic connections. See Tania Sengupta, 'Between Country and City: Fluid Spaces of Provincial Administrative Towns in Nineteenth-century Bengal', *Urban History* 39, no. 1 (February, 2012): 56–82.

> the people nor added to their comforts. Their ancestors in their unreformed village-homes were on the whole better off than they are now.[94]

Technology was viewed as debilitating, discriminatory, and insensitive to dharmic or religious sentiments. When the floating pontoon bridge was built over the River Ganges in 1874 linking the twin cities of Calcutta and Howrah, it was hailed as a technological wonder. The Howrah Bridge became the icon of the city's technological revolution and the subject matter of numerous popular vernacular songs and pamphlets of the time as we shall see later. But the educated were markedly reticent. It finds cursory mention in Tagore's otherwise quite meticulous observations on the city's transportation networks.[95] Other writings complain how the mighty Bhagirathi has to bear the burden of speeding and heavy trains that tear across her breast. Ganges water, so holy to the Hindus, accordingly was being defiled everyday by the throwing of the city's organic rubbish into it, as well as the industrial waste arising from the numerous jute mills that lined the river.[96]

While it would seem that the tram was introduced in Calcutta for the convenience of the increasing number of clerks and office workers and shops and businesses, mechanized travel in general came under much criticism in the educated writings. To begin with, there was observed a direct and inverse corelation between health and motorized travel in the city. Prankrishna Dutta was quick to blame the trams and other rental vehicles for the explosion of diabetes among the population. Tagore too notes the injurious effects of travel by tram on the youth of his days. Both recalled an earlier time when people could easily cover long distances by

94 Sir Bepin Krishna Bose, *Stray Thoughts on Some Incidents in My Life* (Madras, 1923), pp. 3–4.

95 Tagore briefly mentions a new Howrah bridge being proposed after the First World War (in fact, it was built during the Second World War and completed between 1938 and 1943). K. Tagore, *Kolikatay Chalafera*, p. 118.

96 Sharma, *Sahar Chitra*, pp. 48–9.

foot and stay healthy as a result.[97] The Tagores of Jorasanko were particularly irked by the digging up of roads in the vicinity of their ancestral residence:

> I remember vividly the nuisance caused to householders by the Company [the Calcutta Tramway Company] digging up the roads and shutting off all the entrances into the smaller streets feeding the main roads.[98]

The Calcutta Tramway Company (CTC) was a typical *sahib company* (white man's company), writes Kshitindranath, and did not initially entertain the repeated complaints made by the residents in the affected streets. It was only when a prominent member of the Tagore household like Jyotirindranath Tagore threatened to file a case of inconvenience against the company that they relented and amendments were made.[99]

Kshitindranath's own experience of mechanized travel, including that of trams, ranged from the lukewarm to negative. While it was fun to watch the steam-powered earliest trams, riding on them proved positively unpleasant because of the noise of locomotion, the shrill tram whistle, and 'all the juddering'. The later electric-powered trams proved equally disappointing with their 'unimaginative' speed and efficiency, and suffocating and emotionless mechanical feel.

> ... there was no romanticism in reaching the destination so quickly—there was such little time between boarding and alighting ... it might be great for speeding up business but I do not like the electric trams of recent times—its high speed renders it with a deadening and unappealing character.[100]

[97] P. Dutta, *Kolikatar Itibritta*, p. 96; K. Tagore, *Kolikatay Chalafera*, p. 80. Kshitindranath in fact believed that the first experiment in 1864 of introducing horse-drawn trams did not succeed because people preferred to walk rather than pay for tram travel.

[98] K. Tagore, *Kolikatay Chalafera*, p. 81.

[99] K. Tagore, *Kolikatay Chalafera*, pp. 81–2.

[100] K. Tagore, *Kolikatay Chalafera*, pp. 89–90. He also writes in a similar vein of the annoyance caused by motor cars. See pp. 98–101. Tagore also complains of the nuisance created by motor cars and motor cycles, pp. 98–101, 105–6).

For Calcutta's people technology came at the bitter cost of rising tax burdens. Its streets were engulfed in darkness after sunset causing tremendous difficulties for pedestrians and traffic, and encouraging crime. Oil lamps used in public spaces were either too few or regularly pilfered to be of any use.[101] Gas lights were first introduced in Calcutta in 1857 by the Oriental Gas Company. These remained the principal mode of public lighting till electric lights replaced them in 1900. As the new gas lights were being planned, taxes were proposed for these novel civic amenities. Residents of houses paying a rent of over five rupees had to pay a 4 per cent tax on their rent for the new gas lights. Those with oil lamps on their streets had to pay a similar 2 per cent tax as the number of oil lamps in these streets were being increased. Bengali Commissioners of the Municipality themselves were vehemently opposed, pointing out how householders, already overburdened with the recent steep rise in the house assessment tax, would be unwilling to pay more. They also pointed out that drainage, rather than lighting, needed prioritizing.[102] The newspapers were distraught, underlining the futility of even complaining.[103] The *Hindoo Patriot* protested loudly in 1858 that

> [t]he evils of taxation are fast escaping from the Pandora's Box of the legislative council. Today the city requires good roads; tax the householders! Tomorrow the roads required to be watered—tax again!—the next day the streets are found awfully dark for the purpose of good government—haul up the citizen for an additional pressure of the screw!—the day after the stink of the drains is discovered to be too nauseating for refined noses—give another

[101] Mahendranath Dutta, *Kolikatar Puratan Kahini O Pratha*, reprint edition (Calcutta: Mahendra Publishing Committee, 1975; original edition 1929), see pp. 20–5. Apparently, even illumination from gas lamps were not that effective in lighting up streets. K. Tagore, *Kolikatay Chalafera*, pp. 27–8.

[102] *Report of the Commissioners for the Improvement of the Town of Calcutta* (hereafter *RCIC*), *1854*, p. 10.

[103] 'If it turns out that the king who is meant to protect his subjects has harmful intentions, then there is no point in shedding tears.' *Sarbasubhakari Patrika*, Bhadra 1262 B.S. [1855], reprinted in Benoy Ghosh, *Samayik Patre Banglar Samajchitra* (Calcutta, 1980), vol. 3, pp. 94–5.

> strain to the throat of the liege! The liege in the meantime gets black in the face—his eyes stand out of their sockets—his tongue lolls out ruefully ...[104]

The crushing burden of municipal taxes was generally felt by a wide spectrum of city dwellers. Thus, poets composing street songs echoed the frustrations of the middle-class groups in the city, mentioning a wide range of taxes that the urban populace were plagued by, from income tax to taxes for water, streets, and police, in addition to those for lights. Inability to pay the taxes, they lamented, led to disproportionate fines and even seizure of property and eviction.[105]

Ironically, the fruits of technological progress did not flow with speed and ease for the northern part of the city where the bulk of the Indian population lived. The engineering infrastructure for drainage, disposal of garbage, lighting, and supply of safe drinking water took a long time to reach the Indian residents of the city. Gas lamps thus were much brighter than the older oil lamps, but they were costly with the lamps, posts, and brackets being imported from England.[106] They were prioritized in business districts and the pleasure areas of the White Town—the Eden Gardens, Strand, and the Maidan—but proved a rarer presence in the northern part of the city.[107] The Oriental Gas Company complained that the 'bendy lanes and streets of the Northern Division' did not lend themselves naturally to the laying of gas pipes. While the main thoroughfares were prioritized, the smaller streets and lanes used by pedestrians continued to be lit only by the dimmer oil lamps.[108]

[104] *Hindoo Patriot*, 13 March 1856, cited in Alok Ray (ed.), *Nineteenth Century Studies* (Calcutta, 1974), Chapter 5, p. 64.

[105] Aminchandra Datta, *Howrah Ghater Poler Kobi* (Calcutta: Kabita Kaumudi Press, 1874), p. 11.

[106] Each gas post, with lamps and fittings, cost thirty-five rupees. *RCIC, 1861*, p. 24.

[107] Thus, for example, there were fifty-six gas streetlights in Chowringhee Road as compared to forty in the much longer Chitpore Road, and nineteen in Park Street compared to only eight in Pathuriaghata Street. *RCIC, 1861*, Appendices XII and XIII.

[108] *RCIC, 1861*, pp. 25–31.

It was not till 1874 that the first sewers were built in the Black Town. Safe drinking water was introduced in the northern quarters in 1870. Until then, Mahendranath Dutta recalls, residents had to resort to water drawn from the Ganges or the Hendua Tank and delivered by human water-carriers or *bhaaries*. Water drawn from wells (with considerable risk of groundwater contamination) was used for other household needs. It was not by accident, he notes, that cholera subsided in the city following the introduction of filtered tap water.[109] Kshitindranath Tagore remembers the nuisance caused in his childhood (in the last decade of the nineteenth century) by rubbish collecting on the doorsteps of householders because of the inadequacy of the waste-disposal services. Petitions were sent repeatedly to the government, he writes, but to no avail.[110] In reality things would have been more improved by then, but the memory of discrimination lived on in writings as late as in 1921:

> The sahib tollah [area] in the city is neat and tidy
> It has all things paved and nicely organised
> The roads are comfortable to walk on ...
> Peace reigns in this splendid kingdom
> Electricity has been tied to the posts there
> Lighting up electric garlands ...
> Now you will be astonished to hear of Chowringhee
> There are mehters on standby duty daily
> And look at the scene in the Bangali tollah!
> Putrid stench fills the alleys and byways
> Animal carcasses rot by the road side
> What a great and healthy way to live life![111]

[109] Mahendranath Dutta, *Kolikatar Puratan Kahini O Pratha*, pp. 5–6. Rabindranath Tagore too recalls in his childhood memoirs, an entire ground floor room being filled up with earthenware pots containing a year's supply of drinking water brought in from the Ganges during the less polluting winter months. Rabindranath Tagore, 'Chhelebela', in *Rabindra Rachanabali*, Centenary Edition, vol. 10 (Calcutta: West Bengal Government [Saraswati Press], 1961), p. 132.

[110] K. Tagore, *Kolikatay Chalafera*, p. 5.

[111] Devendra Sharma, *Sahar Chitra* (Calcutta, 1921), p. 29.

Traditional ways of living were being profoundly changed in the city. Concerns of hygiene, order, and efficiency underwrote municipal projects of improvement while older sensibilities of caste hierarchies, ritual practices, and spatial organization continued to inform people's daily experiences.

The Nimtala Burning Ghat controversy can be taken as a case in point. As one of the principal burning ghats for Hindus since 1828, Nimtala was under constant surveillance of the municipal government for reasons of hygiene. When improvements organized by the Hindu community in 1857 proved very limited, the government proposed the building of a mechanized incinerator for the performance of death rituals.[112] The proposal was met with fiery resistance from the Hindus, with Ramgopal Ghosh delivering an impassioned speech in opposition to the move before the Justices of Peace Committee, which went to live on in public memory for years later.[113] The government ultimately backed down, while a subscription of 35,000 rupees was raised by Ghosh from the Hindu community in 1865 to finance improvements—including the building of high walls to conceal the grounds from public view—in the ghat.[114]

Calcutta suffered from a chronic shortage of clean water in the nineteenth century. Residents relied on dug out or natural water reservoirs, in addition to river water. The town's water supply when set up in 1848, came from two reservoirs where river water was pumped in and then supplied by means of aqueducts to the city, with the overflow filling up some public tanks.[115] The ducts stopped short of reaching the end of Chitpore and Lower Circular Roads, as the engine was not powerful enough to pump water any

[112] In 1857, approximately 6,000 rupees was collected for the improvements. See Mitra, *Gokul Chandra Mitra O Sekaler Kolikata*, pp. 45–6.

[113] See D. Ray, *Debganer Martye Agaman*, p. 400.

[114] *ARCM for 1866*. The Kalighat burning ghat by contrast, was easier to manage as the municipality was able to acquire its lease and then subject it to sanitary regulations. *Administrative Report of the Municipality of the Suburbs of Calcutta*, 1874–5, p. 31.

[115] *RCIC, 1848*, Appendix 11, p. 27.

further.[116] The crisis was partially solved ten years later by the arrival of a 25-horsepower engine from England, which was set up to supply water to underground pipes leading to the northern part of the city.[117] From 1870 onwards, 800 hydrants along public roads and lanes maintained a constant and liberal supply of clean filtered water.[118]

Despite the novelty of such a facility, there was initially some reluctance to use filtered hydrant water among inhabitants. There were, in fact, stories doing the rounds of *bheesties* or water-carriers mixing in some mud with the filtered water to make their masters believe that it was holy river water.[119] Widespread use of the municipal water supply could take root only after prominent leaders of Bengali society had authorized it. The Dharma Sabha declared the supply of filtered water fit for all uses except religious ceremonies.[120] Dwarkanath Vidyabhushan, editor of *Somprakash*, also sanctioned its use in accordance with Hindu dharma and ritual in his newspaper.[121] The introduction of a municipal water supply, however, signalled a decline in the maintenance of the many large tanks in Calcutta and its suburbs, which were privately owned but had been, for centuries, open for communal uses of bathing, fishing, and washing pots. The problem was acute particularly in the suburbs where filtered water took some time to reach.[122]

[116] An opportunity for additionally buying a discarded engine and pumps belonging to the old paper mills at Cossipore had to be abandoned for shortage of funds; *RCIC, 1850*, Third and Fourth Half-yearly Reports. Wealthy inhabitants like Rani Rashmoni and Nawab Nazeem contributed, with the rani covering fully for an aqueduct running the entire length of the densely populated Jaun Bazar Street, from the Chowringhee to Circular Road. *RCIC, 1854*, pp. 13–14.

[117] *RCIC, 1861*, pp. 76–7.

[118] *Report of the Municipality of Calcutta for the Quarters ending June 1876* (hereafter *Calcutta Municipal Quarterly Reports*).

[119] *Calcutta Municipal Quarterly Reports Ending June 1876.*

[120] Report of Health Officer, Appendix 12, *ARCM for 1870*.

[121] D. Ray, *Debganer Martye Agaman*, p. 361.

[122] The vice-chairman of the Calcutta Municipality recognized this problem and suggested the taking over of the tanks via long-term leases

In the tract *Sahar Chitra* (Picture of the City) by an unknown Brahmin scholar, the author laments the decline of earlier rituals and customs in a section called 'Happiness in the East' or Prachya Sukh. In keeping with the contemporary trends among the literate, the tract outlines a hyper-romantic portrayal of a more traditional Hindu habitual world that was being lost to technology and modern ways of living. The familiar hyperboles of material abundance and domestic bliss in the bygone era, constituting key elements of the nationalist critique of colonial economy, are present. Thus, images of barns full of grain, sheds full of cattle, and ponds full of fish are presented alongside well-kept houses—where women excelled in housework and ritual worship of family deities—with lovely gardens.

But plugged in is another critique—of the material cultures of modernity. The work asserts the benefits of traditional rituals of daily sweepings and sprinkling of water in Bengali homes, and the use of cow dung as disinfectant; the resorting to ayurvedic instead of modern medicine, and the preference for the indigenous *kaviraj* (physician) instead of the medical doctor. In contrasting the controversial newer municipal market, also known as Hogg Market, with the older and more established Nutan Bazar belonging to Rajendra Mullick, the author offers a comparative estimate of the moral economies of the two markets. The Nutan Bazar was motivated by Hindu dharmic rather than profit motives. It thus had a guesthouse in the city offering free meals and accommodation for all where a significant part of the market's profits were spent. Despite the glamour and the huge range of rare and luxury consumer goods available at the Municipal/Hogg Market, the Nutan Bazar outdid the former by its virtuous reputation.[123]

The fundamental transformation in social structures and distribution of caste privileges in a ritually ordered society following

---

so as to repair and maintain them as reservoirs of safe drinking water for the public, cutting out presumed secondary activities such as washing utensils, bathing, and fishing. *Administrative Report of the Municipality of the Suburbs of Calcutta, 1874–5*, p. 23.

123 Sharma, *Sahar Chitra*, pp. 75–7. The debate over markets crops up again in Chapter 4.

the establishment of a colonial political economy has been studied by scholars.[124] Initially, the upheaval caused by intermixing and changing social structures of patronage and influence was reflected in the attempts to reorganize Calcutta's society into rival factions or dals. There was an expectation that dals would fulfil the purpose of preservation of dharma or ideology of the social order. The group leaders or *dalapatis* oversaw the maintenance of ritual law and order, and negotiated a fine balance between caste and class status.[125] With the colonial regime affording many opportunities to mercantile enterprise, low-caste members of society could rise in status upsetting traditional social divides. Caste elders passed customary decrees for the containment of such disruption, doggerels poked fun at social aspirants, and insults and honours were carefully managed within a very intricate framework of ritual etiquette.[126]

But as the players in the field increased in number, and newer groups benefitting from the dispensation of colonial education came to dictate discussion of social matters, traditional hierarchies were eroded further. Caste was also losing its symbolical and ritual importance in public life—in educational, professional, cultural, political, and intellectual activities—although it still mattered in the private realm—in marriage and ritual ceremonies—by the mid-nineteenth century.[127] Earlier socially disenfranchised groups enjoyed the heady freedom to move from the older restrictive caste

[124] See, for example, Rajat K. Ray, *Social Conflict and Political Unrest in Bengal, 1875–1927* (New Delhi: Oxford University Press, 1984); John Broomfield, *Elite Conflict in a Plural Society: Twentieth Century Bengal* (Berkeley and Los Angeles: University of California Press, 1968); S.N. Mukherjee, 'Class, Caste and Politics in Calcutta, 1815–1838', in *Elites in South Asia*, edited by Edmund Leach and S.N. Mukherjee (Cambridge: Cambridge University Press, 1970), pp. 33–78.

[125] S.N. Mukherjee, 'Bhadralok and Their Dals—Politics of Social Factions in Calcutta, c.1820–1856', in *The Urban Experience: Calcutta*, edited by Pradip Sinha (Calcutta: Riddhi-India, 1987), pp. 192–212.

[126] For an excellent account of these processes, see Sumanta Banerjee, *Parlour and the Streets.*

[127] P. Sinha, *Calcutta in Urban History*, pp. 93, 97–8.

and familial networks to grab new opportunities offered by the secular state.

A close look at the caste composition of the city's residents in the early decades of the twentieth century gives us an idea of its prevailing social profile. While Brahmans and Kayasthas (including the Kaibartas) dominated the urban population, there was a significant presence of the lower castes of Chamars, Goalas, and Subarnabaniks, followed by the Kahars, Tantis, and Telis.[128]

The impact of the revolutionary changes introduced by technology and modernization of civic amenities were equally profound in everyday lived lives in Calcutta. The availability of common water from municipal taps, and open access to public transport and entertainment halls heightened social anxieties. The right to use hydrant water by all was thus contested on Calcutta's streets, sometimes leading to vicious scuffles.[129] An increasing number of clerks, petty office-goers, and business people resorted to the tramway from the 1880s onwards. As public tramways and omnibuses replaced the highly selective constricted spaces of hired palanquins and hackney carriages, the prospect of close proximity and bodily contact with the general public unnerved the privileged. The rapidly expanding Calcutta Tramway Company was sensitive to the needs of its passengers and introduced first- and second-class carriages on the trams for its varied customers. Thus, High Court judges, barristers, and advocates could travel comfortably on trams alongside less privileged workers. As late as the early twentieth century, high-caste viewers complained of menial methars (scavengers) populating movie theatres.[130]

Despite bhadralok complaints, it was beyond doubt that modern ways of living and being in the city, drawing on Western civic patterns, had come to stay. The technological and material changes in urban life that had been introduced by the municipal fathers were challenging earlier modes of living, breaking down hierarchies,

[128] *Census of the Town and Suburbs of Calcutta, 1911*, p. 48.

[129] In a street affray regarding the right to use a public hydrant, one of the disputants received a blow from a stick, which turned out to be fatal. *Report on the State of the Police in Calcutta, 1892*, p. 7.

[130] Sharma, *Sahar Chitra*, p. 90.

and opening up ritualized closed spaces and segregated clannish lifestyles. But the process was cyclical. Over time, as the changes congealed, newer social formations engendered by technology and the new civic infrastructure that came into being furthered modernization and innovation. Disruption was also conducive to the opening up of a more participatory and wider public sphere where the city's population could openly discuss, debate, and negotiate issues related to the changing urban world, as we shall see in the next chapter.

Experiences of Belonging and Unbelonging: Migrants, New Urban Communities, and the City

Riding on the back of a strong regional identity and at the heart of a cultural efflorescence that defined the 'modern' in historical terms in India, Calcutta represented the bastion of refined bhadralok culture and the Bengali language its haloed bearer in the nineteenth century. A booming print and publishing industry carried the variable fruits of this flourishing vernacular identity across all layers of a widening literate society. And yet, by 1901, 36.3 per cent of city's residents spoke Hindustani, while native Bengali speakers constituted barely more than half the population.[131] In economic terms too—serving principally as petty clerks, traders, and labourers in the informal sectors—Bengalis felt cornered by rich Marwaris at the higher and up-country north Indian populations at the lower end of the urban economy. The resentment spilled out in popular literature, and unfriendly doggerels and epithets directed against these communities.

The colonial capital had opened up multifarious opportunities for enterprise in the city that was not necessarily open to Bengalis alone. Other communities migrated from various parts of India—Rajasthan, United Provinces, Orissa, Bihar, and East Bengal—to make the most of the economic scene in the British capital. Up-country migrants in particular were displacing Bengalis in

[131] *Census of India, 1901*, vol. 7, no. 4, p. 72. Also see *Census of the Town and Suburbs of Calcutta, 1911*, pp. 47–8.

low paid and menial jobs such as police constables and scavengers. Those perceived as exploiters and 'outsiders'—such as the Marwaris—even became the targets of merciless assault on occasions. Displacement and competition among the Bengalis and the so-called non-Bengalis invariably resulted in mutual acrimony and typecasting. The social costs of migration were calibrated ceaselessly in the city's newspapers, literature, and popular culture. The dire economic situation of the interwar years intensified uncertainties with rising prices, shortages of essential items, and profiteering.

The cosmopolitan city that took shape in the eighteenth and early nineteenth centuries owed its origins to primarily mercantile and maritime interests. Calcutta had a rich diversity of immigrant population from Europe, which, besides the British, comprised Germans, Austro-Hungarians, French, Armenians, 'Jews', and Russians. But perhaps the largest constituency of immigrants was made up of the Chinese, who in 1911 numbered 2,349 and lived mostly in the Kalutola area.[132] Unsurprisingly, the marts (Burrabazar), ports (Watgunj), and cantonment (Alipore) areas contained the largest numbers of immigrant populations, where nine-tenths of the population was 'foreign born'.[133]

Calcutta's earliest Indian merchant and comprador groups were composed of migrants. Jagat Seth was a north-Indian Khattri, Manohar Das was an Agarwal banker from Benares, the Oswals were Marwaris from Rajasthan. Many prominent traders were associated with the Burrabazar area. By the nineteenth century, the term *patti*s rather than paras, the latter with a purely Bengali association, was acquiring greater prominence in the Burrabazar area. It was also coming to acquire a more landlocked and local character than a maritime, cosmopolitan one.[134] Over time, Bengalis were eventually pushed out and could be found in riverine marts lining the river (Dharmahatta, trading in split bamboos;

[132] 'Jews' form a racial category in British census reports and other official documentation; *Census of the Town and Suburbs of Calcutta, 1911*, pp. 16, 42–3.

[133] *Census of the Town and Suburbs of Calcutta, 1911*, p. 16.

[134] P. Sinha, *Calcutta in Urban History*, pp. 54–5, 56–7.

Baniatola, trading in spice; and Ahiritollah, trading in grain) and in the northern bazaars.

The early years of the twentieth century registered very different patterns of displacement and immigration in the city. Within just a decade, from 1901 to 1911, the number of immigrants—mostly male—in Calcutta rose by 5.7 per cent. Suburbs populated mostly by migrant labour, such as Manicktola, Garden Reach, and Cossipur–Chitpore, also showed dramatic increase.[135] With the expansion of the jute mills and rising demand for labour, the number of immigrants grew rapidly in the city at the beginning of the twentieth century. Nearly a quarter of Calcutta's population was engaged in industry, a vast majority of them being employed as jute spinners and weavers.[136] In 1911, Bihar supplied 155,000 and the United Provinces some 90,000, over a third of the latter coming from the districts of Benares, Azamgarh, Ghazipur, and Jaunpur. Migrants from the Bikaner and Jaipur areas of Rajputana were also proving a steady stream from the start of the twentieth century onwards.[137] With this mainly Urdu- and Hindi-speaking immigrant labour community, Bengali was hard-pushed to hold its own in the polyglot city.

Their presence in urban spaces was heightened by the tendency to concentrate in certain areas as they preferred to live with friends and family in already congested quarters rather than seek newer accommodation.[138] Thus, Biharis tended to congregate in the wards of Kalutola, Muchipara, and Entally; those from the United Provinces in Jorabagan, Burrabazar, Kalutola, and Watgunj; those from Bombay and the Punjab in Burrabazar and Kalutola; and those from the central parts of India and Rajputana in Jorabagan and Burrabazar.[139] High densities of Bengali populations, on the

[135] *Census of the Town and Suburbs of Calcutta, 1911*, p. 3.

[136] *Census of the Town and Suburbs of Calcutta, 1911*, p. 62.

[137] The number of immigrants from these areas rose from 15,000 to 21,000 between 1901 and 1911, with the Agarwalas and Mahesris accounting for a growth of 150 per cent; *Census of the Town and Suburbs of Calcutta, 1911*, pp. 15–16, 48.

[138] *Census of the Town and Suburbs of Calcutta, 1911*, p. 10.

[139] *Census of the Town and Suburbs of Calcutta, 1911*, p. 16.

other hand, were recorded in the northeastern parts—Shampukur, Kumartuli, Bartala, Sukea Street, Muchipara, and Paddapukur—and in Bhawanipore in the south.[140] Their tendency to live in linguistic, regional, ethnic, and occupational enclaves allowed migrants to hold on to their traditional sense of social and religious affiliations, resisting to a certain extent the effect of the cosmopolitan city as an agent of change.

But over the latter half of the nineteenth century, in literary rhetoric and popular culture, the city was being claimed back by Bengalis themselves. In an intensely competitive economic environment, enterprising and prosperous migrant communities came under attack. In literary representations, two groups in particular are relentlessly targeted—the Marwaris and East Bengalis. Disparaging soubriquets, such as *meros* and *bangals* respectively, were applied to these communities and became part of everyday vocabulary. Alienation of migrants helped displace anxieties and readjust the mental maps of the city's Bengali residents, enabling the acceptance of the increasingly mixed population in their midst.

Humour was frequently deployed to counteract the impact of migration. Fun was thus made of East Bengalis in *Debganer Martye Agaman*, which featured an attempt to trick a supposedly naïve and rustic East Bengali man by a shoe-shop owner. The man, however, eventually claimed his urban credentials as a face-saver (he was a product of Dhaka, which could also boast of tap water and shoe shops), asserting that he had not been fooled.[141] The bucolic image of East Bengali migrants pervaded literary depictions and was rendered more acutely comical by the exaggeration and distortion in presenting the Bangal dialect. By contrast, up-country migrants from north India are shown as possessing a wily and shrewd business sense that allowed them to lead a life of penury while amassing huge fortunes.[142]

Bengalis from East Bengal themselves initially tended to cluster together on their arrival in Calcutta. It was common for students to house together. When Anandamohan Bose, later a member

[140] *Census of the Town and Suburbs of Calcutta, 1911*, p. 47.

[141] D. Ray, *Debganer Martye Agaman*, p. 290.

[142] D. Ray, *Debganer Martye Agaman*, pp. 304–5.

of the Bengal Legislative Council, arrived from Mymensingh to study at Presidency College, a house in Chhutarpara Lane was rented for him and a few other boys connected with the family. Over time, this house became a meeting point for all East Bengal students.[143] A strong sense of community identity based on region (Oriyas, Biharis, Marwaris), religion, and occupation (the various paras—kansaripara, jelepara, and so on—and later methars, carters, gowalahs, taxiwallahs, tram workers, hackney-carriage drivers) also characterized other migrant groups who drew on their own support and professional networks in the city and beyond.[144]

Marwaris—a generic term for people from Rajasthan, although specifically indicating people from the Jodhpur–Marwar area—became a more serious target of attack from the end of the nineteenth century onwards. Speculative practices such as gambling in rain and cotton prices had already made the Marwaris unpopular, but their refusal to participate in the boycott of cotton products from Manchester during the Swadeshi Movement and the artificial rise in the price of cloth in the 1917–18 period aggravated the Bengali bitterness. The vernacular press named and shamed the community and as we shall see in Chapter 6, riots broke out that targeted specifically Marwari shops, residences, and individuals.[145] In addition, the adulteration of ghee or clarified butter, often used for religious purposes, with animal fat by Marwari tradesmen proved incendiary.[146] Bengalis felt under siege and hysteric newspaper reports about the imminent decline and extinction of the race from poisonous food items flourished.[147] What compounded

[143] Sarkar, *Life of Anandamohan Bose*, pp. 11, 15.

[144] See Chapter 4. Also see Anne Hardgrove, *Community and Public Culture: The Marwaris of Calcutta* (New Delhi: Oxford University Press, 2004), pp. 31–3, for the experience of the Marwaris.

[145] Thus the *Nayak*, 21 May 1918, and the *Dainik Basumati*, 12 September 1918, squarely blamed the Marwaris for speculating in cotton-piece goods. Reports from the Native Newspapers (Bengal), 1918–19.

[146] Hardgrove, *Community and Public Culture*, pp. 160–7.

[147] See for example the report in *Hitavadi*, 19 September 1919. Reports from the Native Newspapers (Bengal), 1918–19.

the problem were the acute shortages and rising prices in food and cloth, which had made painfully visible the gap between prosperous Marwari tradesmen and shopkeepers on the one hand and service-oriented Bengalis stagnating in middle to low income jobs on the other. Even menial jobs, it was felt, of washermen and artisans were being taken over by 'outsiders' from north India and Rajasthan, pushing Bengalis to the margins of existence.[148]

The experiences lived on in collective memory, finding expression in literature and contemporary memoirs. In popular perception, Marwaris came to be associated with greed, ruthlessness, and corruption. The *Sahar Chitra* pamphlet published in 1923 complains about how the railway had allowed Calcutta to be infiltrated by the Marwaris of Burrabazar. Pretending to be traders, the author claims, they ruin Bengal. The critique is hostile: they are lackeys of the European merchants, devoid of any ethics, and only look after their own interests.[149] Kshitindranath Tagore's memoir has an elaborate description of the ghee adulteration incident of 1917, painting the Marwaris in quite unfavourable terms.[150]

* * *

Modern urban planning, technology, and the introduction of civic infrastructures shook up traditional ways of living and being for Bengalis in Calcutta in the nineteenth century. While fundamentally reconfiguring their everyday lives, the city had a profound impact on the older social order—breaking down caste hierarchies, opening up closed ritual spaces, homegenizing access to public amenities, and introducing scientific methods in running the city. But the process was neither smooth nor without opposition. Educated Bengalis found modernization stifling and inconvenient, strategically proffering the 'golden days' of the ritually ordered past as ideal. The modern civic order, to a certain extent, bound together unrelated individuals in relationships of exteriority as in

[148] *Bangali,* 12 September 1919. Reports from the Native Newspapers (Bengal), 1918–19

[149] Sharma, *Sahar Chitra,* p. 51.

[150] K. Tagore, *Kolikatay Chalafera,* pp. 123–5.

a bourgeois public sphere. It facilitated exchange and debate in a wide range of arenas from street songs to newspapers, but also sporadically led to violence. Imperfect aggregation of a civil society and strong surviving pockets of caste, region, and religion-based identities lived on to reveal themselves in moments of tension and unrest as we shall see in some of the later chapters.

2

Songs, the City, and the Everyday

Urban social space in Calcutta in the nineteenth century was a contested terrain. This chapter shows how Bengalis themselves were intervening in the urban processes by participating in a wide and vibrant popular culture. These constituted, this chapter argues, a series of negotiations as much with colonial perceptions of space, community, and gender as with varied local understandings of the same, and marked the emergence of a vibrant and extremely vocal Bengali public sphere at the end of the nineteenth century. The educated bhadralok were never at home in the city. They rarely wrote about Calcutta, except by way of ridicule and despair. Despite the novelty of the metropolitan experience, Calcutta was looked upon as a place of licentiousness and alcoholism, decay and deprivation, and an upturned social order. Such narratives functioned as counterweights to the fantasies of access and movement that had propelled ambitions of social ascendancy and autonomy among the city's diverse groups, including women. Popular topical print on the city, on the other hand, represented a joyous celebration of city life. Urban ruin and corruption was treated in this literature as the inevitable outcome of greed and worthlessness of the educated. Folk artists and street performers were also an intrinsic part of this urban parade. Through song, dance, painting, and poetry, they laid as much claim to the city's spaces as their social superiors. Popular urban street cultures thus highlight the tensions, differences, and aspirations of its varied residents, opening up the city as heterogeneous and problematic. The chapter considers these contending claims to the city and outlines newer formations of the body social through these activities. The gradual consolidation of these communities and changes in social structures, it argues, led in turn to the politicization of their new identities.

Calcutta, in the late nineteenth century, was a melting pot of migrant workers, artisans, servants, boatmen, labourers, petty traders and shopkeepers, and an army of clerks. And yet, we know rather little of the responses of its more humble inhabitants to these tumultuous developments. What was the reaction of these people to the changing world around them? Contemporary songs on Calcutta, some of which were later captured in print, provide some entry-points into this mental world of the city's lower social orders. They show how singing and songs in Calcutta in the late nineteenth century animated the urban domain with widely shared discourses on the city—on women, material changes, natural disasters, and sexuality—validating the experience of a recently urbanized world seen from below. The incidents and experiences narrated in the songs offered common reference points around which public debate could crystallize and urban sensibilities shaped. The study thus also traces the emergence of an urban public just under the educated layers that was visible and vocal, and quite organically located in the city's open public spaces—streets, markets, and open grounds.

In all of the songs, the city is the fundamental organizing category of the subject matter, and, in their presentation, the producers assumed shared interests between the listener, performer, and writer. Both the specificity and the temporality of the songs discussed here made them unique, not as fleeting moments of city life, but as critical experiential frames through which city dwellers could capture the tremendous social and material changes occurring around them. In a recent essay, Ranajit Guha talks of the significance of the 'everyday' in Calcutta's colonial urban life.[1] Recurrent emphases on the everyday, the ordinary, and the routine in the midst of the major events being described offer some mundane but some extraordinarily piquant images of life in the city. While some were sung extempore or from handwritten song sheets, others were printed for performance and sale. Both genres were highly stylized and faithful to traditional formats of composition, but also very distinct as newer 'urban' variants, as evident in the imagery deployed and chosen themes. The chapter studies some such songs from this period, exploring the interstices between a largely pre-modern, pastoral, and deeply indigenous sensibility, and the onset of a rushed modernity and urbanity in nineteenth-century Calcutta, the consequences of living and working in a harsh colonial environment, and their wider significance for the newly emergent public sphere in the city.

Traditional street entertainment based on both religious and more sensual themes had been around for a while, but there emerged new urban variants in Calcutta in the very late eighteenth and early nineteenth centuries in the form of *kobi*-songs (kobi meaning poet) that were adapted from older and more sober pastoral versions to include sharply observant and amusing accounts of everyday experiences of city life and staged in front of vast adulatory crowds. Often the songs could turn loudly and unambiguously critical, packed with pungent hatred of the city's more well-off denizens, immigrants, and not unsurprisingly, erring women. There was yet another category of songs on the city that developed independent of this performative tradition from the late nineteenth century onwards and shared by significant reading/singing and listening groups. Printed as short pamphlets of no more than ten pages and composed in sometimes stylized and sometimes rudimentary, colloquial Bengali, they offered perspectives and comments on dramatic happenings or major developments that presumably affected all city dwellers.

[1] Ranajit Guha, 'A Colonial City and Its Time(s)', *Indian Economic and Social History Review* 45, no. 3 (2008): 329–51.

As bridges spanned mighty rivers, and electricity dispelled evening darkness, people were awestruck by these events and wrote and sang prolifically about them. Unlike the educated middle classes lamenting the passing of old days,[2] there was a joyous celebration of city life. Poems and songs composed in the traditional style of rhymed couplets marked the construction of the Pontoon Bridge over Hooghly in 1874,[3] the illumination of the Howrah Bridge in 1879, the laying of the tramway in the city in 1880, and even the municipal drains in Calcutta in 1874. But frailty in the face of natural disasters, disease, and death also drove home the ephemeral nature of modern civilization. The cyclones of 1867 and 1877, the scare of worms in edible fish in 1875, and the spread of dengue fever in 1872 and 1874 fanned the fears of an impending apocalyptic doom, where the city's residents had to pay for their sins.

Not just the physical and material, but the social and cultural topography of the city was also fast altering. The increasingly visible and disturbing presence of women in public spaces triggered images of a world turned upside down in contemporary popular art and literature. It seemed indicative of the moral decay of the new urban world. Migrants, in the shape of up-country labour and numerous menial servicemen and women in the city, constituted another source of anxiety. Most importantly, the opening up of urban space as a sphere of arguably freer[4] circulation and exchange, not bound by caste and ritual restrictions, and subject to the same municipal regime, inserted new aspirants into the scene who challenged the comfortable

[2] See, for example, Rajnarayan Bose, *Sekal Ar Ekal* [Those Times and These Times] (Calcutta, 1874), and Prankrishna Dutta, *Kolikatar Itibritta* (Calcutta: Pustak Bipani, 1981), originally serialized in *Navyabharat* between 1901 and 1903.

[3] Aghorchandra Das Ghose, *Ekei Bole Pole* [The Ideal Bridge]; Aminchandra Datta, *Howrah Ghater Poler Kobi* [Poet of the Bridge]; Nandalal Ray, *Nutan Poler Tappa* and *Poler Pnachali;* Jaharilal Shil, *Nutan Poler Pnachali* (last three indicating songs dedicated to the Bridge). All were published from Calcutta in 1874.

[4] Not 'free' in its fullest sense though, as like all colonial cities, aspects of race, authority, and power continued to impinge upon and restrict the urban infrastructure.

boundaries of the educated and propertied classes. Surprisingly, the colonial state in this literature appears as a benign law dispenser and provider of urban essentials. It is the Bengali elite—as its corrupt, petty executive and facilitator—that come under much criticism.

The educated Bengalis too wrote about Calcutta, but their concerns were very different. Their acknowledgement of the technological marvels of the British Empire was apathetic, at best tardy. When they did speak about these, it was to complain about the inconvenience caused by the city being dug up all over or the lack of a clean water supply.[5] Registering mixed feelings about Calcutta with its abundant wealth and opportunity, and an alien lifestyle rivalling one that was habitual and sanctified by custom, their writings closely interrogated their own social and cultural investment in the city. There was one shared concern, however, and that was about the increasing presence of women in public places and the perceived moral corruption of the urban fabric.

One such literary response, the *Kalikata Kamalalaya*, recorded the changing times as indexed in contemporary popular perception. Set up as a dialogue between a city dweller and a villager, with the latter confronting the former as his alter ego, the work posed the author's own self-doubts to a wider readership. Under the onslaught of the countryman's impeccable reasoning, the city man puts up a tough but spirited defence of his city, but the response is riddled with ambiguity. Such divided selves were to form an endemic feature of educated writings in the times to come.[6] Anxiety persisted particularly on the upsetting of Hindu ways of life and codes.[7] The idealized urban/rural divide working

[5] Kshitindranath Tagore, *Kolikatay Chalafera* (Calcutta: Adi Brahma Samaj Press, 1930), p. 81; Atul Sur, *Tinsho Bochharer Kolkata: Patabhumi o Itikatha* (Calcutta: Ujjval Sahitya Mandir, 1988), p. 40.

[6] For a useful discussion on this, see Partha Chatterjee, *The Nation and its Fragments: Colonial and Postcolonial Histories* (Princeton: Princeton University Press, 1993).

[7] P. Dutta, *Kolikatar Itibritta*, pp. 127–53.

in the author's imagination above is obvious, and recurs in other writings.[8]

An important investigative angle therefore is that of social ordering in the city. How did the city's non-elite inhabitants fit into their new roles? The fluid boundaries of urban existence caused, the chapter argues, many to challenge the shifting structures of the city's population, gender and caste hierarchies, governance, and social patronage networks. The increasing visibility and enterprise of such actors produced a social geography that was much more complex than what a simple acceptance of modern civic bourgeois ethos would suggest. In fact, their vigorous presence rendered the streets of Calcutta a contested site for class, caste, community, and gender encounters. The songs covered here bring to light the many perceptions of different lower social layers in urban Calcutta in the nineteenth century and the ways in which they were responding to the changes occurring around them through street songs that reflected on the city.

Street Performances, Doggerels, Humour, and the City

Sumanta Banerjee's seminal work has highlighted a world of pungent lower-order hatred of the urban successful.[9] The street culture of Calcutta in the early part of the nineteenth century was a vociferous one. Basic to all of them was mocking laughter, sometimes light-hearted, but often pointed and taking the form of hostile derision, and evoking images startlingly similar to a Rabelaisian carnival world.[10] The initial patrons for such street cultures were

[8] Yogendra Das Chaudhuri, *Kantalaler Kolikata Darshan*, 2 vols (Calcutta, n.d.).

[9] Sumanta Banerjee, *Parlour and the Streets: Elite and Popular Culture in Nineteenth Century Calcutta* (Calcutta: Seagull Books, 1998).

[10] Bakhtin has shown how a world of folk humour, mockery, and abuse in performances was intrinsic to the medieval carnival in Europe, almost entirely deriving from 'the life of the belly, the buttocks and the genital organs'. See Mikhail Bakhtin, *Rabelais and His World* (Cambridge, Massachussetts: Massachussetts Institute of Technology Press, 1968), p. 21.

the first generation of the rich in Calcutta—old landed aristocracy, East India Company compradors, and commercial barons of the city, who still strongly identified themselves with country life. But these were quick to find wide support among the city's far less prosperous residents.

Doggerels and street humour on the city were unrelenting and acrid in their critique of the overflowing wealth and corruption among some residents. Thus, 'forgery, cheating and lies, these three together make up Calcutta'. Again, on the numerous notorious addictive hubs of leisurely smoking and drinking that had sprung up all over the city: 'Baghbazar, Konnagar, Battala and Bowbazar are the centres of hemp-smoking, opium pills, drinking, and opium-smoking, respectively. If anyone fails to make a pilgrimage to these places, he is the worst sinner on heaven, hell, and earth.'[11] When Nandakumar failed to look after his guests at his grandly publicized charity dinner, he was mocked: 'Nandakumar was so brilliant with his estimate of one lakh [one hundred thousand] Brahmins, wasn't he?; the result: some were treated with fish-heads and others, the butts of guns.'[12]

Contemporaries noted in particular the power of street musicians and singers to hurl abuse in the rudest colloquial on perceived wrongdoers, ranging from parsimonious patrons to wealthy cheats, even reflecting the personal rivalries between different aristocratic groups or dals.[13] Thus, when the well-known

[11] *Jal, juyochuri, mithye kotha, Ei tin niye Kolikata*; And again, *Baghbajare gnajar adda, gulir Konnagare; Battalae mader adda, chondur Bowbajare; Ei shob mohatirtha je na chokhey herey, Tar moto mahapapi nai trisangsarey*. Harihar Seth, *Praceen Kolikata* (Calcutta: Prabasi Press, 1934), pp. 314, 322.

[12] *Jal, juyochuri, mithye kotha, Ei tin niye Kolikata*. Seth, *Praceen Kolikata*, p. 314. Rai Bahadur Pramathanath Mullick, *Sachitra Kolikatar Katha* vol. 2 (Calcutta, 1935), p. 13.

[13] Social and intellectual life in early nineteenth-century Calcutta was dominated by a Hindu brahmanical culture of aristocratic families. They were almost invariably merchants, bankers, banias (comprador merchants), and landowners from high-caste groups, and served as leaders or dalapatis of local caste societies or dals. They built palatial residences

Raja Nabakrishna Deb, merchant and top servant to the East India Company, lost a court case against another landed notable, Chudamani Dutta, drummers paraded triumphantly in front of the Deb residence with the corpse of the latter, beating to the rhythm of a doggerel that congratulated Chudamani even in his death.[14] But the critical net could also well be cast further afield, in highlighting the evils widespread in the larger society and government—as when an appropriately contemptuous doggerel circulated in the city following the passing of the notorious Insolvency Act in 1830 by the East India Company.[15]

Rival pantomime or *sawng* performances emerging from the city's occupationally organized residential quarters (for example, *dorjipara* or tailor colony) during the lively Gajan festival dedicated to Shiva, were far from benign in their representations of contemporary city life, and instead 'specialised in throwing the spotlight on social, administrative, municipal corruption and wrongdoings in religion and education, the sharp wit of the songs lashing

---

and lived opulent lifestyles, acting like miniature feudal chiefs and providing patronage and protection to their caste members. As de-facto units of social and political importance, the government recognized the dals and consulted them on important matters. See S.N. Mukherjee, 'Class, Caste and Politics in Calcutta, 1815–1838', in *Elites in South Asia*, edited by Edmund Leach and S.N. Mukherjee (Cambridge: Cambridge University Press, 1970), pp. 33–78. Also see S.N. Mukherjee, 'Bhadralok and Their Dals—Politics of Social Factions in Calcutta, c.1820–1856', in *The Urban Experience: Calcutta*, edited by Pradip Sinha (Calcutta: Riddhi-India, 1987), pp. 192–212.

[14] *Yam jinte yayre Chuda, Yam jinte yay; Japtap karaki, marte janle hoy.* [Chuda thus goes on to win against Yama, the God of Death; even daily worship and ritual is not enough to guarantee a death as glorious as this.] See Mullick, *Sachitra Kalikatar Katha*, vol. 2, p. 59.

[15] The act allowed the Company to seize personal fortunes at the slightest pretext, and was responsible for the dissolution of the prominent Agency House Palmer & Co. in 1830. See Mullick, *Sachitra Kalikatar Katha*, vol. 2, pp. 83, 167.

mercilessly at their targets', a memoir recalls.[16] One such procession emerging from the Bowbazar jelepara (boatmen's colony) area, had a participant performing as an untouchable female scavenger or *methrani* and singing a song aimed at the Calcutta Municipality, and threatening the high-caste educated Bengalis manning its middling and lower rungs:

> My name is Hari Methrani
> I am the grandma of the Municipality
> If anyone accuses us of being abusive
> We quit work in unison[17]
> Our caste is very well bonded.
> But the *babus* [derisive term for educated Bengalis] are different.
> They shamelessly lick the half-eaten plates of sahibs [European bosses]
> Despite their gratuitous kicks.
> And then they retort 'do not touch us methrani',
> ... Oh we will wed Brahmin priests
> And marry off the Sens with the Deys [implying caste disorder].[18]

The female sweeper had an analogous presence in other contemporary popular folk forms as well such as Bengali indigenous theatre or *jatra*, where the play would invariably begin with her

[16] The author recalls this from his childhood days in the early twentieth century. Sur, *Tinsho Bochharer Kolkata*, p. 77. The powerful ability of urban festive tableaux to showcase contemporary events and messages has been noted for other South Asian locations. See, for example, Raminder Kaur, *Performative Politics and the Cultures of Hinduism: Public Uses of Religion in Western India* (London: Anthem Press, 2005), especially Chapter 3.

[17] The threat represented here was more than dramatic. Sweepers in colonial Calcutta were in constant conflict with the municipal administration, struck work repeatedly, and were notorious for bringing the city to a standstill. See, for example, *ARCM for 1867*, Appendix VIII, p. 5; *Administrative Report of the Municipality of the Suburbs of Calcutta, 1873–4*, pp.22–3. Vijay Prashad discusses colonial Delhi Municipality's similar dependence on manual labour when it came to the organization of sanitation. See Vijay Prashad, 'The Technology of Sanitation in Colonial Delhi', *Modern Asian Studies* 35, no. 1 (2001): 113–55.

[18] Sur, *Tinsho Bochharer Kolkata*, p. 77 (italics mine).

farcical appearance on stage (sometimes alongside other such characters performing menial jobs such as the water seller, coachman, and so on), upbraiding the establishment and singing parodies using a peculiar pidgin Hindi-mixed Bengali[19] and full of swagger and commonsensical social wisdom.

Even for the reticent bhadralok, the lure of the street proved quite tempting and, despite their public condemnations of such exuberant street presence, they did occasionally join in to celebrate the city's tremendous urban surge.[20] As Ranajit Guha has commented recently, 'far from holding back', from the mid-nineteenth century onwards, Calcutta in its writings appears to 'spill over into the streets, join the crowds, and defy the over-Sanskritised sensibilities of the literati by adopting the mode of the everyday speech as its vehicle'.[21] Guha's allusion here was to a very specific work, *Sketches by Hutom* (The Night Owl)—arranged in the style of Dickens' *Sketches by Boz*—by Kaliprasanna Sinha, an intellectual and aristocrat, and published in 1861, which combined witty social observations with closely detailed depictions of city life and everyday mores, and was written in a playful, racy colloquial style.

Kobi Songs: Adapting Older Styles to Newer Experiences

Kobi songs formed an integral part of the vibrant street scene described above. With their antecedents rooted in communal festivities at the end of the harvest season in rural Bengal,[22] kobi songs in the eighteenth and nineteenth centuries came to be sponsored

[19] This was to probably authenticate the figure of the methrani who in real life would usually be an up-country Hindi-speaking migrant from Bihar or the United Provinces.

[20] For the campaign against obscenity in popular cultures in colonial Calcutta see Banerjee, *The Parlour and the Streets*; and Anindita Ghosh, *Power in Print: Popular Publishing and the Politics of Language and Culture in a Colonial Society* (New Delhi: Oxford University Press, 2006).

[21] Guha, 'A Colonial City and Its Time(s)', p. 334.

[22] Dineshchandra Sinha, *Purbabanger Kobigaan*, vol. 1 (Calcutta: Calcutta University Press, 1993), p. 54.

by nouveau riche patrons in Calcutta and around, who saw in this an opportunity for extending and consolidating their newly acquired web of patronage and influence. The songs were usually performed on the occasions of prominent festivals and feasts, organized and hosted by the more prosperous households in Calcutta, although over time the venues became more neutral and public. Itinerant folk poets/songsters or kobis, who had travelled to the city in search of better fortunes, performed before large—often similarly uprooted—urban audiences, and were immensely popular for their ready wit, lyrical prowess, and rhythmic song and dance routines. Arguably, their skills of singing folk songs in rural locations when transported to a bustling modern city proved admirably flexible, as they were quick to adapt their traditional subject matter to contemporary urban life in Calcutta.[23]

The insertion of more earthly, mundane, and current subject matter into the songs from this period onwards was to prove an enduring feature of kobi songs, thriving well into the twentieth century.[24] While still faithful to the conventional formats and themes drawn from Hindu religious texts, kobis made use of tongue-in-cheek allusions and telling imagery to offer commentaries on the city's social scene. An added-on aspect to the songs that the street audience particularly enjoyed was a piece called *kheud*,[25] usually sung extempore, which allowed space for abusive verbal duels between rival poets. The contest lasted several hours and could only come to an end when there was a clear winner, with the audience taking decided, and often clamorous, combative sides.

[23] For a useful account of the historical evolution of kobi songs, see Prafulla Chandra Pal, *Prachin Kobiwalar Gaan*, reprint edition (Calcutta: Calcutta University Press, 1994; original edition 1934) and D. Sinha, *Purbabanger Kobigaan*, the latter particularly focusing on the living traditions in eastern Bengal, present day Bangladesh.

[24] D. Sinha, *Purbabanger Kobigaan*, Chapter 4; P.C. Pal, *Prachin Kobiwalar Gaan*, pp. 48–53.

[25] Variously termed as *lahar*, *tarja*, or *tappa*, these were interludes in the main composition which allowed the sensual, scatological, and abusive to thrive in sharp musical exchanges between performers.

The kobis themselves were veritable stars of their days, and there was tremendous emotional investment on the part of audiences in singers, both on and off stage.[26] They came from modest backgrounds of either lower-caste or lower-order professions, such as cobbler and sweetmeat-maker, and often carried on their normal occupations alongside singing songs. A promising star would apprentice himself to a pre-existing group, and then break apart to forge his own. The songs could be composed by the lead singer himself, but usually professional composers wrote songs on demand for various groups.[27] Traditionally the dig-and-retort format of the songs would allow for verbal duels between rival poets, but these were more formal occasions, with poets singing from prepared song sheets with pre-formulated rejoinders.[28] Later on these became more impromptu, involving offensive exchanges, and were best enjoyed as such. Eventually, the kheud element took over to become the most definitive element of these compositions being spun by the singers themselves on the spot.[29] Contemporaries commented on the astounding ability of kobis,

[26] Rival fan followings are known to have clashed before and after performances. See P.C. Pal, *Prachin Kobiwalar Gaan*, p. 79.

[27] Thus, Ram Basu in his early life had composed songs for another kobi, Bhabani Bene. Brahmin composers often wrote for these kobis, preferring the backstage, because of the stigma associated with kobi performances. Thus Gadadhar Mukhopadhyay is known to have written songs for well-known kobis of the time such as Bhola Moira and Nilu Thakur, and Gorakshanath for Anthony Firingi. See P.C. Pal, *Prachin Kobiwalar Gaan*, p. 29. Also see D. Sinha, *Purbabanger Kobigaan*, pp. 91, 223.

[28] Poets are even known to have consulted each other before writing down their responses to taunts posed by rivals. Even when comparatively more 'instantaneous', rebuttals were composed by songwriters off-stage during recitals, and subsequently fed into the performance.

[29] Later *kobiwal*s reminiscing in the early twentieth century recalled how the audience would demand that the coarser elements of songs be offered and could not spare much patience for the sober thoughts of Puranic tales. As itinerant singers barely making a living out of their profession, he continues, kobis did not have much option but to submit to such demands. See Chandrakumar De, *Saurav* 2, no. 7, Baisakh 1321 B.S. [1914], cited in D. Sinha, *Purbabanger Kobigaan*, p. 79.

often semi-literate or illiterate, to compose sharp rebuttals extempore, keeping their audiences enthralled for hours on end.[30]

While the themes of the songs consistently revolved around familiar mythological and devotional tropes, they offered opportunities for intervention, innovation, and comment, varying widely in their mood, imagery, and delivery. Thus, the illicit love affair between the Hindu god Krishna and his earthly partner, Radha, a married woman, was repeatedly invoked to offer veiled illustrations of real-life clandestine relationships between many babus and married housewives.[31] Singing as Radha, a singer thus underlined the vivid possibilities of infidelity in the marital ranks:

> I have been so enslaved by your flute that I dare to venture into the forest
> The enchanting melody of your tune has slain me.
> I care not for *kul* [kin status], nor for honour;
> ... Your flute has destroyed my cherished chastity.[32]

With the audience increasingly seeking instantaneous pleasure and bodily excitement in the songs, kobis turned to the sensational and erotic themes in Hindu myths, usually with double entendres involved.[33] The description of *biraha*, or Radha's agony and physical desire at separation from her beloved, could be both poetic and erotic. The overlapping imagery of the lone housewife in the family household while the earner husband was elsewhere—presumably Calcutta—for purposes of work was, however, distinctly palpable in such motifs.

> Leaving the young woman alone you left for abroad
> My soul craves with longing for you
> Who will guard my youthful body without you?

[30] *Nabyabharat*, Poush, 1290 B.S. [1883]; Satishchandra Mitra, *Jashohar Khulnar Itihas*, both cited in D. Sinha, *Purbabanger Kobigaan*, pp. 39–40, 43, 65.

[31] This was the medieval Vaishnava theme of *bhakti* where the love between Krishna and Radha served as the metaphor for holy union between God and His devoted follower on earth.

[32] See P.C. Pal, *Prachin Kobiwalar Gaan*, p. 181 (italics mine).

[33] P.C. Pal, *Prachin Kobiwalar Gaan*, pp. 74–7.

Who do I turn to in the absence of my beloved?
Fie on him for not turning up in the springtime
And chasing false dreams in distant lands without sparing a thought for his woman
How could he, being a husband, leave me at the mercy of Madana, the god of love?[34]

A large male service population from the city's hinterland travelled to Calcutta every day, leaving their families back in their village and suburban homes. The possibility of their wives losing their honour in their absence was a constant and gnawing fear. In fact, many believed that thus uncared for, some of the more daring women found solace in clandestine sexual relationships with other men.[35]

Singularly pointed was the simultaneous dig at the practice of cohabitation among young Bengali men with prostitutes, or other lovers, neglecting their faithful wives. Radha thus complains in a song:

So here you are Shyam! Having spent the night elsewhere,
You return with an empty soulless body;
... What reminded you of Radha, why have you come here,
Now that your dawn was spent with someone else?
... Oh, I can't bear to look at your face.[36]

Far away from the sobering influences of domesticity, it was not unusual for petty servicemen to fall prey to the attractions that the

[34] Song by Ramsundar Roy. See P.C. Pal, *Prachin Kobiwalar Gaan*, p. 382. Also see pp. 313, 337 for more examples.

[35] This was not entirely unfounded. Surveys in Bengal in the early 1870s showed a large influx of rural women in Calcutta's brothels, not all of whom had been forced into the profession by economic distress, intimidation, or treachery. A number of upper-caste Hindu women, usually widows, are reported to have strayed from their families on their own volition. West Bengal State Archives Report, Judicial Department, no. 76, 1872, p. 73, cited in Ratnabali Chatterjee, 'The Indian Prostitute as a Colonial Subject: Bengal, 1864–1883', *Canadian Women Studies* 13, no. 1 (1992): 51–55, at 53. A contemporary, Shib Chunder Bose, also mentions this development. See Shib Chunder Bose, *Hindoos As They Are* (Calcutta, 1881), p. 35.

[36] Song by Horu Thakur. See P.C. Pal, *Prachin Kobiwalar Gaan*, p. 91.

red-light area of the city had to offer.[37] But the kobis quite clearly blame the men for the plight brought upon their married womenfolk.[38] Not unsurprisingly, the general import of the songs was very conservative. The values that were constantly driven home were those of marital fidelity and honesty, filial love, and domesticity. They seemed to provide succour to the audience in a rocky social environment.

Singers routinely mobilized the collective interests of the listening public playing to different sub-sets at different points of the performance—women, lovers, office workers, and the socially less privileged. The appeal of the great stars lay in their ability to convey messages to the audience in a singularly direct and authentic manner. As Peter Bailey has argued in the context of music hall songs in nineteenth-century England, it was 'knowingness' or the awareness of shared reference points that enabled linkages 'by pulling the crowd inside a closed yet allusive frame of reference, and implicating them in a select conspiracy of meaning that animate(d) them as a specific audience'.[39] The direct form of address structurally built into the kobi performances, in addition, further facilitated the transmission of messages from singers to audience. Over the course of the nineteenth century, the venues too shifted from the more private domain of influential families to that of market places, riversides, temple courtyards, and even cremation grounds, giving the genre a more decidedly 'street', and thereby inclusive, character.[40]

[37] See Tapan Raychaudhuri, 'Norms of Family Life and Personal Morality among the Bengali Hindu Elite, 1600–1850', in *Aspects of Bengali History and Society*, edited by R. Van M. Baumer, Asian Studies at Hawaii, no. 12 (Hawaii, 1975), p. 23.

[38] Song by Ram Basu. See P.C. Pal, *Prachin Kobiwalar Gaan*, pp. 226–7. The reference to the 'monthly flower' or the menstrual cycle, and the dangers that desertion can bring in connection with it, is a recurrent feature in the songs.

[39] Peter Bailey, *Popular Culture and Performance in the Victorian City* (Cambridge: Cambridge University Press, 1998), p. 137.

[40] D. Sinha, *Purbabanger Kobigaan*, pp. 65, 71, 84, 87, 100.

Everyday subject matter and shared concerns created an intimate world of exchange of ideas and sentiments. Songs, thus, complained of the curse of endless taxes, and also described the plight caused by natural disasters such as cyclones and floods.[41] The change in the urban landscape brought about by technological innovations was reported with great awe: machine-powered steamers and railways and the telegraph that could send instant messages were hailed as stupefying wonders. In comparing the human body to a train and the mind to an engine, and the human quest for salvation as a railway journey, the technological metaphor was raised to new heights and machines embraced as the new emblem of spiritual enquiry.[42]

The songs were rendered to a background of rhythmic music, using a combination of traditional folk percussion and metal instruments, as well as the violin.[43] Rhythmic dance routines performed to fast-beating music often accompanied the chorus.[44] The intoxicating beat of the music drawing audiences to the performance sites has been reported by contemporaries.[45] The stage presence of the singers was significant not so much in terms of costume as in the degree of role-playing involved. Narrating highly charged emotive or dramatic sequences involving violent fights or tearful betrayals, the performative skills of the singer were as closely tested as the vocal. Not surprisingly, late nineteenth-century audiences recall 'seeing' rather than 'hearing' kobigaan.[46] Bhadralok

[41] See, for example, extract from a contemporary kobi song on the cyclone of 1876 in Noakhali as cited in D. Sinha, *Purbabanger Kobigaan*, p. 59.

[42] See D. Sinha, *Purbabanger Kobigaan*, pp. 115–17. Information cited from manuscripts in the author's private collection, dating from 1886–9.

[43] Earlier renderings were to the accompaniment of violin and *khol-kartal* (twin clapping metal discs and percussion instrument made out of clay and animal skin). In the late nineteenth century, *dhol* (barrel-shaped folk drum) and *knashi* (a clanging bell-metal dish) were used. D. Sinha, *Purbabanger Kobigaan*, p. 61.

[44] P.C. Pal, *Prachin Kobiwalar Gaan*, p. 67.

[45] 'Kobigaan', *Saurav*, 16:10, 1335 B.S. (1928), cited in D. Sinha, *Purbabanger Kobigaan*, p. 264.

[46] 'Kobigaan', *Bandhab*, Poush 1282 B.S. (1875), cited in D. Sinha, *Purbabanger Kobigaan*, pp. 72–3.

observers, however, deplored the lack of classical restraint in kobi songs, describing them as 'indistinct, indecent and discordant', sung out loud in shrill, nasal tones and irritating to the extreme because of 'the neck-curling, furrowing of eyebrows, and grinding of teeth' involved.[47]

The kheud element of the kobi songs, where abuse hurled at rival poets flew freely and generously, egged on by the audience, contains rich commentaries on the patrons as well as the songsters. Thus Bhola Moira, a famous songster, took little care to disguise his contempt for 'Lalababu' (real name Krishna Chandra Singha), a wealthy descendant of a prominent aristocratic family, for his alleged miserly habits:

> What a babu that Lalababu of Calcutta is!
> He prefers to have his roasted aubergines without salt [as it is expensive].
> That rascal is nothing but a lowly [low-caste] *hadi*.
> Who does not hesitate to squeeze the last drop out of a jaggery-laden ant, nor feast like a bee on free honey.[48]

In addition, Calcutta, with its numerous caste-based factions and power groups, comes alive in the slander accompanying the songs. The kobi compositions are useful as encoded records of contemporary caste politics of the city. To begin with, caste and occupational identities were quite self-consciously attached to most kobi names, offering a transparent social map of the composers. Thus, we have Gonjla Guin (cow-owner), Keshta Muchi (cobbler), Bhabani Bene (spice-trader), and Bhola Moira (sweetmeat maker). But caste identities could also be mobilized during the extempore to insult or gain an edge over rivals.

The attacks on colleagues in the profession could be savage, and toe-curlingly personal. Any physical irregularity or evident

47 'Kobigaan', *Bandhab*, Poush 1282 B.S. (1875); and 'Mymensingher Kobigaan', *Saurav*, n.d., cited in D. Sinha, *Purbabanger Kobigaan*, pp. 72 and 90 respectively (italics mine).

48 P.C. Pal, *Prachin Kobiwalar Gaan*, p. 38. Krishna Chandra was the grandson of the onetime East India Company *dewan* (topmost revenue official in India), Gangagovind.

social vulnerability of poets provided ready ammunition to their competitors. Unflattering nicknames based on such characteristics and coined by rival songsters thus came to be attached to most kobis. Mahesh Kana[49] and Loke Kana (*kana*, meaning blind), Gopal Ure (Ure being an uncomplimentary version of the word 'Oriya', indicating a resident of Orissa), and Kukur Mukho Gora (dog-faced Gora) are instances of such individualized insults. The digs at migrants extended to even those coming to the city from the eastern districts of Bengal, disparagingly referred to as Bangals.[50]

The repeated assaults by more than one contemporary Bengali kobi on the only non-Indian songster among them all, Anthony Firingi, showcases the dislike for immigrants and foreigners in the city in no uncertain terms. Portuguese by birth, Heinsman Anthony settled in the vicinity of Calcutta with a local Brahmin woman, and then trained himself in kobi singing, eventually becoming quite a star in the process. But his evidently forcible entry into this world earned him much displeasure from his colleagues. In contemporary songs, he was variously portrayed as a stealer of coffins, accused of adopting the manner of Bengalis, and warned to refrain from the invoking of Hindu divinities.[51] Women singers, admittedly rare in the profession, too were not spared.[52] Bhola Moira is thus known to have insulted a particularly prominent female poet, Joggeswari, by referring to her as a shameless, bellowing cow looking for favour from the patron babus.[53]

The kobi songs represent a microcosm of social and caste rivalries and aspirations, as well as the miseries and joys of urban

[49] Mahesh Kana was blind from birth. P.C. Pal, *Prachin Kobiwalar Gaan*, p. 97.

[50] D. Sinha, *Purbabanger Kobigaan*, p. 52, citing from Haricharan Acharya, *Banger Kobir Lorai*, 1920.

[51] P.C. Pal, *Prachin Kobiwalar Gaan*, pp. 112, 86, and 39.

[52] One memoir recalls stories of women kobis singing in boats set afloat in the private lake of Gokul Mitra on the occasion of *Ras Mela* (festival celebrating the union of Radha and Krishna), around the end of the eighteenth century. Sur, *Tinsho Bochharer Kolkata*, p. 67.

[53] P.C. Pal, *Prachin Kobiwalar Gaan*, pp. 83–4.

living. With its high proportion of migrants, communal bonds in Calcutta were uncertain and variable, but the sociability of listeners at musical performances in the streets, fairgrounds, and marketplaces was comforting. For people caught up in the social and geographical upheavals of agrarian disorder and urban migration, the words of the songs could provide a direct link with their past, access to and knowledge of a new social world, and visions of a more egalitarian social order. In an analogous study of Calcutta' street songs by lower-caste sects by Bauls, Kartabhajas, and Sahebdhanis, Hugh Urban too has observed the evocation of community identity and a certain moral economy, in the face of material adversity.[54]

A broader metalanguage underlying the kobi songs was that of 'knowingness', as Peter Bailey suggests in the context of the nineteenth-century music hall songs of the working classes in England. In Bailey's study, 'knowingness' represented a new alertness that was part of the cosmopolitan urban sensibility that had to 'know' its world in order to survive.[55] The 'knowing intimacy' displayed in popular song motifs and tropes with urban themes, thus enabled sizeable constituencies to collectively identify with the songsters. The kobi songs eventually lost out to theatre in the city and migrated to east Bengal, although some formats continued to be used on stage.[56]

Printed Street Songs: News, the Urban, and the Sensational

Underscoring the fundamental importance of the ephemeral in literature, such as gossip or sensation, Ranajit Guha highlights

[54] Hugh Urban, 'The Marketplace and the Temple: Economic Metaphors and Religious Meanings in the Folk Songs of Colonial Bengal', *Journal of Asian Studies* 60, no. 4 (November 2001): 1085–114.

[55] Peter Bailey, 'Conspiracies of Meaning: Music-hall and the Knowingness of Popular Culture', *Past and Present*, no. 144 (August 1994): 138–70.

[56] *Saurav*, 2: 7, Baisakh, 1321 B.S. (1914), cited in D. Sinha, *Purbabanger Kobigaan*, p. 81.

the role of 'immediacy'—the now—inherent in it in the bringing together of an 'urban public' in nineteenth-century Calcutta:

> As a phenomenon it lives only for the day ... in a state of utter transience. Consequently, it is the 'now', the vehicle of its circulation, rather than the messages circulated, that enables this discourse to weld the mass of its interlocutors together into an urban public. The instantaneous exchange of information in myriad bits, with no particular demand to make on reflection, generates a concern which, for all its indefiniteness or volatility—or, precisely because of these—constitutes the very ground of that publicness. It is not what people are talking about that is vital to such gossip, but the fact that they are talking to one another in a state of average intelligibility.[57]

Guha here is concerned with one of the sections in the contemporary commentary—*Hutom Pnechar Naksa,* or Sketches of the Night-Owl—which focused on *hujuk* or temporary excitement, offering both politically significant news such as the 'Mutiny' of 1857, and the arrival of the deposed Nawab of Oudh in Calcutta, as well as rumours, gossip, and sensational trivia, such as the stir caused by the birth of a seven-legged calf in the city.[58] Such consuming mass interest in freak events, scandals, and the sensational, which also later reappeared as part and parcel of the booming print scene in Calcutta, thus served a very specific purpose. It allowed the residents of the city to listen in and exchange ideas on contemporary events that forged brief solidarities based on everyday concerns and extraordinary occurrences. The first chapter of Hutom's book starts with an extract from a contemporary tappa, where the singer proclaims in broken Hindustani how the city makes everyone canny and experienced.[59] 'Knowingness' emerges as a theme once again.

[57] Guha, 'A Colonial City and its Time(s)', pp. 341–2.

[58] Kaliprasanna Sinha, *Hutom Pnechar Naksha*, edited by Arun Nag (Calcutta: Subarnarekha, 1991; originally published in 1861) pp. 123–76.

[59] K. Sinha, *Hutom Pnechar Naksha*, p. 31. The original words used are: '*kahai Tunowa—sahar shikhawe kotowali*' ('Tunowa says the city teaches you to be canny.' The last word literally means policing, but was clearly being idiomatically expressed here to mean awareness.)

Trying to make sense of the new city, there emerged a flood of cheap literature in Calcutta towards the end of the nineteenth century, recording the dramatically transformed social, material, and technological realities in metropolitan life. The literary genres in which this found expression were various, from novels, dramas, satires, and songs to periodical pamphlet literature. Of these, by far the most articulate and emblematic were the songs based on contemporary events and themes, which had had an immediate and visible impact on city life. Authors were invariably among the more well known who had made a name for themselves in the writing trade, moving seamlessly between songs, dramas, novellas, and trivia. The language is stylized but with a tendency to slip into coarse imagery and vocabulary, racy alliteration, as well as sensationalized rhetoric—all suggestive of a non-serious, superficial readership.[60]

Small pamphlets of no more than fifteen to twenty pages gave shape to the emotions, anxieties, and concerns of residents during catastrophic events or spectacular occasions, and translated for them through familiar idioms their own lived experiences. It is thus significant that the songs almost invariably employed mythological tropes to 'understand' a seemingly baffling course of events, whereby cosmic and extraterrestrial occurrences shaped the destiny of mortals on earth. In some ways, it is possible thus to see the genre as a legacy of the mythology-based *pnachali* (composed in rhymed couplets) and kobi songs, but using more modern themes and indices.[61] Overall, however, the sensibilities were more pastoral and moral rather than modern and urban.[62] Although locating the

[60] Isvarchandra Sarkar, *Kartike Jhoder Pnachali* [The Song of the Autumn Storm] (Calcutta: Harihar Press, 1867), pp. 4, 14.

[61] For example, the metaphor of the train being used to describe a storm alongside that of the roaring tiger. See Tarinicharan Das, *Jongule Jhod* [The Rampaging Storm] (Calcutta: Gyandipak Press, 1867), pp. 3–5.

[62] Thus, when describing the impact of the storm on the city in 1867, authors chose to depict the damage done to crops, cattlesheds, fishes, and modest residential clusters rather than the ruin brought upon the trading and financial sectors that received extensive coverage in the contemporary press and official reportage.

specific readership/s for this genre is difficult, it is possible to infer from their considerable print runs the prevalence of well-known popular authors in the field, as well as evidence of wide readership of such ephemeral vernacular literature in contemporary Bengal, that they reached a substantial audience of not very well educated, marginally literate readers.[63]

Alongside mainstream newspapers, I would like to argue, these pamphlets too circulated select news from the city, acting as equally valid, if more expressive, emotive registers of urban experiences and events. There is some element of journalistic-style fact-based reportage involved, as of ships thrown up on land in the cyclone pamphlets of 1864,[64] which betrays the genre's closer location to actual events than the mythological tropes it employed as metanarrative (see Figure 2.1). Clearly, too, a larger global repertoire of contemporary images was mobilized to display the canny worldliness of authors, reporting volcanic eruptions in Africa while discussing natural disasters,[65] and the subway under the Thames when talking of British technological feats.[66]

Scandals and major events in the city, as we shall see in further detail in the following chapter, provided much fodder. For the burgeoning popular press in the city, this was ready material for authors and printers alike wanting to make quick money. The print world at Battala reacted with predictable delight, with songs

[63] Typical print runs were between 2,000 and 3,000. See for example *Quarterly Reports of the Bengal Library* for 1874, 1879. For a detailed discussion of readership of cheap ephemeral Bengali tracts in late nineteenth-century Bengal, see A. Ghosh, *Power in Print*.

[64] See Maheshchandra Das De, *Hay Ki Adbhut Jhod!* [Alas! What a Strange Storm!] (Calcutta: Harihar Press, 1867), pp. 4–5. This is verifiable from other official and non-official sources such as Lieutenant Colonel J.E. Gastrell and Henry F. Blanford, *Report on the Calcutta Cyclone of the 5th of October, 1864* (Calcutta: 1866; printed and published for the Government of Bengal by Order of the Lieutenant Governor), and W.D.K. Macknight, *A Description of the Calcutta Cyclone of 5th October, 1864* (Liverpool, 1867).

[65] Das De, *Hay Ki Adbhut Jhod!*, p. 10.

[66] Aghorchandra Das Ghose, *Ekei Bole Pole! Ya Bolle Tai Kolle!!!* [The Ideal Bridge! They Did As Promised] (Calcutta, 1874), p. 12.

FIGURE 2.1 Ships Were Actually Thrown Up on the Shore by the 1864 Cyclone
Source: Anonymous, *48 Photographs Showing the Effects of the Great Cyclone of 1864* (Calcutta, 1865). Courtesy of the National Library, Kolkata.

and plays being published within months of the incidents being reported.[67] As a sphere peopled not by well-educated and cultured Bengali gentlemen, but by street people, prostitutes, labouring menials, and illiterate theatregoers, it was brought together by sensational events. While dealing with the ordinary and everyday, such events compelled discussion on serious social themes

[67] See, for example, Maheshchandra Das De, *Mama Bhaginir Natak* (Calcutta: Harihar Press, 1878); Natabar Das, *Makkel Mama* (Calcutta: Kar Press, 1878). These were based on the infamous case of an illicit relationship between a Upendranath Bose, an attorney at the Calcutta High Court, and the wife of his nephew, Kshetramoni, fought as a very public courtroom drama in 1878.

of general interest, and oversaw the intermingling of different social worlds.

Although produced partly for private consumption, as with other ephemeral literature of this kind, the genre was meant to be read and/or sung aloud, and perhaps even performed. The importance of songs within the vernacular print culture in Bengal during this time cannot be overstated. Local jatras, or folk theatre, and later the urban Bengali stage we know, found songs irresistible and initial city theatre was purely musical in format. Songs subsequently lived on for a considerable while as necessary interruptions—often as comical interludes—within the structural format of stage plays.

References to songs being sung in streets on contemporary themes can be found in the works themselves.[68] And although direct evidence of these songs being actually sung is wanting, it would not be hard to imagine them being sung during communal festivities or in private gatherings—especially as there are detailed directions on vocal styles, stage entries and exits, and characterization.[69] Thus, there are instructions on both real and imaginary ragas (moods) and talas (rhythm) in which the songs should be sung, some of the latter being quite cheeky in their play of words. Alongside the more serious and conventional guidance on style, rhythm, and mood were also more playful directions from the author. The cyclone songs were thus to be sung in *raginis* or musical moods such as *kothay jabo* (where shall I escape?) and *gelo re* (reference to impending disaster), while the rhythms were to be *Sri Durga bole pran tyajibo* (invoking Goddess Durga when I die) and *shaamaal, shaamaal* (be warned! be warned!). At once irreverent and relevant in their import, such light-hearted nonsense must have been used to predispose readers to the casual nature of the reading material in their hands. The direct form of address was also frequently used as characteristic of oral traditions.

[68] Badalbehari Chattopadhyay, *Bishom Dhnoka, Maachhe Poka* [What A Betrayal! Worms in Fishes!] (Calcutta, 1875), p. 10.

[69] See, for example, Nandalal Ray, *Nutan Poler Tappa* [Song of the New Bridge] (Calcutta: Sudharnab Press, 1874).

Decadence and Disasters: Women, Sin, and Tropes of Retributive Justice

The standard literary tropes for talking about the times were those of rot—moral and material—some of which we have encountered above. In popular imagination, the city had to pay for such sins. So when catastrophe struck in the shape of natural disasters, writers pointed to the inexorable hand of fate.[70] In 1864 and 1867, Calcutta was hit by devastating cyclones resulting in the loss of valuable lives and property. Within a month of their appearance the vernacular presses of the city were reporting the events in their inimitable style. Predictably, the structural format of the songs was one of divine retribution for the world having lost its values, although the genre also simultaneously represented an extant culture of reminiscing and discussion of past calamities that sometimes survived in public memory for decades after the actual event had taken place.[71] In the guise of offering graphic descriptions of the catastrophe itself, the authors presented their personal views on society, morals, and politics, acting as valuable registers of the communities that they represented.

In many ways, the poets affirmed, the storm had acted as a leveller, not sparing anyone, rich or poor, and both built-up areas and temporary shantytowns had suffered badly. The babus had been chastised, and prostitutes and babus alike were being tyrannized by builders claiming exorbitant rates for reconstruction of fallen buildings in the aftermath of the storm.[72] The storm was unrelenting in its exposure of the city's sin and immorality in these imaginary renderings—its aftermath finding illicit lovers in cheap hotel

[70] See, for example, Maheshchandra Das De, *Hay Ki Adbhut Jhod!*, p. 2; and his *Eki Asambhab Kartike Jhod* (Calcutta, 1867), pp. 1, 8, 14. Yet another author writing on his own admission on both occasions and mobilizing similar tropes is Sarkar, *Kartike Jhoder Pnachali*, p. 5.

[71] Kshitindranath Tagore recalls listening to vivid descriptions of the 1865 cyclone in his childhood. See his *Kolikatay Chalafera*, p. 30. The cyclone songs too offer internal references to works being composed on previous occasions of cyclones.

[72] Das De, *Eki Asambhab Kartike Jhod*, pp. 10–11.

rooms, and even an elderly brother-in-law locked in a clandestine embrace with the younger brother's wife.[73] The recurring unnatural and fantastic image is that of a world turned upside down.[74]

Fearing for the loss of their own flimsy residences and imminent death in a foreign land without the comforting presence of family and friends, the writers echoed the sentiments of many migrants to the city eking out a modest living amidst much adversity.[75] The city as a temporary, unfriendly, and uncertain place was further reaffirmed in allusions to the inevitable desecration of forgotten and forsaken decomposed bodies through post-mortem operations that would inevitably be carried out by the state, with one author fearing such a fate in the event of his dying from a collapsing house.[76] The songs also offer a vivid glimpse of the more modern civic markers of urban dislocation caused by the storm in overflowing drains, torn telegraph lines, and broken gas lamps in the city.[77]

Songs and tracts on worm-ridden fish, which afflicted the city in 1875, also relied on similar tropes of cosmic intervention to right a reversed world order. Despite those (invariably men) circulating in the wider public and seemingly wiser world reporting that scanty rainfall over the past few years had caused fishes to pick up the disease from the dried up and unclean river beds, women in the narratives—and presumably also the expected readership of

[73] Sarkar, *Kartike Jhoder Pnachali*, pp. 3–5.

[74] In this upturned world, owls sang tuneful melodies and birds roared like lions; Brahmins forgot to worship while the low-caste *chandal*s housed shrines; Shudras took over the professions of the twice-born; and the king fled his kingdom as lowly washermen donned expensive shawls. See Sarkar, *Kartike Jhoder Pnachali*, p. 15.

[75] T. Das, *Jongule Jhod*, p. 7. The personal dislocation of the poet could be real or imagined here, although the linguistic style of his composition indicates that he could have been originally a resident of eastern Bengal.

[76] T. Das, *Jongule Jhod*, p. 8. The heavy state presence is felt in at least one other work, which portrays a vivid picture of police searching for bodies amidst the ruins left behind by the storm. Das De, *Eki Asambhab Kartike Jhod*, p. 12.

[77] T. Das, *Jongule Jhod*, pp. 6, 15.

the tracts—firmly believe that the catastrophe had been brought upon the city people by their own wrongdoings.[78] Cast variously as a curse resulting from the insult by a group of fishermen to the smallpox goddess, Sitala, and the challenging of Kali by the River Ganga, the virulent spread of disease amongst fish in the riverine tracts of eastern Bengal and even the Hooghly was seen as causing untold misery amongst the fish-loving Bengalis.[79] As with the cyclone, this calamity too had acted as a leveller, affecting all—those who could afford fish and those who could not.[80]

The image of a beleaguered Bengali population trying to cope with the absence of fish, that vital ingredient in Bengali cuisine and celebrated by poets and litterateurs ad infinitum, is touching and designed to readily evoke the empathy of readers sharing the misfortune. The weakening of constitution and vitality resulting from a long-term deficiency of fish in household diets, it was thought, would have a disastrous impact on Bengalis as a race. Reduced to a meal of rice, lentil, and vegetables, one author feared, Bengalis would turn into Hindustanis or *khottas*, both offensive terms describing the supposedly inferior Hindi-speaking up-country migrants in the city.[81] Buried in the narrative is also a veiled dislike for the usually East Bengali migrant fisherfolk, who

[78] Badalbehari Chattopadhyay, *Bishom Dhnoka, Maachhe Poka*, p. 9.

[79] See, for example, Dvijabar Sarman, *Machher Basanta* [Smallpox Afflicted Fish] (Calcutta: Kabita Kaumudi Press, 1875); Jaharilal Shil, *Machher Poka* [Worms in Fishes] (Calcutta, 1875); Badalbehari Chattopadhyay, *Bishom Dhnoka, Maachhe Poka*; Aminchandra Datta, *Mechho Basante Mechhonir Darpachurna* [The Fisherwoman's Pride has been Slain because of the Smallpox in Fishes] (Calcutta: Kabita Kaumudi Press, 1875). Trains had been banned from bringing in fishes from eastern Bengal, but the waterborne trade must have persisted. Aminchandra Datta, *Mechho Basante Mechhonir Darpachurna*, p. 4.

[80] There is also a pertinent side note on widows who are happiest as others are now forced to share their dietary deprivation—Hindu Bengali widows being customarily barred from consuming fish—with the tone here being more sympathetic than satiric. See J. Shil, *Machher Poka*, p. 10.

[81] Jaharilal Shil, *Machher Basante Jele Mechhonir Khed* [The Fisherwoman's Repentance on Smallpox in Fishes] (Calcutta: Sudharnab Press, 1875), p. 3.

were depicted as involved in malpractices and artificially inflating the price of fish even in the best of times.[82]

Not surprisingly, women bear the burden of sin, guilt, and atonement in this literature. Bengalis can be delivered from the disaster if their married women in every household can fast for a day, chant from the current tract, worship Sitala, and forego fish for a period of three months.[83] The image of the craving, consumerist housewife in Hindu reformist literature is found echoed in the representation of the aggressive fisherwoman whose insatiable demands, it was asserted, had led to the current debacle. Without her relentless wants, fishermen would not have indulged in malpractices and brought the reprisal upon themselves. In a powerful direct address to his male readership, one author thus cautions men to keep their wives under control:

> ... 'Be warned' says the author to his male readers.
> The women of inferior households invariably ignore their husbands;
> Indulged beyond repair their confidence is increased.
> [As we have seen in the case of the fisherwoman insulting her husband ...]
> It is not a good idea to pamper your woman;
> Irrespective of high and low families.[84]

Long Live the British: Paying Tribute to Colonial Technology

Historiographies of the East–West encounter in colonial India have centred on the image of a despairing colonized elite being

[82] J. Shil, *Machher Basante Jele Mechhonir Khed*, pp. 9–11; Aminchandra Datta, *Mechho Basante Mechhonir Darpachurna*, pp. 7, 10–11. The motif crops up elsewhere too within the genre as when cheeky references are made to East Bengali boatmen plying ferry boats on the Hooghly who are made redundant when a bridge is built across the river. Jaharilal Shil, *Nutan Poler Pnachali* (Calcutta, 1874), p. 5; Das Ghose, *Ekei Bole Pole!*, p. 9.

[83] Sarman, *Machher Basanta*, pp. 11–12.

[84] J. Shil, *Machher Basante Jele Mechhonir Khed*, pp. 8–9. Brackets mine.

crushed under the ruthless wheels of Western modernity. The printed songs discussed here celebrating urban technological achievements, however, establish alternative images of this cultural encounter in nineteenth-century Calcutta. At a time when Calcutta was rapidly transforming beyond recognition with its tramways and gaslights, parks and avenues, and unprecedented levels of commercialization in daily life, we see how non-elite groups reflected upon and engaged with these changes through participation in and patronage of street songs that became immensely popular in the contemporary urban culture. In fact, the city's technological innovations also find expression in other street songs of the time. Hugh Urban has shown how marginal religious sects in late nineteenth-century Calcutta used both the material layout of the city and new technology like the railway as allegory in describing the human body and its journey through a world of suffering and death.[85]

While the theme of gloom dominates the moral and social imaginary of the city folk elsewhere, the songs of praise lavished on the unmitigated technological success in the metropolis are unequivocal in their stance. In 1874, the Hooghly River that ran alongside Calcutta was spanned, for the first time, by a wooden bridge supported by a series of boats. It had taken three years to build, and was 1,528 feet between abutments, with a roadway for carriages 48 feet in width, as well as footpaths. The middle section was movable, so as to allow the passage of vessels up and down the river.[86] The resulting floating pontoon bridge amazed Calcutta's residents. Songs, dramas, and poems celebrating the event, and congratulating the British for achieving this 'miracle' were published the same year. A recurrent incredulity was expressed at the ability to 'float iron on water', a task where even the gods had failed.[87] One such song ran as follows:

85 Urban, 'The Marketplace and the Temple', 1085–114.

86 L.S.S. O'Malley and Monmohan Chakravarti, *Bengal District Gazetteer: Howrah*, (Calcutta, 1909).

87 J. Shil, *Nutan Poler Pnachali*, pp. 6, 9; Nandalal Ray, *Poler Pnachali* (Calcutta, 1874), p. 4, and *Nutan Poler Tappa*, pp. 1–2, 5.

> Oh what a pole [bridge] has been built by the sahib company
> How could a bridge be built over the Ganges?
> Even Vishwakarma [the builder-god] has admitted defeat ...
> Such intelligence and skill ... there is no problem anymore
> All can easily cross the river now ...
> The bridge has brought happiness upon this earth.[88]

Commendation was due for easing up communication across the river, especially reducing the rush of ferry traffic during office hours.[89] Robust and reliable even in times of storm and reducing the anxieties of crossing by ferry boat in choppy waters, authors noted, the pavements and wooden floors of the bridge also made it easier for pedestrians in wet and muddy conditions.[90] Most importantly, travel, initially at least, was toll free, much to the relief of the poor.[91]

Another work marvelled at the city's sophisticated underground drainage system, along with gaslights and motorcars. The author revels at the thought of covered sewers, clean surroundings, and most importantly, 'peaceful nights without mosquitoes'.[92]

An incredible amount of painstaking detail marks the songs that are both technological and also immensely visual in nature, inviting the listeners/readers to come and investigate for themselves. The writings on the city's underground drains thus carry minute descriptions of the different stages of construction—from the digging and groundwater extraction, to the erection of wooden arches for containing the pipes, and the fine brickwork.[93] There must have been a consuming interest in the actual

[88] Nandalal Ray, *Nutan Poler Tappa*, p. 1.

[89] Das Ghose, *Ekei Bole Pole*, p. 6.

[90] J. Shil, *Nutan Poler Pnachali*, pp. 4–5; Nandalal Ray, *Poler Pnachali*, p. 4, and *Nutan Poler Tappa*, p. 8.

[91] Das Ghose, *Ekei Bole Pole*, p. 9; J. Shil, *Nutan Poler Pnachali*, p. 8; Aminchandra Datta, *Howrah Ghater Poler Kobi*, p.11. Newspapers complained when there was a tax imposed later on of one pice, asking for it to be reduced to half a pice. *Saptahik Samachar*, from *Indian Newspaper Reports (Bengal)*, *1874–75*, week ending 16 January 1875.

[92] Aghorchandra Das Ghose, *Drener Pnachali* (Calcutta, 1874), 1874, pp. 5–6.

[93] Das Ghose, *Drener Pnachali*, pp. 3–4.

FIGURE 2.2 The Pontoon Bridge on the Hooghly, Calcutta; Johnston and Hoffman, Postcard from the 1890s
Source: Photo 514/(1) © The British Library Board. Courtesy of the British Library, London.

mechanics and building processes for the authors to present them so elaborately, as seen in a vivid and loving portrayal of the Howrah Bridge (see Figure 2.2):

> Wrapped in copper sheets and shaped as a[n inverted] boat
> The bridge is afloat on the river.
> Iron chains running below secure it onto anchors.
> [While] Arranged diagonally on a series of boats are a collection of mighty supports
> Resembling the mythical moonbeam-drinking bird.
> The actual bridge rests on this structure
> Itself a fine weave of beams and rafters.
> There are attractive footpaths on both sides
> Lined with charming railings.[94]

94 Aminchandra Datta, *Howrah Ghater Poler Kobi*, p. 3

The rendering, however, even if based on the factual, was done in the style of the marvellous and fantastic, impressing upon the audience the breathtaking nature of the changes happening around them. Thus, there are images of people travelling in hordes to see the Howrah Bridge, particularly its illumination at night, and talking ceaselessly about it.

Part panegyric and part pnachali style, the works sang enthusiastically of the achievements of the British, comparing the Raj to King Rama's regime and scoffed at the pretentious babus who mimicked the superficial English culture without obviously internalizing any of their technological prowess.[95] Positive racial attributes showered on the ruling nation—steely determination, fortitude, courage—are compared with lack of the same qualities in Bengalis.[96] Thus, the British are just and fair in their rule, benevolent, and mindful of the woes of their subjects, and authors fervently hoped that their rule in India would remain permanent.[97] Being the supreme amongst humankind, accordingly, it is hardly surprising that they look down upon Bengalis as an ignorant and lowly race.[98] While the temptation may be to read this simply as an inward critique of Bengalis looking for redemption, the eulogy is entrenched enough—recurring with remarkable consistency in invariably every single tract—to prompt other more ambiguous understandings.

The admiration expressed was incessant and compulsive. Frequent cross referencing in the tracts meant that while highlighting the wonders of one marvel, poets would also sing of others. The Howrah Bridge composers thus also paid tributes to the steam train, telegraph, and gaslights, 'refine [*sic*]' tap water and drains.[99] One work listed on the cover page all the machines it was going to cover—from railways, telegraph, and steamships

95 See Das Ghose, *Ekei Bole Pole*, p. 5, for a biting critique of the coat-and-fob-chain-donning, cigarette-smoking, meat-eating, pidgin-English-speaking, and fashionable-stick-wielding babu dandies.

96 J. Shil, *Nutan Poler Pnachali*, pp. 3–4, 8.

97 Das Ghose, *Ekei Bole Pole*, p. 12.

98 J. Shil, *Nutan Poler Pnachali*, p.7.

99 Nandalal Ray, *Poler Pnachali*, p. 3; Das Ghose, *Ekei Bole Pole*, p. 8.

to the travelling balloon, jute and sugar presses, and road rolling machines.[100] Just about anything seemed possible:

> If they wish to they [the British] can even build a staircase to the heavens,
> We have already seen how they can make men fly in balloons in the sky.
> Now only if they could bring back the dead to life
> [I am sure] all would accept them as Gods on earth.[101]

There must have been a buzz in the city about the numerous engineering feats flooding the urban space and constituting an integral part of everyday life. But such jubilation, arguably, could also be rhetorical, containing underlying anxieties about machinery and technology.[102] As Bernhard Rieger has pointed out in an illuminating study, such rapid and dramatic innovations could also prove to be a worrying source of uncertainty, engendering 'ambivalent appreciations of new technology', whereby the tropes of both 'wonder' and 'debacle' could coexist.[103]

It is perhaps also why the songs apply familiar and comfortable mythological tropes to comprehend and transmit the overwhelming experiences to an audience struggling to make sense of it all. The Howrah Bridge is thus compared to Rama's bridge;[104] and the reticence of the otherwise mighty Ganga River at her seeming inability to avenge herself, despite

[100] Das Ghose, *Drener Pnachali.*

[101] Nandalal Ray, *Nutan Poler Tappa,* p. 5.

[102] Hugh Urban has noted the agony expressed in the extractive and crippling power of foreign technology in Baul street songs. Urban, 'The Marketplace and the Temple', 1097.

[103] Rieger discusses these attitudes in the context of innovations in aviation, passenger shipping, and films. See Bernhard Rieger, '"Modern Wonders": Technological Innovation and Public Ambivalence in Britain and Germany, 1890s to 1933', *History Workshop Journal* 55, no. 1 (Spring 2003): 152–76.

[104] In Hindu mythology, Rama is believed to have built a stone bridge across the seas in a mission to rescue his wife, Sita, from the demon-king, Ravana. Aminchandra Datta, *Howrah Ghater Poler Kobi,* p. 2; J. Shil, *Nutan Poler Pnachali,* p. 9; Nandalal Ray, *Poler Pnachali,* p. 4.

being fettered by iron chains, explained away by her cosmic flight from the mortal world.[105] In one tract, the author in the end chastises those who, in their uncritical admiration of the rulers, forget their religious scriptures or *shastras* and defy their dharma. While drawing attention to the current plight of the Gods, particularly the Ganges, he triumphantly reminds all of a cosmic resurrection for her and other divinities at the end of the Kali Age, as enumerated in the shastras.[106] Another pleads with the Goddess not to wreak havoc in revenge and instead remain within the celestial top-knot of Shiva—implying her not lost but temporarily hidden powers.[107]

Songs and the City: A Widening Urban Public Sphere in Colonial Calcutta

Urban social space in Calcutta in the nineteenth century was a contested terrain. With huge influxes of immigrants in the city, the new organization of work schedules and space politics, restrictive laws regulating movements in certain areas under the pretext of policing, the thriving sex industry and its attendant opium dens and alcohol shops, and the increased visibility of women—Calcutta seemed a disconcerting place. The forceful entry of such diverse social constituencies, each with different claims to social and political authority, into a fractured, heterogeneous public sphere, signalled turmoil and struggle.

Writing in the mid-nineteenth century, Kaliprasanna Sinha, with his sharp eye for recording street life, described a Durga Puja procession in the city:

[105] Nandalal Ray, *Poler Pnachali*, p. 4. The reference here alludes to the Puranic tale of Ganges being chastised by Lord Shiva when he catches her in his topknot and tames her destructive powers.

[106] Accordingly, as non-believers, the British were not required to be mindful of the divine status of the river merely seeing the bridge over it as augmenting communication, but it was different for Hindus. See J. Shil, *Nutan Poler Pnachali*, pp. 7, 10.

[107] Nandalal Ray, *Nutan Poler Tappa*, p. 2

> The main street of Chitpur gradually filled up with people. The prostitutes standing on the roof tops and verandahs watched the gaiety while smoking from their silver decorated hubble-bubbles; the people on the streets alternated between seeing the moving image [of the Goddess] and the standing images of the prostitutes.[108]

The dense urban experience is something that finds repeated literary representation in Bengali writings alongside official discourse. The comfortable and assuring social boundaries regulating caste and community identities in the villages had broken down on account of the forced proximity of the urban spatial ordering. In addition, the blurring of distinctions between the *chhotolok* (lower classes) and bhadralok haunted the social imagination of the prosperous. The seeming social anarchy and commotion prevailing in the streets did not help. Despite legislation initiated by the bhadralok to stifle public expression of revelry and dissent, marginal social groups repeatedly spill over and out of their ascribed roles and locales into the streets.[109] As Swati Chattopadhyay comments in her recent study of architecture in colonial Calcutta, 'The densely linked urban form had become too easy for the lower-class culture to infiltrate through the many interstices of the urban fabric.'[110]

The same textual evidence of the widening participation in *public spaces* can also be read as testimony to a widening of the *public sphere*. By the end of the nineteenth century, a vibrant street presence and increasing visibility in print of marginal social groups matched the growing social and economic opportunities presented by the colonial metropolis of Calcutta. They constituted a significant layer in the urban experience, even self-consciously acknowledging the tremendous role that the city played in their

[108] K. Sinha, *Hutom Pnechar Naksha*, p. 117.

[109] 'The Society for the Suppression of Obscenity' set up in 1873 thus was the main mover in the passing of a law prohibiting sawng processions.

[110] Swati Chattopadyay, *Representing Calcutta: Modernity, Nationalism and the Colonial Uncanny* (London and New York: Routledge, 2005), p. 260.

everyday lives. Popular street and print culture, particularly songs, consistently foreground the city as a site for discussions on social and topical themes. Intimate matters packed within a literary mode—sometimes light-hearted—ensured accessibility and provoked responses. Despite anxieties about surviving in a harsh environment, Calcutta's material munificence and technological marvels provoked awe and admiration. And there was no doubt about the way in which the new urban regime fundamentally dominated, reconfigured, and regulated the lives of its residents.

This chapter shows how, contrary to the urban experience of the educated middle classes, the city afforded opportunities to other social groups to claim a space for themselves in a very public manner. These were literate and semi-literate groups operating below the level of educated literary associations and newspapers, and positioning themselves quite clearly in that social bracket. Their concerns were not with the high arts, literatures, and sciences that constituted 'useful knowledge' for the many bhadralok societies crowding the frontal stage of the public sphere, but more with aspects of day to day living.[111] The songs are very petty bourgeois in their sensibility, sharing concerns about boat fares, taxes, price of fish, and sanitation, as well as the importance of controlling wives. They are also deeply involved in the local and the everyday, as opposed to grand views on society, history, and culture like the bhadralok.

For a beleaguered and uprooted population, the songs helped to translate their angst into a comfortable familiarity, provided vital maps of the urban terrain, and helped in the navigation of a rapidly changing world. In this sense, the songs represented a certain level of dexterity, a canny sense of manoeuvring a space in the highly contested social landscape of the colonial urban metropolis—reinforcing a sense of belonging to certain communities, helping to clarify multiple positions on women, migrants, bhadralok, and the colonial government.

Male anxiety of rampant female sexuality that is endemic in bhadralok writings is an aspect, however, that was shared by the

[111] Like the Bethune Society or the Society for Acquisition of General Knowledge.

street songs, being mostly male-authored as they were. Gentle chastisement of wayward women in the songs was complemented by simultaneous airing of such concerns in the cheap circulating print literature on social scandals. Sensational stories of sexual intrigue cautioned against the hasty upsetting of traditional terms of domesticity and gender relations, as well as reckless licentiousness. Motifs of reprisal in the shape of natural phenomena collectively inflicted on the city were used in the songs as sobering reminders of its sins.

* * *

Street songs on the city in colonial Calcutta were then essential sites for the construction of urban discourses and the shaping of various community, caste, and social identities. Alongside the more elevated platforms of the press and literary and civic societies of the educated, they too presented an opportunity for public debates on the contemporary urban experience and significantly shaped the ways in which various non-elite groups made sense of themselves and their new environment. The city in the songs is the fundamental organizing category, the common referential frame for writers, performers, and listeners alike, and while singing about the everyday the songs offer occasion for reflection on various aspects of city life.

3

Sexuality, Scandals, and the Urban Order

The telling of popular stories on the urban experience was inimical to the shaping of the city's social order. It helped outline a new public sphere and announce the presence of new social and political actors in Calcutta. Scandal narratives can be taken as a case in point. Contemporary scandals, involving transgression of normative sexual and gender boundaries, emerging more publicly than ever before in the city's law courts, and reported with speed and sensation in the journalistic and commercial print world, gripped popular imagination and worked collective anxieties to a feverish pitch. Debates about sexuality in both private and public spaces in popular and reformist print helped the airing of ideas, opinions, and concerns in unsettling times, reshaping the fundaments of vital social institutions such as family and domesticity, while also enabling the increased visibility of women in the urban public sphere.

Apart from general themes of corruption and depravity among the 'gentle folk' or bhadralok—of which there are endless examples—short skits dwelling on sensational topical events were popular. The current chapter is drawn from a representative body of low-brow scandal literature focusing on some key events during the late nineteenth and early twentieth centuries.

The horrific Elokeshi–Mohunta scandal of 1874, the murder in the red-light area of Sonagatchi in 1875, and cases of serial killing of prostitutes in the early twentieth century rippled the city's social and moral fabric. The high news value of such reportage, especially for a widespread male readership, cannot be ignored. The press and publishing industry banked on the sensational murders rendering their own moral judgement on individual cases. As Sumanta Banerjee points out, 'Thus, the theme of prostitute-killing became a hook to hang a morality tale, sending out the message that such women had to pay the price for their freewheeling habits.'[1]

But sensationalism alone is an inadequate explanation for the popularity of themes of erotic violence, sexual transgression, and physical violation. The public discourses surrounding these cases also resonated with, and, in turn, gave shape to emergent cultural constructions of conjugality and sexuality, domesticity and family, gender and class, morality and purity. The new law courts and trial procedures together with the press helped turn private affairs into public spectacles, and opened them up for discussion and litigation. Scandals were thus 'created', both in the courtroom and in print, with both the moral and the legal communities scrutinizing and passing judgement on the lapses involved. As Tanika Sarkar has pointed out, a scandal going public has immense social, political, and cultural ramifications for the public sphere:

> A trial makes scandalous disclosures, publicizes intimate transgressions. Its reception has the same function as enlarging the scope of gossip, pulling it out of hidden, intimate, familiar circles into the realm of public concern and argument. An event is something that creates a shared field of discussion and thereby creates an interpretative community that reads the text of the event. An event of a 'gossipable' kind adds a peculiarly intimate twist to it. If gossip flourishes within an intimate group and draws its discussants into a tighter circle of acquaintances and concerns, a scandal has the same function within an anonymous, abstract public: it draws an unseen community of concerned people closer together

[1] Sumanta Banerjee, *Crime and Urbanization: Calcutta in the Nineteenth Century* (New Delhi: Tulika Books, 2006), p. 65.

> by focusing on intimate issues about its constituents. The range of its reception defines the space of the public sphere.[2]

This chapter is also about intimate violence and the role it plays in entrenching patriarchal structures in a highly unstable urban society. With huge influxes of single male immigrants in the city, the thriving sex industry and its attendant opium dens and alcohol shops, and the increased visibility of women, Calcutta seemed a disconcerting place to many residents. Violence directed at female partners and housewives for infidelity—real or alleged—seemed one way of retaining male control in sexual relationships. Murders and grievous bodily harm of women in a fit of jealous rage, in particular, fill up the Calcutta Police reports. As will be seen further, intimate corporeal chastisement functioned to police both the porous borders that had been opened up by urban discourses of choice and social aspiration for women, as well as soothe the corresponding anxieties regarding displaced families, peripatetic workers, and lone female partners and wives.

A related issue that comes up for debate when discussing norms of conjugality and sexuality in late nineteenth-century Calcutta is that of prostitutes. The presence of prostitutes in the city was a source of huge anxiety for reformers of that period. Their geographical and social expulsion to the margins of the city was matched by a more alarming development in later decades—that of their wanton physical harm. And yet, as this chapter shows, prostitutes were a vital cog in the urban economy and society, propping up familial structures and offering sexual comforts to a largely labouring single male population in the city. By acting as a foil to settled domesticity, they enhanced the virtues of the middle-class housewife and strengthened the conjugal bond between husband and wife. Contemporary popular print takes cognizance of their contributions, painting them with empathy and demonstrating their vigorous presence in street cultures, as an integral part of the wider urban experience.

[2] Tanika Sarkar, 'Talking about Scandals: Religion, Law and Love in Late Nineteenth century Bengal', *Studies in History* 13, no. 1 (1997): 63–95, at 66.

Scandals: Debates on Conjugality, Fidelity, Transgression

It is true that certain forms of a participatory politics had not entirely taken shape as yet, and exercise of critical reason by private individuals in public—following the model postulated by Jürgen Habermas—was mainly articulated through the new literary vernacular prose in elite journals and writings.[3] But as scholars have pointed out, the making of the public sphere in Bengal saw a remarkable downward reach in the 1870s. Farces, pamphlets, tracts, and lyrics pouring out of the cheaper vernacular presses were written and published by men (and even a few women) lacking higher education, who began to wield the more accessible everyday colloquial Bengali language in their writings to their commercial and social advantage, 'as soon as they ... [had] an interesting story to tell'.[4] A widening listening and performing culture of the streets added further interpretative layers to the stories. Within the structural format of the plays, we have interlopers in the form of curious neighbours, concerned citizens, barbers and washermen, prostitutes, and housewives offering their own views on the scandals. Baul and kobi songs are also depicted as picking up the themes of the scandals and spreading their messages far and wide.

When, in 1878, Upendranath Bose was tried for adultery with his nephew's wife, Kshetramoni, the popular press was vitriolic in its critique of the romance, blaming both in equal proportions for it. Upendranath, described as *borolok* (high in wealth and status) in the farces and songs was mocked mercilessly for his public humiliation in a court of law, and his ultimate prison sentence.[5]

[3] Jürgen Habermas, *The Structural Transformation of the Public Sphere* (Cambridge: Cambridge University Press, 1989).

[4] T. Sarkar, 'Talking about Scandals', 72. Also see Anindita Ghosh, *Power in Print: Popular Publishing and the Politics of Language and Culture in a Colonial Society* (New Delhi: Oxford University Press, 2006).

[5] Upendranath was sentenced to prison for a year. References are drawn here to the similar shaming of other powerful figures like the Tarakeshwar Mohunta of the Elokeshi–Mohunta case a few years earlier. Maheshchandra Das De, *Mama Bhaginir Natak* (Calcutta: Harihar Press, 1878), p. 8.

Kshetramoni was represented as a fallen woman of easy morals with a voracious appetite for luxury and good living.[6] Her husband, Jogen, was only a young *munsif* (an officer handling civil suits at the lowest judicial level) at the district court, while Upendranath had considerable wealth. Kshetramoni's condemnation was rendered more acute by her background. While in Elokeshi's case songsters and playwrights were ready to make concessions for her promiscuity through commensurate narrative moves, as discussed further, Kshetramoni was less fortunate. Daughter of a magistrate and brought up in Calcutta, she must have represented, for the writers, a perfect example of the new breed of educated women that they so despised. One author directly blames education for fomenting illicit romances in 'every household'.[7]

The scandal was also reported in Bengali newspapers with some show of reluctance and, according to an editorial in the *Somprakash*, only 'to satisfy the curiosity of the readers'.[8] Far from depicting 'an enlightened interest in social questions', another paper commented, the 'morbid curiosity' it had excited among 'all classes of the native population' reflected merely the public's 'love of scandal'.[9] As could doubtless happen with scandals of today, the reportage might have actually augmented circulation of the newspapers in question, but the educated middle classes felt dragged down by one of their own:

> Upendra babu has cast a stain on our pure society; he was a kayastha by caste, a man of means and education, and a lawyer; no one dreamt that he would perpetrate so grave a crime.[10]

The Elokeshi–Mohunta case that hit the city in 1873 exploded these worries on to a talkative public sphere, when a young, married

[6] Das De, *Mama Bhaginir Natak*, p. 7; Natabar Das, *Makkel Mama* (Calcutta, 1878), p. 5.

[7] Das De, *Mama Bhaginir Natak*, p. 8.

[8] Editorial, *Somprakash*, 12 August 1878. *Indian Newspaper Reports (Bengal)*, week ending 17 August 1878.

[9] *Sadharani*, 18 August 1878. *Indian Newspaper Reports (Bengal)*, week ending 17 August 1878.

[10] *Sahachar*, 19 August 1878. *Indian Newspaper Reports (Bengal)*, week ending 17 August 1878. Blame was also laid at the door of the father of Kshetramoni, Iswarchandra Mitra, for refusing to cooperate with the apparently wronged husband, Jogen. Editorial, *Somprakash*, 12 August 1878.

woman by the name of Elokeshi was beheaded by her husband, Nabin, on suspicions of adultery. The priest or *mohunta* of the temple at Tarakeshwar was later convicted of seducing Elokeshi, and Nabin deported for life to the Andamans. In the popular cultural world, however, despite being the murderer, Nabin was exonerated as he had acted in defence of Hindu conjugality and saved Elokeshi from a life of shame, while the mohunta stood accused. As meticulously studied by Tanika Sarkar, the case allowed intense and open discussion on Hindu conjugality, religion, and colonial law, drawing in participants from all levels of society. Newspapers, farces, theatre, songs, popular art, and crafts were all mobilized to present different opinions and interpretations of the event.[11]

An interesting aspect of such cases is the increasing visibility of courts and trials, which became public through newspapers and filtered into the popular domain through songs and gossip, rumour and suggestion. Quite a few of the scandal plays were simply a duplication of the trials and the subsequent disciplinary proceedings. There were fervent debates about the contributions of the characters involved in the scandal and the various judgments delivered in the courts of law.

The Elokeshi–Mohunta case trials were serialized in newspapers, reportage appearing as they happened, with the public closely watching their progress. There was another interesting aspect to the court proceedings, as Sarkar points out. The trials were celebrated in farces and in paintings as great social levellers.[12] Nabin was the poor Brahmin youth who had finally managed, with the aid of colonial law and justice, to expose the powerful mohunta.[13] The mohunta's prison sentence, his hard labour, and his humiliation at the hands of the judges, the prison guards, and the police were the exclusive themes of several farces and of many songs and artwork (see Figure 3.1).

[11] T. Sarkar, 'Talking about Scandals'. Sripantha lists in total thirty-four scandal plays related to this event. Sripantha, *Mohanto Elokeshi Sambad* (Calcutta: Ananda Publishers, 1984).

[12] T. Sarkar, 'Talking about Scandals', 82.

[13] The mohunta was sentenced to three years of hard labour and had to pay a fine of 2,000 rupees despite being represented by an English barrister. The plays celebrated the impartiality of colonial justice and the legal system. See, for example, Nimaichand Shil, *Tirthamahima* (Calcutta: New Sanskrit Press, 1873), pp. 82–3.

FIGURE 3.1 Courtroom Scene of the Elokeshi Murder Case, Kalighat Painting, c. 1875
Source: Courtesy of the Victoria and Albert Museum, London.

On a wider scale, this was also about the right of the colonial state to decide cases that were so intrinsic to Hindu customary law, the importance of including Indians as jury in critical cases, the exposure of corruption in religious institutions, and the role of religion in regulating the domestic domain. Sarkar argues that the 1870s marked a more open and fluid space for debate on social issues before everything became subsumed within the nationalist–indigenist perspective at the turn of the century, resting squarely on the defence of Hindu patriarchy as the last-remaining autonomous, non-colonized space.[14] As others have shown, this was the period when an inwardly turned and politically subdued intelligentsia, thoroughly disillusioned with the colonial regime, reflected on its past and future and tested the fundaments of its social and religious institutions.[15] It was in this highly charged political context that the scandal was being reviewed. 'Hindu conjugal sexuality and its Other—adultery and/ or rape—became,' argues Sarkar, 'an important register to test the morality of fundamental social and religious institutions, and acquired political meaning.'[16]

Unlike Sarkar's focus on the centrality of Hindu religion and colonial law to the scandal, this chapter underlines the subtext of love and loyalty, transgression and revenge—themes that are undeniably thrown up by the Elokeshi–Mohunta plays, and themes that cannot be explained by prescriptive laws and Hindu conjugal norms alone. Male romancing and its obverse of violence were as critical tools for maintaining patriarchal control as any customary or colonial law. While part of the debate might have been about the state's interference in the intimate sphere and the tightening of the Hindu conjugal world as a response, it was also about the uncertainties in familial life and normative

[14] T. Sarkar, 'Talking about Scandals', 70, 74. Also see Tanika Sarkar, *Hindu Wife, Hindu Nation: Community, Religion and Cultural Nationalism* (Bloomington: Indiana University Press, 2001).

[15] Sumit Sarkar, '"Kaliyuga", "Chakri" and "Bhakti": Ramakrishna and His Times', in *Writing Social History* (New Delhi: Oxford University Press, 1999).

[16] T. Sarkar, 'Talking about Scandals', 75–6.

domesticity that had been caused by the circumstances of urban work and living, and the temporary, fragile nature of sexual bonding in the new age. There are too many indications that suggest a wider and unsettling investment in patriarchal society that make such violence appear normative, not worrisome. In several of the plays, Nabin's horrific crime is tempered by his 'hot-headedness'—a characteristic that authors paint with great indulgence and empathy.[17] In one play, the owner of an opium den even contemplates how, if he had the right to legislate, he would make laws that would automatically clear a husband for hacking to death a disloyal wife.[18] As a highly visible index the Elokeshi case helped calibrate the categories of legitimate male violence, gendered loyalty, and the limits of sexual freedom for women.

One variable that muddied the debate in all of this, however, was the aspect of love.[19] Despite creating minor upsets, Nabin's undying love for his wife captivated popular imagination. Nabin had apparently given running away with the sullied Elokeshi a thought before killing her.[20] It also allowed the flourishing of a powerful discourse. In killing Elokeshi, according to this interpretation, Nabin had acted as a 'true husband', since a life of dishonour is worse for a woman than death.

But what comes across more emphatically in the plays is a language of force and ownership of the female body. In one play deploying aliases, on hearing how the mohunta had planned to block his escape with Purnakeshi (alias Elokeshi), Bipin (alias Nabin) exclaims:

> ... I'll see how he [the mohunta] can snatch you away from me. If I cannot enjoy Purnakeshi, the mohunt cannot too. He cannot

[17] N. Shil, *Tirthamahima*, pp. 55, 69, 72, 77; Bholanath Mukhopadhyay, *Mohanter Chakra Bhraman Natak* (Calcutta: Sudharnab Press, 1874), pp. 43, 46, 49.

[18] B. Mukhopadhyay, *Mohanter Chakra Bhraman Natak*, pp. 62–3.

[19] Sarkar hints at this but does not elaborate it. T. Sarkar, 'Talking about Scandals', 92–4.

[20] N. Shil, *Tirthamahima*, pp. 76–7; B. Mukhopadhyay, *Mohanter Chakra Bhraman Natak*, p. 44.

> make a fallen woman of you. [Bipin strikes Purnakeshi's neck with a fish knife].
> ... [striking again] Dear love, is it possible that the mohunta will enjoy you instead of me? Let us see him do so! [Purnakeshi's fall and death].[21]

Where love, or at least sexual jealousy, most mattered was the intimate sphere of bodily relations. Nabin's was a crime of passion, and it is here that the scandal cast its widest net and where there existed an almost unconditional consensus on the act of murder. Patriarchy reacted to the scandal by consenting to the reclamation of the disloyal female through death. As her lover and husband, Nabin owned Elokeshi's body and alone had the right to claim it, even when dead. Nabin was not a thoughtless murderer, and his words and actions were celebrated 'not as the sign of unreason and weakness, but of noble and strong love'.[22]

The scandal touched a raw nerve for an anxious and cornered masculine order, constantly living in the fear of losing its women to the pressures of urban living. Nabin worked in a printing press in Calcutta[23] and had to spend long periods away from his wife who stayed with her natal family in the suburbs. The distance and loneliness of spouses is amplified in the plays by referring to Calcutta as *bidesh* (foreign land).[24] The temporary residences in the city—mostly in the nature of tiled huts—where such petty workers lived were unfit for housing wives, and unsafe too.[25] In one play, Nabin warns other young husbands in the city:

> ... If I knew, I would not have left my newly-wed wife here ... [I hope] many have learned lessons from my predicament.[26]

[21] N. Shil, *Tirthamahima*, pp. 83–4. Similar sentiments are also expressed in B. Mukhopadhyay, *Mohanter Chakra Bhraman Natak*, p. 51.

[22] T. Sarkar, 'Talking about Scandals', 93.

[23] See B. Mukhopadhyay, *Mohanter Chakra Bhraman Natak*.

[24] N. Shil, *Tirthamahima*, p. 28. We also saw this sentiment reflect in the city songs in the last chapter.

[25] N. Shil, *Tirthamahima*, p. 58.

[26] B. Mukhopadhyay, *Mohanter Chakra Bhraman Natak*, p. 40.

The printing establishment was heavily invested in this discussion, as authors themselves admit, mostly in favour of Nabin.[27] But there was also more widespread support. When Nabin's life sentence was remitted after three years, songs welcomed the judgment and hailed his return to Bengal.[28] Another worry that surfaces here is that of migrants, a sentiment also encountered in the previous chapter. At least in one play, the mohunta is depicted as a migrant from the Bihar–UP region, who had grown up in Bengal.[29]

By contrast, love was definitely written out of Elokeshi's affair with the mohunta. Her representations were caught between two extremes—that of a submissive, unwilling victim of pressures from her natal family (in some accounts she was drugged before she was raped, or physically forced), or a fallen and despicable woman worthy only of the deepest contempt. Some are distinctly misogynistic representations where not only Elokeshi but also her mother-in-law is blamed for arranging the rendezvous between Elokeshi and the mohunta, and then actually exploiting it for financial gain.[30] But Elokeshi's own and active participation in the scandal was removed by a series of such erasures. Any agency on her part could only be described in terms of promiscuity and brazen sexual liberties. Elokeshi was no simple victim figure here, and love had no place in such an equation. The mohunta, of course, was villainized to no end—painted as a vile figure living a life of sin and licentiousness, routinely exploiting women pilgrims, and misusing the funds of the temple.[31]

[27] Jaharilal Shil, *Mohanter Sarbanash, Nabiner Poush Mash* (Calcutta, 1876), p. 7; also see B. Mukhopadhyay, *Mohanter Chakra Bhraman Natak*, pp. 59, 61.

[28] J. Shil, *Mohanter Sarbanash, Nabiner Poush Mash.*

[29] Harimohan Chattopadhyay, *Mohanta Pakshe Bhutanandi* (Calcutta: Calcutta Press, 1873), p. 2.

[30] See for example, H. Chattopadhyay, *Mohanta Pakshe Bhutanandi*, p. 18; Nandalal Ray, *Nabin Mohanta Elokeshi Natak*, second edition (Calcutta, 1875), pp. 1–2, 28; B. Mukhopadhyay, *Mohanter Chakra Bhraman Natak*, p. 20.

[31] See, for example, Aghorchandra Das Ghose, *Mohanter Khed* (Calcutta: Gyanollas Press, 1873); Krishnaraj Ray, *Mohanter Bilap* (Calcutta, 1878).

Scholarship on sexually motivated murders in the nineteenth century has focused on male domination and patriarchal control of women as fundamental motivations for such actions.[32] The nineteenth century in Britain and America saw the rise of widespread campaigns against the brutalization and sexual violation of wives.[33] Feminist thinkers and social purity reformers condemned physical and sexual cruelty toward wives, which they argued, arose from a husband's ownership of his wife's body. Women were encouraged and supported in seeking divorce from aggressive and violent husbands, and the state responded slowly, but accordingly, with appropriate legislation.

India, by contrast, during the same period, witnessed very little legislative action, the raising of the age of consent for consensual sex from 10 to 12 in 1891 being perhaps the only notable exception. But here too, the failure of the Age of Consent Act and the state to protect women and the furious uproar it generated in traditional society has been reported by scholars.[34] Unable to legislate in the intimate sphere to pre-empt violence, the colonial government resorted to the harshest measures to set up a few cases as exemplars. Interestingly, these did not apply to all.

[32] See, for example, Jane Caputi, 'The Sexual Politics of Murder', *Gender and Society* 3, no. 4 (December 1989): 437–56; Judith Walkowitz, 'Jack the Ripper and the Myth of Male Violence', *Feminist Studies* 8, no. 3 (Fall 1982): 543–74; Deborah Cameron and Elizabeth Frazer, *The Lust to Kill: A Feminist Investigation of Sexual Murder* (New York: Polity Press, 1987).

[33] The Protective Agency for Women and Children was founded in Chicago in 1885 and played a leading role in this respect. In England, at the instance of the prominent suffragist Frances Cobbe, a Protection Bill was drafted and introduced in Parliament in 1879, and ultimately passed with an important proviso—that the bill would not protect adulterous women. See Elizabeth Pleck, *Domestic Tyranny: The Making of Social Policy against Family Violence from Colonial Times to the Present* (Oxford: Oxford University Press, 1987), Chapter 3, pp. 88–107.

[34] Tanika Sarkar, 'Rhetoric against Age of Consent: Resisting Colonial Reason and Death of a Child Wife', *Economic and Political Weekly* 28, no. 36 (4 September 1993): 1869–78; Dagmar Engels, 'The Age of Consent Act of 1891: Colonial Ideology in Bengal', *South Asia Research* 3, no. 2 (November 1983): 107–31.

What impact did this have on intimate violence, especially within the unstable social environment of a city like Calcutta—with its highly unequal sex ratios, and a surplus of lone males—where sexual relationships could be stretched and tested, and denial of favours or unfaithfulness could lead to extreme reprisals? The brutal murders of women—wives and prostitutes, lovers and temporary partners—demonstrate how sexual relationships served as a nodal point through which male supremacy and normative gender hierarchies could be reproduced and reaffirmed in the face of challenges. In the face of a colonial state hesitant to legislate in the sphere of social and customary law, sexual violence thus served to critically constitute the regulatory order of gender and—as we shall see later in the chapter—also class. In the meantime, women remained exposed to summary judgements being delivered by the patriarchal order, even paying the highest price of death, a theme that is further explored in the next section in the Sonagatchi murder case.

Sonagatchi Murder: A Case of Intimate Violence

Murders of intimates by men is understood in many studies to be about an assertion of male 'proprietary rights', especially where they involve sexual partners.[35] Being merely conceived of as some sort of extended domestic violence in the eyes of law therefore, these crimes often seem less socially threatening than murder in other situations.[36] Martin Wiener has shown, however, the judicial processes by which more restrained and civilized gentlemen were cultivated in Victorian Britain, their new 'manliness' being measured in terms of their self-control even when faced with extreme provocation, especially from women. The impact was felt

[35] K. Polk, *When Men Kill: Scenarios of Masculine Violence* (Cambridge: Cambridge University Press, 1994); R. Shoemaker, 'Male Honour and the Decline of Public Violence in 18th-century London', *Social History* 26, no. 2 (2001): 190–208.

[36] Shani D'Cruze, Sandra Walklate, and Samantha Pegg, *Murder: Social and Historical Approaches to Understanding Murder and Murderers* (Cullompton: Willian Publishing, 2006), p. 105.

more among the working classes who were believed to be more prone to violence, and hence, in greater need of disciplining and guidance. The middle and upper classes were theoretically self-policing, the lower classes were not. Evidence would suggest that the working model was extended to a certain extent to India in the nineteenth century. Marking the murderous violence of a small number of mostly poor, labouring men or social outcastes effectively masked the private violence of the more 'respectable, as we shall see, while the state took on the benign patriarchal role of protecting women from dangerous masculinities.

In 1875, a few years after the Elokeshi–Mohunta case, another outrageous and daring murder rocked Calcutta when a young man by the name of Kalicharan Rakshit entered his mistress Golap's house in broad daylight and hacked her to pieces in the presence of her servants. He did this apparently because Golap had ended their 'relationship' and had been for some time refusing to entertain him. Rakshit later confessed to killing another young girl living with him in a drunken fit and disposing of the body in the river.[37] The particularly brutal nature of the crime—which in contemporary Victorian juridical circles was associated with 'rough men' and those from the labouring classes—must have played a role in sealing the fate of the appeal.[38]

While the crime itself was horrific enough, what rendered it even more sensational in its reportage was the nature of its execution. Rakshit had apparently walked in unopposed into the house of a woman he knew, brushed past her attendant, taken the stairs to the upper-floor room where Golap lived, and then proceeded to hack her to death with a fish-knife, ignoring the protests of her servants. Having finished her, he went off raging and roaring to

[37] *ARPC, 1875*, pp. 20–1.

[38] Martin Wiener, *Men of Blood: Violence, Manliness and Criminal Justice in Victorian England* (Cambridge: Cambridge University Press, 2004), p. 232. Wiener reports how—in a case somewhat analogous to Sonagatchi because of the outrageous nature of the attack—a labourer stabbed his estranged wife fourteen times in broad daylight leading the permanent undersecretary to note how 'brutal' the murder was. The sentence passed was one of hanging.

the terrace declaring to one and all that he had committed this crime, and challenging anyone to come near him. He was eventually caught by a policeman to whom he submitted meekly, and led off through the crowded streets to safe custody.

Out of the two murders—the one committed by Nabin and the other by Kalicharan—the Sonagatchi case has received less attention. And yet, for its sheer audacity, raw brutality, and passionate nature of crime, the murder of Golap too had considerable impact. One local press commissioned two pamphlets—one on the murder itself and another on the trial and conviction, both written by the same author and published in 1875.[39] While detailing the ghastly nature of the murder and chiding the perpetrator for attacking a 'weak and defenceless woman', the author, however, in the end makes use of the opportunity to present a very conservative message to young men:

> All of you out there, do remember
> How the woman bewitches by weakening your mind.
> This is the price of abandoning your family and loved ones.
> Coming in contact with a prostitute is a sin;
> ... You lose both your present and your future.
> And are in grave danger of losing your life.[40]

Sympathy for the victim is thus strongly overshadowed by her sinful life. The bottom line is clear, that such women did not deserve to live. Death following disgrace seems to be the logical conclusion to this narrative, the moral tale further driven home by the appalling murder.

The account of the coroner's inquiry and the trial is incredibly factual, citing penal codes, names of individual judges, doctors, and lawyers involved, and trial dates. While the case against Rakshit is outlined in great detail—including postmortem reports, witness statements, and the confession of the accused—his defence is summarized in a few lines. Rakshit is apparently unrepentant, even on hearing his sentence of death

[39] Akhilchandra Datta, *Sonagajir Khun* and *Sonagajir Khunir Fnasir Hukum* (Calcutta, 1875), printed and published by the Kabita Kaumudi Press.

[40] Akhilchandra Datta, *Sonagajir Khun*, p. 11.

by hanging, and mutters mockingly in approval, 'Good, good, good!'[41] Outright and unambiguous sympathy for the defendant, however, is not apparent.

The reportage on the Sonagatchi case in the pamphlets is intriguing. To begin with, compared to the Elokeshi, case, the commentary is reduced, almost non-existent. While Nabin, the murderer and husband of Elokeshi, was acquitted in the public mind of his crime, the stance is not so clear in the case of Golap. Nabin was to be exonerated as he was acting in defence of Hindu conjugality and fighting the corruption amongst certain sections of contemporary priesthood. But Rakshit was sinful of cohabiting with a prostitute outside wedlock, and therefore, less worthy of sympathy.

And yet, even here it is possible to trace a hint of sympathy for him as the author makes a direct connection between the killing and Golap's betrayal, suggesting 'there must have been a reason' (*thakibe kono karon*) almost justifying the act.[42] In particular, the reporting of the arrogance with which Rakshit greeted his sentence seems to betray a certain admiration for the accused. Cases such as these helped society police the boundaries of normative conjugality, sending off strong warnings to errant men and women. Also, extended beyond the realms of family and home, it seemed to send off a further note of statutory caution, especially to women, about loyalty and fidelity to sexual partners. In Sonagatchi, it came perilously close to imposing the conjugal framework on a libertine profession.

There appeared to exist very little disagreement about the relative degrees of male and female complicity in sexual sin, and the violence engendered by women was the rightful punishment for the exercise of their sexual liberty. The subtext seemed to be that of the limits of sexual freedom for women. The warning is stark: the lurid details of the murder, where Golap had been hit in the body (ten wounds), and the repetitive moralizing drives home the dangers of polygamous bonding. While it is the woman who takes the terrible blows, it is young men who are warned of the dangers lurking in the prostitute quarters. Her unfaithfulness justifies the crime, the murder her preordained payment for sin.

[41] Akhilchandra Datta, *Sonagajir Khunir Fnasir Hukum*, p. 12.

[42] Akhilchandra Datta, *Sonagajir Khun*, p. 5

The Sonagatchi case was not isolated. Murders of women by partners/lovers/husbands in a fit of jealous rage were continuously reported in contemporary newspapers and recorded in police reports. 1855, thus, saw the brutal murder of his wife by a scavenger who suspected her of adultery. She had been stabbed repeatedly with a carver knife.[43] In 1870 alone there were three separate cases: of a prostitute killed by a police constable, a woman murdered by her former servant and lover, and a seaman from Manila slitting the throat of his mistress, Victoria Gregory.[44] In another tragic case, Umbica Churn Bose, a native of Barisal, who was besotted by a girl from his native village, followed her to Calcutta when she became a day scholar at Bethune School and, after several attempts to renew the intimacy, stabbed her fatally as she was alighting from the school omnibus. He was later executed.[45] In a daring instance, just five years after, and in almost an imitation of Sonagatchi, a woman was hacked to pieces with a billhook in broad daylight as she was walking down a crowded thoroughfare by her rejected suitor. No one interfered.[46]

Aspects of class and gender can be seen at work here, with reference to the penal outcome, in a lot of these cases. Unable to legislate in the intimate sphere to pre-empt violence, the colonial government resorted to the harshest measures to clamp down on perpetrators, to set up a few cases as exemplars. The heavy hand of colonial justice can be felt in assaults and murders involving lower class men as compared to comparable situations in middle-class households where the affairs were hushed up, or the perpetrators received mitigated sentences. Police reports betray tales of middle-class intervention—sometimes with success—and attempts to rescue bhadralok male perpetrators of domestic violence. Thus, in 1888, the son of a prominent Sanskrit scholar and pundit in Calcutta was charged with the murder of his child-wife and eventually executed, but not before his father had attempted to pass this off as suicide.[47] In yet another case in 1895, where a

43 *ARPC, 1855*, p. 15.

44 *ARPC, 1870*, pp. 2–4. Also see *ARPC, 1882*, pp. 7–8.

45 *ARPC 1891*, p. 6.

46 *ARPC, 1880*, p. 6.

47 *ARPC, 1888*, p. 6.

girl-wife was murdered by her husband for wishing to return to her parents, the sentence of hanging passed by the Sessions Court was eventually commuted to transportation for life on appeal to the High Court.[48] The middle classes appear blatantly protected, even when caught red-handed. When a certain Jadunath Ganguly killed his mistress in a pre-planned murder with a sword, the jury at the initial trial found him guilty of the lesser crime of culpable homicide because he was a Brahmin.[49]

Historians of crime agree that over similar chronologies, lower-status men have become more directly criminalized as higher-status men have had better success in keeping their intimate violence out of court.[50] Strange has shown how in Australia in the late nineteenth and early twentieth centuries, despite the contemporary mandatory sentence for murder, which was hanging, there was a domestic discount operating through discretionary recommendations for mercy by juries. This loophole, Strange argues, allowed the criminal justice system to thrive as a patriarchal and class organ, where men exercised their judgement to distinguish between 'respectable' and 'deviant' masculinities.[51]

Scandals such as Sonagatchi were also about sexuality in the city and the sexually permissive culture it seemed to nurture in its bowels.[52] Was aggressive, brutal sexuality of men acceptable? How willing were women as sexual partners in this violent, erotic world? And how far could these partnerships be regarded as possible and

[48] *ARPC, 1895*, p. 11.

[49] An appeal launched at the High Court against the judgment, however, saw him subsequently convicted and executed. *ARPC, 1876*, p. 10.

[50] See for instance, P. King, *Crime, Justice and Discretion in England, 1740–1820* (Oxford: Oxford University Press, 2000).

[51] C. Strange, 'Masculinities, Intimate Femicide and the Death Penalty in Australia, 1890–1920', *British Journal of Criminology* 43, no. 2 (2003): 310–39.

[52] For similar concerns being raised in early nineteenth-century New York over the murder of a prostitute, see the excellent article by Patricia Cline Cohen, 'The Helen Jewett Murder: Violence, Gender, and Sexual Licentiousness in Antebellum America', *NWSA Journal* 2, no. 3 (Summer, 1990): 374–89. See also Frank Mort, 'Scandalous Events: Metropolitan Culture and Moral Change in Post-Second World War London', *Representations* 93, no. 1 (Winter, 2006): 106–37, for a discussion of crime, permissive culture, and sexuality in a much later time frame.

desirable alternatives to the cult of domesticity and conjugal life? Initial pointers may be made towards a squeezed male labouring and low-ranking service population in the city, which was a product of economic deprivation, social uprooting, single living, and the sexual instabilities resulting from both isolation and an unbalanced gender ratio. This is further developed later on in the chapter.

A related but less burning issue was the problem of young men wasting themselves in the red-light district. Wayward youth was the recurrent theme of an entire category of street and reformist literature of the period. Rakshit was a case in point. A son of a wealthy man, he inherited part of the estate when his father died in 1872. Since then he had allegedly led 'a riotous and dissipated life', and, at some point, must have arrived in Calcutta to pursue his pleasures.[53] In a case remarkably similar to the Sonagatchi incident, yet another prostitute, Kusum, was stabbed to death by her eighteen-year-old lover, Tinkari, in 1885. Son of a homeopathic doctor, Tinkari was a school student, deemed 'a restrained boy' by his teachers and hailing from 'a peaceful and law-abiding family'; his fate touched a raw nerve with Calcutta's middle classes, many of whom felt that it was easy for youth to become corrupt in the city when unchaperoned. The young Saralabala Sarkar, writer and nationalist, remembers how 'everyone was struck, as if by thunderbolt' when the verdict of death by hanging was declared. On the day of the execution, Saralabala's mother refrained from cooking and fasted as a token of protest.[54] Such was the wave of empathy felt that a signed petition was sent—although to no avail—by 'prominent citizens' to the lieutenant governor of Bengal, seeking his prerogative of mercy and intervention in the case.[55].

Prostitutes in Urban Culture: Proxy Wives to Harlots

While the previous section highlighted the relative absence of women in the city and the problems arising thereof, here the focus

[53] *ARPC, 1875*, p. 4.

[54] Saralabala Sarkar, *Saralabala Sarkar Rachana Sangraha*, vol. 1 (Calcutta: Ananda Publishers, 1989), p. 938

[55] *ARPC*, 1885, pp. 2–3.

is on the presence of a very significant and critical category of women whose vigorous symbolical existence in the world of popular culture was matched by an equally strongly felt presence in the city's everyday life. Calcutta's prostitutes recurrently appear in a range of nineteenth- and early twentieth-century archives, from official documentation to newspapers, reformist pamphlets, songs, illustrations, and popular print. And yet, their dynamic presence in the city has been almost written off by their marginalized location in dominant narratives.

The metaphors and categories of nineteenth-century European reformers—crime, scrutiny, poverty, disease, and sanitation—have continued to influence discussions of prostitution amongst scholars. While there has emerged important scholarship on prostitution in colonial India, the process of marginalization of the trade has usually been studied under the twin framework of puritanical reformist drives and aggressive colonial medicine.[56] Such approaches have masked other and more positive contributions of these women to the urban culture and economy that so vilified them. By servicing and supporting both service and wage labour with their own domestic and sexual labour, the institution served as 'illegal marriage' and the prostitutes as 'proxy wives'.[57] The labour of prostitutes thus sustained the structures of colonialism and capitalism through their intimate and intricate links with the migrant work force in the city.

[56] For an account of the reformist campaign see Sumanta Banerjee, *Dangerous Outcast: The Prostitute in Nineteenth Century Bengal* (Calcutta: Seagull Books, 1998). For the marginalization of prostitutes by the Contagious Diseases Act (CDA) see Kenneth Balhatchet, *Race, Sex and Class under the Raj* (New York: Weidenfield and Nicholson, 1980); Philippa Levine, 'Venereal Disease, Prostitution and the Politics of Empire: The Case of British India', *Journal of the History of Sexuality* 4, no. 4 (1994): 579–602; Ashwini Tambe, *Codes of Misconduct: Regulating Prostitution in Late Colonial Bombay* (Minneapolis: University of Minnesota Press, 2009).

[57] This has been argued in other contexts too. See Luise White, 'Women's Domestic Labour in a Colonial City: Prostitution in Colonial Nairobi, 1900–1950', in *Patriarchy and Class: African Women at Home and in the Workplace*, edited by Jane Parpart and Sharon Stichter (Boulder, CO: Westview Press, 1988), pp. 139–60.

The prostitute in the nineteenth century was a vital part of Calcutta's social and economic fabric. To begin with, the hidden sexual economies of prostitution were invaluable in a city composed largely of males. In the 1881 census, men were returned twice as numerous as females and this continued to be the pattern for the next two decades.[58] By 1911—if women of child-bearing age are taken into consideration—there were three men to every woman among the immigrants in Calcutta.[59] For the floating male population of the city, prostitutes also provided another key service in that their quarters served as 'second homes' for their clients.[60] A substantial majority catered to a petty bourgeois and working-class clientele—clerks, textile workers, seamen—and even formed semi-permanent relationships with them as seen earlier in the cases of intimate violence involving prostitutes. For the huge army of petty office workers in the city, prostitutes provided the comforts of home and family.[61] Labourers too formed a significant proportion of customers.[62]

[58] Women comprised 33 per cent of the total population of Calcutta in 1881. See *Census of the Town and Suburbs of Calcutta, 1881*, pp. 21, 25. Roughly the same results are available for 1891 (H.F.J.T. Maguire, *Census of the Town and Suburbs of Calcutta 1891*, p. 21) and 1911, with the proportion of women of child bearing age (15–40) constituting only 15 per cent of the total population that year (see L.S.S. O'Malley, *Census of the Town and Suburbs of Calcutta, 1911*, p. 2).

[59] *Census of the Town and Suburbs of Calcutta, 1911*, p. 17.

[60] See Meghnad Gupta, *Raater Kolkata* (Calcutta, 1923), pp. 32–4. Gupta's data supplies the following ratios of males to females in the city: 55:2 (1872); 55:6 (1881); 50:7 (1901); 47:5 (1911). In 1921 there was one prostitute available for every forty males. Prafullachandra Basu, *The Middle Class People in Calcutta, and Their Effects upon the Health and Morals of the Rising Generation* (Calcutta: Chuckervertty, Chatterjee & Co., 1925), p. 74.

[61] R.J. Minney, *Nightlife of Calcutta* (Calcutta: The Muston Company, 1919), p. 22. Minney estimates 90 per cent of the clientele of prostitutes in the city came from the clerical groups.

[62] See Aghor Chandra Ghosh, *Pnachali Kamalkali: Choudda Ain* (Calcutta, 1873); Chandrakanta Sikdar, *Ki Mojar Shonibar* [What a Fun Saturday], (Calcutta, 1863), p. 47.

According to one unofficial estimate, the number of women in the profession in the city and its suburbs in 1921 was 15,000. Twenty years ago, at the turn of the century, 'one in every fifteen women over ten years of age was a prostitute', the account goes on to suggest. Wards displaying the highest concentration, such as Jorabagan and Knasaripara, recorded one in every four to five women as prostitutes.[63] Official estimates confirm that prostitutes constituted 21 per cent of the female workforce and 4.5 per cent of the total women in the city in 1911.[64] In the first half of the nineteenth century, these were mostly women from elite, high-caste *kulin* families, but from the 1870s onwards, lower-caste, poorer women tended to dominate the trade.[65] Recurrent famines, destruction of artisanal trades, and discriminatory wages in agricultural labour pushed more and more women to the growing metropolis, to work not only as labourers in the city's businesses and industry, but also as prostitutes and domestic servants.[66] Starting off in the Sonagatchi area of Chitpore, the trade migrated southwards over time spreading to Bowbazar, Colinga Bazar, and even Bhawanipore, which was an upcoming and desirable residential area in the early decades of the twentieth century.[67]

As Samita Sen has shown, solitary women migrants to cities like Calcutta came to typify the female industrial workforce in the early decades of the twentieth century. Destitute widows, oppressed daughters and sisters, and rejected, battered, and barren wives migrated to escape their natal and marital families.[68] While in the city, they were badly paid in their jobs, made redundant easily,

63 Herbert Anderson, *Calcutta Vice* (Calcutta, 1921), pp. 2–3. The chapters of the book were originally serialized in the *Bengalee*.

64 *Census of the Town and Suburbs of Calcutta, 1911*, p. 64.

65 See Usha Chakravarty, *Condition of Bengali Women around the Second Half of the Nineteenth Century* (Calcutta, 1963), p. 97; Ratnabali Chatterjee, 'Prostitution in Nineteenth Century Bengal: Construction of Class and Gender', *Social Scientist* 21, no. 9/11 (Sep–Oct, 1993), p. 161; Sumanta Banerjee, *Dangerous Outcast*, pp. 82–3.

66 R. Chatterjee, 'Prostitution in Nineteenth Century Bengal'.

67 Anderson, *Calcutta Vice*, pp. 13–14.

68 Samita Sen, '"Without His Consent?": Marriage and Women's Migration in Colonial India', *International Labour and Working-Class History* 65 (April, 2004): 77–104.

and generally led a precarious existence. They either had to thus supplement their income through other means or resort to prostitution to make ends meet. In 1881, registered prostitutes numbered 12,228, but in reality the figure would have been much higher if we take into account those in part-time trade.[69] Having broken their rural ties and living outside of kin and caste pressures, prostitution seemed a relatively workable option for women trying to rebuild their lives in the colonial urban economy. In the middle-class Bengali and official mind, mill towns and working-class neighbourhoods became associated with prostitution, ruining of rural and communitarian social codes, and the collapse of all caste and gender hierarchies.

Unlike in Victorian England where prostitutes, to a certain extent, were shunned by the more respectable working-class sections—a wedge rendered more secure by the Contagious Diseases Acts (CDA)—in Calcutta, the prostitute was, initially at least, very much a part and parcel of her mixed-class neighbourhood.[70] As palatial mansions owned by the rich were given over to the trade and owners moved out to newer areas, prostitutes came to reside in the midst of dense residential clusters in Jorasanko, Jorabagan, and Shyampukur. Their living quarters ran along principal streets, and businessmen and aristocracy alike invested in the trade as landlords and rentiers.[71] According to one estimate, each mansion

69 *Census of the Town and Suburbs of Calcutta, 1881*, p. 46. This number was also affected by the fact that the CDA was still partially in force at the time of the census and not all would have come forward for identification. By the 1891 census the number had shot up to 20,126. See *Census of the Town and Suburbs of Calcutta, 1891*, p. 31.

70 Judith Walkowitz, *Prostitution and Victorian Society: Women, Class and the State* (Cambridge: Cambridge University Press, 1980), p. 208. Although, overall, Walkowitz believes that prostitutes were perceived as an integral part of their working-class location—both in a physical and social sense—she does admit that feelings about them were mixed in working-class neighbourhoods.

71 Anderson, *Calcutta Vice*, p. 20; S.N. Mukherjee, *Calcutta: Essays in Urban History* (Calcutta: Subarnarekha, 1993), p. 32. There was a move in the first decade of the twentieth century to remove houses of ill fame from some 'principal streets' by declaring them 'public thoroughfares'. See Anderson, *Calcutta Vice*, pp. 19–29.

housed over a hundred women.[72] The pre-eminent family of Tagores of Jorasanko are known to have owned several brothels in Calcutta.[73] Besides, there were numerous huts and rented rooms from where prostitutes operated, which were scattered throughout the city.[74] Depending on size such houses had anything from five to fifteen tenant-prostitutes.[75] Managed (and occasionally owned) by housemistresses or *bariwalis*, the women occupied single rooms either paying rent out of their income or offering services to clients in lieu of food and lodging.[76]

For the largely male and better (relative to women) paid workforce in the city—clerks, technicians, assistants, and managers in the colonial establishments—women were needed for sexual gratification and providing the 'comforts of home'.[77] In the 1870s the male migrant population in the city was estimated at half a million, while prostitutes numbered some 30,000 only.[78] It was a symbiotic relationship between the two groups. Self-respecting better-paid workers left behind their wives in the villages—partly because city housing was unaffordable but also because norms of upward mobility meant the inculcation of seclusion

[72] Minney, *Nightlife of Calcutta*, p. 22.

[73] S.N. Mukherjee, *Calcutta: Essays in Urban History*, pp. 12–13.

[74] Police records show that brothels and 'disorderly' houses flourished in Calcutta in the mid-nineteenth century, much to the annoyance of neighbours. *ARPC*, p. 12.

[75] J.N. Ghosh, *Social Evil in Calcutta* (Calcutta, 1923), p. 23.

[76] Depending on size, rooms would vary from five to fifteen in number with as many tenants staying in a single house. J.N. Ghosh, *Social Evil in Calcutta*, p. 23; Anderson, *Calcutta Vice*, pp. 20–1.

[77] In her brilliant and classic study, Luise White has shown how prostitutes in colonial Nairobi provided not just sexual services but also domestic comforts—such as food and bathwater—to an uprooted and marginalized workforce without a place to stay in the city, thus 'selling' their homes as well as their bodies. See Luise White, *The Comforts of Home: Prostitution in Colonial Nairobi* (Chicago: University of Chicago Press, 1990), especially Chapter 3.

[78] Home Public, 20 February 1869, 112–15; Home Sanitary, June 1875, 32–4. Cited in Sumanta Banerjee, *Dangerous Outcast*, p. 147.

by women, commensurate with status, in rural households.[79] Women migrants in Calcutta and other industrial colonial cities, on the other hand, were also mostly without families, and in need of male shelter. There is evidence that some lived with male workers for protection, and came to be branded as 'prostitutes' in official reports, even if that was not actually the case.[80] But the arrangement could very well have worked for professional prostitutes in varying degrees. In a violent and unstable world, male partners—however temporary—offered some security, and the women, in turn, could continue to entice men with sex and a homely environment. The arrangement worked particularly well if the police were to be avoided.[81]

Women operated from minimal and impoverished establishments in the city but offering privacy and relative safety.[82] Clients were supplied at the end of the day not only with alcohol and sexual

79 Structures of alternative domesticity offered by prostitutes have also been discussed by Bidisha Ray, 'Contesting Respectability: Sexuality, Corporeality and Non-"bhadra" Cultures in Colonial Bengal', unpublished PhD dissertation, University of Manchester, 2008, pp. 148–9.

80 Samita Sen, '"Without His Consent?', 83–4. For a fuller discussion of such flexible living arrangements in mill towns, see Samita Sen, *Women and Labour in Late Colonial India: The Bengal Jute Industry* (Cambridge: Cambridge University Press, 1999), Chapter 5.

81 Thus, during the 1860s there were numerous cases where prostitutes could avoid the provisions of the CDA by proving their attachment to a man, Sumanta Banerjee, *Dangerous Outcast*, p. 154. If, however, attachment could be linked to a policeman, this worked even better. One common saying among prostitutes went thus: 'If you want to eat fish, choose hilsa. If you want to take a lover choose a policeman' (*Machh khabi to ilish. Nang dhorbi to pulish*). Cited from his private collection and translated by Sumanta Banerjee, *Dangerous Outcast*, p. 109.

82 Thus, labourers earning eight paisa a day and sleeping on coarse mats had the option of spending their nights on 'luxurious' beds of prostitutes. A.C. Ghosh, *Pnachali Kamalkali: Choudda Ain*, cited in Sumanta Banerjee, *Dangerous Outcast*, p. 151.

services, but also food and domestic comfort.[83] Usually the man would shop for the food. Flatbreads (rotis), fish fries, and meat feature in the diet of customers in popular literature.[84] Favourite customers could be offered rice cooked in ghee or clarified butter which gave it a yellowish tinge. In prostitute parlance such men would be referred to as *holdey bhatar* or 'yellow husband' to imply a particularly close relationship.[85] As a contemporary tract notes:

> ... If there were no prostitutes in this world, how could we carry on? It is only because of them that I [we] continue to make a living in Calcutta ...[86]

In popular culture the discursive lines defining virtue continue to be unclearly drawn well past the mid-nineteenth century, despite the reformist trend. Prostitutes are vilified, but more for their extortionate nature than for leading immoral lives.[87] Even during the height of the venereal diseases scare in the 1860s, authors of Battala tracts are sympathetic to their plight while being mildly

[83] The aroma of deep fried flat bread (*luchis*) and spiced mutton filling the air offer deeply sensory images of the red-light areas in the evening. See Gupta, *Raater Kolkata*, pp. 30–1. Domestic servants employed by brothels and sometimes the women themselves were known to be regular customers in local liquor shops, stocking up bottles of country liquor for their nightly customers. Anderson, *Calcutta Vice*, pp. 36–7.

[84] See Babulal Nath, *Dekhle Hashte Hobe* (Calcutta: Anandodoy Press, 1872), p. 4; Aminchandra Datta, *Mechho Basante Mechhonir Darpachurna* (Calcutta: Kabita Kaumudi Press, 1875), p. 10; Jaharilal Shil, *Machher Poka* (Calcutta, 1875), p. 11. See also Durgacharan Ray, *Debganer Marte Agaman* (Calcutta: Deys Publishing, 2001; original edition 1886), p. 353. Food invariably crops up in cheap, commercial tracts discussing the prostitute quarters. Mouthwatering snacks such as fried fish and potato cakes, mixtures and boiled egg, kheer, sweets, and so on find mention and are represented in loving detail. Prostitutes would often buy these (and alcohol) for their clients. See Aghorchandra Das Ghose, *Chai Belful* (Calcutta: Anondodoy Press, 1872) and D. Ray, *Debganer Martye Agaman*, pp. 366–7.

[85] Sumanta Banerjee, *Dangerous Outcast*, p. 112.

[86] Nath, *Dekhle Hashte Hobe*, p. 7.

[87] See, for example, Chandicharan Ghose, *Barangana Er Samul Ghatika Orthat Beshyai Sarbanasher Mul* (Calcutta, 1874), pp. 3–8; Nath, *Dekhle Hashte Hobe*, pp. 5, 9.

concerned about the risks posed by prostitutes to the health of their customers.[88] While subjected to violence and exploitation themselves, the general perception among members of the prostitutes' own social strata was that of a 'fairly quiet and orderly' workforce.[89]

Prostitution provided women with readier access to money and social independence than their working-class counterparts. While to a large extent operating within an arena of male supremacy and frequently subject to sexual abuse and physical violence, better-off women could control the trade and often lived together as part of a distinct subgroup. When troubled by clients or police, they could act in their own defence, both individually and collectively. When a client abused a prostitute in the Sonagatchi area, he was dragged—by her orders—to her house and severely beaten. He was found lying dead next morning in the courtyard of his own house with a broken thigh and other injuries.[90] Those maintained as mistresses by wealthy men enjoyed generous salaries and even personal well-furnished homes with cooks and servants in their employ.[91] Most of the women with a higher social status could read and write as well.[92] They performed religious festivals with great pomp and splendour, funding processions in the city.[93]

A strong female subculture was a distinguishing feature of prostitution in nineteenth-century Calcutta. Sumanta Banerjee has uncovered a world of coquetry, sexual enjoyment, critique,

88 Thus, in one tract on the CDA, the author advises prostitutes to submit to registration and examination for the sake of the trade. A.C. Ghosh, *Pnachali Kamalkali: Choudda Ain*.

89 This was the impression of the guide who took an Englishman on a tour of night-time Calcutta, exploring the city very much in the tradition of the European flâneur, later recording and publishing an account of his sojourn. Minney, *Nightlife of Calcutta*, p. 22.

90 *ARPC, 1896*, p. 5. But the woman was not charged as the police surgeon deemed that the death had occurred from a fall and not violence.

91 They could hire priests and even partners on their payroll, according to one fictional account. See D. Ray, *Debganer Martye Agaman*, pp. 353–4.

92 Some could boast of monthly incomes of 200 to 1,000 rupees. J.N. Ghosh, *Social Evil in Calcutta*, pp. 22, 24.

93 J.N. Ghosh, *Social Evil in Calcutta*, p. 31.

and sarcasm in prostitute songs and sayings of the time.[94] But prostitutes were gradually eroded of humanity and, to a certain extent, rights, through a series of measures including the governmental attempt to regulate the trade in the 1860s as we shall see further. Courts even refused to be involved in cases that required them to uphold the sanctity of a contract made between a prostitute and her clients, leaving the women without adequate legal protection. The grounds cited for such a move was that it 'infringed public policy and offended public morality'.[95]

In the late eighteenth and early nineteenth centuries, prostitutes were not considered 'immoral' and in fact continued to operate very much along the lines of medieval feudal patterns in the modern metropolis of Calcutta. While the aristocracy and the more prosperous had their private courtesans and dancing girls, the bazaar prostitute served the poorer and labouring man. Their degradation came about via the twin forces of industrialization—and hence regulation of the trade and its potential for criminalization—and the *bhadra*-fication (gentrification) of Bengali society.

Although prostitutes had been vilified earlier, they formed the targets of concerted reformist campaigns from the 1880s onwards. As the state moved in to legalize and regulate certain practices and criminalize others within the trade, the educated middle classes joined the campaign to contain the apparent scourge that was prostitution in the city. Though inhabiting a world apart, prostitutes posed a perennial threat to the safety and sanctity of middle-class homes and colonial civility, representing a distressing street disorder that threatened to infect the normality and inviolability of respectable urban life.

As more well-off men started building their own homes in the city from the mid-nineteenth century onwards and bringing over

[94] Sumanta Banerjee, *Dangerous Outcast*, pp. 108–13. See also Debjit Bandyopadhyay, *Beshya Sangeet, Baiji Sangeet* (Calcutta: Subarnarekha, 1999).

[95] Such a stand was taken by the government at the instance of a Bengali judge, Rashomoy Dutta, in 1854. There remained unresolved many cases where prostitutes had not been paid by clients despite previous understandings. Sumanta Banerjee, *Dangerous Outcast*, pp. 130–1.

their wives and families, their needs for prostitutes declined.[96] Instead, prostitutes came to be seen as a source of pollution and constant temptation to middle-class sons and husbands, and young men in general. Within the emerging upper-caste Hindu nationalist discourses of the late nineteenth century, the prostitute was also the *bhadramahila*'s (genteel woman) other and needed to be constructed as such to provide binaries of chaste and unchaste, modest and immodest.[97] The contrast between the seductive and aggressive harlot and the virtuous wife languishing at home formed the subject matter of many reformist pamphlets.

The hesitant but visible inroads of modern Western ideals of intimate romance and companionship within marriage between husband and wife in middle-class urban households may have also signalled the end of clandestine relationships with prostitutes. Recent studies have underlined the emerging importance of romance in conjugal relations in the late nineteenth century, partly brought on by English influence, but also the changed structures of urban employment that made older forms of kinship-driven joint-family structures untenable.[98] Relationships with prostitutes, however, remained unchanged with the vast majority of the clerical and working-class clientele continuing to depend on them.

There needs something to be said about the urban geography of prostitution in colonial Calcutta. While the older neighbourhoods were concentrated in the Chitpore area, where prostitutes usually

[96] R. Chatterjee, 'Prostitution in Nineteenth Century Bengal', p. 161; Tapan Raychaudhuri, 'Love in a Colonial Climate: Marriage, Sex and Romance in Nineteenth-century Bengal', *Modern Asian Studies* 34, no. 2 (2000): 349–78, 369.

[97] Chatterjee, 'Prostitution in Nineteenth Century Bengal', p. 167; Sumanta Banerjee, 'Marginalisation of Women's Popular Culture', in *Recasting Women: Essays in Colonial History*, edited by Kumkum Sangari and Sudesh Vaid (New Delhi: Kali for Women, 1989), pp. 127–77.

[98] Raychaudhuri, 'Love in a Colonial Climate', 349–78; Rochona Majumdar, *Marriage and Modernity: Family Values in Colonial Bengal* (Durham and London: Duke University Press, 2009).

lived in rented rooms in aristocratic mansions, newer and upcoming areas were more 'visible'. The older prostitutes depended on established clientele, or presented themselves in the overhanging verandahs (in smaller houses it would be the front stoop or raised open-style porch), while the newer groups—resettled in residential pockets further south—from the end of the nineteenth century preferred 'walking the streets' rather than solicitations.[99] As a result, residents became less tolerant and prostitution less insulated from 'respectable' groups.[100] The open nature of their operations in the newer locations not only earned them the censure of the middle classes, but also made the prostitutes more vulnerable to criminals as we shall see further.[101] Middle-class perceptions invariably also conflated a range of working-class and poor urban women with prostitutes ranging from housemaids and jute-mill and godown workers to *paanwallis* or female sellers of paan, light betel-leaf refreshments.[102] 'Gratification of lust' and not income was seen as the primary motive in such clandestine prostitution.

From the early twentieth century, there arose a movement to reclaim the red-light areas on the grounds of civic morality. But the campaign for the shutting down and relocation of the 'houses of ill fame' was fraught with inconsistencies and debates as members of the Municipal Corporation deliberated the wisdom of directing uprooted prostitutes to specified areas in the city. So much was the paranoia regarding the possibility of immoral women 'infecting' respectable neighbourhoods if relocated that in some cases—such as Chitpore and Burrabazar—the process was actually stalled.[103] Overall, the need

99 J.N. Ghosh, *Social Evil in Calcutta*, p. 28; Anderson, *Calcutta Vice*, pp. 12–13; D. Ray, *Debganer Martye Agaman*, pp. 352, 365.

100 A slightly earlier and an extreme case of such intolerance is that of a Heeralal Basack who killed his thirteen-year-old wife and then committed suicide apparently because of the latter's habit of hobnobbing with 'women of bad character' residing in the house opposite. It is possible that the wife was soliciting customers as well, but that is not clear. *ARPC, 1869*, p. 2.

101 J.N. Ghosh, *Social Evil in Calcutta*, pp. 9, 28. The reformist language is organized in an ironic twist whereby prospective clients are seen as 'victims' and 'prey' to the prostitutes.

102 J.N. Ghosh, *Social Evil in Calcutta*, pp. 9–10.

103 Anderson, *Calcutta Vice*, p. 27.

to keep professedly disreputable areas away from respectable neighbourhoods was consistent. As one reformer comments:

> Segregated areas may be assigned to the fallen women. This will answer many a good purpose.... Scattered as they are all over the city, prostitutes habitations are a great source of trouble and annoyance to ... respectable residents. If they were segregated in particular areas far from the respectable residential quarters, it will be comparatively an easy task for the police and the authorities to control the immoral traffic and thus check its hideous growth.[104]

Prostitution was seen to disgrace 'the important and growingly beautiful suburb' of Bhawanipore, where nearly one thousand women operated in the 1920s.[105] The Bengal Act III of 1907 that was put into service empowered the police to clear all 'main thoroughfares' of 'disorderly houses', once streets had been declared so on the recommendations of the corporation. Colinga Bazar Street with 100 such houses, which was cleared using this legislation in 1910, came to be seen as a minor victory among reformers.[106] A decade later, nine other streets had been similarly cleared, taking the total to ten.[107]

But there appear to have been more vested interests involved, such as the principal Marwari Associations, which wanted 'houses of ill fame' or 'bad houses' removed from Chitpore. As the Marwaris argued, moral issues aside, converting the houses to shops, places of business, and residential quarters would be of long-term commercial benefit to the local community.[108]

Over time the intimacy and personalized nature of the trade disappeared as prostitutes came to constitute a rather industrialized sex trade that supported the burgeoning metropolis and its sharply increased migrant workforce. In the meantime, the state was beginning to capitalize a casual labour market and reconstitute the prostitute's body within legal and medical discourses, which rendered her doubly vulnerable and passive. The commoditization of sexual relations was partly the indirect fallout of the CDA, Act XIV of

104 J.N. Ghosh, *Social Evil in Calcutta*, p. 37.
105 Anderson, *Calcutta Vice*, p. 14.
106 Anderson, *Calcutta Vice*, pp. 30–2.
107 Anderson, *Calcutta Vice*, p. 24.
108 Anderson, *Calcutta Vice*, pp. 20, 25.

1868, which required prostitutes to register and present themselves for medical examination, ostensibly to check the spread of venereal disease, particularly among the British soldiers who visited them. The draconian nature of the act, the humiliating physical examination of prostitutes, and—if suspected of being diseased—the forced incarceration, caused many to flee from the city and take refuge in surrounding suburbs where the act was not operative.

The fear of contracting venereal disease and the reformist bent in the educated classes initially caused them to support the legislation. But as the dragnet was cast wider and came to harass a range of women who were not part of the trade—including mistresses of the more prosperous—the bhadralok protested.[109] In the popular press, literature circulating on Act XIV or *Choudda Ain*, captured this ambivalence. Thus, *Bahoba Choudda Ain* (Jubilations for Act XIV) and *Badmaesh Jobdo* (The Wicked Have Been Disciplined)—the latter by the Brahmo reformist and author, Prankrishna Dutta—as the titles indicate, and as the style and author profiles suggest, are symptomatic of the sensibilities that celebrated the imposition of the Act. And yet, in their sympathetic portrayal of the victimized women, the hypocrisy of the middle classes, and above all the undoubted lure of the prostitute's world, there is a double voicedness that problematizes any stance of unanimous condemnation.[110]

They describe, arguably with a twinge of sadness, how the red-light district has become virtually deserted—missing the hubbub of hawkers, snack shops, and alcohol sellers, and above all, the

[109] See Sumanta Banerjee, *Dangerous Outcast*, pp. 169–70. The act was finally repealed in 1888.

[110] Anon., *Bahoba Choudda Ain* (Jubilations for Act XIV) (Calcutta, 1869). Bordering on the scurrilous, the tract however betrays the voyeuristic interest of both readers and authors in the process of the medical examination by government doctors at the police station. In the dramatized version, the women listening in and egging on a prostitute narrating her experience are from respectable households, barely able to hide their unwholesome curiosity. From the narratological perspective, all of this undercuts their presumed worth and moral superiority. See p. 10; Prankrishna Dutta, *Badmaesh Jobdo* [The Wicked Have Been Disciplined], Calcutta, n.d., reprinted in *Dushprapya Sahitya Sangraha*, vol. 2 (Reflect Publications: Calcutta, 1992), pp. 5–11.

clientele—as the women have fled to Farasdanga (Chandernagore, a French enclave close to Calcutta), Hooghly, Serampore, and other suburbs. There are moving descriptions of those left behind—visibly upset and with their heads in their hands instead of promenading on the streets.[111] Another work by a popular author of the commercial press, Aghor Chandra Das Ghosh, is openly sympathetic and advises—through the words of the love-god, Madana—the prostitutes to accept the new regulations and come back to the city. It recounts the aggressive behaviour of police and the sad plight of women who have little choice but to present themselves at the police station when summoned.[112]

Murders of 'Lowly' Women: Sexual Violence, Class, and Gender

In the early decades of the twentieth century, the prostitutes stood fundamentally vulnerable—maligned and criminalized in the eyes of law and society. In police literature, they came to be increasingly associated with crimes, even as cheap pornographic novels and illustrations constituted them as erotic, dehumanized subject matter.[113] Hounded by the state and maligned by society, bereft of family and friends, prostitutes became a symbol of the powerlessness of women in the new industrial order. Reformists by the early twentieth century were trying to set up correction homes and rescue women from the trade. But a parallel and disturbing trend was evidenced in the increasing brutalization of the prostitute's world in the early decades of the twentieth century. The schizophrenic stand stemmed from attitudes of both pity and loathing of the sordid world that the prostitutes lived in.[114]

[111] P. Dutta, *Badmaesh Jobdo*, pp. 5–11.

[112] A.C. Ghosh, *Pnachali Kamalkali: Choudda Ain*, cited in Sumanta Banerjee, *Dangerous Outcast*, p. 151.

[113] See Sanjay Sircar, 'Mou-rani: A Lost 1940s Bengali Pornographic Street Text', *South Asian Popular Culture* 4, no. 1 (2006): 87–90.

[114] This can be evidenced in the title of reformist tracts urging the imminent need for rescuing the 'fallen women'; See Anderson, *Calcutta Vice* and J.N. Ghosh, *Social Evil in Calcutta*.

As the government became more vigilant over intimate violence in the domestic and pseudo-domestic spheres, class and gender malevolence was displaced on to other marginal domains of intimacy. Between 1917 and 1919 Calcutta was shocked by a series of prostitute murders, which also involved the theft of gold jewellery. Seven women were murdered in a row and their ornaments stolen in Upper Chitpore Road and nearby lanes and even as far as Kalighat and Rambagan. In each case the criminals escaped without leaving a trace. The victims were killed by methods of gagging or strangulation using their own sari ends. About roughly a decade later, another spate of similar killings ensued between 1928 and 1929. Once again, jewellery was missing as the prostitutes lay murdered in their own living quarters. The criminals dressed well and travelled in taxis and horse-drawn phaetons, posing as prosperous and cultured men, to gain the confidence of their victims before striking.[115]

Isolated instances of murder and robbing of prostitutes were known to the police since as early as the mid-nineteenth century. But they seem to have acquired intensity around the beginning of the twentieth century.[116] In some cases, prostitutes were not killed but drugged and their possessions stolen. Lethal poison, such as potassium cyanide, could also be used as in the 1929 killings, but more commonly used drugs and intoxicants included the less harmful and indigenous *dhatura* (stramonium extracted from the plant of the same name) or bhang and *siddhi* (intoxicating drinks made from cannabis and Indian hemp), and morphine. In rare instances, the throats of the drugged women could also be slit with a sharp knife.[117] In police and criminal parlance, such

[115] Rai Sahib Satyendranath Mukherjee, *Murder of Prostitutes for Gain* (Calcutta: Jnan Printing Works, 1935).

[116] See, for example, *ARPC, 1855*, p.16; *ARPC, 1858*, p.2. Priyanath Mukhopadhyay, the police detective, who in later life serialized crime stories drawn from his own experiences, reported such murders of prostitutes for their ornaments. See Priyanath Mukhopadhyay, 'Bishom Samasya' [A Grave Problem], in *Darogar Daptar*, edited by Arun Mukhopadhyay (Calcutta: Ananda Publishers, 2004), vol. 1, pp. 22–35; vol. 2, pp. 450–63.

[117] Minney, *Nightlife of Calcutta*, p. 22.

crime was known as *ranger kaj* or 'colourful crime', a strange misnomer for what were really rather grisly and tragic executions, but perhaps also indicative of the deeper, more dismissive, and even misogynistic attitude towards the practising women in the trade.[118]

Police photographs—ostensibly taken as dispassionate forensic evidence—suggest interiors that are suffused with death, poverty, and dereliction. Sensory indexing of crime scenes in crime stories and reportage offer powerful after-effects of the murder as the unbearable odour of decomposition, the spectacle of a strangulated body, and the obvious disorder in the immediate moments preceding or following the death haunts the reader.[119] Together they build up an image of an outcome that was inevitable, even predictable, where violent deaths could be legitimately bracketed off with depraved lives, desperation, and lowly living.

Young women residing in lodgings were cut off from the family system. Their living arrangements—usually without male partners or children—while ideally suited to their business, also made them particularly vulnerable. The layout of the prostitute quarters, the narrow and dark lanes in which they stood, the open nature of the residences that permitted anyone to walk in and out as they pleased, all made for rather facilitating circumstances in which to commit this kind of crime. It was also lucrative. As prostitutes preferred to convert their cash income into gold ornaments and store them in their own rooms instead of using banks, they were easy targets. In fact, they veritably—though unwittingly—attracted criminals by flaunting their elaborately ornamented selves in public while attracting customers.[120]

118 Also variously known as *ronger kormo*. Killing of prostitutes by smothering was known as *chapar kormo*. *ARPC 1872*, p. 23.

119 Crime stories by the contemporary Calcutta police detective, Priyanath Mukhopadhyay, are replete with such dispassionate but elaborate forensic detailing. See A. Mukhopadhyay (ed.), P. Mukhopadhyay, *Darogar Daptar*. The works of Priyanath are discussed in considerable depth in Chapter 5.

120 R.S.S. Mukherjee, *Murder of Prostitutes for Gain*, pp. 1–5.

The police focus in the initial investigations always invariably rested on the immediate neighbourhood of the prostitute quarters—on *paanwallahs*, or male paan sellers, pimps, and drivers of hackney carriages and taxis who were seen to be in league with burglars, thieves, and murderers. This was a mirror of both police and middle-class prejudice, which saw illicit sex and crime going hand in hand in these disreputable parts of the city. The finger of suspicion even fell on the prostitutes themselves, who were not considered very much apart from this criminal class, living cheek by jowl with them.[121] The dangerous social proximity of the victims with the professional criminal classes in the area made them intrinsically risk prone and therefore less worthy of pity. Curiously, the pawnbrokers or *poddars*, who were more directly involved in such crimes, were harder to get. There was a thriving trade in stolen ornaments that could be sold directly to the poddars who would melt it down to bullion to avoid identification. They kept no records of such transactions and could very well avoid the law.[122]

And yet, as they police themselves confess, professional murderers of women for their ornaments seldom came from the groups the force routinely identified as criminals. They came from more prosperous classes—*sircars* (middling-level clerks) and writers with reasonable salaries in government service or mercantile firms.[123] Others were educated but unemployed youth, petty merchants, and the like.[124] The mixed social profile of the murderers also of course included more variants—there was the entertainer who earned his living by cross-dressing and dancing, small time

[121] In an interesting case reported in a contemporary police diary, when a prostitute when a prostitute was found dead in her residence, it was suspected that she was murdered by a local paan seller and his associate, as well as another prostitute neighbour, and that her ornaments were stolen. In the end, it turned out that the prostitute had died of heart attack. P. Mukhopadhyay, 'Bishom Samasya', vol. 1, pp. 173–87.

[122] See A. Mukhopadhyay (ed.), P. Mukhopadhyay, *Darogar Daptar*, vol. 1, p. 525; pp. 22–35.

[123] *ARPC, 1860–61* and *1861–62*, p. 6.

[124] R.S.S. Mukherjee, *Murder of Prostitutes for Gain*, pp. 96–100.

cheats, smiths, and butlers—that were in keeping with the police profiling.[125] But the flamboyant posturing of the murderers, their knowledge of chemical drugs and poison like morphine and cyanide, their attire[126]—all point towards middle-class roots of the crimes. Drugging and robbing prostitutes was a new trend amongst these groups.[127]

The secrecy and potential impunity with which the murders were committed (it proved hard initially even for veteran detectives to catch the murderers) point to a certain level of audacity and recklessness on the part of the perpetrators. Handbooks published for the police underlined the tricky nature of the cases, and the cunning of criminals that had to be matched by superb standards of police intelligence and investigative skills. The murders also show deep-seated sexual and class antagonisms, and the sharpening of divides between 'pure' and 'impure' women, which ring-fenced the latter as legitimate game for criminals. In a tragic reversal of stereotypes in contemporary reformist literature where the prostitutes 'preyed' on young men, the Calcutta prostitutes in the early twentieth century lived in constant fear of murderers lurking among their clientele. Within the subaltern circles there appears to have existed, in fact, a deep empathy for the suffering women, as evident in the following exchange, appearing in a strangely voyeuristic account of nightly Calcutta, between a flâneur-style British sightseer, and his local guide:

> 'The women are afraid now', my guide told me. 'Many have had their throats cut and the precious fripperies taken.'

[125] R.S.S. Mukherjee, *Murder of Prostitutes for Gain*, pp. 69, 96; *ARPC, 1890*, p. 5.

[126] In one case, the murderer, Serish Chunder Pattuck, was caught while selling off stolen jewellery to a poddar (money changer). The rather expensive shoes that he had left behind in the prostitute quarters were also instrumental in tracing him. *ARPC, 1894*, p. 7. The use of hydrocyanic acid is also reported in other contemporary Calcutta murders involving well-to-do gentlemen. See P. Mukhopadhyay, 'Pathe Khun' [Murder on the Streets], *Darogar Daptar*, vol. 1.

[127] *ARPC, 1865–6*, p. 3. Judging by the caste suggested in the surnames as well as the formal character of the first names, Nilkanto and Hurris Chunder Dutt, were also possibly from literate middle-class backgrounds.

'And do not the women cut throats too and rob and steal?'
'No', said my guide firmly, 'they are fairly quiet and orderly.'[128]

In the murder cases encountered above, violence reconfirmed both patriarchal and class control, extending dominant contemporary cultures of marginalization of women's sexuality within domestic settings to the non-domestic, commercial domain of lowly paid sex-workers in the city. While men's sexual prerogatives were being tested by colonial law within the marital sphere from the 1890s onwards, they found other avenues of expression.[129] The lowly prostitute thus emerged as a legitimate target for sexual aggression and murder, and the murders themselves in turn became manifest as grotesque sites of social and moral disturbances engendered by particular urban lifestyles. Pathologized by reformists, police, and urban planners alike as easily available and street characters, their poverty added to the prostitutes' moral blight, and opened up their bodies for both gratuitous and motivated desecration. The middle-class criminals thus challenged the colonial state in less-policed private spheres of intimacy with a certain degree of abandon, playing cat-and-mouse games with the law, and laying arrogant claim to not just the body but also the material wealth of the prostitute.

It may be possible to see how, in addition, the murders were about mobilizing access to an urban fantasy generated by particular environments and settings such as Calcutta's red-light and other pleasure districts such as the race course and cheap theatre.[130] The standard of living for most paid workers was humble, but more youthful groups—unemployed students surviving on parental aid, those taking up new but tightly paid jobs, or living as dependents in bigger

[128] Minney, *Nightlife of Calcutta*, p. 22.

[129] Martin Wiener has noted how in Victorian England, as more middle- and middling-class women claimed social respectability and became—juridically speaking—'out of bounds' for men, prostitutes became exposed to violence, sexual and otherwise. Wiener, *Men of Blood*, pp. 93, 104–5, 108.

[130] Theatre was very popular and a mostly weekend affair, with Saturdays being referred to as 'theatre days'. Kironmoy Raha, 'Calcutta Theatre: 1835–1944', in *Calcutta: The Living City*, edited by Sukanta Chaudhuri, vol. 1 (Calcutta: Oxford University Press, 1990), p. 192.

joint families—were always on the lookout for supplementing their income for leisure purposes in a city where cost of living was high in the aftermath of the First World War and after.[131] The prototype of depressed lower-middle-class gentility, increasingly feeling squeezed out of its lifestyle bracket, transforming to deranged and homicidal masculinity has been pointed out in the context of other contemporary city murders, and might well have played a role here.[132]

While men's aberrant behaviour was located in the moral quicksands and easy lure of the city, lowly women were regarded as predictable victims of the unstable social environments that had produced them. Not only was sexual enjoyment of and access to such women seen as a class privilege, when sexed subjectivity was conjoint with stigmatized existence, sexual violence became doubly normative.[133] Priyanath Mukhopadhyay, the legendary police detective and crime writer spanning the late nineteenth and early twentieth centuries, who will be further examined in Chapter 5, typically represents such a standpoint. Erring women from lowly classes are thus depicted in his narratives as paying for their sinful, immoral lives either as victims of murder or as wretched destitutes.[134] Priyanath presents prostitutes in particular as wily and untrustworthy, often not deserving of our sympathy.[135]

[131] This is discussed further in Chapter 5.

[132] See Julie English Early, 'A New Man for a New Century: Dr Crippen and the Principles of Masculinity', in *Disorder in the Court: Trials and Sexual Conflict at the Turn of the Century*, edited by Nancy Erber and George Robb (New York: New York University Press, 1999), pp. 209–30; and Mort, 'Scandalous Events'. The first involved the murder of his wife by a doctor in 1910 and the second was a case of serial murder of women and prostitutes in North Kensington in 1953 by an outwardly 'respectable' gentleman living in depressed circumstances.

[133] The thesis is also applicable in the context of sexual violence perpetrated on low-caste Dalit women in India, as discussed by Anupama Rao, 'Violence and Humanity: Or, Vulnerability as Political Subjectivity,' *Social Research* 78, no. 2 (2011): 607–32.

[134] A. Mukhopadhyay (ed.), P. Mukhopadhyay, *Darogar Daptar*, vol. 1, pp. 121, 404.

[135] A. Mukhopadhyay (ed.), P. Mukhopadhyay, *Darogar Daptar*, vol. 2, p. 52.

The Calcutta murders bypass the titillating 'sexual script' of sex and violence, male dominance and female passivity, and the crossing of class borders, the centre points of the Ripper murders a few decades earlier, even though the same elements are present.[136] The lurid details of the strangulations and poisoning, the often unclothed and sometimes mutilated bodies, could have made for sensational press but the cases seem to remain confined in police reports and crime stories written by policemen. This might have been the product of a more evolved journalism, but is perhaps also suggestive of a conflicted empathy for the victims: on the one hand, most perpetrators were well-to-do middle-class men, although their social status is muddied by their criminality and their despicable motive of robbing destitute women; on the other, the victims came from the lowest social rungs and lived in sin, and as such perhaps deserved the fate they were met with.

* * *

In a sense, this chapter was about the presence and absence of women in colonial Calcutta, and the problems and possibilities opened up in each case. Central to these debates was the entrenched practice of prostitution in the city with which contemporary understandings of sexuality were inextricably linked. Scandals and murders revolving round sexual themes helped crystallize ideas on conjugality and sexuality, love and sin in the city. The problematic role played by violence in intimate spheres and the predominance of class categories in shaping contemporary attitudes towards sexual violence was evident in the courtroom and the wider public sphere. The vernacular press at all levels of readership prompted open debates and discussion on these themes, settling unease and reframing the terms of sexual relationships in urban settings. The chapter shows how the city was coming to terms with its women in the midst of fundamental changes in urban lifestyles and governance—including the role of litigation in establishing conjugal norms, criminalization resulting from medical regulation of prostitutes, and the brutalization of those at the margins of the urban economy.

136 Walkowitz, 'Jack the Ripper and the Myth of Male Violence', 546.

4

Battle for the Streets

Contesting Municipal Regimes

A new conceptualization of the streets was a formative element in the creation, not merely of colonial power but of a new sense of the public in colonial Calcutta. A significant site for the articulation of what has increasingly been called the 'everyday state', streets also constituted strategic locations for its questioning and contestation. With the state's recurrent attempt to regulate and control streets, and that of the people to defy that order, Calcutta's streets became the crucial sites in this war between the state and its people. A wide range of the city's residents—pedestrians, householders, and low-paid occupational groups such as hackney-carriage drivers, scavengers, and milkmen—clashed over municipal laws that were affecting the ways in which they moved, lived, and earned a wage in the city's streets. Unlike what has been argued in recent literature on colonial Indian cities, this chapter proposes that such opposition represented significant questioning of the new urban regime and its values at all levels in society.[1] Far from being the unassailable

[1] See, for example, Prashant Kidambi, *The Making of an Indian Metropolis: Colonial Governance and Public Culture in Bombay, 1890–1920* (Aldershot:

harbinger of modernity in the subcontinent, colonial Calcutta comes across as a hesitant experiment in metropolitanism—made up of a series of makeshift arrangements, half-hearted implementation, and often status quo.

The following pages explore the multiple points of contestation between Calcutta's residents and the municipal government over new urban laws and regulations that came to increasingly control people's daily lives in public and private spaces. Not only was the orderly circulation of traffic necessitating the exclusion and marginalization of more conventional forms of transport by the turn of the century, modern civic mores were imposing new codes of hygiene, conduct, and deportment in public spaces, trades, and domestic realms that were overpowering in their reach. Legislation restricted encroachment on thoroughfares, banished beggars and entertainers, and delineated specific use of 'public' spaces such as parks and stations. An organized network of streets and roads, open squares and gardens, civic buildings, ports, and markets announced a new regime of the modern metropolitan city.

Gods, People, and Traffic: Conflicts and (Im)Possible Resolutions

Ranajit Guha's recent study of festivals in colonial Calcutta discusses how the constraints of industrial time or the sahib's (white man's) time impinged on civil society. The regular and routine everyday of the imperial capital, when contrasted with the turbulence visible

---

Ashgate, 2007); Stephen Legg, *Spaces of Colonialism: Delhi's Urban Governmentalities* (Oxford: Blackwell Publishing, 2004); Swati Chattopadyay, *Representing Calcutta: Modernity, Nationalism and the Colonial Uncanny* (London and New York: Routledge, 2005). Sandip Hazareesingh studies contestations of colonial urban civic models in Bombay, but predominantly takes on board the responses of the nationalist urban elite, focusing on newspapers, cinema, and other middle-class fora for espousing what he calls 'civic nationalism'. See Sandip Hazareesingh, *The Colonial City and the Challenge of Modernity: Urban Hegemonies and Civic Contestations in Bombay City (1900–1925)* (Hyderabad: Orient Longman, 2007).

in works such as Hutom's *Naksha* or *Sketches* that we encountered in Chapter 2, and in other pamphlet literature of the time, is significant. Guha notes how the colonial metropolis—its military, judicial, administrative, and financial institutions

> ... relied critically on the local population to keep the regime and its accessories serviced, and the wheels of power turning in every department, from law and order through banking and trade to education. Six days a week, this vast collaboration was visible in the movement of these employees commuting in large numbers between the residential parts of the city and its administrative and commercial quarters ...[2]

In Guha's analysis, one part of the everyday was assimilated to official time and alienated from civil society. The other part of this everyday that the *Naksha* celebrates is to be found outside work time—in holidays and festivals.

> What was still left to the subject population to live outside the working day, which was taken up with servicing an alien state machine, was only a truncated and diminished everyday. It was restored to its fullness only when official time, embodied in the kerani's [clerk's] six-day week, was suspended, that is, when there was a festival in the city .... All the dispersed moments of the day-to-day ... are gathered in a festival to make up the fullness of a community's time. This may be celebrated, as it often is, with excess and abandon.... Here, the drudgery of office work contrasted sharply with the exuberance of the festivals ...[3]

Popular festivals and entertainment dominating Calcutta's streets on religious occasions are indeed reported in great detail in contemporary accounts of the city. The main thoroughfares—usually reserved for office traffic and commerce at other times—were completely taken over during festivals, when processions marched on from the houses of local aristocrats and men of means who tried to outdo each other in these festivities. For those hosting the ceremonies, it became a mode of negotiating power and patronage in local society. People from all social levels—from the highest in the British officialdom

[2] Ranajit Guha, 'A Colonial City and Its Time(s)', *Indian Economic and Social History Review* 45, no. 3 (2008): 329–51, 343.

[3] Guha, 'A Colonial City and Its Time(s)', 347–8.

and Hindu aristocracy to the pauper on the street who came for a free meal—attended, as informal power networks were showcased and tested.[4] For rootless migrants in the city, festivals such as the Durga Puja (worship of Goddess Durga) provided a sense of solace, a time for gathering round as a community. Later on, the Pujas turned more communitarian (*barowari*), knitting together locality and community in a more cohesive fashion. Worship was organized through smaller initiatives and based on public subscription. As a recent study notes, it 'increased the social weight of the ritual and pushed the festivities onto a wider social plane', although this participation may have been more troubled than claimed here.[5] The old aristocracy resented the rise of the nouveau riche in the city, especially those from the lower castes, and queried the legitimacy of their festivities.[6]

Different localities/communities were invested in the festivals through the various performances and competitions that were attached to the festivities. Thus the sawngs of Chadak or the kobi songs on the occasion of Ras (celebrating the birth of Krishna) or Durga Puja fought each other lustily to establish the eminence of their respective artistes and community in the public arena.[7] An integral part of the Puja was the *kadamati* (wet mud) ritual of games and songs, which happened on the ninth (*navami*) day of the festival. Following the ritual sacrifice of animals, male participants rolled and wrestled on the bloodied ground, in a macabre display of valour. Later they descended on the streets in processions, carrying the sacrificed animal heads, and singing songs deemed abusive and obscene by some contemporary observers.[8] For the few days of the Puja, the

[4] Kaliprasanna Sinha, *Hutom Pnechar Naksha*, edited by Arun Nag (Calcutta: Ananda Publishers, 1991; originally published 1861), pp. 236–8, 241–3.

[5] Tithi Bhattacharya, 'Tracking the Goddess: Religion, Community, and Identity in the Durga Puja Ceremonies of Nineteenth-Century Calcutta', *The Journal of Asian Studies* 66, no. 4 (November, 2007): 919–62, 950.

[6] K. Sinha, *Hutom Pnechar Naksha*, p. 235. This point has been made earlier in Chapter 1.

[7] K. Sinha, *Hutom Pnechar Naksha*, pp. 88–90, 244–5.

[8] Prankrishna Dutta, *Kolikatar Itibritta* (Calcutta: Pustak Bipani, 1981), pp. 135–6; Mahendranath Dutta, *Kolikatar Puratan Kahini O Pratha* (Calcutta: Mahendra Publishing Committee, 1975; original edition 1929), p. 39.

streets remained impenetrable because of the traffic and milling crowds attending various musicals and folk theatre.[9]

Small pamphlets published on the occasion of the Durga Puja paint a sharp contrast between the indulgent festivities in Calcutta and the more sober affairs in rural locations. While the urban scenarios feature the dandy and the alcoholic, the village scenes depict moments of warm family reunions and meditative contemplation.[10] The rural Pujas were quieter affairs, conducted on smaller budgets, and involving small close-knit village communities who voluntarily offered their subscriptions in return for food and access to the worship and rituals.[11] Overloaded boats and trains carried many migrant workers back home to their families and ancestral villages.[12]

Ras and Ratha Yatra (Chariot Journey) festivals held around the same time, during the monsoon, were also prominent public events hosted by the aristocracy but open to all. Recalling his childhood days at the start of the twentieth century, noted scholar Atul Sur remembers the Ratha Yatra festivals organized by the Basak family and that of Rani Rasmoni, and the Ras Melas or fairs hosted by Gokul Mitra and Ruplal Mullick. There were fairs, entertainment, and pantomimes on their residential grounds. Earlier accounts by Hutom (the Night-Owl) and Prankrishna Dutta at the turn of the twentieth century are consistent in their reportage about the vast crowds carrying flags and festive umbrellas, following the chariots on the streets, singing devotional songs, and playing music.[13] The unpaved muddy street of Chitpore did not add to the comfort of either the administration or the public. Such was the scale of

[9] K. Sinha, *Hutom Pnechar Naksha*, p. 244–5.

[10] See, for example, Baboo Airabat Pakshiraj, *Durga Puja: Ek Bitkel Mahakavya* (Calcutta: Albert Press, 1876); Jogendranath Basumullick, *Ebar Pujor Boro Dhum* (Calcutta, 1875); and Abinashchandra Chattopadhyay, *Pujar Utsav* (Calcutta: Albert Press, 1876).

[11] P. Dutta, *Kolikatar Itibritta*, p. 111.

[12] Beharilal Bandyopadhyay, *Asmaner Naksha: Palligramastha Babuder Durgotsav* (Calcutta: Budhodoy Press, 1868), pp. 78, 82–3.

[13] K. Sinha, *Hutom Pnechar Naksha*, pp. 233–4; P. Dutta, *Kolikatar Itibritta*, pp. 142–3.

attending crowds during the Chariot Festival that the municipal administration in 1834 banned such processions from the main streets of Calcutta.[14]

The repressive police presence crops up repeatedly in Hutom's portrayal of the festivals, from the collection of bribes to their use of whips to control the crowds:[15]

> Gradually the gajan processions dispersed under the orders of the police. The Superintendent, who was on a horse, whisked out his watch and declared that the time was over. This was the sign for the declaration of the 'martial law': anyone caught playing drums after this time would be incarcerated in the police station ... the city became quiet. Many slung their drums over their shoulders and carried them quietly home. The onlookers returned home, grumbling about the administration.[16]

Like the banning of the chariot festival, the Gajan and Chadak festivals too were closely watched, controlled, and then ultimately banned in 1863.[17] Of all the public festivals, the hook-swinging festivities were the most dreaded by the colonial government. Contemporaries record the community spirit of the Gajan processions as they emerged from Kalighat and made their way to the north of the city, stopping by ordinary households and temples alike. Pantomime processions invariably emerged at the same time, attracting huge crowds.[18] The militant stance of the weapon-wielding and parading *sannyasis* or holy men, the collective expressions of pain and jubilation during hook-swinging, and the subversive nature of the pantomime shows (as seen in Chapter 2) accompanying the processions—all made for a volatile public presence. In Hutom's words again:

> The Chitpore Road becomes muddy at the slightest provocation of rain—on top of that drummers have emerged with the *gajan*. A man carrying a heavy brass plate is followed by little boys beating

[14] Atul Sur, *Tinsho Bochhorer Kolkata: Patabhumi O Itikatha* (Calcutta: Ujjval Sahitya Mandir, 1988), pp. 47, 67.

[15] K. Sinha, *Hutom Pnechar Naksha*, pp. 39, 247, 258.

[16] K. Sinha, *Hutom Pnechar Naksha*, p. 50.

[17] P. Dutta, *Kolikatar Itibritta*, p. 151.

[18] P. Dutta, *Kolikatar Itibritta*, p. 150.

> it with clubs. Behind that is an unruly mass of flags and carriers. Low caste *hadis* are singing *bhajans* ... devoted to Shiva to the accompaniment of drums. They are followed by the patron's armed personnel.... Then there are the impersonations of Shiv and Parvati with their bodies covered in ash and sporting tin foil snakes on their heads. They are followed by the incense burning and dancing *sannyasis* with their bodies pierced by metal.[19]

This is not the city as depicted in the writings of European travellers and commentators, residing as it did in the narrow impenetrable alleys of the Black Town. But then neither was it a city that this intellectual and author of the Black Town seemed particularly happy about. Despite the apparent jollity of the festival narratives in Hutom's work, one can clearly sense a mood bristling with resentment and class antagonism. The overwhelming presence of bodies and sounds (and both are almost formulaic in their presence in Hutom's accounts of the different festivals), defying and occupying space in the streets, was detrimental to law and order. For the city's elites the streets were becoming socially and sexually charged arenas, resonant with excitement and risk. The defiant multitudes that thronged the streets during the festivals could no longer be tucked away from public view, but had to be managed and controlled. Bans were operative on some processions as seen above and passes mandatory for still others.

Police presence became entrenched in public gatherings from the 1860s onwards, and anti-obscenity acts closely monitored the bodily deportment and content of public entertainment.[20] By the 1870s, the Ras and Chadak festivals had almost completely disappeared from the city to settle in their 'minor' reincarnations in the suburbs.[21] Patronage of fairs (melas) by individuals, communities, or groups on private grounds of estates, however, continued

[19] K. Sinha, *Hutom Pnechar Naksha*, p. 49 (italics mine).

[20] Passes were needed for musical processions since 1835, while hook-swinging and sawngs came to be banned in 1865 and 1874 respectively. Sumanta Banerjee, *Crime and Urbanization: Calcutta in the Nineteenth Century* (New Delhi: Tulika Books, 2006), pp. 119–22.

[21] *Administrative Report of the Municipality of the Suburbs of Calcutta for 1872–3*, p. 49.

well into the end of the nineteenth century. The energetic Ramlila celebrations—commemorating the slaying of the demon Ravana by the eponymous hero of the epic Ramayana—reported by Hutom on the private grounds of Nursingh Bahadur of Posta continued into the 1870s and beyond, although by that time it had come to be sponsored by the traders and moneylenders of Burrabazar.[22]

Martin Daunton has shown for late Victorian England how, changing house designs, street layouts, the policing of popular culture, and the provision of regulated spaces all went hand in hand with the emergence of more private, introverted domains for residents, in which the streets became more 'socially neutral rather than social arenas in their own right', and assemblages more passive than participatory.[23] The same social and civic ethos can be seen driving the municipal engine in nineteenth-century Calcutta, with an added dimension—that of the political. The post-1857 colonial government was wary of crowds and preferred to keep a close watch on potentially seditious public spaces.[24] As we shall see later, banned from street demonstrations or assemblies, many nationalist groups continued to meet in private drawing rooms or *baithak khanas* to discuss strategies and agenda.

Traffic was an important constituent of the street scene, and central to the discursive articulations of state power and modernity on the one hand and challenges to it on the other. Technology and machines, and their intrusions into the everyday lives of people represented not just newer material cultures to be absorbed over time, but also the fraught nature of their mobilization in the urban economy. The haste with which mechanized vehicles were introduced and the relentless securing of the urban landscape—both physical and human—for their smooth running was detrimental

[22] *Administrative Report of the Municipality of the Suburbs of Calcutta for 1872–3*, p. 49.

[23] M.J. Daunton, 'Public Space and Private Space: The Victorian City and the Working Class Household', in *The Pursuit of Urban History*, edited by D. Fraser and A. Sutcliffe (London: Edward Arnold, 1983), pp. 212–33, 218–19.

[24] C.A. Bayly, *Information and Empire: Intelligence Gathering and Social Communication in India, 1780–1870* (Cambridge: Cambridge University Press, 2000).

and confusing to pre-industrial modes of passage, occupations, lifestyles, and sensibilities. As Arnold comments in a recent article, 'With its ox-carts, bicycles, trams, and cars, traffic represented both the excitement, bewilderment, and danger of the modern city, and a mixed-up temporality, a heterogeneous time and place in which the modern and pre-modern uneasily coexisted.'[25]

Mechanized vehicles were introduced in Calcutta from the end of the nineteenth century onwards, beginning with trams in 1873. Initially proposing to carry only goods but later taking on passengers, the earliest trams were horse-drawn. Electric trams were introduced in 1902, after a brief experiment with steam engines.[26] Motor cars arrived in 1896, and motorized buses ran for the first time in 1922, succeeding a long tradition of horse-drawn omnibuses that had been operating in the city since 1830.[27] By 1914 Calcutta had 517 cars, 240 taxis, 152 motorcycles, and 21 trucks.[28] By 1925, there were 280 buses.[29] Development of traffic in other Indian cities around the same time shows a similar rise.[30] By 1936 British India had around 124,315 registered motor vehicles.[31]

But other forms of transport continued alongside for a long time, hindering the speed of circulation in the city, and leading to endless traffic jams (see Figure 4.1). The heterogeneity of traffic in Calcutta was read as a sign of urban dystopia by European observers in the early twentieth century.[32] The continued presence

[25] David Arnold, 'The Problem of Traffic: The Street Life of Modernity in Late Colonial India', *Modern Asian Studies* 46, no. 1, Special Issue (January, 2012): 119–41, 122.

[26] Radharaman Mitra, *Kolikata Darpan* (Calcutta: Subarnarekha, 1988), pp. 179–84.

[27] Radharaman Mitra, *Kolikata Darpan*, pp. 187–9.

[28] *Annual Report on the Police Administration of the Town of Calcutta, 1913*, p. 8, cited in Arnold, 'The Problem of Traffic', 124.

[29] Radharaman Mitra, *Kolikata Darpan*, p. 189.

[30] For Bombay, for example, see Meera Kosambi, *Bombay in Transition: The Growth and Social Ecology of a Colonial City, 1880–1980* (Stockholm: Almqvist and Wiksell International, 1986).

[31] Arnold, 'The Problem of Traffic', 124.

[32] Arnold, 'The Problem of Traffic', 126–7.

FIGURE 4.1 Mid-day Traffic on Canning Street in Calcutta's Premium Business District, 1914
Source: From E.P. Richards, *Report by Request of the Trust on the Condition, Improvement and Town Planning of the City of Calcutta and Contiguous Areas* (Calcutta: Calcutta Improvement Trust, 1914), X775 © The British Library Board. Courtesy of the British Library, London.

of the cheaper bullock carts (mostly used for trade purposes) and horse-drawn hackneys, as well as 'careless' pedestrians frustrated the colonial administration and led to strict laws and punitive measures to tackle the problems. In metropolitan Britain too, the Police Acts of the 1830s and 1867 were responsible for increased powers of intervention in the regulation of traffic and street activity but the late nineteenth-century impression, as one scholar notes, was still one of relative freedom, considerable anarchy, and laissez-faire on the streets.[33]

In Calcutta during the same period, the law acted differently. 'Street offences' appears as a new category of crime in police records from the 1870s onwards with a very high conviction rate, mostly for disregard of sanitary rules, driving without lights after dark, and obstruction of narrow, crowded thoroughfares by carters

[33] Patrick Joyce, *The Rule of Freedom: Liberalism and the Modern City* (London and New York: Verso, 2003), p. 217.

and hawkers. It was the largest category of cognizable crime in the city with a high proportion of arrests actually translating into convictions: 97.82 per cent in 1884.[34] In 1888 alone, there were 2,930 convictions for driving without lights and for driving on the wrong side of the road, and 666 convictions for bathing in prohibited tanks and at stand-posts.[35] As for the regulation of traffic, the police departments were almost exclusively involved, until the formation much later on of specific regulatory associations and acts. Arnold notes how '... the amount of effort involved in even attempting to regulate road traffic remains a striking (if barely noticed) feature of late-colonial law enforcement and policing'.[36]

Indeed, overall and for the better part of the nineteenth century, the city police were as much consumed by civic as by criminal offences, their daytime duties being very different from their night-time obligations. As explained exhaustively in the annual police report of 1842:

> Their [police's] day duty should consist in preventing breaches of peace, arresting persons against whom a hue and cry has been raised, keeping the streets free of obstructions from Carriages and other vehicles, preventing people from bathing in the Aqueducts, taking up drunken and disorderly persons, and faquirs, and others making an obscene and disgusting exposure of their persons, also mendicants wandering about the streets, and endeavouring by the exposure of wounds and personal deformities to obtain alms, dissolving assemblies in streets and highways.[37]

In 1886, the police were given greater powers owing to an amendment in the Police Act, which allowed them to arrest drunken and riotous persons, and those guilty of 'outraging public decency' by committing 'nuisances' in the public streets.[38] Within two years, the frequency of arrests and prosecutions for

34 *ARPC, 1884*, p. 10.
35 *ARPC, 1888*, p. 3.
36 Arnold, 'The Problem of Traffic', 137.
37 *ARPC, 1842*, see Appendix A, p. 9.
38 *ARPC, 1886*, p. 3.

civic crimes had increased alarmingly. Lambert, the then police commissioner, admitted that the large increase in the number of arrests were 'a matter of regret'.[39]

In all of this, the streets emerge as veritable theatres of war, with the administration and residents alike fighting for control. Scholars have argued how streets formed sites of intense clashes between residents and the government for other colonial situations. Brenda Yeoh has shown how smooth avenues for trade and commerce in colonial Singapore could also function as sites of protest, celebration, and custom.[40] The observation of Rudolf Mrázek, in the context of colonial Indonesia is noteworthy as well: 'Modern roads in the Indies, besides the many wonderful things that they did, became from the moment of their inception a battlefield and a space where the Dutch in the colony were clearly uncertain of themselves.'[41]

Police were in perpetual conflict with the drivers and owners of bullock carts in the business centre of the northern part of the town, with Police Commissioner Lambert commenting in 1888:

> ... when I see that, day after day, the same classes of offences are constantly occurring in the same locality, it seems a question, whether some increased severity on the part of the Courts would not sensibly diminish these public nuisances, and thereby render police interference less necessary.[42]

The colonial plan of rolling out a smooth technological revolution in urban transport, where a grateful native community helped to push the programme through, was clearly on the docks. As Mrázek puts it, in the context of the new electric tramway in the Dutch Indies, the 'dream' was to keep it 'running upon the landscape ... calm

39 *ARPC, 1888*, p. 3.

40 Brenda Yeoh, *Contesting Space: Power Relations and the Urban Built Environment in Colonial Singapore* (Singapore: Singapore University Press, 1996).

41 Rudolf Mrázek, *Engineers of Happy Land: Technology and Nationalism in a Colony* (Princeton, NJ: Princeton University Press, 2002), p. 8.

42 *ARPC, 1888*, p. 3.

and orderly, between one and the next point [stop] of an undoubted modernity'.[43] And yet the only way in which such dreams could be realized was by regulation, whereby recalcitrant drivers, commuters or pedestrians were brought within the folds of the modern, mechanized traffic regime.

Hackney carriages were tolerated but proved a major source of consternation. There was no doubt a problem with hackney carriages, which busily plied the road as precursors of modern cabs, with 159 casualties caused by careless driving as early as 1854–5, out of which there were ten deaths, and twenty-four cases of severe injuries.[44] Almost two decades later the figures were similar, with nineteen deaths reported.[45] Carriages were also hauled up for driving on the wrong side of the road, with 130 cases reported in 1863–4.[46] The narrow streets and bad road conditions played their due role, but officials were quick to blame the locals, both drivers and pedestrians:

> There appears to be in general a great indifference to life, by persons driving in the public streets, it being usually thought sufficient to call out to a person likely to be driven over, to pull up is seldom thought of: the Natives however are inveterately careless as to getting out of the way of carriages ...[47]

The Hackney Carriage Act that was passed in 1864 targeted those driving negligently and without lights, and saw the start of a wave of prosecutions much to the consternation of drivers.[48] The revised Hackney Carriage Act of 1866 continued the assault, with a further revision in 1911 to include rickshaws within

[43] Mrázek, *Engineers of Happy Land*, p. 10.

[44] *ARPC, 1854–5*, p. 9. The hackney carriages were notorious for the speed at which they travelled, and their bullying of pedestrians, including abuse and even the use of whips. See Durgacharan Ray, *Debganer Martye Agaman* (Calcutta, 2001; original edition, 1886), p. 274.

[45] *ARPC, 1877*, p. 14. Also see *ARPC 1878*, p. 14 for similar comments.

[46] *ARPC, 1863–4*, p. 13.

[47] *ARPC, 1854–5*, p. 10.

[48] There were 364 cases that year. *ARPC, 1864–5*, pp. 12–13.

its remit.[49] Carriages were also fined for obstructing passenger ghats when they rode up to the head of the side road, although it was really their inability to park elsewhere because of privileged parking of European carriages on the same stretch that caused the offence.[50] Regulations and fines for traditional passenger and cargo boats were also somewhat unfairly imposed.[51] Thus, boats and dinghies were arbitrarily fined when mooring within the port, when in reality, they could not moor elsewhere ever since the extension of and establishment of the jetties.[52] By 1909 it was no longer proving feasible to prosecute for road obstructions in busy trade areas like Fenwick and Burrabazar, and alternative methods were sought to redress the problem.[53]

Mechanized vehicles added an almost routine, everyday aspect to the risks posed by streets. With the arrival of tram cars and motor vehicles, the figures of street accidents show an exponential rise.[54] In 1883 there were 43 injured by tramcars in the streets of Calcutta, but the police themselves conceded that the problem was caused by the extension of the tramway into so many narrow thoroughfares (see Figure 4.2).[55] In fact, constant police supervision

[49] Sixty-two cases were reported that year. *ARPC, 1867*, p. 62; A.P. Muddiman, 'British India: Acts of Legislative Council', *Journal of Comparative Legislation and International Law*, Third Series, 3, no. 1 (1921): 125–35, 131.

[50] *ARPC 1873*. See the appended police magistrate's report for that year, p. 2.

[51] Thus, for passenger boats alone there were 1,676 cases in 1866. *ARPC*, 1866, Appendix B, p. 12.

[52] *ARPC, 1873*. See the appended police magistrate's report for that year, p. 2.

[53] *ARPC, 1909*, pp. 1–2 of the lieutenant governor's report.

[54] A similar rise can be noted across India, although the Calcutta figures appear to be the highest. Arnold, 'The Problem of Traffic', 130–1. For Bombay in particular, see Sandip Hazareesingh, *The Colonial City and the Challenge of Modernity*, pp. 62–9.

[55] By 1911 the tramway had been extended to Alipore, Tollygunge, and Behala, as well as to Howrah. See *Census of the Town and Suburbs of Calcutta, 1911*, p. 4.

FIGURE 4.2 Chitpore Road with Trams Running in 1914. Narrow Footpaths Compound the Difficulty of the Pedestrians
Source: From E.P. Richards, *Report by Request of the Trust on the Condition, Improvement and Town Planning of the City of Calcutta and Contiguous Areas* (Calcutta: Calcutta Improvement Trust, 1914), X775 © The British Library Board. Courtesy of the British Library, London.

was needed for their smooth running.[56] A total of 240 drivers were prosecuted successfully in 1903 for rash and negligent driving.[57] In 1908 there were 13 cases of death and injury caused by motor cars.[58] In 1910, out of the 61 persons killed in road accidents, horse-drawn carriages were responsible for 31, tramcars for 17, and

56 *ARPC, 1884*, p. 16; *ARPC, 1883*, p. 19.
57 *ARPC, 1903*, p. 2.
58 *ARPC, 1908*, p. 4.

TABLE 4.1 Injury and Death Rates in Traffic Accidents in Calcutta in 1914

Conveyance	Deaths	Injuries
Motor cars	32	358
Trams	12	240
Hackney carriages	4	131
Private horse-drawn carriages	10	166
Other conveyances	9	93

Source: Compiled from data in *The Annual Report of the State of Police of the Town of Calcutta during the Year 1914*.

motor cars for 13.[59] In 1914, there were 67 killed and 988 injured in traffic accidents (see Table 4.1),[60] and yet, in 1918 the number of motor vehicles plying in the city remained unabated at over five thousand, including 863 motorcycles.[61]

While we do find drivers of tram cars and hackney carriages charged with rash and negligent driving, there is another narrative running here, that of 'careless' natives—and this is despite the recklessness and culpability of European drivers being so often evident. It was especially the 'poorer classes' who appear to come under fire for sleeping on the streets, for their lack of 'road sense',

59 *ARPC, 1910*, p. 3.

60 *ARPC, 1914*, p. 13.

61 In fact, the traffic in general had increased so much in volume that the government had to sanction a new Public Vehicles Department under a Deputy Commissioner of Police (DCP), comprising of two branches—one for motor vehicles, and the other for hackney carriages—each with its own Assistant Commissioner of Police. *ARPC, 1918*, 'Resolution by Under Secretary to the Government of Bengal, Political Department, Police Branch', p. 2.

62 *ARPC, 1884*, p. 16.

63 *ARPC, 1902*, pp. 9–10.

64 *ARPC, 1909*, p. 6. In the case of the Dutch Indies too, those caught up in road accidents caused by motorcycles and cars are variously described as 'confused' or drunk, and even 'absolute idiots'. See Mrázek, *Engineers of Happy Land*, p. 21.

and for 'habitually allow[ing] their children to play in the streets', leading to high rates of injury and mortality.[62] In 1902, thus, in two cases of children being run over and killed by trams, the drivers were acquitted.[63] The larger onus of being safe on the roads rested with the pedestrian population, which it seemed were best just 'not being there'. Especially with motor cars, people appeared utterly incapable of responding to their speed and majesty with the veneration due. In 1909, five deaths were caused by motor cars in Calcutta. In three cases the coroner exonerated the drivers, and in the remaining two this was found to be accidental. In all five cases the persons injured were described as 'old and decrepit'.[64] The pedestrian and the pauper were clearly the lowest of the low in the hierarchy of those with access to the streets, as the traffic became more and more assertive.[65]

A milestone in traffic management was signalled with a highly critical report on Calcutta's 'street-less state' being authored by the urban planner E.P. Richards in 1914.[66] It complained how Calcutta, despite the great increase in its commerce and commercial traffic, had not changed anything by way of planning, changing, or adding new streets, with the result that the busiest parts of the city remained impassable during the rush hours. Bullock carts pouring in at the rate of 5,000 each day from the suburbs for trade purposes posed a tremendous challenge.[67] Compounded with the fact that the city had 2,500 acres of 'streetless' and congested

[65] By contrast, in England, even as the responsibility for walking safely on the streets came to rest increasingly on the shoulders of the pedestrian, there was a parallel belief in the free access of all to the highway, even those on foot. In a court ruling in 1865 thus, a widow was granted financial compensation when her husband was struck down by an omnibus. Joyce, *The Rule of Freedom*, pp. 217–18.

[66] There was a simultaneous move to reappraise traffic problems in other Indian cities, although it was acknowledged widely that nowhere was the problem as acute as in Calcutta. Arnold, 'The Problem of Traffic', 129.

[67] E.P. Richards, *Report by Request of the Trust on the Condition, Improvement and Town Planning of the City of Calcutta and Contiguous Areas* (Calcutta: Calcutta Improvement Trust, 1914), p. 116.

property and streets that were in desperate need of widening, Calcutta was in a seemingly hopeless state.[68]

The proposed regulatory traffic regime signalled the ascendancy of European town-planning models in its conception—recommending the widening of streets, freer and quicker circulation, and more arterial roads. More critically, in its privileging of motor traffic over other road-users from bullock carts to pedestrians, it signalled the presence of bodies and traffic in the streets that were irresponsible, undisciplined, and yet to be 'modern'. But the world of urban planning was often far removed from the reality of life on the streets.

To begin with, bullock and ox carts were cheap and essential in Calcutta to haul heavy loads of raw jute from landing stages on the Hooghly to mills in the northern suburbs, and could only be replaced when motor cars began to prove more remunerative. Second, Calcutta's streets were narrow to the point that they could only carry a minimum load of traffic and bear certain speed, without risking accidents. Third, while accidents were blamed on 'the persistency with which natives avoid footpaths and walk in the middle of the road',[69] contemporaries recall how pedestrians were forced to walk on the roads because of insufficient or muddy pavements, and were arrested by police as a result.[70] While pavements in the White Town were built with stone slabs, almost the entire area of the Black Town north of Bowbazar had mud pavements.[71] Later, in an interim and ad hoc measure during the

[68] Richards, *Report on the Condition, Improvement and Town Planning of Calcutta*, p. 35.

[69] *ARPC, 1877*, p. 14. Also see *ARPC 1878*, p. 14 for similar comments.

[70] Sur, *Tinsho Bochhorer Kolkata*, pp. 82–3. Both the roads and pavements became impossible to use because they became muddy if it rained and also because of the daily municipal sprinkling of water to control the dust. Calcutta was apparently promised stone pavements by Curzon on the occasion of the Golden Jubilee celebration of Victoria's rule. Kshitindranath Tagore, *Kolikatay Chalafera: Sekale aar Ekale* (Calcutta: Adi Brahmo Samaj Press, 1930), pp. 35–6, 38.

[71] Cemented pavements appeared in this part of the city for the first time during the First World War. Sur, *Tinsho Bochhorer Kolkata*, p. 82.

war, when pavements were covered with sharp red stone chips, it prompted the urban planner and consultant Patrick Geddes to write a letter to the Calcutta Improvement Trust (CIT) in 1915. In it he pointed out the thoroughly impractical nature of the pavements for Indian pedestrians, most of whom walked barefoot or donned footwear unsuitable for walking on them. Besides, given the high volume of pedestrian traffic in India and the ritual caste requirements of avoiding bodily contact in certain circumstances, Geddes argued, the pavements were too narrow even if deemed suitable by European standards. He suggested the widening of pavements to about 17 to 20 feet.[72] Regulations and fines for traditional passenger and cargo boats were also somewhat unfairly imposed.[73] Thus, boats and dinghies were arbitrarily fined when mooring within the port, but in reality, they could not moor elsewhere ever since the extension of and establishment of the jetties.[74]

A note from the lieutenant governor of Bengal in 1875 cautioned the force that the police should not unduly harass the town's population who are on the whole law-abiding and arrests should only be made if sufficient evidence exists. There was no real excuse for 'off-handed rudeness, roughness or violent demeanour on the part of the police', the order reminded traffic and police personnel.[75] Three years later the mood had changed. In 1878, Souttar, the new commissioner of police for Calcutta, insisted that police should be allowed to make arrests:

> It would no doubt be good if so many arrests were not needed. But in a town like Calcutta it is especially in public interest that the streets be kept free from obstruction, that orders relating to conservancy be attended to, and that boatmen and drivers of carts and public vehicles be subservient to rule. It must not be overlooked that to deprive a chowkidar of his summary powers of arrest *is practically*

72 *Annual Report of the Calcutta Improvement Trust, 1915*, p. 53.

73 Thus, for passenger boats alone there were 1,676 cases in 1866. *ARPC, 1866*, Appendix B, p. 12.

74 *ARPC, 1873*. See the appended police magistrate's report for that year, p. 2.

75 *ARPC, 1875*, p. 5 of the lieutenant governor's report.

> *to surround him with petty offenders, who would be completely masters of the situation, in the bazaars, in the streets, and in all public places* [italics mine].[76]

As Kaviraj has pointed out in a recent study, the municipal sign was an important weapon against this spontaneous 'indiscipline'. While it was impossible for the police alone to implement such a huge municipal regime by themselves, the gradual inculcation of rules through street signs acting as 'the voice of the state' was deemed plausible. The municipal sign became a powerful tool in the process, regulating public conduct, arrogating to itself the powers of 'a constant relentless surveillance of everyday behaviour ... [and] popular conduct', and 'symbolising the presence of a distinctly Weberian rationalist intelligence ... without which the ... order of modern life threatened to dissolve into chaos ...'[77] Atul Sur remembered from his childhood how municipal signs on road junctions carried warning notices from the police commissioner in four different languages. It instructed people to use pavements or face punishment.[78]

But Kaviraj also points out the irrelevance of the municipal notices and the modern civic regime to many inhabitants, for '... those who promulgated the notice had one conception of what public space meant, and those who defiled it had another. In their appropriate contexts, both concepts made sense'.[79] By posing the urban order as disciplined, rational, hygienic, and technologically advanced, colonial modernity denigrated all that went against it. The duality between city and country that resulted, posited a fundamental contradiction between rural and urban norms and lifestyles. And yet, for most inhabitants the mechanized and scientific city was a relatively new experience, one that had to be tested and tried out, resisted and ignored, before being accepted.

76 *ARPC, 1878*, p. 2.

77 Sudipta Kaviraj, 'Filth and the Public Sphere: Concepts and Practices About Space in Calcutta', *Public Culture* 10, no. 1 (1997): 83–117, 85.

78 Sur, *Tinsho Bochhorer Kolkata*, pp. 82–3.

79 Kaviraj,'Filth and the Public Sphere', 84.

Privy Wars: Sanitary Regimes and Their Contestation

Calcutta in the colonial archive earned a reputation for its filth and disease-ridden habitat, its insanitary condition being cited as one of the principal reasons for the proposed shift of the imperial capital to Delhi. The city's residents, however, blamed piecemeal municipal regulations. Sewerage issues and supply of clean filtered water had been a longstanding problem in the city. Increasing rates of taxation for the maintenance of municipal services had also become a thorny issue. But nowhere, perhaps, was the war so intensely fought as in the regulation of privies, house drains, and sewers of built or *pucca* buildings, with private latrines in particular coming under the strictest of surveillance.

In the traditional Indian system, excrement collected in receptacles placed some way below privies were emptied intermittently by scavengers. But under the municipal administration *tolah methars*, or contracted scavengers, serving private premises would collect rubbish and night-soil from privies more regularly.[80] Every householder had to pay 5–12 annas for the removal of the night-soil service but this was hard for the poorer classes of artisans, labourers, and domestic servants whose wages did not exceed 7 to 12 rupees per month.[81] The collection of rubbish was often a problem as people tended to dump rubbish in front of their gates till collection, while night-soil was disposed of by householders through unauthorized 'secret' sluices emptying into deep drains.[82]

In the case of the majority of Calcutta's population, however, private privies were a luxury and instead communal privies—not served by methars—and drains were resorted to. Crude earthwork ditches and open drains running along the side of roads became, over time, elongated cesspools where, in addition to privies, house sinks and cook rooms also drained. Paucity of brick-lined sewers meant that the impurities leaked into the subsoil, and tight

80 *RCIC, 1848*, Appendix 11, pp. 34–5, 38.

81 *Administrative Report of the Municipality of the Suburbs of Calcutta for 1874–5*, p. 35.

82 *RCIC, 1848*, Appendix 11, p. 35.

finances meant these drains were not regularly maintained. In 1850, approximately 75 miles of drains were cleaned after 10–12 years.[83] The decay of traps of house drains at the street boundaries of property allowed odour to escape to the footpaths.[84]

Many regulations relating to the sanitary condition of the town already formed, at the start of the 1860s, a regular part of the police administration and not conservancy operations.[85] But the Conservancy Act VI of 1863, which came into force for tackling these problems, was more targeted and listed an elaborate set of offences. Amongst others, it forbade Calcutta's residents from throwing night-soil into public drains and carcasses into rivers, and required them to abide by strict municipal regulations when it came to the construction of private privies. A fine of fifty rupees was imposed on landowners for keeping their land or premises in a filthy condition, and every day at the rate of ten rupees thereafter, allowing two days from the serving of the notice.[86] The act forbade people from keeping privy doors or trap doors opening onto any street as they had earlier been to facilitate sewage collection by tolah methars.[87] The offence of throwing night-soil into conservancy drains was taken very seriously by the police and, if caught, could be prosecuted in police courts and often severely punished.

The act claimed the largest number of offenders in the city under any single category for a long time. Most sanitary offences related to sewage flowing on to public streets, keeping animals without licence for profit, and retaining offensive matter in the house for more than 24 hours. Conservancy cases rose dramatically over the course of the latter part of the nineteenth century, from 4,455 in 1866 to 14,690 in 1872 (see Table 4.2).[88]

83 *RCIC, 1850.*

84 *Report of the Commission Appointed under Section 28 of Act IV (B.C.) of 1876 to Enquire Into Certain Matters Connected with the Sanitation of the Town of Calcutta* (Calcutta, 1885). Hereafter *Sanitation Commission 1885*, p. 22.

85 *RCIC, 1861*, p. 47.

86 *ARCM for 1867*, Appendix VIII, pp. 5–6.

87 *Sanitation Commission 1885*, p. 33.

88 *ARPC, 1866*, Appendix B, p. 12; *ARPC, 1872*, Statement A, p. 38.

TABLE 4.2 Convictions and Fines for Municipal Conservancy Offences by Year

Offence	1860	1862	Offence	1876
Not removing filth from houses	413: Rs 885			
Throwing filth into public drains		111: Rs 244	Throwing night-soil into public drains	34: Rs 44
Licensed tatties in a filthy state		52: Rs 346	For allowing sewage to flow on public streets	110: Rs 81
Removing night soil after fixed hours	37: Rs 66	881: Rs 2,268*	Retaining night-soil longer than 24 hours	424: Rs 263

Source: Compiled from *RCIC for 1860 and 1862; Report of the Municipality of Calcutta for the Quarters ending March 1876.*
Note: *This was half the sum of all fines levied that year.

The town had been struggling with its sewage and drainage systems ever since the setting up of its municipal administration. Two drainage scheme proposals had to be abandoned in the 1850s because of the high costs involved.[89] While a dense network of sewers were fully operational in the southern part of the city from the mid-nineteenth century onwards, filth in the Northern Division had to be collected and disposed off via sewers in the municipal depots where they were taken, eventually finding their

[89] This included the costly Cowie Drainage Report of 1857. See D.B. Smith, *Report on the Drainage and Conservancy of Calcutta* (Calcutta, 1869), p. 2. Similar reluctance to spend on sanitation and drainage while simultaneously being critical of filth has been reported by scholars for other British territories. See Liora Bigon, 'Sanitation and Street Layout in Early Colonial Lagos: British and Indigenous Conceptions, 1851–1900', *Planning Perspectives* 20, no. 3 (2005): 247–69.

way to the salt water lakes.[90] Drainage works commenced here in 1869, and by 1874 main sewers ran from Canning Street and Mirzapore Street south to the extreme north end of Bagh Bazar.[91] An integral part of the new drainage regime was the accompanying law by which householders and owners of private premises had to have their privies connected to public sewers instead of resorting to drains. The escape of odour from stables and cook rooms were also to be minimized by the insertion of trapped inlets.

Despite the law requiring householders to connect and notice being routinely served to properties abutting on the new sewers as they were being built, the figures of connected premises were dismal. In 1881, slightly over 20,000 homes in Calcutta were connected to the sewers, representing only half the total number of premises in the city. Out of these, up until 1885, not more than 2,829 privies—about 8 per cent of the number of total private privies in the city—had been connected.[92] Even if we counted one privy per premise, it means only just over one-tenth of the premises connected to the sewers had bothered to get their privies connected. A street as densely populated and long as the Chitpore Road had none of its 424 premises connected by 1872.[93]

There were technical problems. A principal feature of the underground drainage scheme was that all privies should be directly connected with the sewers. But the advance in drainage works could not be matched by a critical supply of water needed to flush the sewers to keep them healthy. The water supply and the velocity of motion required for the carriage of impurities was insufficient to flush the privies. This made the connections inconvenient and risky.[94] Following a report in 1876, the connection with privies

[90] These were collected earlier on in open carts and then from the late 1870s onwards in closed odourless metal tubs.

[91] *ARCM for 1874*, p. 3.

[92] *Sanitation Commission 1885*, pp. 21, 32.

[93] *ARCM for 1872*. See Appendix I, Annual Report of the Drainage Department, for figures conveying the highly unequal distribution of sewers and drainage facilities between the northern and southern divisions of the town.

[94] *Sanitation Commission 1885*, p. 16.

was therefore practically prohibited.[95] A special Conservancy Committee appointed in 1882 recommended more regular flushing, but it remained a perennial problem for lack of powerful engines and high level of the main sewers at Palmer's Bridge.[96] Those householders without connections found themselves in a particular predicament—paying, over and above the water rate, extra fees for the collection of night-soil from their homes.[97] The problem was compounded by the fact that methars were in very short supply, with the ratio of methars to privies standing at 1:30 in 1878.[98]

But there were other factors at work too. Bengalis resented heavily the intrusion of the municipal administration into their homes. The general attitude of Bengalis to domestic inspection and sanitary measures was summed up by an administrative report in 1873 thus:

> Perhaps no people are so averse to domiciliary visits as the Bengalis, and when to an intrusion into their private apartments for purposes of inspection is added the service of summons and consequent attendance in court and fine for an offence, the gravity of which they do not in most instances appreciate, the natural irritation and ill-feeling which may be created by over-zeal will easily be understood.[99]

It seems that 'the great sanitary machinery of the city work[ed] ... for the most part on the public highway alone, and the greater portion of the town area ... [was] left in primitive filth'. But as

95 *Sanitation Commission 1885*, p. 32.

96 *Sanitation Commission 1885*, p. 15.

97 These ranged from 8 annas to Rs 2 a month for tiled huts, and from 8 annas to Rs 8 a month for pucca houses. The 1885 Sanitation Commission reported that these were very high rates yielding an annual surplus of over one lakh rupees in 1878. *Sanitation Commission 1885*, p. 32.

98 *Sanitation Commission 1885*, p. 37.

99 While written with empathy, the report does summarize quite well the nature of opposition that municipal officers and workers might have faced from householders. *Administrative Report of the Municipality of the Suburbs of Calcutta for 1872–3* (Calcutta, 1873), Report by R.C. Sterndale, pp. 22–3.

neither the municipal water supply nor the sewers could be carried into private land without the consent of the landlord, 'drainage stop[ed] ... at the boundaries of private property'.[100]

In fact, there was 'violent opposition' from householders to the progress of works, particularly in the bustees. A major clash seems to have occurred over the zamindari privies that were maintained for the tenants of bustees by landowners. These were unlicensed semi-public latrines erected by the owners of bustees for their tenants, and an addition made to the rent for the collection of night-soil. House owners resented the costs they had to bear for the laying on of water to houses and petitioned the Secretary of State in Council to repeal the Act of 1870 that had made this into law.[101] The 1863 act had also given the municipality the power to compel house owners to make 'efficient roadways' between existing blocks of huts, if needed on sanitary grounds. But this again was not fully implemented for fear of opposition.[102] There were also numerous complaints from residents regarding the appearance of cracks and other defects in their properties because of drainage works.[103]

Admittedly, 'fines [were] ... no good and offenders ... usually wealthy natives who ... [could] afford to pay'.[104] The Health Officer in 1869 asked for harsher measures to be taken against the 'wealthy and educated delinquents' so that they could feel the weight of the law.[105] But '... owing to the deficient water supply the Corporation were not in a position to compel the owners to connect their privies with the sewers'.[106] By contrast, in Bombay and Madras, municipalities worked more confidently and had greater powers overall to demolish huts on grounds of overcrowding and oversee the construction of newer blocks.[107]

[100] *Calcutta Municipal Quarterly Reports Ending March 1876.*

[101] This was refused. *ARCM for 1870*, p. 23.

[102] *ARCM for 1870*, p. 23.

[103] *ARCM for 1869*, Appendix C.

[104] *ARCM for 1867*, Appendix VIII, pp. 5–6.

[105] *ARCM for 1869.*

[106] *Sanitation Commission 1885*, p. 33.

[107] *Administrative Report of the Municipality of the Suburbs of Calcutta, 1872–3*, p. 24. For Bombay see Kidambi, *The Making of an Indian*

The vital role played by city sewers in regulating cultural economies of health and social relations has been profitably studied in the context of modern Europe.[108] Studies on the mid-nineteenth century reconstruction of the Paris sewers, for instance, have shown how the process—which ran between 1850 and 1870—fundamentally shaped class relations and cultural practices in the city. Urban policies and the management of sanitation and disease also led to a radical reworking of relations between the body and urban form.[109] More crucially, far from representing an unproblematic emblem of modernity, the city sewers provoked loud and contentious debate, accompanied by a halting and ambivalent reorientation of attitudes towards public health and customary beliefs.[110] For colonial India too it is not impossible to see how urban sanitation regimes were not just about the imposition of municipal authority but also a civilizational conflict over cultural practices.[111]

There is a need to pause here and reflect on the changing composition of the Municipal Corporation after 1875. The extension

---

Metropolis, Chapter 5; For Madras see M. Satish Kumar, 'The Evolution of Spatial Ordering in Colonial Madras', in *Postcolonial Geographies*, edited by Cheryl McEwan and Alison Blunt, pp. 85–98 (London and NY: Continuum, 2002), pp. 95–7.

[108] David Inglis, 'Sewers and Sensibilities: The Bourgeois Faecal Experience in the Nineteenth-century City', in *The City and the Senses: Urban Culture Since 1500*, edited by Alexander Cowan and Jill Steward (Aldershot: Ashgate, 2007), pp. 105–30; Alexander M. Martin, 'Sewage and the City: Filth, Smell and Representations of Urban Life in Moscow, 1770–1880', *The Russian* Review 67, no. 2 (2008): 243–74. Also see Alain Corbin, *The Foul and the Fragrant: Odour and the French Social Imagination* (Cambridge, Massachusetts: Harvard University Press, 1986).

[109] See the excellent article on this by Matthew Gandy, 'The Paris Sewers and the Rationalisation of Urban Space', *Transactions of the Institute of British Geographers* 24, no. 1 (April, 1999): 23–44.

[110] David S. Barnes, *The Great Stink of Paris and the Nineteenth Century Struggle Against Filth and Germs* (Baltimore: Johns Hopkins University Press, 2006).

[111] Colonial law and regulation was often at variance with other local practices such as in tanneries, slaughterhouses, and burial grounds.

of the local administration to include Indian representation meant that between 1876 and 1899, two-thirds of the members of the Municipal Commission were elected by rate payers, and were mostly comprised of Hindu Bengalis. So positing any simple dichotomies between Bengali residents and the corporation becomes slightly more problematic. For this study, however, what is significant is that the privy wars relate mostly to the pre-1875 period when the administration was largely European. The degree of opposition to the corporation temporarily died down after 1876, especially after sewer connections were made non-mandatory.[112]

The Bengalis could not really fathom the fuss with the privies: the system had existed for several decades without doing anyone any harm. As one administrative report noted: 'There is ... no subject on which the middle class residents ... are seemingly more averse to change than in the regulation and improvement of their privy accommodation.'[113] Bengali newspapers were critical when commenting on the draconian and even discriminatory sanitary regimes in the city. Accordingly, incidents of Bengali men being harassed and apprehended, marched to police stations, and ultimately fined by magistrates for urinating on the streets were common, and yet, Englishmen went scot-free despite being guilty of the same offence.[114] Popular pamphlets blamed the Municipal Commission and judiciary for disproportionate fines over small offences, and overseeing relentless pursuit of transgressors on every road and alleyway and general disruption.[115]

Even earlier, Hutom had noted, in his characteristic razor-sharp style, how the government had begun to meddle with both public

[112] As studied by Mark Harrison, the conflicts during this period were played out for the most part within the corporation itself between the Hindu-Bengali and European members. See Mark Harrisson, *Public Health in British India: Anglo-Indian Preventive Medicine, 1859–1914* (Cambridge: Cambridge University Press, 1994), Chapter 8.

[113] *Administrative Report of the Municipality of the Suburbs of Calcutta for 1874–5*, pp. 33–4.

[114] *Sangvad Prabhakar*, 18 April 1862, cited in Benoy Ghosh, *Samayik Patre Banglar Samajchitra* (Calcutta, 1980), vol. 2, p. 176. See also, D. Ray, *Debganer Martye Agaman*, p. 309.

[115] Devendra Sharma, *Sahar Chitra* (Calcutta, 1921), pp. 22–3.

and private hygiene in the city, while not doing enough in other areas of maintenance.

> Oh Mother Bhagavati, leave this city and do not ever enter again,
> Calcutta seems to be turning into a circus every day.
> The Justices believe themselves sincerely effecting a fair deal,
> And yet it is impossible to open one's eyes or mouth
> While walking on the streets because of the dust.
> One is forbidden from urinating or defecating on the streets,
> Or drawing water from the aqueducts.
> There is a licence tax payable per head,
> And night-soil cannot be left overnight in latrines.
> Health Officers, Latrine Magistrates, and Income tax assessors have made our lives excruciating
> On top of that the Governor has an eye on our excrements!
> This is intolerable O Divine Mother.
> It has become impossible to live here anymore.
> ... Hutom Das has therefore decided to ditch the city for the skies
> Where he can fly like a free bird.[116]

Recent studies have posited the idea of 'dirt' as coterminous also with 'danger', and as inhabiting the space beyond the auspicious boundaries of the home or the 'outside' in Indian cultural traditions. Thus, the sanctified enclosure named 'home' is both produced and marked by household rubbish that forms its borders.[117] The outside by contrast is not a hospitable world. As Kaviraj points out for the nineteenth and twentieth centuries in India, 'To the normal anxieties of people accustomed to living in caste society, which obviated the need to meet utter strangers and improvise responses to untried situations, the new kind of colonial city sparked fears of miscegenation and unpredictability. The world outside was [in this view] ... inhospitable and full of danger ...'[118]

Especially in the context of the earliest colonial metropolis of Calcutta, this approach proves particularly useful. Practical

[116] K. Sinha, *Hutom Pnechar Naksha*, p. 248.

[117] Kaviraj, 'Filth and the Public Sphere 94. Also see Dipesh Chakrabarty, 'Open Space/Public Place: Garbage, Modernity and India', *South Asia: Journal of South Asian Studies* 14, no. 1 (1991): 15–31, see 19–26.

[118] Kaviraj, 'Filth and the Public Sphere', 97–8.

difficulties—as encountered earlier—aside, there was evidently a certain mindset at work that banished rubbish to the public domain, and rendered dirt as 'invisible'. The same mindset also saw diseases rampant in the city rather than the emotionally invested site of the village, and believed in the shastric rather than technological scientific power of purification.[119]

The campaign against sanitary regimes represented the entrenched conflict of interest between Calcutta's residents and its government—as in Bombay—where fledgling nationalist leaders tested their earliest battlegrounds. Mark Harrison has shown how the middle-class *grihasthas* or householders were most vocal in their opposition to European domination in the Commission, exemplified in the career of the nationalist Surendranath Banerjea and his newspaper, the *Bengalee*. This was also an opportunity for the informal galvanization of critical voices amongst the city's residents who resisted—by action and word—the municipal diktats regulating their intimate bodily habits in their own homes. The idea of the Hindu residence as the private sanctum of the resident householder where municipal laws were most unwelcome intruders seems to have evoked extraordinarily aggressive sentiments and mobilized opposition to the new rules.

Urban Order and Disorder: Unorganized Strikes and Trade Disputes

Recent literature on colonial Indian cities have highlighted the tightening grip of technologies of governance in the urban sphere be it in sanitation, housing, or general policing.[120] In Calcutta, in contrast to Bombay and Delhi, the municipal authorities struggled

[119] Calcutta was thus seen to make people dyspeptic. K. Sinha, *Hutom Pnechar Naksha*, p. 44; Also see P. Dutta, *Kolikatar Itibritta*, p. 99. Filtered water supply thus could only be declared 'pure' once the shastric pundits had okayed it.

[120] See Kidambi, *The Making of an Indian Metropolis*, Chapter 5, 'The Ultimate Masters of the City: Policing Public Order'; Legg, *Spaces of Colonialism*, Chapters 3–4.

to be the 'ultimate masters'. Traditions of collective protest and strikes run as far back as the early decades of the nineteenth century in the city. Various occupational and caste groups brought the city to a complete halt over the long stretch of the nineteenth and the early twentieth centuries, affecting basic services such as transport and sanitation, and demanding lesser regulation and intervention in their trades. Together they throw up a narrative of remarkable community organization, initiative, and action within specific occupations, with sufficient clout being wielded by clan and caste leaders. Again, in all of these disputes, the streets emerge as the centre stage of action (or inaction, as the case may be), a strategic location for the defiance of the municipal regime that ran the city, and marking as important a political statement as the state's recurrent attempt to impose regulatory order upon it.

The earliest strike was that of the palanquin or *palki* (wooden cubicles carried at the end of long poles by bearers) bearers in 1827. Palanquin bearers, mostly from Orissa and plying the trade in terms of clan-based regulations (for example, assignment of particular city areas to bearers from particular clans) operated in the city in the first half of the nineteenth century. They lived together in tight residential clusters with the *ada* or palki station situated in their midst. Palkis were much in demand, and especially used by clerks and women.[121] In 1827, in an effort to regulate this prosperous business, the government made it mandatory for bearers to obtain licences in lieu of fees and fixed the hourly rates for hiring palanquins.

The strike that followed was initially quite resolute. The bearers openly and visibly challenged the administration by gathering together in large groups in prominent places like the Maidan opposite Fort William and the passenger jetties.[122] Bengali

[121] K. Tagore, *Kolikatay Chalafera*, pp. 54–9. Tagore calls them 'clannish'.

[122] Apparently, the bearers were accusing the government of immorally 'taxing [their] bodily labour'. *Calcutta Gazette*, 28 May 1827 (original report in *Sambad Timir Nasak*), cited in Sumanta Banerjee, *The Wicked City: Crime and Punishment in Colonial Calcutta* (New Delhi: Orient Blackswan, 2009), p. 332.

newspapers were sympathetic to the cause and reported how the bearers, being unable to read the 'English clock', could potentially be misled by their more 'respectable' customers who could, and therefore be duped into accepting less for their services.[123] But the government was firm. Several striking bearers were arrested and the rest broken into agreeing to the new rules after five days.

In response to the government's Hackney Carriage Act in March 1864, applying to chiefly the horse-driven carriages, but which also extended to palanquins, hackney drivers and palanquin bearers struck work.[124] The act required compulsory registration and the fixation of appropriate licence plates to the carriages, and set limits to the number of passengers on board, and speed—no more than 4 miles per hour. Both groups were already under considerable pressure paying significant amounts in tax.[125] The first to strike were the palanquin bearers, two days before the act was to come into operation. There was apparently a 'monster meeting' held in the Calcutta Maidan involving both hackney drivers and palki bearers, and a one anna subscription per man raised to set up a petition to the viceroy.

In each case the strikes were broken but not before they had posed considerable challenges to the city's administration.[126] Both

[123] *Samachar Darpan,* 2 June 1827, reprinted in Brajendranath Bandyopadhyay (ed.), *Samvadpatre Sekaler Katha,* vol. 1 (Calcutta: Bangiya Sahitya Parishat, 1970), p. 304.

[124] By 1881 there were 4,085 registered palki bearers and 3,659 hackney-carriage drivers in Calcutta, although together with those unregistered or wrongly enumerated under some other category, these figures nearly doubled. See *Census of the Town of Calcutta and Its Suburbs 1881,* pp. 44–5.

[125] The horse and carriage tax varied from 12 annas for a medium-sized pony to Rs 4 and 8 annas for a four-wheeled carriage on wheels, payable quarterly. But the municipal administration admitted in 1860 that the collection of the tax was proving difficult. *RCIC, 1861,* p. 37.

[126] Other colonial cities were also subject to such threats, and Calcutta was not alone in this. Singapore thus saw protracted struggles between rickshaw pullers and the city administration in the early decades of the twentieth century, with strikes bringing the city to its knees. See James F. Warren, *Rickshaw Coolie: A People's History of Singapore, 1880–1940* (Singapore: Singapore University Press, 2003), pp. 105–33; Tilman

constituted the chief means of transport in nineteenth-century Calcutta, and frantic efforts to placate leaders behind the scenes are evident. Faced with the prospect of the strike and failing to persuade the leaders, the government took a different approach. If the Registrar of Hackney Carriages is to be believed, at his instigation, the hackney carriages, far from joining the strike, actually stayed on in the streets and did a profitable business much to the detriment of the palanquins.[127]

Clearly, the problem remained unresolved, as the hackney-carriage drivers went on another strike in 1873, and both groups together struck work again in 1901–2. The chief reason for the later strikes was the habitual blackmailing by the police of carters and drivers for purported traffic offences, but the complaint against police harassment and extortion was recognized. A full inquiry was held and the force shaken up—so much so that enough policemen failed to report eligible infringements of the law.[128]

Carters were also affected by similar regulations as those for the hackney-carriage drivers. In 1850, drivers of bullock carts struck for two days, forcing the government to withdraw the taxes imposed on them. The *Sangbad Prabhakar* reported this triumphantly in its editorial columns.[129] Following the construction of the Howrah Pontoon Bridge, cartmen devised a clever strategy to avoid penalization. They increasingly registered in Howrah on the other side of the river Ganges, while actually carrying on their business in Calcutta. The police found it frustrating that vehicles registered elsewhere could not be prosecuted if caught violating traffic regulations.[130]

Frasch, 'Tracks in the City: Technology, Mobility and Society in Colonial Rangoon and Singapore', *Modern Asian Studies* 46, no. 1 (2012, Special Issue): 97–118, at 104–5.

[127] 'Report from the Registrar of Hackney Carriages to the Commissioner of Police', dated 30 August 1865, cited in Sumanta Banerjee, *The Wicked City*, pp. 334–5.

[128] *ARPC*, 1901, p. 2.

[129] *Sangbad Prabhakar*, 6 Falgun, 1257 B.S., reprinted in B. Ghosh (ed.), *Samayik Patre Banglar Samajchitra*, vol. 1, p. 61.

[130] Letter from Stuart Hogg, Commissioner of Police, Calcutta, to Secretary, Government of Bengal, Judicial Files, Proceedings, February

Workers in the unorganized sector and the urban poor thus seem well organized and focused in their efforts—not exactly helpless. The presence of clan leaders or sardars among the Oriyas—perhaps the single largest workforce in the city in the late eighteenth and early nineteenth centuries, supplying cooks, water-bearers, gardeners, and the like—who set down trade rules, settled disputes, and intervened on behalf of the community in negotiations with the British rules, gave a certain focus and purpose to them.[131] They could raise subscriptions, arrange for written petitions, and cohere together in times of trouble. But others too seem to have been strongly knit together in occupational groups with the display of similar abilities to organize large-scale protest. Other trades too worked like vast de facto trade guilds or pressure groups. In the early 1830s about two thousand salt workers assembled in front of Governor-General Bentinck's residence to protest against the oppressive practices of Dwarkanath Tagore in his salt-estate.[132]

While traditions of non-violent collective protest against the government in colonial India are known to have been operative in various economic and political contexts before the late nineteenth century, its peculiar urban manifestation during this period saw it embedded in specific occupational, manual service groups, vital to the capital's sustenance.[133] The specific use of striking work as a tool for protest and negotiation seems to have been known in north India as early as 1810, when the residents of Benares

---

1875, West Bengal State Archives (henceforth WBSA), cited in Sumanta Banerjee, *The Wicked City*, p. 336.

[131] Oriyas comprised 2.5 per cent of Calcutta's population even as late as 1881, offering such services in the city during the summer season (working as farmers in their own villages during the winter). See *Census of the Town and Suburbs of Calcutta 1881*, pp. 41–2.

[132] Abanti Kumar Sanyal, 'Babur Bangshabichar', *Ekshan* (Autumn, 1976), cited in Sumanta Banerjee, *The Wicked City*, p. 359.

[133] For studies of such protest for earlier periods (late eighteenth and early nineteenth centuries) in agrarian settings, see, among others, the monumental work by Ranajit Guha, *Elementary Aspects of Peasant Insurgency in Colonial India* (New Delhi: Oxford University Press, 1983).

protested against the imposition of a house tax in the city, resulting in its withdrawal soon after. Some twenty to thirty thousand people participated in the protest, led by their caste panchayats, abandoning their homes and gathering in a field to demand the repeal of the oppressive tax. Making a public spectacle of their suffering, the residents hoped to appeal to the moral judgement of the authorities and drive home the legitimacy of their claim.[134] For both, the striking transport workers of Calcutta and the Benares residents, the strategies deployed seem to have been similar: abandonment of usual occupations/businesses, vast gathering in open spaces, and mobilization of caste clout—the last being a point I will return to later.

One of the most intractable groups the administration faced, however, were the scavengers of the Conservancy Department, who represented a crucial workforce that helped keep the city clean.[135] Night-soil in Calcutta was collected from houses and public latrines and kept in private depots outside houses, to be eventually retrieved by the municipal administration. But scavengers who carried out this vital task refused to be regulated by municipal regulations and struck work repeatedly, most prominently in 1867 and 1877. The first strike followed the establishment of municipal depots that year which recruited methars directly instead of the tolah depots run by clan leaders. The new regime was stricter. Registers were to be maintained at each depot, so that methars could not avoid detection if they failed to bring in their filled tubs for a single day. The independent and more prosperous methars apparently agreed to the new plan, but tolah methars at first refused and struck work. With the administration remaining firm and resistance seemingly dying down in due course, however,

[134] Richard Heitler, 'The Varanasi House Tax Hartal of 1810–11', *Indian Economic and Social History Review* 9, no. 3 (1972): 239–57. Heitler sees in the non-violent nature of the protest and its moral appeal, a precursor to later Gandhian techniques of hartal.

[135] In 1911, there were 15,381 registered sweepers and scavengers in the city, but in the late nineteenth century there was also a large informal segment in the workforce, which might have accounted for a larger number. See *Census of the Town and Suburbs of Calcutta, 1911*, p. 68.

the authorities were convinced that 'a most unmanageable set of men' had been brought under their firm control.[136]

In 1867, it is with some triumph that the Health Officer of Calcutta reported that the methars had been finally brought under control with a complete reorganization of the Night-Soil Department:

> Up to that epoch any attempt made towards the abatement of the disgusting nuisances created by the Mehters met from that class of men with the most stubborn and passive resistance. All means had been tried to induce them to take the initiative in the measures proposed by me, but in vain. Attempts at conciliation were made, but they were laughed at, and fines even had no effect whatever upon them.[137]

But tolah methars remained instrumental in challenging the administration, especially as the latter were so dependent on them. Ten years later, in 1877, the methars struck work again when the municipality tried to introduce the *halalcore* system that had been pioneered so well in Bombay a few years earlier. The system meant that all methars in the city had to be licensed, bringing them under the direct control of local authorities, and restricting their operations to particular beats. But the attempt was hasty and not all relevant parties were consulted. The tolah methars were enraged, night-soil was not collected for several weeks and when the local authority tried to recruit fresh methars from distant areas, they were met with threats and the new and potential recruits were intimidated. A special methar corps had to be organized, which proved costly to the government.[138] Further tightening of the system resulted, with a supervisory team of sanitary peons (overseeing 200 houses in each beat), *jemadars* or intermediary sanitary officers, and inspectors overseeing their work.[139]

[136] *ARCM for 1867*, Appendix VIII, Health Officer's Report, pp. 4–5.

[137] Report by the Health Officer of Calcutta, 29 April 1867, *ARCM for 1866*. In Bombay, the methars were more amenable as they could be turned out of their quarters—owned by the municipality—if found to be erring in their duties. *Administrative Report of the Suburbs of Calcutta for 1875–6*, p. 29.

[138] *ARCM for 1877*, pp. 48–9; *Calcutta Municipality Quarterly Report Ending 9 July, 1877*, pp. 4–5

[139] *Calcutta Municipal Quarterly Report*, 1 October 1877. Pulakesh Roy, 'The Story of the Mehter Strike in Calcutta in 1877', *Revolt Studies* 1, no. 1 (1985).

The new regulations were designed no doubt to break the ties of caste and clan between the clan leaders and tolah recruits, make the methars directly answerable to the administration and minimize the resistance of clan leaders to the introduction of any innovation in technology or organization that would restrict their profits. But in reality, the tolah methars persisted in sabotaging the new sanitary measures. The municipal night-soil collectors continued to be assaulted, intimidated, and even falsely prosecuted in courts by the tolah methars.[140] In the event of a householder attempting to employ someone else following dispute between the former and a methar, the new potential recruit was threatened by the panchayat which forbade him to work in that tolah.[141]

Such tactics worked for other groups too. Bheesties, or water-carriers, were thus not just content with striking work when fined by the municipality for not watering the streets properly, but also prevented other bheesties from being recruited.[142] The situation came to such a standstill that the administration was even considering an arrangement whereby residents would water their own streets and be remunerated for their services.[143] When the bheesties struck work again in 1866, refusing to be mustered twice a day, they were replaced by coolies with buckets and watering carts.[144]

The image of a municipal administration being repeatedly brought to its knees by its manual workers is evident in the frustration that is expressed in its annual reports. The problem was compounded by the fact that municipal workers in the city were being lost to the railways in large numbers in the 1870s.

140 *Administrative Report of the Suburbs of Calcutta for 1874–5*, p. 36.

141 *Administrative Report of the Suburbs of Calcutta for 1873–4*, p. 23.

142 *RCIC, 1860*, p. 71. In February 1866, when the bheesties struck work for being mustered twice a day, they had to be replaced by coolies. Report by the Health Officer of Calcutta, 29 April 1867, *ARCM for 1866*.

143 *RCIC, 1860*, p. 71.

144 *ARCM for 1866*, health officer's report, p. 9. Apparently, the bheesties had been encouraged to strike by the absence from the city of the Health Officer who was in Bhagalpur trying to recruit methars for the Conservancy Department.

Out of all these groups, the milkmen or the *goalas* were described in official reports as 'the most inveterate and hardened offenders'.[145] Their resistance reached almost mythical proportions it seems with the circulation of stories such as this within the municipal establishment: when fined an exemplary fine of twenty-five rupees, a goala paid the fine and bowing to the magistrate said:

> ... all right [*sic*] your worship, I can re-coup myself by putting a little more water in your honor's milk. We can afford to be generous now as you have given us a plentiful supply of water which does not spoil the milk.[146]

Perpetual and habitual violation of municipal laws by milkmen frustrated the authorities. Goalas come under attack for practising *phooka* (injecting salt into the cows) and for flaying goats alive,[147] in addition to the neglect of sanitary conditions in cowsheds—over-crowding, infrequent clearing of dung, and filthy tanks, as well as the torturing and abusing of cattle in public streets.[148] But the administration itself faced an assault from the Bengali newspapers with the *Hindoo Patriot* calling the vice chairman of the municipality 'a tyrant in many respects', in reporting the allegedly forceful implementation of sanitary measures in areas inhabited by milkmen.[149] A rather defeated Sterndale admitted: '... [I]t is hardly too much to say that more money has been and is being wasted in litigation, paying fines, and vain efforts to resist the pressure of improvement than would have probably sufficed to remove the

145 *ARCM for 1872*, p.13.

146 *ARCM for 1871*, Appendix IV, Health Officer's Annual Report, p. 3.

147 *ARPC, 1889*, p. 8; *ARPC, 1883*, p. 9. Interestingly, the government itself destroyed 7,000 and 8,900 stray dogs in Calcutta in 1907 and 1909 respectively. *ARPC, 1907*, p. 5; *ARPC, 1909*, p. 6.

148 *ARCM for 1872*, pp. 10–12. Cases against offenders for the torture and abuse of cattle were reported as rising steadily. *ARPC 1862–3*, p. 12 (279 cases); *ARPC 1863–4*, p. 13 (396 cases); *ARPC 1864–5*, p. 13 (452 cases); *ARPC 1866*, p. 12 (859 cases).

149 *Administrative Report of the Suburbs of Calcutta for 1879–80*, pp. 51–2.

old cow-houses and build new ones in new ground in the first instance.'[150]

Trouble was posed by butchers too when they opposed the introduction of compulsory licences for the use of the municipal slaughterhouse recently installed in Tengra. The municipality reacted by enforcing the Suburban Slaughter House Act of 1869 and closing down the slaughterhouses at Narkeldanga. An appeal made by the butchers against this decision was upheld by the judge of 24 Parganas, and the Narkeldanga and Kurryah slaughterhouses were subsequently reopened.[151] Those that had applied to operate from Tengra, reverted to the suburban slaughterhouses, with the exception of two butchers only.[152] It was not until 1871 that the butchers could be compelled to use the Tengra slaughterhouse when the licenses for the suburban slaughter houses eventually ran out.[153]

The municipality faced much opposition to the enforcement of bye-laws to bazaar improvement. An establishment comprising of four inspectors of Bazaars and Nuisances, with two peons each, had been appointed in 1850, but to no avail.[154] 'In fact, so formidable had the combination of [bazaar owners] become that legislation had to be resorted to for the settlement of the question.'[155] When notices were served on the bazaars for measures such as removal of obstructions or encroachments, clearing of roads and paths, cleaning of blocked drains and rubbish heaps, they were either ignored or resisted. In Madhub Dutt's bazaar, the Health Officer's Assistant and Surveyor 'were turned out of the bazaar in a most offensive manner,

[150] *Administrative Report of the Suburbs of Calcutta for 1879–80*, p. 57.

[151] *ARCM for 1869*, p. 31.

[152] *ARCM for 1870*, p. 10. It was claimed in the report that these two 'faithful(s)' were the 'leaders' of the *kassai* (butcher) community, who were fortunate to have the municipal stamp of approval on their meat.

[153] *ARCM for 1871*.

[154] *RCIC, 1850*. Third Half-yearly Report.

[155] A new act, the Bengal Council Act of 1866, Act VI, had to be passed to introduce fresh legislation for enforcement. *ARCM, 1866*, health officer's report, p. 6.

and prevented from carrying out orders …'.[156] The owner ultimately relented, however, and stone floors had to be built for the fish stalls and broad walks installed in the bazaar. Passive resistance techniques were employed repeatedly, including foot-dragging. While the municipality wondered whether appealing to the good sense of the aristocratic and 'enlightened' owners of the bazaars—rather than their servants or employees—might improve their chances of reform, the actions of the bazaar operatives and stall owners outlined a narrative of considerable protest and opposition.[157]

In all of these strikes and protests in the unorganized sector of manual labour in the city, the role of community and caste ties is noticeable. While an organized trade union was yet to emerge and would not do so until the start of the twentieth century, clan-based fiats mobilized group solidarity among workers. In a survey of collective protest and strike in the railway sector in the nineteenth century, Ian Kerr underlines the importance of a range of factors—violence, poor conditions, non-payment of wages, and such like—in encouraging solidarity among workers during the pre-history of trade unionism.[158] But he also shows how caste and regional solidarities could cut across class and drive some of these conflicts, prompting Curzon to suggest that 'the railways must mix up races and religions' while recruiting.[159] While the still rather thin literature on working-class protest in the nineteenth century tends to focus on the industrial sector, it is important to recognize the remarkable evidence of communitarian ties in protest action among manual-labour groups in non-industrial

[156] *ARCM for 1866*, p. 6.

[157] Bazaars such as Ranee's Postah owned by the Rajah of Burdwan, and the new Postah Bazar owned by Baboo Rajendra Mullick were among those that posed problems. *ARCM for 1867*, pp. 10–11.

[158] Ian J. Kerr, 'Working Class Protest in 19th Century India: Example of Railway', *Economic and Political Weekly* 20, no. 4 (26 January 1985): PE34–PE40.

[159] Cited in Kerr, 'Working Class Protest in 19th Century India', PE38. Curzon was reacting to a particularly successful series of strikes by Brahmin signallers between 1897 and 1899.

sectors of the urban economy.[160] This is especially necessary as the overwhelming and enduring reality of the informal sector in Indian urban economies seems to have bypassed the attention of most scholarship.[161]

In fact, there is much evidence of parallel structures of command and control existing in the city, especially within occupational groups and trades, which were beyond the pale of laws and rules recognized by the government and local administration. Professional and trade disputes seem to have been frequently settled by intimidation and violence among scavengers, bricklayers, and other groups.[162] Street brawls and rioting among rival groups of carters were reported even in the early decades of the twentieth century.[163] In a sensational case in 1897, reported in the *Bengalee*, a Marwari man was waylaid in Harrison Road and severely beaten by men with lathis. It appears that they had been hired by a distant relative, following a disagreement and a prolonged court case over the settlement of accounts between two other businessmen.[164]

Rival bazaars were often in dispute with each other. Motilal Seal had originally purchased the Dharamtala Bazar from a certain Mr Jackson, but experienced difficulty in re-establishing it. Strong opposition was offered by Ananda Narayan Ghose who attempted

[160] For Bengal, these studies are focused on the jute industry. See Dipesh Chakrabarty, 'Communal Riots and Labour', *Past and Present* 91 (May, 1981): 140–69; Ranajit Dasgupta, 'Structure of the Labour Market in Colonial India', *Economic and Political Weekly* 16, nos 44/46 (November, 1981): 1781–806.

[161] A notable exception of course is the work of Jan Breman. See Jan Breman, 'A Dualistic Labour System? A Critique of the "Informal Sector" Concept', *Economic and Political Weekly* part 1, 11, no. 48 (27 November 1976): 1870–6; part 2, 11, no. 49 (4 December 1976): 1905–8; part 3, 11, no. 50 (11 December 1976): 1933–9; and his *Footloose Labour: Working in India's Informal Economy* (Cambridge: Cambridge University Press, 1996), pp. 5–7.

[162] *ARPC, 1893*, p. 11.

[163] Seventeen cases of rioting and unlawful assembly were reported among carters, who were regarded as 'a turbulent section of the population'. *ARPC, 1911*, p. 12.

[164] *ARPC, 1897*, p. 6. Also see the *Bengalee*, 3 July 1897.

to establish a rival bazaar called Anandabazar, resulting in fights between rival *lathial* (armed mercenary) groups.[165] Another armed fight broke out between a more established bazaar called Simla Bazar (started originally under a Simul tree) and a newer one that came to be known as Chhatubabur Bazar. The latter began life from 1882 onwards on open ground owned by Chhatubabu, an aristocrat, where fisherfolk and vegetable sellers used to temporarily occupy space between autumn and winter. Over time it acquired a semi-permanent nature and threatened the fortunes of the older Simla market.[166]

Perhaps the best known of the contemporary bazaar rivalries is that between the well-known Dharamtala Bazar and the newly established Municipal or Hogg Market, named after the corporation chairman, Stuart Hogg, in 1873–4. The Dharamtala market, then under the ownership of Hiralal Sil, was a thriving bazaar making huge profits, its cost in 1873 estimated as 12 lakh rupees.[167] Contemporary Bengali opinion affirmed that the Dharamtala butchers formed a critical group in the competition and the success of the new market depended heavily on them.[168] In fact, the new market had been set up to ensure that only meat from regulated abattoirs—and therefore, of acceptable standards for the consumption of the European community in Calcutta—could be provisioned there. The corporation's tight supervision of the market would enable just that.

But there was a catch. For Hogg's plan to work, it necessitated a simultaneous move by the butchers of Dharamtala—from whom

[165] Kissory Chund Mitter, *Mutty Lal Seal* (Calcutta: Toolat, 1993; original edition Calcutta, 1869), p. 16,

[166] Simla Bazar disappeared when Bethune College purchased the land on which it used to operate. Mahendranath Dutta, *Kolikatar Purano Kahini O Pratha*, pp. 59–60.

[167] Anon., *The Battle of the Markets: Bajarer Ladai* (Calcutta: Smith Co. Press, 1873), p. 7.

[168] In the pamphlets, thus, the vendor selling aubergines is paid two rupees to secure his loyalty, and the vendor selling potatoes fifty, while the butchers are paid 300–700 rupees. Anon., *The Battle of the Markets*, pp. 2–4.

Europeans had always obtained high quality meat—to the new market.[169] When this proved difficult, Hogg bought the Dharamtala market to stop it from being a competitor.[170] But the rivalry, while it lasted, was widely reported in both the vernacular and English press and debated in vernacular pamphlet dramas of the time. The various versions and interpretations in circulation were highly polarized.

The English side blamed the *daroga* or inspector of the Dharamtala market for forcibly extracting agreements from its vendors binding them to his market for the next five years. Apparently most complied, with the exception of the butchers. Led by Mullah Gholam Ghous, they refused to give in. When two of them were then expelled from the market in December 1873, the rest of the butchers threatened to leave en masse. They were housed temporarily on open ground opposite the market and rehoused in the new Municipal Market when it opened a few weeks later.[171]

The contending version offered by Bengalis accused the daroga of the Municipal Market of accosting the vendors of the Dharamtala Bazar and forcing them to resettle in the new market. The Bengali pamphlets portray vendors of the Dharamtala market seeking the protection of the owner, Hiralal Shil, who promises armed guards to them. The pamphlets also report other illegal means employed by Hogg, such as increasing taxes to pay for the new market, getting the municipality to cover the costs of the inaugural party for Europeans, and bribing and intimidating shop and stall owners to move to his new market.[172] This was an impression echoed in

169 But official literature offers another version. Apparently, situated as the Dharamtala market was at the corner of Dharamtala Street and Chowringhee Road and hemmed in by houses on all sides, the need was felt for a bigger and more accessible bazaar. The plan was thus approved for a new market to be opened between Jaun Bazar and Lindsay Street. *ARCM, 1871*, pp. 6–7.

170 D. Ray, *Debganer Martye Agaman*, pp. 289, 291–2. The Municipal Market was renamed Hogg Market in 1903 after the retirement of Stuart Hogg as municipal commissioner. Sur, *Tinsho Bochhorer Kolkata*, p. 158.

171 *ARCM for 1874*, pp. 8–9.

172 Surendranath Bandyopadhyay, *Great Market War Orthat Pradhan Bajarer Ladai* (Calcutta, n.d.); Anon., *The Battle of the Markets.*

contemporary local newspapers. The *Biswadut* thus accused Hogg of drawing on public funds to counter the pressures from Hiralal Shil.[173]

The pamphlet dramas seemed to suggest a bhadralok–nationalist critique of the municipality's actions as well. There is a damning indictment of Hogg by the Indian Justices of Peace, such as Rajendralal Mitra and Krishnadas Pal, who refuse to sanction the extra twenty thousand rupees that Hogg asks for. The same figures also regard the setting up of the Canning Market and Tramways a waste of public money. The crushing burden of the city's improvement on the rate-payer is repeatedly underlined.[174]

* * *

The institution of modern ways of living and being in the city drawing largely on the British metropolitan experience impacted fundamentally on the lives of Calcutta's inhabitants in the late nineteenth and early twentieth centuries. Municipal regulation intruded on people's livelihoods, mobility, and even intimate bodily habits. But the streets that emerged as the principal sites for the implementation of the new urban regime were also the most potent locations for its resistance. The city's residents were less impressed it would seem by the enthusiasm professed by the City Fathers. As milkmen, scavengers, hackney-carriage drivers, and householders challenged the regulations, they were also grappling with phenomenal changes in their own conceptions of space, sanitation, ritual, and authority. In the process, a new urban public was being shaped that could question the state and negotiate its own rights in the civic sphere, a development that is discernible across many social levels. It was the city which made it possible, by bringing an urban public together which was increasingly finding a common antagonist in the colonial state—a point to be further explored in Chapter 6.

173 *Biswadut*, 7 April, in *Indian Newspaper Reports (Bengal), 1874–75*, week ending 17 April 1875.

174 Anon., *The Battle of the Markets*, pp. 27–8.

5

Criminality, Class, and Moral Anxieties

Calcutta by the late nineteenth century represented the quintessential city of 'forgery, cheating and lies'.[1] It was even gaining a darker reputation for more physical violence and murder, with anonymity in a bustling city providing the perfect cover for criminal activity. This chapter investigates the possibilities opened up by crime in the new metropolis and how crime in turn shaped the urban sphere. Examining criminal activities in the city as recoverable from police reports and police diaries affords glimpses of a city being reordered by its material wealth, social aspirations, and moral attitudes. Criminal activities both defined and challenged the normative urban civic, familial, and moral order and offered a choice of lifestyle to the city's residents. The educated middle class and the colonial government joined hands in stamping out such corruption and crime as they saw fit, thus propping themselves up as the moral guardians of the new urban community. But the tremendous lure of ill-gotten fortunes posed considerable challenges to the securing of normative social hierarchies. The surge of crimes

[1] *'Jal, juachuri ar mithye kotha, ei tin niye Kolkata.'*

among the seemingly respectable shook up earlier strangleholds of moral authority, opening up these groups to public scrutiny and critique. Taken together, such cases disrupted both the traditional stereotypes that dominated earlier police imaginaries as well as received social geographies of the city that demarcated troubled areas from untroubled ones.

Police diaries written, published, and serialized (*Darogar Daptar*, 1892–1904), by a Bengali policeman and detective, Priyanath Mukhopadhyay, offer in-depth social insight into the world of criminals in the city, underlining in the process his own investment as a bhadralok in his investigations. The pages of the *Daptar* proved an important discursive space for sharing news and views on crime, highlighting the values and priorities of the changing urban society. Crime stories are significant for me as they point towards newer social configurations that were no longer wholly shaped by the traditional demarcations of class and poverty. The connections between social and moral decline in urban settings were not so straightforward anymore at the turn of the twentieth century. While such stories would have unleashed social and moral anxieties for the upwardly mobile and established classes, they would have also to a certain extent challenged the self-representations of the respectable and middling groups.

Anonymity, Opportunity, and Crime in the New Urban Order

Crime confirmed the image of Calcutta in popular perception as an anonymous place that fostered the loosening of domestic, neighbourly, and community ties. While on the one hand, the anonymity of the city allowed the shaking off of older, often clannish ties of community and family, on the other hand, it encouraged the formation of new ones of avarice, opportunism, and self-aggrandizement. Even in crimes where the victim was known to the perpetrator, the compulsions of a harsh urban environment rendered their relationship disaggregated and impersonal. Coupled with this, desire for material goods in a rapidly growing consumerist culture acted as an overpowering incentive for crimes by non-professionals.

A recent study of crime in nineteenth-century Calcutta traces back its antecedents to the days of the East India Company in the eighteenth century.[2] For the earlier part of the nineteenth century and for the greater part of the eighteenth century, crime was knowable and visible. Earlier dacoities had been bolder and more dramatic in nature. Legendary dacoits were well known to the police and admired by the local population for their daring exploits.[3] Further visibility of crime was ensured by means of public naming and shaming. Culprits would be driven around in carts and their crimes announced by beating tom-toms. Public hangings and brandings by means of hot iron too were not unknown.[4] Mid-century onwards, the print media could be harnessed in virulent campaigns against noted criminals, aligning readerships into opinion camps and offering extra-juridical but equally important social verdicts on important cases.

Following vigilant policing, clearing of jungles, and a strategic redesigning of Calcutta that afforded better protection to the capital,[5] the nature of crime in the city underwent a fundamental change. To begin with, crime went underground and became more specialized, with professionals acting either on their own or in small groups. Break-ins and burglaries became so rampant by the late 1860s, especially in the commercial sector, that they began to be listed prominently alongside murders and culpable

[2] Sumanta Banerjee, *Crime and Urbanization: Calcutta in the Nineteenth Century* (New Delhi: Tulika Books, 2006).

[3] Some kind of 'social banditry' seems to have been in vogue. Those like Roghu and Bishe Dakat (dacoit) apparently sent prior warnings to their victims, usually much-disliked rural landlords or zamindars, and later distributed the spoils among the local population.

[4] Sumanta Banerjee, *Crime and Urbanization*, p. 18. In one case, five convicted burglars were sentenced to be hanged in a bazaar close to the house where the crime had been committed by way of setting an example. See pp. 29–30.

[5] Business houses were shifted further west to a more protected area—in what is known today as Clive Street—which formed the commercial centre of the city.

homicide in police reports. In 1872, for instance, recorded burglaries in Calcutta and its suburbs grossed at 235.[6]

Godowns and cotton merchants had become targets as more cash could be found here.[7] Police reports accused businessmen of being lackadaisical—for employing people without checking their credentials, for not taking interest in subsequent proceedings after informing the police, regarding their loss with stoical indifference, and locking up their shops at dusk with only a country-made padlock.[8] Residential houses were also attractive and house-breakers over time emerged as experts in picking locks.[9] Ranging from simple burglaries, which were committed by cutting the mat walls or the string that fastens the door of a house, to entering the houses of Europeans posing as servants, there emerged a range of sub-specializations over time, commensurate with the thriving business of house break-ins in the city.[10] In addition to the regular professionals, there are other instances of non-professionals operating as lone individuals as in the impressive case of a house-breaking and theft in Bowbazar Street where a man made off with money and valuables from a poddar's shop and could not be traced.[11]

[6] *ARPC, 1872*, p. 21.

[7] *ARPC, 1867*, pp. 6–7.

[8] *ARPC, 1875*, p. 6; *ARPC 1872*, p. 22.

[9] The terms *pheeter kormo* or *geela jharrah* were used for housebreakings using false keys, with expertise among native picklocks functioning in direct contrast to the hopelessly bad quality of native padlocks. *ARPC, 1872*, p. 22. For an interesting account of how burglars managed to continuously innovate with the help of technology, see Sumanta Banerjee, 'Urban Technology and the Changing Forms of Crime in Early Colonial Calcutta', *Social Scientist* 38, nos 3/4 (March–April 2010): 25–36.

[10] See *ARPC, 1872*, p. 22, for different terminologies in vogue for such micro specializations such as *phoot* (quick job) and *rynee* (doing a European's house).

[11] *ARPC, 1876*, p. 7. After befriending the poddar and renting a small room close to his shop, the burglar had managed to cut through a wood and brick partition to reach the money changer's shop.

The commercial sector in the city encountered a range of regular thefts. Carters, coolies, and hackney-men stole goods entrusted in their care.[12] There occurred routine stealing of cargo goods by drivers of bullock carts, who changed the original registration tin plates, disposed of the goods in the suburbs or railway stations, and then returned to their masters with the proper registration number restored. Substituting of licence plates with the branding of cart numbers onto its woodwork did not prove successful, as cart-men began branding their own fictitious numbers to avoid detection.[13] Theft of cloth, copper, and other goods from agency houses—with men posing as coolies and making away with bags of money that banks required them to carry, wholesale thefts of bales of goods when left in exposed places prior to carting or shipping—led to serious losses and proved a headache to the police. A range of indigenous terms in vogue lent pedigree to and proved the intensity of the crimes.[14]

Obscurity provided the perfect cover for all kinds of cons, financial and material. Thus, there were the *ghat marra* or those who stole people's clothes and belongings as they bathed in the river ghats in Calcutta,[15] and the practice of drugging new arrivals in Calcutta after luring them to the suburbs and then robbing them.[16] A string of specifically urban cons and thefts with imaginative schemes that were prevalent in the city is provided by S. Wauchope, Officiating Commissioner of Police, in the department's annual report for 1872.[17] These ranged from pickpocketing

[12] *ARPC, 1860–61* and *1861–62*, p. 6.

[13] *ARPC, 1889*, p. 7; *ARPC, 1879*, pp. 7–8.

[14] Thus, carter crimes were *churkee marrah*; pilfering was *chichkay, phoser kormo*, or *chootkee kormo*; money loots involving coolies were *doee er kormo*; and wholesale theft of goods from storage was *dhole marrah*. *ARPC 1872*, pp. 22–3.

[15] *ARPC, 1859–60* and *1860–61*, p. 5.

[16] *ARPC, 1889*, p. 5.

[17] *ARPC, 1872*, pp. 18–28. Such crimes are detailed in a series of police reports towards the end of the nineteenth century, which shows that figures were on the rise. See another police commissioner thus reporting that 'a considerable number of professional cheats obtain a decent livelihood by preying on the unwary and simple in Calcutta'. *ARPC, 1877*, pp. 9–10.

(*pokit tolah* or *geera kattah*) and petty pilfering to theft of ornaments (*bauer jharra*), and *cheeteer kormo*, 'a clever, sleight-of-hand trick in which the performer selects a country bumpkin, induces him to show him his money, and substitutes double pice for rupees'. The last mentioned trick was apparently 'carried out to perfection by Calcutta professionals in the mofussil'.[18] In *jeeb budlee*, a well-dressed man recruited a vagabond from the streets as a servant and then went on a shopping spree, finally taking off with the unpaid for goods using some pretext, and leaving his servant behind as hostage, never to return.[19]

More stunning crimes were performed under the cover of respectability and ostentation. The most common kinds were those of mock nawabs parading in villas outside the suburbs, *nilamwalas* doing mock auctions, non-existent companies trading in goods and money, and *tupkawalas* selling brass items as gold to unwary strangers.[20] Occasionally, some sensational cases received momentary attention, such as that of the well known diamond merchant, A.M. Jacob, defrauding the Nizam of Hyderabad of about 20 lakhs of rupees regarding the purchase of the 'Imperial diamond'.[21] Setting up of false mercantile establishments, encouraging people to deliver goods and then absconding with them was a category of crime that required extraordinary levels of police intervention as we shall see further.

In the absence of an established culture of banking, people preferred to store cash and valuables in their own premises or carry it on their person. But such weakness proved costly as in the case of a durwan or gatekeeper who was murdered by the gardener of an uninhabited house in Garden Reach in 1887. The murdered individual, a resident of north India, had been accumulating his cash savings and was about to depart to his native village with the money.[22]

[18] *ARPC, 1872*, pp. 22–3.

[19] *ARPC 1872*, p. 23. More urban cons and theft styles are reported in *ARPC 1878*, pp. 22–3.

[20] *ARPC, 1877*, pp. 9–10; *ARPC, 1889*, p. 6; *ARPC, 1872*, p. 23.

[21] *ARPC 1891*, p. 11.

[22] *ARPC, 1887*, p. 7.

Those handling money in the commercial sector and transporting large amounts of cash from one part of the city to another were particularly vulnerable. A collecting clerk for an ironmonger carrying 500 rupees in cash was accosted and attacked in 1862 by a gang of up-countrymen with swords and sharp weapons during the evening. He died instantly. In another case, the same year, a *gomasta* (commercial bill-collector) was murdered by a colleague in the same shawl business in a pre-planned enterprise.[23]

In a particularly unfortunate case, a reliable postman who went missing with registered post and money orders worth 2,000 rupees was later found murdered in a flimsy residential building in Burrabazar. The suspect, Gangabhushan alias Chinsukram, proved elusive but was finally tracked down in a room above a paan shop in the courtesan quarter. His real name was Ramsaran, and he had used decoys to trick the police more than once. Although proving quite a match for the police, he was later arrested, convicted, and sent to the Andamans with a life sentence. The nerve-centre of the trading community in the city ironically proved a good cover for Ramsaran who took up several temporary residences, adopted aliases, and frequently changed location in the busy commercial district. The name suggests he was probably a migrant from northern India, although it is not clear if he had a regular profession in the city.[24]

Neighbours, relatives, and employees are seen as ruthlessly preying on their victims. Cases such as a relative turning up to live with a family from Gorakhpur and then murdering the old couple with a plan to rob the family grain shop were typical.[25] Servants, though often unfairly stereotyped in domestic manuals, constituted one category of such mobile criminality, swiftly moving from one employment to another and untraceable in the absence of vigilant

[23] *ARPC, 1862*, Appendix A, pp. i–iv.

[24] Priyanath Mukhopadhyay,'Daak Chor' [Postal Thief] (Falgun 1301 B.S. 1894) in *Darogar Daptar*, edited by Arun Mukhopadhyay (Calcutta: Ananda Publishers, 2004), vol. 1, pp.345–61. Priyanath, who was a police officer, refers to the event actually happening in May 1883, about a decade earlier.

[25] *ARPC, 1894*, p. 7.

recordkeeping by households.[26] Cases of servants earning the trust of a household and then making off with family ornaments were known.[27] It was even possible for outsiders to acquire access to the family house via conniving servants.[28]

There are also numerous instances of young women and children being brutally murdered for gold ornaments and jewellery from the 1880s onwards.[29] Police reports reveal, for instance, a ruthless case of a child bride being murdered by neighbours and then buried under the floor of their house along with the ornaments.[30] It was common for children to be lured away from the safety of their homes, murdered for their ornaments, and then drowned in the many tanks scattered throughout Calcutta.[31] Police complained repeatedly of children being exposed to considerable risk by being allowed to play in the streets wearing gold and silver ornaments.[32]

Crime, thus, offered easy avenues to impoverished and marginal groups, affording opportunities for their survival and material betterment. As we shall see in the next section, it bred professional criminals and encouraged an upscaling of violence. In addition, criminal activities considerably loosened the obligatory ties of kin, clan, and community in a city of displaced populations. The anonymous interface between perpetrator and victim proved

[26] Housekeeping manuals meant for the consumption of middle-class housewives constantly warned them against servants, thus naturalizing the attributes of dishonesty and criminality in them. See Swapna Banerjee, *Men, Women and Domestics: Articulating Middle-class Identity in Colonial Bengal* (New Delhi: Oxford University Press, 2004), pp. 176–7.

[27] *ARPC, 1882*, p. 12; *ARPC, 1979*, p. 10.

[28] Thus, in one instance, two residents of the United Provinces made off with 3,000 rupees from the office room of the Head Clerk of Alipore Zoo. In accessing the keys to the cupboard where the cash-box was kept, they earned the help of a servant in lieu of a share of the stolen money. The criminals were later traced to their native villages and caught. See P. Mukhopadhyay, 'Chatur Chor' [Sly Thief] (Agrahayan 1301 B.S. 1894), *Darogar Daptar*, vol. 1, pp. 304–16.

[29] *ARPC 1892*, p. 11.

[30] *ARPC, 1874*, pp. 4–5; *ARPC, 1879*, p. 10.

[31] See for example *ARPC, 1891*, p. 12; *ARPC, 1888*, p. 6; *ARPC, 1899*, p. 4.

[32] *ARPC, 1888*, p. 8.

instrumental over time in encouraging aggressive collectivities that were riotous and could attack, burn, and kill when mobilized, as we shall see in Chapter 6.

Constructing the 'Criminal': Class and Ethnographic Taxonomies

The municipal administration and police in Calcutta in the nineteenth century was overwhelmed by criminal activities and struggled to maintain law and order in this important commercial centre. The structure and attitudes of policing, however, reveal more about perceptions of crime rather than their actual suppression. In the official imagination, and borrowing very much from metropolitan policing ideologies, the rot lay within the underclasses,[33] and mid-nineteenth century onwards there was a feverish desire to physically banish unruliness and crime to the margins of the ordered urban space.[34]

As a colonial metropolis with an immense resource base, that Calcutta should experience its fair share of thefts and murders is not surprising. But 1870s onwards, there appears to have occurred a significant rise in house break-ins and burglaries as seen above.[35] The police blamed this on the increasing number of up-country coolies employed in the suburbs—in the works in the port commissioner's docks and the extension of the Kakurgachie and Eastern Bengal State Railway—and the influx of many 'bad characters' and thieves operating among them. The closure of the jute mills at Garden Reach throwing about 4,000 labourers out of work, it was suggested, had also led to an increase

[33] See, for example, Judith Walkowitz, *City of Dreadful Delight: Narratives of Sexual Danger in Late-Victorian London* (Chicago: University of Chicago Press, 1992).

[34] Thus Chief Magistrate Elliott complained that he was powerless to do anything about the 'bad characters' under the surveillance of the police, and that if he had his way would have sent all 'vagrants'—indigenous and European back to their respective homelands. *ARPC, 1854*, p. 4.

[35] See *ARPC, 1872*.

in crime.[36] At around the same time, another stand was taken on crime in the city: the identification of a 'professional criminal class'[37]—described as 'pests of the society' who should be severely punished to deter them from further criminal activities.[38]

The idea of the habitual criminal crystallized materially in the form of registers of 'known offenders' kept by the police from about 1875–6 onwards.[39] Records were maintained both at the police stations and suburban courts, and subsidiary registers tracked subsequent movements of offenders after release.[40] The mid-nineteenth century official terminology for this category is 'bad characters' or *budmashes*.[41] It is significant that while European criminals or those with criminal propensities in India were branded as 'vagrants' or 'loafers'—a rather neutral term suggesting peripatetic, usually unemployed individuals who could be reformed by workhouse regimes—the same category of perceived troublemakers among the indigenous were 'budmashes', a far more loaded term implying miscreants. Anthropometry and fingerprinting, introduced into police work in 1892 and 1899 respectively, further systematized the classification of native urban criminals along

[36] *ARPC, 1907*, pp. 8–9. Also see *ARPC, 1886*, p. 11.

[37] See lieutenant governor's report in *ARPC, 1902*, p. 2, and *ARPC, 1903*, p. 1.

[38] Lieutenant Governor's report in *ARPC, 1902*, p. 2.

[39] No doubt this was very much in keeping with the spirit of the recent Criminal Tribes Act of 1871, which saw the registration, surveillance, and control of nomadic tribes identified as 'criminal' in India, with the aim of turning them into settled, agrarian, and loyal revenue-paying subjects of the British Empire. See Anand A. Yang, *Crime and Criminality in British India* (Tucson: University of Arizona Press, 1985).

[40] *ARPC, 1854*, p. 4; *ARPC, 1876*, p. 19.

[41] *ARPC, 1876*, p. 21. The classification of criminals along class and ethnographic lines in wider and other colonial Indian contexts has been studied by scholars. See, for example, Andrea Major, 'State and Criminal Tribes in Colonial Punjab: Surveillance, Control and the Reclamation of the Dangerous Classes', *Modern Asian Studies* 33, no. 3 (1999): 657–88; M. Radhakrishna, *Dishonoured by History: 'Criminal Tribes' and British Colonial Policy* (New Delhi: Orient Longman, 2001).

ethnological lines.[42] Fingerprinting, when finally instituted in the city's policing, was prolifically used in solving crimes against property. Within two years the numbers of offenders who had to provide impressions had doubled, reaching over two thousand.[43]

The location of thugs and criminals residing within the lower depths of society in colonial India was intimately tied up with concepts of caste, class, community, and official knowledge of these categories. The Annual Police Reports for the Town of Calcutta, thus, attempt to distinguish between different religious communities in their role as criminals, with one police commissioner claiming that Muslims were twice as likely to offend as Hindus, although the figures do not bear this out.[44] There is also an explicit association made between poverty and faith in this regard, especially within the limits of the city. As the commissioner goes on to note, '... the poorer classes, such as coolies, carters, khalassies [sailors], &c. [*sic*] which contribute most largely to the criminal population are to a great extent composed of the adherents of Islam.'[45] In fact, statistics on thefts and house break-ins reveal Hindus outnumbering Muslims in both categories.[46] Taking a typical report on overall convictions in the second half of the nineteenth century, we find 4,436 Muslims convicted in respect of 5,333 Hindus.[47]

These classificatory schemes were not just confined within official circles but found wider resonance in Bengali society. Writing in the 1890s, the real-life policeman Priyanath

[42] *ARPC, 1893*, p. 18. Fingerprinting was in fact initiated in Bengal under Edward Henry, Inspector-General of Police for the province. Edmund Cox, *Police and Crime in India* (London, 1911), p. 209. Also see Chandak Sengoopta, *Imprint of the Raj: How Fingerprinting Was Born in Colonial India* (London: Macmillan, 2003) Chapter 5, pp. 120–70.

[43] *ARPC, 1900*, pp. 3–4; *ARPC, 1903*, p. 3.

[44] This was, in fact, C.T. Metcalf acting as Officiating Police Commissioner in 1875. *ARPC, 1876*, p. 13.

[45] *ARPC, 1876*, p. 13.

[46] Thus, for theft, only 19 Muslims were convicted as compared to 25 Hindus, while for house break-ins, 425 Muslims figured as compared to 449 Hindus. *ARPC, 1872*, p. 4.

[47] *ARPC, 1878*, p. 3.

Mukhopadhyay's crime stories, serialized and extremely popular, pitched such social bracketing at evidently empathetic readers. Speaking of the infamous coffee houses in the northern part of the city, he writes:

> Mecchuabazar has a lot of large temporary tiled huts in one area. The interior of these have wooden benches configured around an empty space at the centre with Chinese porcelain utensils interspersing this arrangement. Muslims from all parts of the world ... sit on these benches before their coffee filled porcelain cups. It is impossible to find civilised or educated people here. This area has been established for the entertainment, and this coffee prepared for the enjoyment of those Muslims who have been banished from their own lands for their criminality—whether be it Arabia, Iran, Persia, Africa, Punjab or [even] Calcutta. Who else will pay 8 annas for what is worth 2? This is the place for those who have ease in earning money [via ill-gotten means], those who can crack open skulls with a smile, those who are sought after to settle rivalries between zamindars [as mercenaries], those who can be hired by clients to insult respectable men, those who do not despise robbery or accept stolen goods, those who defy the police and the jail, and for whom the jails are ever ready.[48]

The relentless search for ethnographic taxonomies of crime is also evident in the caste- and region-based identification of criminal 'gangs' operating in the city, responsible for dacoity, house-breaking, and theft. The Bedyas, a central-Indian tribe relocated and interred in Dacca, on their release were believed to be responsible for innumerable burglaries and dacoities committed in the suburbs of Calcutta in the 1860s.[49] Even four decades later, such tools of nomenclature seemed operative. Several groups nabbed in 1904 thus find their way into reports as, 'The Dome Gang (9, residents of Benares); The Brahmin Gang (12, residents of UP);

[48] P. Mukhopadhyay, 'Jamalaye Ferta Manush' [The Man Who Came Back from the Dead] (Jaistha 1299 B.S. 1892), *Darogar Daptar*, vol. 1, pp. 15–16.

[49] The Bedyas were thought to be skilled in the art of removing ornaments from the arms and feet of sleeping women without waking them. *ARPC 1863*, p. 6.

The Bhur Gang (34, residents of UP)' with their caste rather than crime being used as the classificatory tool.[50] Interestingly, criminality from the start of the twentieth century also became more visibly tied to regions of domicile, as operative in phrases such as 'the Calcutta–Howrah gang of 10, and the Urya gang of 13'.[51]

The Calcutta Police Commissioner, W.M. Souttar, in the annual police report of 1878, further reiterated racialized spaces in the operation of crime by locating petty commercial pilfering by local boatmen and carters in areas skirting the Strand Road to the north of the city; heavy thefts, forgeries, and embezzlements by indigenous carriers centred in Burrabazar and its neighbourhood; and Burmese, Chinese, Jews, Armenians, Moguls, Malays, Arabs, Kabulees, 'a very Babel of tongues', in Bowbazar committing acts of violence. In the European quarters—mostly in the Collingabazar and Taltollah area—men specializing in acts of intimidation, extortion and theft abounded, alongside 'a disreputable set of Jews—Russian, German, and Greek'—who lived off the earnings of their imported European prostitutes. Red-light areas were automatically seen as dens for criminals, with prostitutes living cheek by jowl with petty thieves, and such like. Authorities were keen to impose a certain level of public decorum on prostitutes, to contain them within certain areas, and to break up collusions between prostitutes and thieves. This was partly achieved with the Contagious Diseases Act of 1868.[52]

The educated Bengali middle class lent credence to such official imaginations. Reminiscences of Kshitindranath Tagore, from the prominent Jorasanko household in an area adjacent to the notorious sections of Chitpore Road and Mechhuabazar, recalls the excess of riotous seamen and prostitutes in the area in his childhood days. The black sailors in particular were looked upon with much fear. Kshitindranath remembered how, as a child, taking a narrow lane connecting Mechhuabazar to Colootollah, he came upon a group of

[50] *ARPC, 1904*, pp. 9–10.

[51] *ARPC, 1905*, p. 12. Three gangs of professional thieves nabbed in 1907, operating in the Northern Division of the city, are also located similarly. It is reported that they came from north India, Malda, and Jessore. *ARPC, 1907*, pp. 8–9.

[52] *ARPC, 1878*, p. 23.

them drinking tea in a roadside stall. Too scared to retreat, he recalls holding his breath and rushing past them towards his destination.[53]

In reality, such neat spatializations and categorizations did not work. The city grew in an unpredictable manner, the ranks of 'criminals' swelled with an even greater influx of migrant population who came to the city to work in the mills and factories, and newer categories of crime blurred the easy divisions between the classes. Notorious red-light districts also simultaneously housed aristocratic residents, and indeed, some stately mansions were rented out to prostitutes who openly carried on their trade within the premises. Even the police themselves admitted that mofussil criminals, operating in the small towns and the countryside, were easy to catch because they operated in fixed localities, to which they were presumably bound by ties of caste and community. By contrast, in Calcutta a thief or burglar

> ... has neither home nor surroundings, [spending] one night at a chundoo shop, then at a ghat; now with a prostitute, then in a lodging house with aliases innumerable. Concealed during the day like a jackal, he issues forth on dark nights and is very difficult to catch.[54]

The construction of the Howrah Bridge and railways, in addition, facilitated rapid movement of criminals.[55] Nor did criminals usually operate in 'gangs'. Most 'serious' crimes were committed by individuals, supported by a local network of accomplices, usually known to the police. Inadequacies in police understandings of the topology of crime were to cost the administration dearly with the rise of political activities in the city from the start of the twentieth century onwards.[56]

[53] Kshitindranath Tagore, *Kolikatay Chalafera: Sekale aar Ekale* (Calcutta: Adi Barhmo Samaj Press, 1930), pp. 40, 44.

[54] *ARPC, 1874*, p. 18. Also, *ARPC, 1875*, p. 17, for similar comments.

[55] *ARPC, 1854–55*, p. 6.

[56] It is interesting that the earlier revolutionary activities in the city were traced to 'gangs' in police records—similar to the ethnic groupings seen above—pointing to the limited scope and relative inflexibility of contemporary police parlance in designating crime and criminals.

Disciplinary structures in the city were thus far from all powerful and severely lacking in more accurate and sensitive operational knowledge of their environs.[57] As we shall see, they were challenged, stretched, and openly flouted by indigenous discourses and parallel understandings of jurisprudence, rights, and ethics. In addition, the peculiar hybridized space of the modern metropolitan city in the colony did not lend itself to easy categorization. The inadequate and obdurate functioning of the colonial police administration perhaps finds its most abiding representation in the memoirs of a Bengali sub-inspector of the Detective Branch serving the Calcutta force at the turn of the nineteenth century, examined below. Despite the structural limitations under which we must consider the reminiscences of an ex-colonial officer, the narrative is remarkable for highlighting the endless snags and follies in an otherwise powerful arm of administration.

Middle-class Criminals and the City: Bourgeoisfication of Crime

While the specific class construction of criminals continue to feature in police records along such predictable lines down to the early twentieth century, migrant workers and European vagabonds were gradually being joined by more sophisticated law breakers from within the bhadralok ranks. The administration was firm in dealing with them, although themes of genteel poverty, unfortunate waywardness, or terrible moral dilemmas markedly tempered the representations of such criminals in police records and crime fiction alike. But the increased visibility of middle-class crimes in the courtroom and serialized police tales, journals, and gossip, reconfigured lines of respectability in the popular imagination (as seen previously in the 'scandal' cases). Identification and public naming and shaming of bhadralok frauds and forgeries loosened up the moral and social hold of

[57] Colonial Calcutta offers thus a very different prototype to colonial Delhi as studied by Legg. Stephen Legg, *Spaces of Colonialism: Delhi's Urban Governmentalities* (Oxford: Blackwell Publishing, 2004).

this class.[58] While lower-class criminals were well known to the police as 'habituals', middle-class criminals came to be regarded as 'professionals', specializing in certain domains, and even eliciting a certain degree of respect from the police for their finesse.

Fraudulent firms operated rampantly in the city towards the end of the nineteenth century. One hundred and twenty such bogus firms were found to be functional in Calcutta in 1895 with networks extending as far as Mysore and Bangalore.[59] The proprietors were almost invariably educated Bengalis but the companies operated under European names. Their method was to advertise themselves widely in areas at a considerable distance from Calcutta, offering attractive bargains to customers in lieu of cash to be sent either in advance or on delivery by value-payable parcel post. The victims were sent worthless items by post while the sender absconded with the cash. The address of the firms were usually fictitious or fake, and the residents difficult to trace.[60] A concerted move against the firms was made in 1905 at a higher level and involving the Criminal Investigation Department (CID) based in Simla, which yielded results. Opening up enquiries at the district level encouraged more complainants to come forward and take resort to courts.[61] Prosecutions implicated mostly educated, employed high-caste Hindus, and some Europeans.[62]

Several cases of counterfeiting coins and trademarks can be found in the police reports from the 1870s onwards. In most cases of counterfeiting coins, the basic technique used involved rubbing pice over with quicksilver so as to bear a crude resemblance to

[58] Educated middle-class Bengalis set up societies with the express purpose of self-policing. Thus, the bimonthly journal, *Anusandhan*, appeared in 1887 as an organ of the *Anusandhan Samiti* or the Committee of Inquiry, set up to expose criminals in the previous year. It reported on conning practices in the city and cases of fraud, and claimed to have brought many criminals to justice. Sumanta Banerjee, *Crime and Urbanisation*, pp. 78, 87–9.

[59] *ARPC, 1895*, p. 10.

[60] *ARPC, 1894*, p. 11

[61] *ARPC, 1905*, p. 7.

[62] *ARPC, 1906*, p. 8.

silver money.[63] These were mostly home-bred cottage industries and could be set up using basic technology.[64] Perhaps the most infamous case of the time was that involving Shyamacharan Mukhopadhyay, originally resident of Bakhergunj, who engaged in a profitable coin-forging trade in the 1880s. The circulation of his counterfeit coins had become so rampant that they threatened the circulation of genuine coins in the city. Banks became vigilant and set up a separate department for recording the receipt of forged coins. Innocent users came to be harassed by the police and their premises searched. Shyamacharan used to frequently change his Calcutta residence, worked secretly with a small gang of trusted people (including women), and was immensely crafty in hoodwinking the police. He invariably chose bhadra (gentile) neighbourhoods and was polite and well-spoken in police encounters. After landing on him thrice but unable to find any evidence, the police finally managed to catch him red-handed. Hordes of fake currency, bronze, and iron machines used in forging the coins were found in his house.[65]

Yet another instance of the involvement of the educated in crimes relating to forgery can be traced in the chequered life of an ex-Medical College student who came to Calcutta in 1869 from Chittagong to study Chemistry and, not being able to pay his college fees, honed his recently acquired pharmaceutical skills and applied it to the forging of coins. He served a jail sentence but then returned to the trade with a vengeance. While his cover was that of a perfectly decent gentleman with a day job as a compounder in the Police Hospital, marriage to a 'respectable' widow, and a normal domestic life in his residence at Entally, he had another hidden profession in another location. In a small room in Beniapukur, hired ostensibly for purposes of religious retirement, were discovered a complete set of coining

63 *ARPC, 1871*, p. 2.

64 *ARPC, 1870*, pp. 8–9. Also see P. Mukhopadhyay, 'Stri Ki Purush' [A Man or a Woman?] (Sravan, 1302 B.S. 1895), *Darogar Daptar*, vol. 1, p. 429.

65 P. Mukhopadhyay, 'Kritrim Mudra' [Forged Coins] (Chaitra, 1299 B.S. 1892), *Darogar Daptar*, vol. 1, pp. 38–44.

instruments, moulds, an electroplating battery, chemicals, small bits of silver, and four anna pieces in various stages of completion.[66] Colonial technology could evidently be turned on its head and used to cheat the state which prided itself in being its sole proprietor.

Printing of false currency notes could also be similarly carried on within humble premises using only wooden blocks.[67] Once again regular professions provided cover as in the case of Mahendranath Chatterjee, a musician by occupation, who carried on the business clandestinely within his residence using simple implements.[68] More organized gangs employed the printing press and, because of the conspicuous size of the establishment, operated further away from the city.[69] Again, in these reported cases in the police files, the perpetrators are invariably high-caste, presumably educated Bengalis.

Government officials took advantage of their position for illegal transactions. Many such cases involving high-caste and educated Bengali public servants, such as post office employees, clerks, and other petty service bearers, can be traced in contemporary police reports.[70] One case of forgery involved a financial clerk of Alipore Court who used to convert 'service' postage stamps

[66] *ARPC, 1878*, p. 5.

[67] Currency notes of rupees 5 and 10 were thus being made using a complete set of such simple blocks by Shibu Prasanna Maitra of Sulkea. See *ARPC, 1887*, p. 6. Also see *ARPC, 1889*, p. 9. Priyanath Mukhopadhyay was involved in this case.

[68] A large quantity of paper cut into the size of government currency notes, a water-line plate, and other implements of forgery were found in his house. *ARPC, 1888*, p. 9.

[69] *ARPC, 1897*, p. 8. The forging in this case took place in the village of Mallipota in the Nadia district and involved Hiralal Sircar, Rajani Kant Dutta, and Durga Charan Ballabh. Priyanath reports another case of Motilal Dutta, an elusive forger, who maintained a significant trade using appropriate machinery and materials from his Bakhergunj residence. Dutta's false notes circulated in Calcutta, however, and were used by petty criminals to cheat customers. P. Mukhopadhyay, 'Captain Moti' (Ashad 1302 B.S. 1895), *Darogar Daptar*, vol. 2, pp. 405–18.

[70] See, for example, *ARPC, 1874*, p. 8; *ARPC, 1895*, p. 9.

into more lucrative 'court fees' stamps. The stamps had initially been stolen from the Alipore Jail Press and, using the services of a goldsmith and a dye maker, Baroda Kanta Haldar had managed to transform them. When he ran out of the stolen stamps, Haldar took to converting regular postage stamps to court fees stamps.[71] Another case of a public servant involved in forgery was that of a writer in the Small Cause Court, Harinath Dey, selling fake stamp paper made by gluing old stamps accessed from the record-room on blank paper.[72] Forged documents inducing false payments of large sums of money—such as one involving an employee of the Office of Executive Engineers—were frequently reported and involved laborious investigations although not all could be caught.[73]

A Dangerous City: Anxieties, Aspirations, and Surveillance in a Police Diary

Crime writing draws attention to the ways in which spiralling social aspirations in the city prompted a spate of criminal activities—from fraud to murder—and opened up its deepest recesses. Struck down from its image of a gleaming metropolis, Calcutta, in police annals, is represented as a city of horrific violence and inveterate greed. The popular reception of the city as a vast repository of easily acquirable wealth and a symbol of urban fantasies seem to figure in particular in the lives of poorer migrants who worked and lived in Calcutta under dire circumstances. But it also exposes the desire for material aggrandisement via criminal means among better-off residents, which is frequently seen to be stimulated by Calcutta's urban environment, particularly its pleasure industry—red-light areas, alcohol, and gambling, resulting in treacherous moral quicksand.

[71] *ARPC, 1872*, p. 8.

[72] *ARPC, 1873*, p. 8.

[73] *ARPC, 1876*, p. 9. Another case of an attempt to defraud an insurance company by providing a false death certificate was caught by Rai Jogendra Chandra Mitra, Inspector of the Detective Branch. See *ARPC, 1895*, p. 9.

Scholars have iterated ambivalence in crime writing to criminality and its relation with the dominant social order. The way in which crime literature came to be so eagerly consumed indicates this. The popular appeal of such writing, suggests David Stewart, for instance, in the context of the mid-nineteenth century in America, lies in the way it 'eroticised urban experience' away from the increasingly regimented social order. The exhilaration offered by accounts of the lives of criminals in the darker underbelly of life in the city proved attractive to city-dwellers whose own lives were '... constraining, confining and mind-numbingly dull'.[74] But such transgressive excitement was also balanced by the reader's own desire for safety and security. The genre thus also fed on the fear of crime and of real urban danger.

Calcutta Police Detective Priyanath Mukhopadhyay's monthly serial publication, *Darogar Daptar* or 'Inspector's Files', was issued between 1892 and 1904. Resembling the model of the Vidocq mysteries, these were mostly based on avowedly his own experiences, with some—on his own admittance—being entirely fictional. Priyanath started his early life as an author but then joined the Calcutta Police in 1878 where he served for thirty-three years until 1911.

As the editor-publisher wrote in one of his introductory notes, this was a distinctly European genre that was being offered to Bengali readers for the first time by a home-grown author. Translations of English works were freely available in colonial Calcutta, starting from *Reynold's Mysteries* down to the more recent Poe and Conan Doyle. Priyanath's police tales are sufficiently tinged with this metropolitan influence from across the seas, and Priyanath admits this to his audience: '... for some of the stories I have adopted the form from English and other European stories.'[75]

Priyanath shot to fame in 1889, when he became somewhat of a local celebrity for capturing two notorious European criminals—Warner and Healey—who had proved elusive to the law for some time after committing a series of burglaries and thefts in Calcutta. Following widespread media coverage, Priyanath's popularity was

74 David M. Stewart, 'Cultural Work, City Crime, Reading Pleasure', *American Literary History* 9, no. 4 (1997): 676–701, at 684.

75 A. Mukhopadhyay (ed.), P. Mukhopadhyay, *Darogar Daptar*, Introduction.

further bolstered when he took to writing in later life. Two hundred and six stories in the form of serial publications issued monthly over twelve years, originally from a shop in Sikdarbagan Lane. The monthly issues were between six and forty pages, and cost 3 annas each. The annual subscription rate, including postage, was Rs 1.5.[76] The popularity of the stories is proved by the fact that they were translated into various Indian languages—Assamese, Oriya, Marathi, and others. Fraud authors also tried to fake Priyanath to reap off fringe benefits from his commercial success.

Sukumar Sen claims that *Darogar Daptar* was the first crime fiction to be written in Bengali.[77] But this can be contested. Daroga tales had been around earlier. Girish Chandra Basu's *Sekaler Darogar Kahini* (Daroga Tales from the Past) or *Meanjahn Darogar Ekrarnama* (The Confessions of Meanjahn, Darogah of Police) would be good examples of this inspector-memoir genre, real or otherwise.[78] What sets Priyanath apart was the distinctly urban location of the author in a lot of his narratives. The *Daptar* brought to the surface the seething underbelly of a glittering city, with tales of gruesome murders, petty thefts, burglaries, and conning. Unlike the valiant tales of busting dacoit gangs that the earlier inspectors wrote about, Priyanath's exploits were more about brain than brawn. Crimes committed under the cover of anonymity provided by the city required deductive reasoning, careful combing, and innovative strategies. In the *Daptar*, however, there is less drama and more routine detection, which is time consuming with pure chance often yielding key clues. Detection was a fundamental aspect of his existence in the police force and Priyanath applied himself meticulously to the job.

[76] A. Mukhopadhyay (ed.), P. Mukhopadhyay, *Darogar Daptar*, Introduction. Initially published by Baninath Nandi. Later, proprietor Upendrabhushan Chaudhuri took over in 1899. The compilation studied here has 100 such stories in two volumes, edited by Arun Mukhopadhyay and based on collections in the Hiran Library, Chaitanya Library, and the Bangiya Sahitya Parishad Library of Calcutta, as well as some private collections.

[77] Sukumar Sen, *Crime Kahinir Kalkranti* (Calcutta: Ananda Publishers, 1988), p. 151.

[78] See Girish Chandra Basu, *Sekaler Darogar Kahini*, reprint edition (Calcutta: Pustak Bipani, 1983; originally printed in Nabajivan in 1887–8); Anon., *The Confessions of Meanjahn, Darogah of Police, Dictated by him, Translated by a Mofussilite* (Calcutta, 1869).

Priyanath is quite aware of his movement between fact and fiction as a narrator. Starting off with 'stories', he first backtracks and denies any connection with reality when facing his critics, and then reverts to calling them 'real events'.[79] In addition, he deliberately lets slip comments such as: 'I do not have my eyes on good or bad while writing the truth [readers will have to accept the facts as they are].'[80] It would be difficult to refute that the police tales as narrated by Priyanath are entirely unconnected with actual events. There are several cues to suggest this. To begin with, reference to elaborate and tedious breakdown of routine procedure and events seem to indicate that there was, at some level, a direct transfer from a meticulously maintained police diary to the *Daptar* tales.[81] Priyanath in fact tells us that he maintains the diary under the orders of the *burrasahib* (possibly police commissioner).[82] Second, Priyanath takes great care to blank out the names of living individuals and their descendants as well as residential addresses so as to conceal identities of men and women from 'respectable' classes or prominent individuals. And finally, he refers more than once to both mainstream and second-rank newspapers reporting the crimes narrated by him.

While mostly led by the events that frame him, he is also keen to project his 'detective' persona more prominently. In the English language genre classics of his time, the isolated and alienated detectives are socially consolidated and validated by the use of 'romanticism and intellectualism' by the authors.[83] Unlike Holmes and Dupin, his fictional contemporaries who are fiercely independent,

79 A. Mukhopadhyay (ed.), P. Mukhopadhyay, *Darogar Daptar*, Introduction. Priyanath was thirty-seven years old when he first started writing them.

80 P. Mukhopadhyay, 'Snidhel Chor' [House Boring Thief](Chaitra 1301 B.S. 1894), *Darogar Daptar*, vol. 1, p. 362.

81 There is an actual reference to the writing of his police diary on a daily basis. P. Mukhopadhyay, 'Odbhut Bhikhari' [A Strange Beggar] (Chaitra, 1311 B.S. 1904) in *Darogar Daptar*, vol. 2, p. 526.

82 A. Mukhopadhyay (ed.), P. Mukhopadhyay, *Darogar Daptar*, vol. 2, p. 586.

83 Stephen Knight, *Form and Ideology of Crime Fiction* (London: Macmillan, 1980).

flamboyant, and supremely intelligent figures, Priyanath is quite aware that his work is more routine and mundane. He is a servant of the state, has a larger institutional apparatus to help him, and solves his crimes more by standard police procedure, pure chance, and extraction of confession than a fiendishly clever mind. There is an elaborate style of deductive reasoning—characteristic of the detective-fiction genre—that he repeatedly employs to impress his audience, but they have lost value being applied post facto.[84]

Priyanath followed multiple narrative codes, from crime reportage to social commentary, drama, horror, and detective fiction, drawing on both reader expectations and his own preferences. The police accounts could be representing the state but could also stand apart from it, motivated by their own particular set of moral and social values. While highlighting criminal elements on the margins of society, they could also refer to social injustice and abuse of power at the heart of society, highlighting an alternative sense of moral responsibility.[85]

Unlike his fictional counterparts, Priyanath's less glamorous location gives him empathy, mooring, and a social conscience. Priyanath is a valuable commentator of his time—as a law enforcer, as an educated bhadralok, and as an expert on crime and its causes. His earlier life as the son of a respected Brahmin landlord–merchant in Nadia had given him a strict moral upbringing. The respect commanded by his father in the locality, who was known for his courage, sense of honour, and honesty, inspired the young Priyanath.[86] While he was driven into his profession as a policeman by family misfortunes and not entirely by choice, there is a sense of a mission that drives him. Priyanath projects himself as God-fearing and self-righteous, the moral guardian of society, a model police officer.

[84] See, for example, P. Mukhopadhyay, 'Odbhut Hatya' [Strange Murder], *Darogar Daptar*, vol. 1, pp. 25–6; 'Kripaner Dhon', *Darogar Daptar*, vol. 2, p. 172.

[85] Peter Messent, *The Crime Fiction Handbook* (Chichester: Wiley-Blackwell, 2013), p. 46.

[86] Priyanath Mukhopadhyay, Introduction, 'Tetrish Botshorer Pulish Kahini ba Priyanath Jiboni', in *Phire Dekha*, edited by Arindam Dasgupta, vol. 3 (Calcutta: Subarnarekha, 2011).

Priyanath is not an aloof author. He familiarizes himself with his readers, addressing them intimately and directly on a variety of issues—from apologizing for a gap in the publication to sharing with them his insights on the city, his profession, and human relationships, even admitting lying to elicit confession.[87] He is constantly in dialogue with his readers, encouraging them to either participate in his deductive thinking and observation or to reflect on the social circumstances of his criminals.[88] This interaction with his readers provides the structural framework and discursive environment for his self-conscious moralizing. Crime writing here serves as a moral barometer for testing and maintaining patriarchal, middle-class values.

The police tales probed the psychology and motivations underpinning the nature of evil, passion, and betrayal, and brought to play in his writings anxieties about Calcutta's urban environment. In this, Priyanath admittedly drew heavily on colonial knowledge structures about class, tribe, and criminality, but his compassionate inflections in the narratives suggest other moral truths—about grinding poverty, moral and material uncertainty of ill-gotten fortunes, and upholding family honour and social prestige. While the tales can be read simply as meaningful stories about danger in the city, other narrative registers suggest that they functioned as key interpretative devices for analysing and sharing reflections on the changing nature of social relationships caused by the strains of urban living.

Caught in a web of transient and impersonal associations Calcutta's floating populations—temporary residents and tenants, prostitutes and customers, lowly paid contractual workers, impermanent lovers—all epitomized an urban world in which the anchors of family, locality, and community had been profoundly dislocated. They served as macabre sites of social and moral disturbance, provoking perspectives about greed, jealousy, and loyalty. Elsewhere (in Chapter 3) it was seen how staying in the city engendered volatile and unstable sexual relations, resulting in

[87] A. Mukhopadhyay (ed.), P. Mukhopadhyay, *Darogar Daptar*, vol. 1, p. 268.

[88] A. Mukhopadhyay (ed.), P. Mukhopadhyay, *Darogar Daptar*, see for example vol. 1, p. 141 or vol. 2, p. 148.

violence against partners, usually female. This is a chief concern of Priyanath and the subject matter of some of his tales. But he also suggests the desires and aspirations unleashed by the twin fantasies of easily accessible wealth in the city, and the cover of anonymity—both of which he proves to be unreal. Class barriers break down within this structural format and the moralizing is directed against both the middle and aspiring lower classes seemingly caught in this trap.

Priyanath is driven by a strictly middle-class sense of propriety and social code, as also an agenda of social justice. The criminal poor are painted with empathy. Criminal biographies are routinely inserted in the narratives to 'explain' the seemingly unnatural behaviour of both respectable and not so respectable individuals.[89] Caught between a world of displacement, impoverishment, and depressed gentility on the one hand and tremendous opportunities for illicitly accessing wealth in the city on the other, individuals are seen as inevitably lured towards criminal activities. One reported case involved four masons in Calcutta from the same village in Faridpur who came to live as tenants in a tiled hut in Beliaghata. Later, in a ghastly double murder, they killed both the landlord (a sardar for masons) and his wife and buried them under the soil in their own yard and room. The sardar, it appears, was also a pawnbroker, lending money against ornaments and had a considerable amount of gold and silver jewellery, cash, household utensils, and clothes in his possession. The stolen goods were later found buried under the mud floor of the tenant quarters.[90] Priyanath's rendering here suggests a mixed register of greed and impoverishment.

[89] That these might have been based on real lives is hinted at, when Priyanath says that a recently published, full length 'autobiographical style' biography of one such criminal had not elicited any refutation from any quarters even though the main protagonist of that narrative was still alive. He proceeds on that strength to write yet another 'full length' life story of a criminal who was then serving a life sentence in the Andamans. See P. Mukhopadhyay, 'Snidhel Chor', *Darogar Daptar*, vol. 1, p. 362.

[90] P. Mukhopadhyay, 'Hatya Rahasya' [Murder Mystery] (Asvin 1300 B.S., 1893), *Darogar Daptar*, vol. 1, pp. 118–31. The story carries an extract from the *Statesman* newspaper on the murders—although without a date—to authenticate the events.

But Priyanath is also heavily and simultaneously invested in colonial typologies. Ishan Chandra Ghosh, from the *pankhachari* Kayastha caste of Jessore, is thus presented as a representative member of his community specializing in housebreaking (*snidhel churi*, drilling a hole into the house).[91] Known to the police—regularly in and out of jail and responsible for several innovative burglaries and murders—he earns the admiration of the police for his novel methods of operation, which combined conning with thieving. Ishan would rent temporary shops and houses, target both rich householders and pawnbrokers, plan meticulously, and strike when it was opportune. He usually worked by himself and had been in the trade for several years. Another housebreaker Priyanath catches is reported to be a member of the criminal Bediya tribe, also from Jessore, who apparently specialized in similar crimes.[92]

The criminals that Priyanath writes about do often come from the less prosperous and labouring classes, but there are other typologies on offer—that of propertied landlords, cloth merchants, and sons of zamindars. His own commentaries deployed unstable social registers to 'explain' the crimes—from moral decline, greed, and passion to Gothic monstrosity and wickedness—all of which had to do with behavioural norms rather than simply class.

Perpetrators are hard to bracket off into clear social categories of high and low. Both men and women are involved. In one startling case, a daughter of a respectable and prosperous Brahmo gentleman from Bowbazar is found involved with a bunch of armed fraudsters, and even implicated in murder.[93] Many criminals occupied middling ranks by virtue of either wealth or former social status. Ill-gotten wealth enabled material prosperity evident in the projected lifestyles—hiring of posh carriages,

[91] In his confessional, thus, Ishan (aka Priyanath) admits that he does this for a living and partly out of habit, and that it was too late to change. P. Mukhopadhyay, 'Kriponer Dhon' [The Miser's Hoard], part 2, (Magh, 1306 B.S. 1899), *Darogar Daptar*, vol. 2, p. 179.

[92] P. Mukhopadhyay, 'Shabaish Chor' [Jubiliations for the Thief] (Sravan, 1306 B.S. 1899), *Darogar Daptar*, vol. 2, pp. 84–100.

[93] P. Mukhopadhyay, 'Kal Parinay' [The Fatal Marriage] (Asvin, 1313 B.S. 1906), *Darogar Daptar*, vol. 2, pp. 606–20.

frequenting upmarket shops, and dressing glamorously.[94] In another instance, Priyanath reports the conning of an established jeweller by the daughter of a prostitute known in police circles as Sushila. Posing as the wife of a well-known High Court lawyer, we come to know she had arrived in an impressive horse-drawn brougham carriage and taken away valuable ornaments. She is later tracked down in Chandernagore. Sushila seems a free spirit, who was educated and moved in refined circles. She had also been briefly involved in a relationship with an actual High Court Counsel. She spoke English, behaved like a 'memsahib', had a Muslim cook, and wore Western clothes.[95]

Young men, more often than not, turned to crime to keep up with their permissive lifestyles. Umesh Ray was portrayed as a typical example of wayward youth in the city. A neglected son of a widower, he had migrated to the city from a village in Bankura to take up various positions in middle-class households and 'hotels' (humble food houses, sometimes providing accommodation) as a cook. He did not last long in any situation, however, as he robbed his unsuspecting employers of jewellery and other household objects. His enterprise, daring and wiliness landed him special favours from women (some part of the story is even mildly pornographic), and allowed him to swindle innocent householders and con rail passengers. The earnings from his thefts allowed him to live without work for weeks on end, but he eventually had to pay the price for his sins—landing up in jail in increasing lengths of sentences—from one to six months. Priyanath introduces this as his very first investigation following his appointment as a detective in the Calcutta Police force in 1878. The elaborate commentaries, stylizing, and lurid insertions in the story suggest this could be

94 It was a common trick for fraudsters to appear as well-groomed customers in busy shopping districts and then make off with clothes, jewellery, watches, and other valuable items on the pretext of collecting cash from their homes, seen in the likes of Harimohan Mukhopadhyay, who in reality lived with a prostitute in Harkata. P. Mukhopadhyay, 'Chorer Gari Chora' [Thief Riding a Car] (Kartik 1299 B.S. 1892), *Darogar Daptar*, vol. 2, pp. 36–7.

95 P. Mukhopadhyay, 'Shabaish Buddhi' [Spectacular Brainwork] (Kartik, 1311 B.S. 1904), *Darogar Daptar*, vol. 2, pp. 464–77.

Priyanath's attempt at pitching his narrative net to a wider readership of sensational literature in general.[96]

In another similar case following the death of his parents, young Harihar Das, son of a prosperous spice merchant and landlord of a house in Simuliya (Simla), took to robbing his tenants of jewellery and cash in order to sustain his dissolute lifestyle with a prostitute. He tried all means to sustain this life and did not hesitate to even steal from the prostitute quarters.[97]

Priyanath has empathy for the criminals, but also draws the boundaries of acceptability, warning about greed, lust, and jealousy and the aspirations for crossing of class and gender boundaries. The *Daptar* is overall quite conservative in its tone. Priyanath is a quintessential Brahmin, an upholder of caste order, and harbours presumptions about non-bhadralok low-caste people.[98] *Daptar* tries to restore the moral order, police social borders, and reassure the reader, but the crimes can also be read as a record of both tremendous opportunity and rising social aspirations in the city. Calcutta's pleasure industry is blamed for weakening the moral fibre of its inhabitants, turning upright and honest people into cheats and murderers. The red-light areas, the racing grounds, the alcohol and gambling dens apparently held the youth hostage.[99]

[96] P. Mukhopadhyay, 'Bamun Thakur' [The Brahmin Cook] (Agrahayan 1300 B.S. 1893), *Darogar Daptar*, vol. 1, pp. 144–55.

[97] P. Mukhopadhyay, 'Maar Dhon Churi' [Stealing a Mother's Treasures] (Bhadra, 1300 B.S. 1893), *Darogar Daptar*, vol. 1, pp. 105–17. Interestingly, the tenant from whom Harinath steals is also a victim of changing fortunes in the city. The widow of a cloth merchant who had a shop in Burrabazar, Taramoni, had never felt need in her married life with abundant riches and a two-storeyed house. But following the death of her husband, she lost both the business and the house, and eventually most of the sum of ten thousand rupees that he had left behind. See p. 111.

[98] A. Mukhopadhyay (ed.), P. Mukhopadhyay, *Darogar Daptar*, vol. 2, p. 89.

[99] Betting related to horse-racing had emerged as a favourite occupation in the city and was the cause of financial ruin for many. The racing grounds had opened in the 1820s and by the late nineteenth century the betting business was thriving. Also see P. Mukhopadhyay, 'Ki Na Hoy?' [Anything is Possible] (Bhadra 1306 B.S. 1899), *Darogar Daptar*, vol. 2, pp. 101–16.

This had been a regular motif in reformist literature for explaining a slide into immorality in the late nineteenth century, but seems to have been carried over to explain crime and depravity in the early decades of the twentieth century as well.

Apart from the cases of fraud and forgery seen earlier, the seemingly respectable are also seen to be embroiled in more sinister cases of burglary and murder in the pages of *Darogar Daptar*. It is significant that Priyanath is mindful of protecting the identity of the middle-class offenders, their relatives or accomplices—self-admittedly for the threat of litigation but also perhaps from class-based empathy. Names of streets and localities, prior ancestral residential addresses, and other forms of traceable identification are blanked out in the text using typographic symbols such as asterisks.[100] In other instances he uses false names or deliberately refrains from using authentic names, taking care to explain this to his readers.[101] But Priyanath also respects the private circumstances of 'fallen' aristocratic households and individuals. Gentle chastisement is reserved for the errant. Other more rampant fraud by 'respectable leaders of society' receives his sharpest criticism, although he admits that he is not brave or powerful enough to reveal their names.[102]

The law, however, was not always harsh on bhadralok offenders. The Calcutta Police recorded a case of theft by Gopi Mohun Ghose of a large quantity of jewellery and cash amounting to the massive sum of ten thousand rupees from a certain Badul Bibee. He attempted escaping in a *ghuree* or hackney carriage, but was caught and later arrested and charged by the police. Remarkably, the victim, a prostitute, and possibly his lover, did not want to press charges. In his trial, Ghose was let off lightly. Being of 'good parentage', he was sentenced to be detained till the rising of the

[100] A. Mukhopadhyay (ed.), P. Mukhopadhyay, *Darogar Daptar*, vol. 2, See for example pp. 135, 143, 168.

[101] A. Mukhopadhyay (ed.), P. Mukhopadhyay, *Darogar Daptar*, vol. 2, p. 360; vol. 1, pp. 363, 369.

[102] Priyanath thus reports innovative frauds being engineered in the betting trade related to horse-racing by those from the highest social rungs. P. Mukhopadhyay, 'Ki Na Hoy?', *Darogar Daptar*, vol. 2, p. 115.

court and pay a fine of Rs 500, in default of six months rigorous imprisonment under section 380 of the Indian Penal Code.[103]

An astounding case that emerges in Priyanath's police files is that of Muniruddin, the son of a rich landowner in Jessore. He was married off early to the daughter of a respectable officer of the Munsif Court in Krishnanagar, whose name Priyanath refuses to disclose for fear of spoiling his reputation. But Muniruddin fell into bad company and the material attractions on offer in this principal township of the Nadia district proved a major lure. A decent salaried job did not satisfy his needs and, having exhausted his own inheritance and his wife's jewellery, Muniruddin learnt the trade of housebreaking from an experienced and older practitioner. Together they were responsible for a string of robberies in Nadia.

Muniruddin later moved to Calcutta where his net extended beyond the city to Krishnanager, Jessore, Bardhhaman, and Hooghly. The device that Muniruddin would have used was known as *snidh-kathi*, an iron crowbar, a traditional device used for breaking into mud houses, but now applied to brick-built houses in the city and its suburbs.[104] He was eventually caught, but not before he had managed to escape thrice from jail using his trademark expertise.[105]

Regular salaried jobs in low and middling ranks earned little. It would appear that easier means of amassing fortunes could prove tempting. Priyanath reports the strange case of a young educated newspaper editor and son of a head teacher and scholar, who earned a daytime living by begging incognito on the streets of Calcutta. On discovering his ability to earn more than twenty rupees a day by begging as compared to his monthly salary of thirty, Narendrakrishna resorted to it as a regular profession. He made enough money to buy property in the suburbs, marry, and

[103] *ARPC, 1898*, p. 4.

[104] Boring of a hole big enough to let a person slip in allowed entry into the house's inner quarters, the same passage being used later to spirit away the stolen goods. Jewellery shops and pucca brick houses were invariably targeted rather than mud houses.

[105] P. Mukhopadhyay, 'Snidhel Chor', *Darogar Daptar*, vol. 1, pp. 362–76.

start a family. He was discovered by accident and following a police investigation into his apparent murder.[106]

The pages of the *Daptar* proved an important discursive space for discussing middle-class sexual scandals. While the courts delivered judicial verdicts on such cases involving assaults and murders, vigorous discursive spaces opened up in neighbourhoods, second-rank newspapers, and serial publications like Priyanath's. The legitimacy of the crimes, the morality of the chief actors involved, family honour, and the rites of conjugality all came under the utmost scrutiny and introspection. They condensed competing beliefs about transgressive sexuality set against marriage and the family. Not just the intimate circle of family, friends, and neighbours but larger concentric social circles energetically debated these issues. The *Daptar* pages report milling crowds turning up at crime scenes; entire villages competing to provide information; and wild rumours in circulation which delivered hasty verdicts even before the police had completed their investigation. The dialogical style of *Daptar* was considerably conducive to interchanges between writer and audience.

But Priyanath was himself quite aware of the limits of exposing scandals in bhadra households within its pages. He was attacked by his educated middle-class readers for letting them down. And yet, as Priyanath pointed out, they were evidently being devoured by the same critics. As evidence he points out how his publication of the scandalous story of 'Bamun Thakur' had been sold out completely three times. Sensationalism sold and the *Daptar* did good business in scandals. It revealed a double standard in the claim of his detractors therefore:

> You all know how fast lightning is, but perhaps the scandals of bhadra households travel faster than lightning.... Dear readers! ... [When *Bamun Thakur* was published] I began to receive letters which admonished me for revealing the dark secrets of bhadra households ... [but then the reprint and sale figures of *Bamun Thakur* told another story] ... I had convinced myself then that I would refrain from writing about scandals in respectable families,

106 P. Mukhopadhyay, 'Odbhut Bhikhari', *Darogar Daptar*, vol. 2, pp. 526–36.

> and did well to hold myself to my promise until now when I had to write *Kubuddhi* and *Ranga Bou*.... This is because the tales from bhadra families are realistic representation of the everyday cases I encounter, and without them I would have to stop publishing *Darogar Daptar*. Wherever there is a murder there resides licentiousness, and wherever there is fraud, women are invariably involved. Now then tell me my readers, how can I not write about these things? As I have no other option, then I will write about it even at the risk of offending everyone. But I am certain about one thing. You forbid me to write about such things publicly, but privately harbour the desire that I actually do so that you can read more about them in *Darogar Daptar*. 'Bamun Takur' is shining proof of this.[107]

Reflecting contemporary anxieties, a lot of bhadra scandals involved Hindu Bengali widows. The *Daptar* thus reported the murder of a brother's widow by the other three remaining brothers for her allegedly immoral life in a suburban village close to Kashipur. The corpse had been put inside a large box and left behind in a shipping yard. The trial, in which the brothers managed to defend themselves using legal support, led to only three years of jail sentence for two of the brothers, while the third went scot free.[108] In another brutal case, the young widowed daughter of respectable resident of the Simla locality in Calcutta was horrifically knifed to death by her brother for her clandestine relationship with a man.[109] Priyanath goes to considerable lengths to solve this case, but again with the help of excellent legal support the family was able to escape conviction. The case was followed closely in the local newspapers, and Priyanath might have been addressing this particular audience when he remarked: 'Although Rambabu [the accused] was acquitted, the financial drain caused by his legal expenses proved ample penalty for him. His fortunes never

[107] A. Mukhopadhyay (ed.), P. Mukhopadhyay, *Darogar Daptar*, vol. 2, p. 359 (italics mine).

[108] P. Mukhopadhyay, 'Kata Mundu' [The Severed Head] (Kartik, 1300 B.S. 1893), *Darogar Daptar*, vol. 1, pp. 132–43.

[109] P. Mukhopadhyay, 'Girijasundari' [About Girija] (Baisakh 1301 B.S. 1894), *Darogar Daptar*, vol. 1, pp. 218–32.

returned. Although he is not exactly poverty stricken, his current status is no longer that of a respectable gentleman [*baramanush*].'[110]

Priyanath's reported cases were not untypical from those found in the annual reports of the Calcutta Police at the time. In 1881, a middle-class educated Brahmin cut the throat of the wife of his neighbour. He fled but was traced to a village in Hooghly by sub-Inspector S.C. Mookerjee of the Detective Department.[111] In another sensational contemporary case, Rev. B.C. Ghose of the Church Missionary Society was poisoned by his wife and her lover with arsenic, although this could not be proved for want of evidence.[112] In yet another case, a respectable woman's body was found by the roadside near Eden Garden, with traces of hydrocyanic acid in her stomach. Police suspected that she had probably been poisoned in a house before someone tried to dispose of the body.[113]

In an interesting case that combined two separate incidents of a scandal and murder, Priyanath takes us to the residence of a notable Bengali gentleman where a tin trunk has been found with the decomposed body of a woman inside.[114] The murder had happened in a closely arranged neighbourhood with houses bordering the gentleman's garden, and it transpires that a burglary, a woman's disappearance, and hanging ropes from a terrace are all intricately woven into the case. Satkari and his friend and accomplice, Makhanlal, were both employees in the railway office and tenants in a nearby house. When Satkari catches his wife red-handed with another man, he cuts her to pieces with a hatchet. Later that night, terrified, he with the help of his friend packs her body into a tin trunk with the initial intention of throwing it into the Hooghly. But fear of detection makes them hatch another plan. Makhanlal suggests that they tie the trunk to a ladder that he has seen being let down by the side of the well-known gentleman's house and hauled up on many occasions before. The box ascends to the terrace as they had planned

110 P. Mukhopadhyay, 'Girijasundari', pp. 227, 232.

111 *ARPC, 1881*, pp. 5–6.

112 *ARPC, 1895*, p. 5.

113 *ARPC, 1893*, p. 10.

114 P. Mukhopadhyay, 'Aasmani Laash' [The Corpse from the Heavens] (Jaistha 1300 B.S. 1893), *Darogar Daptar* , vol. 1, pp. 61–75.

and the two retire knowing that even if discovered, the house owner would be able to hush up the affair because of his influence and position in society. Unfortunately for them, their nocturnal activities are witnessed by at least two people, including a burglar, whose statement implicates them squarely. Satkari confesses his crime, while a maidservant in the gentleman's household admits that the rope ladder had been devised by her for transporting her paramour secretly and in the dead of night, to her room. Priyanath leaves this open ended but drops a clear hint at the end of the story that the gentleman's young and widowed daughter and not the maid might have been involved with the rope ladder:

> No one saw the babu's widowed daughter after that. In the end all got to know that she had gone off to Kashi [Benares, a traditional destination for Hindu widows]. But people have been heard saying that this was a strategy to save the honour of the family and that it was not the maid but the widow who had been involved in the scandal. The maid had deliberately taken the blame herself to save her and had intentionally not revealed the name of the man involved.[115]

Priyanath, however, is reluctant to disclose the name of the gentleman involved because of his esteem and reputation in Calcutta, and says so clearly at the start.[116]

Tales of blood and gore, dismemberment, and death excite and repel, titillate and worry. But they also render the city safe through the telling of these tales by a policeman who assures the readers that he is in charge. While there is the visceral element and worked up anxiety, that sense of mastery of the situation calms the recreational reader. But more significantly, for us the police accounts of Priyanath were doing more than that. The *Daptar* renderings were motivated by their author's own particular set of moral and social values. While highlighting criminal elements on the margins of society, his tales also referred to social injustice and abuse of power at its heart, highlighting an alternative sense of collective moral culpability.[117]

115 P. Mukhopadhyay, 'Aasmani Laash', p. 75.
116 P. Mukhopadhyay, 'Aasmani Laash', p. 61.
117 Messent, *The Crime Fiction Handbook*, p. 46.

Mapping the City: Comparative Cartographies of Crime and Safety

A very specific social geography of the town drew lines between 'safe' and 'unsafe' areas. The presumption that the city could be mapped via intense local knowledge of crime and criminals to render it secure and knowable, and mechanisms of surveillance and disciplining distributed accordingly lay at the heart of colonial urban policing in India. Far from representing functional and technical bureaucratic knowledge, they constituted cognitive structures of race, community, and class that was aligned to wider contemporary thinking on criminality in India as seen above. It not only located crime pathologically in certain categories of colonized bodies, but was tested and further honed in the context of the cities with their mix of communities and policing challenges. Stephen Legg has shown how diagrammatic schemes of disciplining in colonial Delhi saw urban space segmented into controllable and knowable parts, emblematic of the administration's confidence in penetrating deep into the urban population and breaking resistance at the core.[118] Similar mappings were operational in other parts of India, and indeed were adopted for the first time ever in the policing of Calcutta in the mid-nineteenth century.

The topology of crime worked out by Calcutta's municipal administration saw the city divided into neat spaces for purposes of efficient policing even before the mid-nineteenth century and resources distributed commensurate with intensity of crimes. In 1842, the then chief magistrate of Calcutta proposed to split the city into three police divisions—the Upper, Middle, and Lower.[119] The arrangement was upheld by S. Wauchope, the first police commissioner of the city, later on in 1856. Geographically, the Upper Division overlapped the Black Town in the north of the city, the Middle Division stretched from the governmental and commercial centre to the European residential quarters in Chowringhee, while

[118] Legg, *Spaces of Colonialism*, especially see Chapter 3, pp. 82–148. Legg's characterization applies to Delhi in the 1930s.

[119] *ARPC, 1842*. See Appendix A, p. 9, cited in Sumanta Banerjee, *The Wicked City*, pp. 91–2.

the Lower Division covered the stretch from the Fort William down to the Kidderpore docks. Each of these areas was identified with its own distinctive nature of prevailing crimes and criminals.

The narrow lanes running behind the palatial mansions of Bengali aristocrats interspersed by slums, prostitute quarters, opium dens, and alcohol shops were believed to house the biggest concentration of criminals of all kinds—a dense habitat of 'swindlers, burglars and cheats', and concerned the police most. The Middle Division stretching right up to the Eurasian quarters and covering the red-light district of Kalingabazar and the traditional pilgrimage centre of Kalighat needed to be kept under surveillance for the operation of pimps and thieves, both Indian and non-Indian. And finally, the southernmost part was reputed to be the haunt of marauding sailors and drunken soldiers, the former associated with the Kidderpore dock area, notorious for its looters and robbers.

Three hundred constables were assigned to each division headed by a European superintendent and under him, in hierarchical order, inspectors (darogas), sergeants (jemadars), and corporals. While the first two divisions were put in charge of a mixed group of European and Indian policemen, the last—housing the exclusive European residential blocks and fort—was to be manned by Europeans only.

Following colonial patterns, Priyanath maps the city in a particular way for his readers, warning them of its dangerous spaces and no-go areas. He himself frequents these quarters, however, for eliciting information, dropping in incognito, and eavesdropping amongst the crowd. Ironically, in his narratives, his presence there as an upholder of the law and a representative of the state renders these spaces in turn apparently more secure. Almost like the Benthamite ideal of Panopticon, Priyanath seems to be everywhere and has access to not only the most private of spaces in domestic households but also the innermost recesses of criminal minds as seen in the previous sections.

It is possible to read this as an attempt to incorporate dangerous urban space into Priyanath's organized vision of the city. While underlining his own power to know the city in ways that his readers cannot, Priyanath is constantly providing visual and historic pointers to the city's evolution—in the form of changed street names, architecture, and topographies. In doing so, he also protects his readers from direct exposure to the areas that are out of bounds of genteel lives.

The *Daptar* creates an illusion of liminal spaces in the city that pose untold dangers and are in constant need of securing, thus justifying Priyanath's presence and the vital role of the police in keeping the residents safe. Mechhuabazar, with its coffee rooms and opium dens for European and Middle-Eastern sailors and labourers, criminal quarters, and prostitute houses, figures in quite a few of his tales. Priyanath's identification of this location as crime prone is to a certain extent not just spatial but also pathological, as was evident in the description of a typical coffee house in the area we saw earlier in the chapter.[120]

There were other structural (not geographic) spaces that were disturbing. *Baganbaris* were recreational houses in the suburbs for the rich and often used as sites of sexual and musical entertainment involving prostitutes. These were spacious homes but in remote locations, not always under the vigilant purview of the owner. In the absence of the landlord, they could be leased out for a few hours or a night by the caretaker or gateman to men in return for payment.[121] Baganbaris could hide vicious murders with considerable ease within its dense shrubbery, water bodies, and garden beds.[122]

Lodges or hotels were ideal locations for harbouring crime. Areas such as Burrabazar and Jorabagan abounded in such large houses where some 200 persons could be living at a time.[123] While these were clustered very close together, the impermanent nature

[120] Mechhuabazar also figures in many of Priyanath Mukhopadhyay's accounts. See 'Chorer Gari Chora', 'Kapten Moti', and 'Snidhel Chor' in *Darogar Daptar*, vol. 1.

[121] See P. Mukhopadhyay, 'Odbhut Hatya', *Darogar Daptar*, vol. 1, pp. 22–35, where a prostitute is murdered for her valuable ornaments and clothing. The watchman on this occasion is paid five rupees (equivalent to his monthly wages) for allowing the men to use the garden house for a few hours that night.

[122] P. Mukhopadyay, 'Orthoi Onortho' [Money is Trouble] (1894), *Darogar Daptar* , vol. 1, pp. 288–303.

[123] In 1881 there were about 200 known boarding houses and hotels in the city. *Census of the Town and Suburbs of Calcutta, 1881*, p. 44.

of the residential lettings, the quick succession of tenants, and the anonymity forced upon neighbours due to such circumstances proved convenient for criminals. With such properties often leased out on behalf of absentee landlords who stayed away from the city, agents handled renting and did not endeavour to verify details provided.[124] Many new arrivals had no records, and were unknown to the police or even to neighbours.[125] It allowed for crimes to be committed within close vicinity of households without the knowledge of other residents.[126] Under the twin covers of anonymity and temporality, tenants could operate with impunity until caught. Criminals could flit from one residence to another as police tried to track them down, as in the case of the coin-forger Shyamacharan and housebreaker Muniruddin.[127]

Almost invariably, these were bachelor dens housing students, small businessmen, and office workers who lived in the city away from families, usually returning to them during weekends and holidays.[128] The living arrangements were minimal and the furniture stark. Food hotels served as functional adjuncts to the lodging houses, serving the inmates daily. Priyanath's opinion of the lodgers and visitors to these hotels brings out sharply once again his position on the societal location of vice:

> None of the people who came to eat here looked like the bhadralok, save one or two genuine ones who driven by hunger and familial responsibility perhaps eked out an honest living at the press works

[124] P. Mukhopadyay, 'Dak Chor' [Postal Thief] (1894), *Darogar Daptar*, vol. 1, p. 354.

[125] *ARPC, 1878*, p. 8; A. Mukhopadhyay (ed.), P. Mukhopadhyay, *Darogar Daptar* , vol. 2, pp. 582–3.

[126] There was thus an instance of a brutal murder of a woman by her lover in the dead of night on the terrace of a lodging house which went undetected until mid-morning the day later, when an occupant of the house overlooking it across the street spotted the supine body lying in the heat of the midday sun and raised the alarm. *ARPC, 1877*.

[127] See P. Mukhopadhyay, 'Snidhel Chor', and 'Kritrim Mudra' in *Darogar Daptar*, vol. 1.

[128] See P. Mukhopadyay, 'Bamun Thakur' (1893), *Darogar Daptar*, vol. 1, pp. 144–5; 'Kapten Moti', *Darogar Daptar*, p. 407, for his descriptions of such places.

> on a meagre salary [in the city]. Any attempt to describe those customers other than them would require writing an entire book. Almost all of them have a place to live. And yet they actually chose to spend their nights with those they would deign to be seen with during the daytime ... it was common to find those coming during the day being away at night time.[129]

But Priyanath's tales also problematize the binary positions on the city—as a setting for fear and attraction, danger, and enchantment. From his perspective, criminals hide behind the cover of anonymity that a big city like Calcutta provides, and the only meaningful way in which the various spaces of the city can be connected are through acts of violence and scam. Priyanath dwells both on the marginal sites of the city where crime was possible on the one hand and seemingly safe zones circumscribed by domesticity and social stability on the other. His tales take us through the poor huts of labourers, sailor dens, and prostitute quarters, as well as seemingly secure internal spaces of middle-class households and aristocratic quarters. In all of this the city is presented as a problem that he then sets about solving.[130] By way of exploiting his readers' fascination for the unpredictable and violent nature of urban life, Priyanath has no reservations in placing such volatility in the centre of settled middle-class neighbourhoods and households. Like fictional counterparts of his generation such as Dupont and Holmes, Priyanath's activities restore order and reason in the city, and contain its opaque threats and irrational excesses.

In the *Daptar*, everyday, familiar and intimate spaces are transformed by crime. Apparently 'safe' places could and did act as sites of brutal murders. Polics records report the case

[129] P. Mukhopadyay, 'Bamun Thakur', *Darogar Daptar,* vol. 1, p. 148.

[130] This classic purpose of detective fiction is also epitomized here thus in Priyanath's tales. For a discussion of this primary motif of detective stories, see David Schmid, 'Imagining Safe Urban Space: The Contribution of Detective Fiction to Radical Geography', *Antipode* 27, no. 3 (1995): 242–69. Also see D. Brand, *The Spectator and the City in Nineteenth Century American Literature* (Cambridge: Cambridge University Press, 1991).

of a man killing his wife by holding her forcibly under water in the Bhistypara tank surrounded by 'well-to-do respectable households' in the midst of a thickly populated cluster of huts without attracting much notice.[131] In another case, a man enticed away his landlady's son, robbed him of ornaments, and drowned him in the Moti-jheel tank in the centre of the race course.[132] There are several instances of the Maidan, the much flaunted open public grounds in the centre of the city, being used to dump bodies.[133] Flexible criminal use of 'regular' urban spaces in the night time—where functional (use of shops and sewers for burglary), ceremonial (theft of jewellery from Kali temple), and leisure spaces (for disposing corpses) during the day could be converted in the night through criminal activities—rather than branded crime pockets in the city is apparent in contemporary police reports.[134] Tanks, gardens, watersides, bye-lanes, and alleys generally acted as convenient dumping ground for dead bodies.[135]

* * *

Anonymity and low social cohesion as rendered by the urban environment fostered a rootless existence, heightening the sense of social dislocation among a chiefly migrant population in the city. As seen in Chapter 3 and again here, the material attractions of Calcutta's pleasure districts, its potential to sustain extravagant lifestyles, and the lure of easily accessible cash and ornaments proved detrimental to the safety of its many residents. The Bengali

[131] *ARPC, 1877*, p. 4.

[132] *ARPC, 1899*, p. 4.

[133] *ARPC, 1908*, p. 15. Also see P. Mukhopadhyay, 'Bolihari Buddhi' [Salutations to Cunning] (Falgun 1300 B.S. 1893), *Darogar Daptar*, vol. 1, pp. 188–201.

[134] Jewellers' shops were favourite targets and often entered through underground passages and sewers. See, for example, *ARPC, 1842*, p. 9; *ARPC, 1870*, pp. 6–7. Also see Sri Rajratna, *Kalighate E Ki Churi* (Calcutta, 1875).

[135] Thus, for example, see *ARPC, 1902*, p. 9; *ARPC, 1906*, p. 12.

detective Priyanath Mukhopadhyay's crime stories recorded these aspirations, with the author acting as both the moral guardian of urban society and its social commentator. The wide circulation of the immensely popular serialized publication of the police tales permitted diverse constituencies to engage with these meaningful narratives about social danger and moral truth to form, in turn, their own competing beliefs of the same. The police diaries were valuable in exposing the rapid loosening of traditional sociabilities in an urban setting and an increasing blurring of 'safe' and 'unsafe' zones in the city. They probed the psychology and motivations underpinning the nature of evil, infidelity, and passion—frequently seen to be stimulated by Calcutta's permissive urban environments—and brought into play anxieties about the city's migrant populations.

6

Collective Protest and Riots

'... in India the street is beginning to stand up ...'
—V.I. Lenin, 5 August 1908 (1963, p. 184)

This last chapter looks at Calcutta during extraordinary moments of crises and transgressions—riots, labour unrest, and nationalist mass movements. As the chapter demonstrates, the symbolical and physical violation of neatly ordered spaces—especially by marginal groups as seen during street protests and mass violence—was both new and shocking to the administration. But even as the latter struggled to deal with the rising levels of urban protest, newer political constituencies were being indelibly etched on the ruins of the older civic order. How did ordered and authoritarian public spaces transform into sites of violence and disorder in the early decades of the twentieth century? Who were the architects of this spectacular transformation? And how did the administration react to this multifaceted, intermittent rioting and protest? The chapter tries to answer these questions by analysing a set of key disturbances in the city over this period pointing primarily to the harsh living conditions, breakdown of trust between the residents, and the administration as well as the inadequacies of urban policing.

Nandini Gooptu has discussed the ways in which the urban poor of north India inserted themselves into contemporary politics because of the interplay of their occupational and communal identities, and their significant marginalization in the urban political economy.[1] The radicalization of poor Muslims and lower-caste Hindus thus occurred as a reaction to a perceived loss of status for these communities. Their increasing activism and presence in public spaces in the early twentieth century later prompted Congress leaders to mobilize their energies for the nationalist cause. In this, however, the narrative inserts the familiar framework of caste, community, and religion in the assertion of marginalized communities.

The approach in this chapter is different. Here the urban experience of these communities is foregrounded as fundamental to the shaping of their collective life in public spaces, taking on board not just their caste and religious identities but also their shared understandings of police repression, municipal policies regulating festivities, housing, and public health, and depressed living circumstances in the city. It is very specifically the urban nature of these experiences that radicalized and mobilized them and brought them into conflict with the law in ways in which their rural counterparts could not envisage. As the disturbances unfolding in the first two decades of the twentieth century show, the allegiances both within and across communal, caste, and class boundaries were fluid, and each crisis drew on its unique set of social alignments. Thus the anti-Marwari 1918 riots were non-communal, but the Bakr-Id riots were not; the bhadralok were targeted in 1907, but were looked upon as effective leaders in a number of strikes at other times, while horizontal links ran among the urban poor irrespective of religion during powerful anti-police, anti-colonial riots.

Police Repression, Racial Violence, and Protest

In 1860, Wauchope, the Police Commissioner of Calcutta, boasted that

> [a] riot by a Calcutta mob is now utterly impossible. Composed of numerous races, without cohesion of a single feeling in common,

[1] Nandini Gooptu, *The Politics of the Urban Poor in Early Twentieth Century India* (Cambridge: Cambridge University Press, 2001).

> although made up of doubtful characters from every part of India, it would be unable to withstand 1500 men all drilled and trained to act in concert.[2]

And yet, within a space of only three decades, Calcutta saw its first in a series of major riots. Assault on the police was already up from the early 1860s onwards.[3] Annual police reports show 120 persons arrested across the year for assault on police in 1880–1.[4] Police constables were also being stabbed in Calcutta's streets.[5] The heavy presence of the army worsened the situation. A serious disturbance was caused at Alipore by sepoys in 1892. When a crowd of spectators gathered on the edge of the parade ground opposite the Agri-Horticultural Society Gardens to witness the ascent of a hot-air balloon, soldiers from the 17th Bengal Infantry—who had also collected there on the occasion of their annual show on the parade grounds—attacked them unprovoked. The police records show the soldiers suddenly attempting to disperse the crowd, using considerable violence, and then passing on to the public road and obstructing traffic. This brought them into conflict with the police and one of them was arrested. The sepoys in retaliation then turned out in force, and committed 'indiscriminate' assaults on the general public and the police.[6] The newspaper *Bengalee*, too, reports several instances of assault by armyment in Calcutta and its suburbs at the end of the nineteenth century.[7]

The colonial government also feared the joining of hands between an unruly labour and other urban groups with a potential for violence—in official papers referred to variously

[2] *ARPC, 1859–60* and *1860–61*, p. 7.

[3] One hundred and fourteen cases were reported in 1862–3. *ARPC, 1862–3*, p. 19.

[4] *ARPC, 1881*, p. 6.

[5] In an interesting case in 1894, a policeman had an exchange with a religious mendicant from Benares for wandering about the chowk with a thick stick in the Burrabazar area. The man initially moved off threatening the policeman, but later that day managed to stab him mortally with a dagger. *ARPC, 1894*, p. 6. In another stray incident, a constable was stabbed to death while on duty at Chitpore Road. *ARPC, 1908*, p. 15.

[6] *ARPC, 1892*, p. 11.

[7] See *Bengalee*, 7 May 1898.

as 'riff-raff', 'rowdies', and 'goondas'—such as petty criminals, unemployed disaffected youth, and unruly groups.[8] The idea of 'mob' action, instead of informed conscious reaction to a particular situation or circumstance, was inherent in official ideology. This enabled them to blame local leaders for inciting sub-groups of population and dismiss any genuine grievances, and locate identifiable, visible, collectives for surveillance.[9] Scholars like Suranjan Das have studied the presence of such ideologies in the enacting of legislation such as the Goonda Act of 1923 or in the characterization of budmashes (those prone to criminal activities).[10]

We have seen earlier in Chapter 4 how the streets, the principal arteries of commerce and administration, were key sites of battle between the residents and the police, be it in matters of strikes, traffic, sanitary practices, or demonstrations. For the residents these constituted acts of defiance, while for the government it was a matter of law and order, its priority being to restore discipline in the streets, making the smooth operation of the modern metropolitan regime possible. In 1886, the police were given greater powers owing to an amendment in the Police Act, which allowed them to arrest with relative ease for disorderly acts.[11] In 1878, the commissioner of police, W.M. Souttar, talked of the importance of the visibility of the chowkidar: 'The chowkidar has to assert his presence in the

[8] Such categorization and classification of urban petty criminals in cities and towns by colonial officials has been studied for the late nineteenth and early twentieth centuries. See Debraj Bhattacharya, 'Kolkata "Underworld" in the Early 20th Century', *Economic and Political Weekly* 39, no. 38 (September 2004): 4276–82; Sugata Nandi, 'Constructing the Criminal: Politics of the Social Imaginary of the Goonda', *Social Scientist* 38, nos 3/4 (March–April 2010): 37–54.

[9] This is also applicable to policing in other Indian cities. See Stephen Legg, *Spaces of Colonialism: Delhi's Urban Governmentalities* (Oxford: Blackwell Publishing, 2004), pp. 124, 132, and 134, for Delhi.

[10] See Suranjan Das, *The Goondas: Towards a Reconstruction of the Calcutta Underworld* (Calcutta: Firma K.L.M. Private Limited, 1996).

[11] *ARPC, 1886*, p. 3.

midst of an undisciplined public if he is to preserve any order by making arrests.'[12]

Bengali newspapers were vocal in their criticism of the police force. As the *Hindoo Patriot* complained:

> Our police are not framed by scrupulousness and they do not fail to convert the slightest power given to them into an engine of oppression and extortion.[13]

A resident of Sibpur, writing in to the same newspaper, described 'rude and illiterate Hindusthanee' (up-country) policemen strutting about the streets of Calcutta's suburbian towns and villages, using 'vulgar abuse' in the presence of passers-by.[14] Police excesses and corruption were regularly reported in the press and print media, with yet another account describing the police as 'an engine of oppression'.[15] Contemporary Bengali proverbs smacked of anti-police sentiments.[16] Confessions extracted through torture, undue fines, and intrusive authoritarian methods had tarnished the organization's reputation from the 1860s onwards.[17] Internal circumstances within the organization might have aggravated such practices. Police reports in the 1860s and 1870s describe itself as a demoralized force, with lower ranks

[12] *ARPC, 1878*, p. 2.

[13] *Hindoo Patriot*, 11 May 1863, cited in Ranjan Chakrabarti, *Authority and Violence in Colonial Bengal: 1800–1860* (Calcutta: Bookland Private Limited, 1997), p. 87.

[14] *Hindoo Patriot*, 15 March 1863, cited in Chakrabarti, *Authority and Violence in Colonial Bengal*, p. 87.

[15] See, for example, *Calcutta Review*, 157 (1884), p. 96.

[16] Thus, proverbs such as '*chhagal ghash khayena ar pulish ghush khayena ekotha ke biswas korbe?*' (Who would believe that a goat does not eat grass or a policeman does not take bribes?), did their rounds. As cited in Chakrabarti, *Authority and Violence in Colonial Bengal*, p. 87.

[17] Basudev Chatterjee, *Crime and Control in Early Colonial Bengal 1770–1860* (Calcutta: K.P. Bagchi and Co., 2000); Also see Sumit Sarkar, *The Swadeshi Movement in Bengal* (New Delhi: Oxford University Press, 2011; original edition 1973), p. 21, for evidence of the heightening racial tensions at the start of the twentieth century.

being more badly paid than labourers and living in small and overcrowded accommodation.[18]

A key feature in these developments was the emergence of strong racial alongside anti-police sentiments in the city that galvanized various groups into common action, a point that is taken up in the subsequent section. Considerable political and racial agitation was reported in the Swadeshi agitation of 1905–7. As we shall see, an important element of the strikes by workers in the period was resentment of white racial supremacy and brutalities in the railways, press, industrial, and mercantile offices. In October 1905, spinners of the Garden Reach jute mill protested against assaults by white overseers and went on a two-day strike.[19] One of the main grievances of the clerks of the East Indian Railway, who went on strike in July 1906, was the use of the term 'native' to designate them. They demanded to be referred to as 'Indians' instead.[20]

Europeans were assaulted in the streets. The joint magistrate of Howrah, while driving home along Strand Road one evening was attacked by a Swadeshi procession that surrounded his trap and he was struck several blows from behind.[21] There was another incident of the pelting of mud at a judge, probably by students again.[22] In Hooghly, a football match disrupted by the orderly of a European excise inspector saw students confronting both the orderly and his employer. The latter it seems hurled 'the filthiest' of abuse at them but went scot free. Instead, the complaining students were faced with expulsion from school by the principal.[23]

[18] *ARPC, 1877*, p. 24. Also see *ARPC, 1867*, pp. 15–20. For a comprehensive account of the challenges facing the colonial police and their internal institutional reforms see Anandswarup Gupta, *The Police in British India, 1861–1947* (New Delhi: Concept Publishing, 1979).

[19] Report on the Agitation against the Partition of Bengal (from Bengal Government No. 205 P. 25 Jan 1906, para 61), Home Public A, June 1906, n. 175.

[20] *Pioneer*, 24 July 1906, cited in Sarkar, *Swadeshi Movement in Bengal*, p. 184.

[21] Report of the Inspector-General of Police, Lower Provinces, on the Agitation against the Partition of Bengal, 1905 (hereafter IGP Report), p. 10.

[22] IGP Report, p. 31.

[23] *Bengalee*, 29 September 1905.

It appears that the general climate of anti-European and anti-police sentiments encouraged attacks from the lower social groups too. Disgruntled hackney-carriage drivers arguing over fares and dismissed servants did not hesitate to vent their anger with bodily insults and assaults.[24] In Howrah, coolies working for an engineering firm laying electrical installation clashed with the supervising European assistants, beating up one of them severely.[25]

But the police were high-handed in dealing with attacks on policemen. When servants of two local notables, one of them a judge and another a councillor, clashed with constables in Grey Street, the former desisted from lodging a complaint at the Police Court. And yet, none other than the police commissioner himself intervened to punish the servant 'offenders'.[26] Amritalal Basu, noted playwright associated with the Star Theatre, wrote a strong letter to the *Bengalee* condemning the police commissioner's intervention.[27] It is against this backdrop of mistrust and growing animosity between the police and Calcutta's residents that we need to place the series of riots and mass protest that were staged on the city's streets in the closing decades of the nineteenth and the opening decades of the twentieth century.

The Politics of the Urban Poor: Anti-police Riots in the City, 1891–1918

To the municipal administration, the urban proletariat was a 'dangerous class', volatile, and capable of bringing instant disruption and chaos to daily life in the city, and therefore in need of constant surveillance. Especially in Calcutta, much wealth and capital was at stake with the giant jute and cotton mills on either side of Hooghly, the flow of trade at the port, and a string of key mercantile financial firms. European businessmen looked to the state and its police force for maintaining overall law and order, even within their own

[24] IGP Report, p. 31.
[25] IGP Report, p. 33.
[26] *Bengalee*, 3 September 1905.
[27] *Bengalee*, 6 September 1905.

labour forces. The city's administration was therefore geared to meet any such sign of destabilization with appropriate force. And yet, from the very end of the nineteenth century onwards, Calcutta came to be besieged by a series of mass riots that tested the law enforcing machinery of the colonial state to the utmost.

The earliest of these were the Shambazar riots of 1891. A rumour that the purchase of some land by a Hindu would result in the removal of a temporary building that was being used as a mosque led to a spontaneous attack on the police in the Shambazar (Nickaripara) area in 1891.[28] The rioters, mostly Jolahas from a muslin-weaving caste in Bihar and UP, were armed with lathis (heavy sticks), bricks, and stones, while the police had only batons, which resulted in one constable being killed and eighteen policemen severely injured. When Police Commissioner Lambert arrived on foot with a group of senior officers and tried to address the crowd, he and several others were struck by missiles thrown at his party and had to retreat.

Another serious riot took place in Chitpore and in the northern part of the town in 1897, involving similar circumstances. When the estate of the Tagores claimed repossession of a piece of land at Talla by court order because the occupying tenant had failed to pay rent, members of the Muslim clergy protested on the grounds that there existed a mosque in the form of a tiled hut on the premises. A series of police demolitions alternating with rebuilding activities by Muslim men ensued.[29] Crowds of several thousands gathered, stopped traffic, and occupied Talla Bridge. Primarily poor Muslim weavers and bricklayers, the protesters were also joined by 'bad characters' whose chief target seemed to be the police although 'several Europeans' were also assaulted in the streets. The military had to be called in as reinforcement

[28] *ARPC, 1891*, pp. 12, 19. These were the events of 16 May 1891. Most of the rioters were, however, acquitted as there was not enough evidence to prosecute them.

[29] Police Commissioner A.H. James to Secretary of the Bengal Government C.W. Bolton, 'Papers on Chitpur Riots', IOR/L/PJ/6/456, no. 1796, pp. 6–7.

as the police were not enough.[30] Once again, top officials including the police commissioner himself (A.H. James) were involved. Confident that he had quelled the disturbance after the first confrontation, and posting a small party in charge at the site, the police commissioner, to his surprise, had to return again and was attacked on a fringe road by a stone-throwing crowd as were some of the military on bicycles. The pattern was not just of a spillover to large stretches of key arterial roads but also that of a spread far south into Mechhuabazar and Beliaghata.

Friction between the police and mill hands was also sparking off trouble in the mill-towns between 1895 and 1896—in Garden Reach, Rishra, and Titagarh. By the end of the week, it was a free-for-all against the police, with riots spreading to the mill towns and turning bloodier, while the rumour was that the Howrah and Garden Reach mill hands were going to join the Calcutta rioters. Prompt action by the government in the form of stationing of police and military at the possible entry points on both sides of the river, however, prevented this from happening.[31]

The mood of the rioters can be felt in the following extract from the police commissioner's report:

> On arriving within 150 yards of the rioters [with a strong contingent of police and fifty men of the Gloucestershire regiment] I halted and sent forward two Muhammadan officers to direct the rioters to disperse, and if they would not do so, to call some of the leaders of the mob. They returned with a man named Sobrati, whom I directed to go back and tell the rioters that, if they did not disperse quietly within five minutes, they would be made to do so by force. He practically refused to obey, and when he got back to the rioters, it was evident that they meant to resist, for after hearing what their

[30] *ARPC, 1897*, p. 9, and Lieutenant Governor's report, p. 4. The riots happened between 30 June and 1 July 1897. See also, Ranajit Dasgupta, 'Material Conditions and Behavioural Aspects of Calcutta Working Class, 1875–1899', Occasional Paper no. 22, Centre for the Study of Social Sciences, Calcutta; *Labour and Working Class in Eastern India* (Calcutta: South Asia Books, 1994).

[31] Police Commissioner A.H. James to Secretary of the Bengal Government, C.W. Bolton, 'Papers on Chitpur Riots', no. 1327/97.

> leader had to say, the whole crowd commenced to cry out 'Ali Ali' and 'Din Din' and brandish their sticks.[32]

So panicked was the establishment that the secretary of state telegrammed the viceroy on the 7th of July, before the question of the Chitpore riots was to be raised in Parliament that week, wanting confirmation of reports from Reuter that 600 had been killed in Calcutta.[33] In reality, eleven were killed and twenty wounded from police firing.[34]

In case of both Chitpore and Shambazar, the police were exposed as tremendously vulnerable within the city limits. In fact, firearms were more readily deployed in the mill-towns with even European factory assistants and officers using them frequently, in addition to the police.[35] Other cities like Delhi too seem better prepared by comparison. Here the police were markedly stronger and more visible. Armoured cars and tanks were used as escort or patrol or for dispersing crowds, and intricate management of potential trouble-spots and communities conducted.[36] Policing in Calcutta was softer by contrast, practiced on foot, bicycles, and horse-drawn carriages, which exposed the force to attack from not only the streets but also the nearby housetops. The lieutenant governor too realized this quickly. One result of the riots was his subsequent decision to arm the city's police with more efficient weapons.[37] Reinforcements were also created in the form of a permanent contingent of Military Police stationed at Barrackpore to check any outbreaks at Calcutta or among the mill hands.[38]

[32] Police Commissioner A.H. James to Secretary of the Bengal Government, C.W. Bolton, 'Papers on Chitpur Riots', p. 6.

[33] Telegram from Secretary of State to Viceroy, dated 7 July 1897. 'Papers on Chitpur Riots', IOR/L/PJ/6/456, no. 1327/97.

[34] Police Commissioner A.H. James to Secretary of the Bengal Govt, C.W. Bolton, 'Papers on Chitpur Riots', no. 1796, p. 9.

[35] See Subho Basu, *Does Class Matter? Colonial Capital and Workers' Resistance in Bengal, 1890–1937* (New Delhi: Oxford University Press, 2004), pp. 116–17

[36] Legg, *Spaces of Colonialism*, pp. 105, 122–40.

[37] *ARPC, 1891*, Lieutenant Governor's Report, pp. 2–3. Also see Home-Public, June 1891, A files, nos 63–7.

[38] *ARPC, 1897*, Lieutenant Governor's Report, p. 4.

The tactics employed by the rioters were bold and opportunist. They cut off arterial roads such as Harrison and Circular Roads, blocked disputed sites, and dispersed and reassembled repeatedly. The violence was vicious and fearless, attacking police commissioners and high officials. Their intimate knowledge of the city as compared to the police—mostly made up of Europeans and up-country, migrant recruits—proved tremendously useful to the rioters. They used alleys and bye-lanes while the police, who had been drilled in using regular streets and roads, and tactics of frontal combat, were left confused and powerless. In Shambazar in 1891, the police were only successful when they abandoned conventional methods, crept up on the rioters from behind using a bye-lane, and attacked them on the flank and rear.[39] Significantly, the rioters indulged in neither looting nor attack on private premises despite being active along main arterial roads.[40] Their targets were clearly Europeans and representatives of the state.

There are repeated instances of a see-saw battle between the police and the rioters as seen in the constant demolition and rebuilding of the 'mosque', and the constant clearances and reassemblies on Harrison Road in 1897. Despite seventy-four being arrested on the first day, the rioters carried on relentlessly. Twenty-five police were at one point besieged in the Municipal Pumping Station without any firearms. Even the police commissioner and his deputy were stoned. Nor did the rioters hesitate to attack a large party of eighty constables. Europeans were clearly vulnerable, although the chief object of attack, the government admitted, was the police. About a dozen were hurt. Two officers of the Gloucestershire Regiment cycling down Upper Circular Road had stones and brickbats thrown at them. The rioters on Harrison Road pulled down the old wooden lamp posts setting fire to them, and blocked the road by rolling onto the centre of the road big drain-pipes that had been left at the sides for later use in construction.[41]

39 *ARPC, 1891*, p. 19.

40 Bolton to Secretary of the Government of India, Home Department, 'Papers on Chitpur Riots', no. 1796, p. 3.

41 Police Commissioner, A.H. James to Secretary of the Bengal Government, C.W. Bolton, 'Papers on Chitpur Riots', no. 1796, pp. 6–7.

The deputy commissioner, H.E.C. Paget, noted the ferocity of the crowd in the Rajabazar area, which included even women and children:

> I saw soon afterwards a most determined attack on one party [of four constables], notwithstanding that they were firing on the mob. The men were struck with bricks and had to fall back.... We dispersed the rioters that were on the spot and proceeded to the Belliaghatta police-station.... On arrival at the Circular Road and Machooa Bazar crossing [with police and military in two brakes], where we had dispersed the mob in the first instance, we drove into some telegraph or railing wires which had been securely fastened from tree to tree across the road. The horses in the front brake were nearly thrown down, and at the same time stones were showered at us from behind the surrounding houses. Some of our men were struck with stones.... We then drove south as far as Sealdah station. Stones [continued to be] ... thrown at us from the lanes leading into Circular Road on the town side. There were women and children in theses lanes, so it was not safe to fire, and we moved on to Union Jute Mills, where we found everything quiet.[42]

When trouble erupted in the city again in 1918 following the publication of a disparaging comment about the Prophet in an English daily, the police and Europeans were once again the targets of attack. There were a good many cases of stabbing with some police officers and a number of constables injured. The deputy commissioner of police, Shaw, was injured by brickbats in Zakaria Street.[43] Another deputy commissioner of police (Bartley) was stabbed. There were attacks on Europeans too, with both military

---

Ironically, using building material parts and debris from construction sites and accessories for urban beautification schemes seem to have been a recurrent theme in these riots. Lamp posts, drain pipes, and railing parts were strategically used to block roads and obstruct patrols. Also see *Hindoo Patriot*, 14 September 1918, for reports of how plant tubs, dustbins, and other footpath accessories were used to barricade streets.

[42] Deputy Police Commissioner, H.E.C. Paget's Report, 2 July 1897, 'Papers on Chitpur Riots', no. 1796, p. 11.

[43] *Hindoo Patriot*, 14 September 1918.

patrols and individuals fearlessly attacked.[44] The Indian Defence Force (IDF) was deployed and the police were compelled to open fire, resulting in injuries. At the Nakhoda mosque, where the Lincolnshire regiment was in charge, firing led to a number of casualties among the rioters. Brickbats were being apparently hurled at the military and police from the rooftop resulting in the order of fire. Twelve were apparently killed.[45]

The characters of both disturbances in 1897 and 1918, however, do not appear particularly religious. The police perceive the *julahas* or weavers as wrongdoers,[46] but in reality, this was the urban poor—Bengalis and non-Bengalis, Hindus and Muslims, migrants and non-migrants alike—who had rioted. In Chitpore, for instance, Hindu representation was not entirely marginal. Amongst those rioters killed was a fifteen-year-old boy, Gajadhar Kurmi, and officials believed that Marwaris had also played a role in stirring up trouble as they had an 'old score to settle with the police'.[47] Up-country Hindu 'budmashes', possibly including mill workers, are also reported as having played a role.[48] Other uncharacteristic

[44] *Bengalee*, 11 September 1918. Two cases of attacks on individuals were reported which involved severe injuries. The victims had to be removed to the Medical College and Campbell hospitals.

[45] Ronaldshay, the governor of Bengal, says this was unfortunate and the officer ordering the fire might have taken a 'doubtful' decision. See Lord Ronaldshay, 'My Bengal Diary', February 1917–November 1919, p. 175. Also see *Bengalee*, 11 September 1918.

[46] These mostly Muslim weavers from the United Provinces were a vital part of the jute industry in Calcutta. See Gyanendra Pandey, *The Construction of Communalism in Colonial North India* (New Delhi: Oxford University Press, 1990), pp. 66–108.

[47] *Amrita Bazar Patrika*, 16 July 1897, p. 5; NAI, Home (Judicial), March 1897, A: nos 31–42; May 1897, B: nos 297–308, cited in Dipesh Chakrabarty, 'Communal Riots and Labour: Bengal's Jute Mill-Hands in the 1890s', *Past and Present*, 91 (May 1981): 140–69, 159. The Marwaris were protesting against the recent police categorization of their rain-gambling activities as crime.

[48] C.W. Bolton, Chief Secretary of Bengal Government to the Secretary of the Government of India, Home Department, 'Papers on Chitpur Riots', no. 1796, p. 1.

participants included those like Cohen, a young Jew, who repeatedly cut off the telephone lines on Harrison Road to prevent communication among the authorities.[49] The profile of the urban poor in the Talla riot emerges as composed of masons, thatchers, bricklayers, coolies, jetty workers, labourers, and methars.[50]

Dipesh Chakrabarty holds that the tensions were also a spillover from the recent anti-cow-killing agitation in some districts (like Shahabad) of the UP and Bihar 1895 onwards.[51] Chakrabarty discusses the key role played by Muslim elite leaders in the riot, emphasizing the lines of communal solidarity that cut vertically across class strata. The Bengal government too believed this to be the case. The demi-official letter from C.W. Bolton, secretary of the Bengal government, to the Government of India, points out how not just *maulvies*, or Muslim religious leaders, but civilian bodies and individuals, including pleaders and barristers with high posts in government, were involved.[52]

But as later scholarship has proven, the role of the Muslim elite in the Shambazar and Chitpore riots was at best partial.[53] The urge to practice restraint and the public condemnations from Muslim leaders following the events at Talla-Chitpore testify to this. When under pressure from the government, the leaders were eager

[49] Police Commissioner A.H. James to Secretary of the Bengal Government, C.W. Bolton, 'Papers on Chitpur Riots', no. 1796, p. 10.

[50] *Ananda Bazaar Patrika*, 18 and 25 July 1897, cited in D. Chakrabarty, 'Communal Riots and Labour', 159. See also Police Commissioner A.H. James to Secretary of the Bengal Government, C.W. Bolton, 'Papers on Chitpur Riots', no. 1796, p. 10.

[51] See D. Chakrabarty, 'Communal Riots and Labour', 142–9. The Hindu workers were also mobilized by Hindu Marwari traders, he argues, a trend later taken up by the Hindu Mahasabha.

[52] C.W. Bolton, Chief Secretary of Bengal Government to the Secretary of the Government of India, Home Department, 'Papers on Chitpur Riots', no. 1813, folio 2.

[53] S. Basu, *Does Class Matter?*; Arjan De Haan, 'Unsettled Settlers: Migrant Workers and Industrial Capitalism in Calcutta', *Modern Asian Studies* 31, no. 4 (1997): 919–49. Also see the critical earlier work of Kenneth McPherson, *The Muslim Microcosm: Calcutta, 1918 to 1935* (Weisbaden: Steiner, 1974).

to demonstrate their loyalty to the administration. A fatwa was issued by Maulvi Syed Mahomed Malee and others, declaring that no building that was not erected on *waqf* land or land expressly dedicated for religious purposes and without proper authorization could serve as a mosque. Circulars were also sent to all imams of mosques in Calcutta to urge their congregations to stay calm over the Chitpore riots.[54] Hindu elites and newspapers, by contrast, were actually encouraging. The *Bengalee* and even ultra-conservative Hindu newspapers like the *Samay* sympathized with the rioters.

Subho Basu has demonstrated the anti-government nature of the early mill disturbances, particularly of the way it fed into the Talla–Chitpore riots the following year. The fellow feeling between Muslim and Hindu mill workers in these riots, the deep suspicion of government institutions, and anger towards factory managers and police in general was widely reported in local newspapers and underlines 'the mutuality of interest that bound the urban poor together'.[55] In the Howrah court, a notice was put up in Persian and Bengali calling upon 'Hindus and Muslims to rise and loot the house of the district magistrate and the deputy district magistrate'.[56]

During the 1918 riots, the involvement of the migrant communities is evident. It is significant that Bengali Hindus and Muslims mostly stayed away.[57] As in 1897, the police and military made preparations, blocking the bridges into the city and having an armed force ready on the scene, following initial rioting in the mill areas.[58] In the thick of the trouble, coolies in Garden Reach area tried persistently to enter Calcutta but were checked by military police.[59] On the 9th of September, a considerable gathering congregated at the Nakhoda mosque. Despite the best efforts made by the leaders, the crowds were palpably beyond control and anti-British slogans were repeatedly chanted. Violent rioting ensued following

54 Police Commissioner A.H. James to Secretary of the Bengal Government, C.W. Bolton, 'Papers on Chitpur Riots', no. 1796, p. 9.

55 S. Basu, *Does Class Matter?*, pp. 122–3.

56 S. Basu, *Does Class Matter?*, p. 122.

57 McPherson, *The Muslim Microcosm*, p. 46.

58 Ronaldshay, 'My Bengal Diary', p. 171.

59 This was the 10th of September. Ronaldshay, 'My Bengal Diary', p. 175.

confrontations with the police and army and some perpetrators were seriously injured.[60] Sporadic rioting continued through the night and cloth shops looted in the surrounding bazaars, with the newspaper *Bengalee* reporting both Hindus and Muslims as being involved. Trouble died down by the 12th. Armed guards and police were sent out in force, including the Calcutta Rifles, Calcutta Scottish, the Lincolns, the Port Defence.[61] A leaflet drawn up by the government urging Muslims to restrain from further agitation was signed by leaders and the imam of the Nakhoda mosque.[62]

Spatial and Customary Tensions in the Urban Sphere: Mosques, Festivals, and Community

Apart from being conditioned by poverty and police repression, the riots also very much have at their centre a symbolical articulation of community. The expression of 'community' as ideological constructs of social organization staged collectively in public spaces from the end of the nineteenth century onwards in various north Indian cities and towns has been the subject of a rich scholarship.[63] Performance of religious festivities or popular protest, such studies have shown, constituted symbolical expressions of community identity in urban 'public arenas'.[64] For Calcutta,

[60] Ronaldshay, 'My Bengal Diary', pp. 172–4.

[61] *Bengalee*, 11 September 1918.

[62] Ronaldshay, 'My Bengal Diary', p. 176.

[63] Sandria Freitag, *Collective Action and Community: Public Arenas and the Emergence of Communalism in North India* (New Delhi: Oxford University Press, 1990); Douglas E. Haynes, *Rhetoric and Ritual in Colonial India: The Shaping of a Public Culture in Surat City, 1852–1928* (Berkeley, Los Angeles, and Oxford: University of California Press, 1991); Philip Lutgendorf, *The Life of a Text: Performing the Ramcaritmanas of Tulsidas* (Berkeley and Los Angeles: University of California Press, 1991).

[64] The most recent study that touches upon this is that of Nandini Gooptu, *The Politics of the Urban Poor in Early Twentieth Century India* (Cambridge: Cambridge University Press, 2001), where ritual collective performances in urban public spaces in north Indian towns in the interwar period are seen as shaping caste and communal identities.

Dipesh Chakrabarty establishes how the mosques and Islamic festivals were the hub of religious and social life for the migrant Muslims from north India. Kenneth McPherson has also noted how the pattern of migrant settlement by occupation and region in Calcutta at the start of the twentieth century fostered the growth of community 'ghettoes' amidst an alien urban environment.[65] As such it is hardly surprising, therefore, that violent anger was vented against extraneous forms of intervention in these socio-religious spaces in the form of imposition of standardized secular civic modes of living—banning ritual sacrifices, disputing the status of proclaimed religious buildings, and the like, as we shall see further in this section. Poor urban Muslims, therefore, fought for their customary rights and religious practices most bitterly in the face of mounting governmental interference.

Official characterization of the late nineteenth century riots in Calcutta and around, which tries to locate in this a specific communal identity and ties it to the more general problem of labour, is misleading. This section argues that the disturbances arose out of a clash between the imposition of modern standards of a uniform civic code and the numerous customary ways of living practised for generations in their original locations in north India by the city's immigrant residents. Besides, communal cooperation between Hindus and Muslims at various stages in the protests point to intersections of other solidarities defined by poverty and declining trust in governance. Sharp rise in the price of basic commodities during the years of the First World War alongside stagnating wages and epidemics thus hit both communities of the urban poor alike.[66] Both were subjected to indiscriminate police repression and the same harsh living conditions. Despite coming to clashes over activities in public space they could occupy the same living quarters, sharing a room with only a mat partition between them.[67] In some ways, these public arenas served as

[65] McPherson, *The Muslim Microcosm*, pp. 17, 34–5.

[66] McPherson, *The Muslim Microcosm*, pp. 33–5, 37. Influenza was the main killer in the war years.

[67] *Samay*, 3 September 1897, in *Indian Newspaper Reports (Bengal)*, 11 September 1897, cited in S. Basu, *Does Class Matter?* p. 123. Also see

alternative worlds to that structured by the colonial urban regime, which provided legitimacy and recognition to a range of actors and value-systems. These were, as yet, not definitively tinged by any sentiment of nationalism but did have a strong anti-government resonance about them.

While not going so far as calling this 'communal', it is possible to agree with Dipesh Chakrabarty that a rising community consciousness can be traced among Muslim mill workers during this period because of labour recruitment patterns (Muslims from Bihar and UP) and a sense of community identity as migrants in a strange land (hence the rallying around the Bakr Id festival and temporary mosques).[68] The intrinsic connections between the mill hands and the rioters in the city can be traced in most late nineteenth- and early twentieth-century disturbances. Either in the form of reinforcement to the city rioters or as followers on from precedents set in Calcutta, the mill hands were ever present on Calcutta's disturbed streets. In times of trouble police postings were organized strategically, therefore placing them at potential chief entry points for the mill populations—bridges and stations—to the city.

Migrant workers in the colonial jute industry in Bengal came mostly from the congested districts of the North Western Provinces and Bihar, some of whom lived in Calcutta. In 1901, the share of up-country men in the labour force for the mills stood at more than 60 per cent.[69] Until 1885–6 jute mill hands were mostly Bengalis. But with the massive expansion of the industry in the 1890s, there was a great demand for labour, which was met by an exodus from north India. Between 1891–2 and 1901–2, the net increase in Hooghly,

---

Parimal Ghosh, *Colonialism, Class and a History of the Calcutta Jute Millhands, 1880–1930* (Chennai: Orient Longman, 2000), Chapters 2 and 3.

68 In 1921, the Muslims of Calcutta numbered approximately 205,000 out of a population of nearly 900,000 in the city. *Census of India, 1921* 6, no. 1, pp. 4, 34. Of course, not all were migrant mill hands, with other crafts and trades such as carpentry, butchery, leatherwork, tailoring, and book binding also absorbing the migrant population.

69 Ranajit Dasgupta, 'Factory Labour in Eastern India: Sources of Supply, 1855–1946, Some Preliminary Findings', *Indian Economic and Social History Review* 13 (1976): 277–324, see 296.

Howrah, Calcutta, and the 24 Paraganas of migrants from Bihar, UP, and Orissa was 182,536, many of whom were entirely new to industrial work.[70] As Dipesh Chakrabarty notes:

> It was natural that their past attitudes, memories and prejudices would also form 'fresh recruits', as it were, in the formation of a social outlook of this group of people. A telling piece of evidence is the argument which a worker at Rishra gave ... as his reason for insisting on killing a cow on Bakr-Id, claiming that 'he had every year sacrificed a cow in his own country, and it was hard that he should now be prohibited from so doing, merely because he had changed his residence'. There was thus an 'immigrant mind' at work.[71]

Sardars or jobbers as recruiters and supervisors of labour drew on and reinforced the networks of community, village, and kin. Ideologies and social norms regulating the pre-industrial lives of the workforce were routinely mobilized by sardars in order to provide a focal point to the uprooted communities as well as to shore up their own standing within them. Amidst a bitterly fought scramble for jobs in the mills in the mid-1890s, the various caste-panchayats of the Hindu migrants and the Muslim ulema, together with the sardars, fulfilled 'the immigrant's need to hold on to certain constants in a hostile and changing environment'. For these socially marginal people, community consciousness was a bulwark against dislocation and insecurity.[72]

For the uprooted and alienated Muslim populations in the mill towns, rituals such as those of the sacrificial slaughter of cows on the occasion of Bakr Id provided one of the few occasions for celebration and a reinforcement of communal and regional solidarities. Any threat to such festivity, therefore, was seen as an assault on the community's right to ritual/customary freedom. The anti-cow-killing agitation in Bihar and UP in the 1890s, as Chakrabarty suggests, no doubt created some tensions, and there appeared heightened activity in both Calcutta and the mill areas

[70] Dasgupta, 'Factory Labour in Eastern India', p. 290, Table 3.

[71] D. Chakrabarty, 'Communal Riots and Labour', 149.

[72] D. Chakrabarty, 'Communal Riots and Labour', 154. For the role of sardars in keeping alive these caste, village, and religious networks, also see McPherson, *The Muslim Microcosm*, p. 35.

over the issue, with frequent clashes occurring during the celebration of Bakr Id.

It is, however, possible to argue that this had more to do with an assertion of ritual rights in tight urban spaces and the challenging of a purportedly secular municipal administration than being narrowly 'communal' in nature. The traditional *qurbani* (sacrifice) of cows in villages with mixed populations of Hindus and Muslims would have been for centuries conducted in secluded and usually segregated areas where Muslims lived. By contrast, the close proximity of the two communities and their shared inhabitation of public spaces in crowded cities, mofussils and mill towns in the late nineteenth century meant potentially volatile consequences. The clash of mutually antagonistic belief-systems in circumstances of extreme deprivation and aggressive communitarian activities provided the flash-point for numerous such disturbances. And the role played in this by harsh managerial and municipal regimes would not be hard to seek.

More often than not, up-country Muslims were severely restricted in their celebration of annual festivities in the mill towns.[73] Similar restrictions applied to Hindus as well, although the conflict ensuing from them is less transparent in official records.[74] Riots occurred over leave during festive periods—when workers preferred to visit their home villages—in the Baranagar, Titagarh, and Kamarhati mills in 1894–5.[75] In Garden Reach, Rishra, and Titagarh again in 1895–6, this happened during the occasion of Bakr Id. In each case, the principal 'trouble makers' were identified as Muslims, and indeed it was largely the migrant Muslim workers in the mills who were targeted by the administration, even though, in two out of the three situations discussed previously, no trouble had actually taken place.[76] The principal grievances of the migrant

73 S. Basu, *Does Class Matter?* pp. 118–25.

74 Thus, in 1896, the Hindu workers of Shamnagar Cotton Mills were refused leave for Rath Yatra but took them by forcibly threatening strike action. Indian Jute Manufacturers Association (IJMA) Report, 1896, pp. 76–80, cited in D. Chakrabarty, 'Communal Riots and Labour', 144.

75 D. Chakrabarty, 'Communal Riots and Labour', 144.

76 In the Garden Reach case in 1896, 100 military troopers and infantry-men were sent out with twenty-seven constables at the request

Muslims, in turn, were directed against the government. But the administration was heavy-handed and insensitive in its handling of the crises, angering the workers.[77]

Mosques in this setting emerged as the symbol and, often, centre of community feeling for Muslims as we have seen in both the Nickaripara and Talla riots. But crucially, the connection between land-grabbing and mosque-building activities was not entirely accidental for the poor migrant Muslims in central Calcutta, as their settlements came under pressure from the local land-market. The government noted how there appeared to exist a '... common practice for Mohammedan tenants of the lower classes in the suburbs of Calcutta to erect such huts ...' and later proclaiming them as mosques without seeking appropriate authorization, which it was keen to put a halt to.[78]

At the munsif's court during the trial of the rioters in 1897, a key question hinged on the veracity of the allegation that the disputed building was a mosque. The judgment noted that although it might have been used as a place for private prayers by the hut's occupant and some of his associates, it was never intended for the public, nor did it appear to have had a history of public worship.[79] Presumably, its recognition as a mosque might have affected the verdict and established the residential claim to it and the surrounding land by a wider community of pious Muslims. Seemingly 'communal' impulses could thus also

---

of the district magistrate, although it later transpired that it was a case of 'false alarm'. Only a minor disturbance occurred in Titagarh, but was restricted to the mill area. S. Basu, *Does Class Matter*, pp. 119, 121.

77 In Rishra in 1895, Muslims of the Standard Jute Mill were restricted from sacrificing cows, the local mosque was surrounded by a police cordon and its imam arrested, and even railway clerks were instructed not to sell tickets to Muslims coming down to Rishra from elsewhere to join in the celebration. S. Basu, *Does Class Matter*, pp. 120–1.

78 Bolton to Secretary of the Government of India, Home Department, 'Papers on Chitpur Riots', no. 1796, p. 3.

79 Judgment of the Officiating Munsif in the Court of the 1st Munsif at Sealdah in the case of the Estate of Hon'ble Prosonno Kumar Tagore vs. Himmat Khan and others, 'Papers on Chitpur Riots', no. 1796, pp. 12–13.

be sparked off by underlying economic factors. In a confidential note to J.P. Hewett, Secretary to the Government of India, Home Department, C.W. Bolton, Secretary to the Government of Bengal, noted how there seems to have appeared a trend where such disputed land was bought by Muslims from Hindu landlords after initial clashes—most notably in the Shambazar case a few years earlier—for the erection of mosques and might have well acted as an incentive later on at Talla in Chitpore.[80]

Throughout the second half of the nineteenth century, former Muslim proprietors were being gradually displaced by rich Marwaris and so the backlash against the demolition of mosques, mobilizing the poor Muslims, could have been a ploy to cling on to the extremely valuable location in the central part of the city.[81] Marwaris in turn made use of the anti-cow-killing agitation to consolidate their own position in the land market. During the 1910 Bakr Id riots, it was the acquisitive capitalist interest of a Marwari merchant—who had not only successfully evicted the largely Muslim population of nearby bustees, but was also keen to trade in more land in the Harrison Road area—that led to the Marwari community's objection to cow-sacrifice in the

[80] In 1893, thus, there occurred similar dispute following the passing of Civil Court decrees for possession of two pieces of land in the same locality, where huts alleged to be mosques had been constructed with local Muslims laying claim to them. The police, in that case, intervened between the parties and it was settled that one plot of land would be purchased by the Muslim community, while the other would be surrendered to the Hindu landlord. Confidential demi-official letter to J.P. Hewett from C.W. Bolton, dated 1 August 1897. In fact, even in Talla, Jyotindra Mohan Tagore initially agreed to make over the land to the Muslims after the riot, but finally withdrew the offer under pressure from the government. See Police Commissioner A.H. James to Secretary of the Bengal Government, C.W. Bolton, 'Papers on Chitpur Riots', no. 1796, pp. 8–9.

[81] The connection between the erection of unauthorized mosques in the city and the scramble for land in central Calcutta between the Gujarati Muslim Memons and the Hindu Marwari merchants has been pointed out by Dipesh Chakrabarty. See D. Chakrabarty, 'Communal Riots and Labour', 166–7.

area, which in turn sparked off the riots, killing six and seriously injuring seventy-six.[82]

The rising wave of pan-Islamism in the city, following British treatment of Turkey and the Caliphate at the end of the First World War eventually brought together two sets of disparate targets for the migrant Muslims—the Marwaris and the British government—when they erupted into riots in September 1918 that was briefly covered earlier.[83] Resentment in the community was sparked off by the appearance of a news item in the *Indian Daily News* that was seen as being disrespectful towards the Prophet. Violent and stirring speeches were delivered at several locations in Calcutta, jihad declared against 'the enemies of Islam' and solidarity expressed with the Indian revolutionaries and the recent martyrdom of Khudiram Bose.[84] While the traditional Muslim leadership remained confused and ambiguous, more uncompromising sections took over, some of whom were based at the newer Urdu presses in the city.[85] A violent speech was made by Jaffar Kalami, a leading journalist of the time, to about 2,000 gathered before the Government House—even while there was a Muslim

[82] The Marwari firm in question, eager to impress prospective Hindu buyers—presumably from the same community—were extremely keen to render this a qurbani-free zone. Hence, the objection. In fact, the trend can be traced back to 1894 when a Marwari-led Cow Protection Society was set up in the Burrabazar area. D. Chakrabarty, 'Communal Riots and Labour', 166–7. For an account of the riots see *ARPC, 1910*, pp. 10–11; also see P. Ghosh, *Colonialism, Class and a History of the Calcutta Jute Millhands*, pp. 178–80.

[83] Confidential demi-official letter to J.P. Hewett from C.W. Bolton, dated 1 August 1897. P. Ghosh, *Colonialism, Class and a History of the Calcutta Jute Millhands*, pp. 164–97. For pan-Islamic sentiments being mobilized in other urban labour/communal disturbance contexts, see Chitra Joshi, 'Bonds of Community, Ties of Religion: Kanpur Textile Workers in the Early Twentieth Century', *Indian Economic and Social History Review* 22, no. 3 (1985): 251–80.

[84] Ronaldshay, 'My Bengal Diary', pp. 158–9. Notices were served banning some of these speakers from public meetings for a year. See pp. 167, 160.

[85] The fractured nature of leadership among Muslims in Calcutta during the period has been covered in detail in McPherson's study. He

delegation inside, negotiating with the governor—urging them to meet the police unarmed and allowing themselves to be shot down.[86] The crowd had followed the deputation to the Government House armed with sticks and umbrellas, urging passers-by to join them, but were eventually stopped by armed police near Tiretta Bazar.[87] Leaders were also palpably unable to control the passion of the crowds gathered in Zakaria Street where the riots initially started, with some eventually seeking police protection.[88]

In the ensuing violence, the police as well as Europeans and Marwaris seem to have been specifically targeted. While there was general looting of mostly cloth and food shops, Marwari stores and homes were singled out for attack. The Manicktala and Beliaghata markets bore the brunt of the assault even as Marwari merchants closed their shops and took refuge inside. Several instances of Marwaris being severely assaulted and killed were reported in newspapers, where individuals had apparently been dragged out of palanquins, motor cars, and carriages and brutally murdered on thoroughfares.[89]

The Marwaris had become unpopular among the poorer sections of Calcutta's residents for a variety of reasons. As seen previously, their land grabbing practices in central Calcutta had led to the eviction of large groups of mostly poorer Muslims towards the industrial suburbs, leading to widespread resentment among

---

points to the appeal of populist leaders, journalists, and associations based on religious, charitable, and trading interests among lower-class Muslims. Urdu newspapers such as the *Naqqash*, *Jamhur*, and the *Sadaqat*, for example, played a lead role in the 1918 agitation. By contrast, the remote aristocratic and Western-educated sections of the community had little power. See McPherson, *The Muslim Microcosm*, pp. 20–32, 40–2.

[86] Ronaldshay, 'My Bengal Diary', pp. 170–1. The deputations later showed unease in leaving the safety of the Government House and join the crowds outside. See p. 174.

[87] *Hindoo Patriot*, 14 September 1918.

[88] Ronaldshay, 'My Bengal Diary', p. 171. Bricks were thrown at the leaders when they tried to calm the crowds.

[89] *Bengalee*, 11 September 1918. A locally well-known Marwari millionaire was savagely attacked when travelling in his car. He later succumbed to his injuries. *Hindoo Patriot*, 14 September 1918.

these communities. Marwari engineering of local Cow Protection Societies in the city further augmented a general climate of hostility towards Muslims. The stockpiling of cotton piece goods by Marwari merchants in an environment of wartime crisis and rise in prices of clothes was reported frequently in local newspapers. What made the situation particularly galling was the governmental reluctance to take action against the Marwari traders. Unscrupulous trading practices in the food sector had also recently weakened the standing of the community, when the contamination of ghee (clarified butter)—routinely used in Hindu ceremonies and rituals—by animal fat was exposed. Deputations were sent to the governor and a mass *hom* or fire sacrifice was organized on the banks of the Ganges with about four thousand Brahmins participating by way of collective ritual atonement.[90]

The rhetoric in both circulating pamphlets and the vernacular press were decidedly anti-British—rather than anti-Hindu—urging for revolution and the courting of police violence.[91] The English proprietor of the *Indian Daily News*, Mr Graham, was singled out for condemnation, with some even demanding that he be exterminated.[92] The Bengal Governor was particularly concerned about '*racial* and religious passions [emphasis mine]' generated by speakers and Muhammadan papers like the *Millat* and *Naqqash*.[93] It was not communal passions against Hindus that motivated the rioters in 1918. The Marwaris had only been targeted as a symbol of immoral profiteering and agents of a morally bankrupt government,

[90] Ronaldshay, 'My Bengal Diary', pp. 77–9. Brahmins of the city sent for priests from Benares who arrived to advise them. The defaulting Marwari firm of Gopiram Bhakal Ram received an exemplary fine of 1 lakh rupees, and proprietors and dealers excommunicated by the Marwari Association.

[91] Ronaldshay, 'My Bengal Diary', pp. 158–60, 163–4, 170–1. Kenneth McPherson too has noted how during the 1918 riots 'the main enemy' were the British. Mcpherson, *The Muslim Microcosm*, pp. 46–7.

[92] Ronaldshay, 'My Bengal Diary', pp. 158–9.

[93] Ronaldshay, 'My Bengal Diary', pp. 156, 158. Urdu pamphlets, inflammatory in tone, were in circulation. See pp. 163–4. The leading journalists of *Rahbar*, *Millat*, and *Jamhur* were eventually banned from the city. Mcpherson, *The Muslim Microcosm*, pp. 44–5.

not as Hindus. Instead, the invocations of martyrdom, passionate street corner speeches, multiple processions, the siting of the initial congregation within the precincts of the holy Nakhoda mosque—all point towards a symbolical posturing of 'community' by a displaced and cornered Muslim community of petty traders, labourers, artisans, and carters that was already under threat from an indifferent municipal regime when the devastating news from Turkey arrived.

While 'nationalism' is an inappropriate term to be tagged on to collective action this early, it is possible to argue that the experience of deprivation and social marginalization in a bustling but ruthless city encouraged alternative ways of configuring these communities that were the very obverse of modern, civic identities that the colonial state hoped to foster. The feeling of uprootedness only served to accentuate their cultural past and rural heritage, and inequalities bred within inflexible, standardized municipal regimes fostered millenarian visions of a more egalitarian order. With an ineffective leadership from the upper strata, popular elements—led by the petty bourgeoisie and journalists—took to the streets to express the grievances of the community. In the unrest studied in this chapter (and also in Chapter 4) it is possible to see how breaking the law was a means of asserting rights way before the radicalization of masses by Swadeshi leaders.

Rising Anti-government Sentiments: The Plague Riots of 1898

The plague in Calcutta in 1898–1907 is a little known chapter as compared to its bigger incarnation in Bombay during the same period. And yet, appearing in Calcutta a little after it did in Bombay, the plague impacted on people if not so much in terms of numbers dead as in terms of the panic created by the prospect of impending governmental measures to control the disease.[94] Following the detection of an outbreak in the city, the municipal health officer

94 The Plague Commission headed by Risley had been set up as early as 1896 to prevent the occurrence of plague in Calcutta by improving the sanitary conditions in the city.

announced stringent measures that included house inspections and possible demolitions, as well as quarantine of suspected patients. In April 1898 the Calcutta Corporation formed ward-level vigilance committees that could enter and search houses for cases. Wild rumours of forcible inoculation and compulsory quarantine, poisoned needles, and killer gases for inhalation circulated as a result. In one case, it was reported that drums were being beaten in the city suggesting that the viceroy was sending regiments to round up bustees and inoculate people.[95] Panic followed and a few days later there was a spectacular large-scale exodus, with 'at least one-fourth of the population of Calcutta fleeing ... [the city] in a state of wild panic'. Stampedes were reported at road, ferry, and rail stations.[96]

There occurred a number of strikes among municipal scavengers in May, as well as carters and hackney-carriage drivers.[97] The entire trade of the city for a time almost came to a standstill for lack of labour supply.[98] These were quickly followed by riots. A large number of workers took to the streets to oppose the plague inoculation drive, with workers from the Calcutta port, the jute presses, and mills, and even peons assembling in various parts of the city and 'behaving in a threatening and defiant way'. Traffic was obstructed, hackney carriages attacked, tramway lines ripped up, and Europeans out and about in the town assaulted. In a particularly tragic case, a young Austrian carrying a handbag was beaten to death on Calcutta's streets for suspicion of being an inoculator.[99]

The government responded by reassuring the Bengali middle classes, allowing 'family hospitals' to be run in 'respectable'

95 *Bengalee*, 14 May 1898.

96 H.M. Crake, Assistant Special Health Officer, *The Calcutta Plague, 1896–1907 with Observations on the Epidemiology of Plague* (Calcutta, 1908), p. 22.

97 *Bengalee*, 7 May 1898.

98 British residents were particularly affected by the striking butchers of New Market on whom they relied for their fresh meat supplies. *Report of the Indian Plague Commission*, vol. 1 (1898–9), Appendix XX, Report on the Plague in Calcutta by J. Nield Cook, p. 469.

99 *Report of the Indian Plague Commission*, vol. 1 (1898–9), Appendix XX, p. 469.

households so that relatives could be cared for in the comfort of their own homes, and calling the bhadralok on board to form part of the vigilante force. No such privileges existed for the larger populations of lower-class people however, who remained terrified. Huts and other temporary constructions in slums were routinely demolished as 'they were impossible to thoroughly disinfect' with thousands displaced every year.[100] The main plague hospital of the city was at Manicktala, which also coincidentally had a burning ghat. So dreaded was this place that in contemporary parlance, 'going to Maniktollah' became equivalent to saying 'going to your death-bed'.[101] Confidential police reports from the districts even admitted that the uneasiness caused by the governmental measures had extended far into the interior.[102]

Resolute battles took place between householders and plague officials carrying out evacuation. There were innumerable cases of evasion and obstruction.[103] Non-consensual removal of suspected plague victims aroused the ire of relatives and onlookers, resulting in burnt ambulances and medicinal supplies.[104] It is significant that on many occasions ambulances bore the brunt of the attack, so much so that a contemporary newspaper suggested that as it had

[100] Thus, for example, 319 huts were destroyed in 1904 displacing some 3,000 people. Letter from R.T. Greer, Chairman of the Calcutta Corporation to the Secretary of the Government of Bengal, Municipal Department, dated 19/21 November 1904, in *Report on Plague in Calcutta for the Year ending 30th June 1904*, p. 1.

[101] *Report of the Indian Plague Commission*, vol. 1 (1898–9), Appendix XX, p. 469.

[102] 'Report on the Plague in Calcutta', Letter from the Chief Secretary to the Government of Bengal, C.W. Bolton, to Hewett of the Bengal Secretariat, dated 18 June 1898, IOR/L/PJ/6/485:1422.

[103] Residents failed to report dead rats or suspected plague incidents. Other refused to allow postmortem of dead friends and relatives, as in one reported case where a *dome* (body-burner employed in Hindu death rituals) was carried away and given ritual cremation by his other dome friends at the burning ghat. *Report of the Indian Plague Commission*, vol. 1 (1898–9), Appendix XX, p. 466.

[104] *ARPC, 1898*, p. 5.

become such a 'symbol of fear and alarm', the ambulance should be done away with and substituted by the more familiar palki or palanquin.[105] The white Bombay ambulance, officials reported, had become a particular bête noire. It was rumoured that patients died as they were made to inhale something while in them.[106]

Indian medics were not spared. Dr S.N. Bose of the Health Department was assaulted and stopped from removing a plague patient by a large number of men.[107] In Champatollah Lane, when a medical student meant to inspect a suspected plague case arrived with the ambulance cart and a medical team, a large crowd of about two hundred gathered forcing the team to leave—the medical student being chased by shouts of '*Mar! Mar!*' (Kill! Kill!)—and burning down the cart. The European officers of the team had bricks thrown at them.[108]

Any governmental official deemed suspicious was indiscriminately set upon. In the Taltollah section of the town, two men, believed to be *ticcawallahs* (vaccinators), were assaulted with lathis.[109] In a significant incident, when two medical officers, Dr Laing and Dr B.B. Sircar, went to inspect the house of a Babu Jogesh Chunder Roy in Bhawanipur, on his application for an Isolation Hospital, a large number of men collected outside the house suspecting them to be inoculators. Although the owner of the house remonstrated with them, some broke into the premises, and commenced searching the house for the doctors, threatening the owner. As the rioters came up the main staircase, in a dramatic confrontation, Dr Laing fired, wounding two who eventually died.[110] The *Bengalee*, in reporting the incident, criticized Laing for his action.[111] In another separate incident in South 24 Parganas, a

[105] *Bengalee*, 21 May 1898.

[106] *Report of the Indian Plague Commission*, vol. 1 (1898–9), Appendix XX, p. 469.

[107] *ARPC, 1898*, p. 5.

[108] *Bengalee*, 14 May 1898.

[109] *ARPC, 1898*, p. 5.

[110] *ARPC, 1898*, p. 10.

[111] *Bengalee*, 28 May 1898.

violent attack was made on a party of Salt and Police Officers who were visiting villages in search of illegally manufactured salt.[112]

The middle classes in Calcutta were divided in their response to the riots vis-à-vis governmental measures. While some sections of the bhadralok press were quick to point to 'badmashes', and protest the innocence of the educated classes, other bhadralok newspapers like the *Bengalee* and *Amrita Bazar Patrika*, which were known for the anti-government stand, were accused of fomenting trouble and also of gross exaggeration by the authorities.[113] Even leading Urdu journals believed that Bengali babus were responsible for the recent trouble.[114]

There is some truth in these allegations. While not directly responsible for inciting the riots, those like Surendranath Banerjee, who had begun to be active in local politics and had recently been elected municipal commissioner, took a public stand on the excesses of the plague administration. In May 1898, his newspaper, *Bengalee*, published an account of a perfectly healthy man, Hari Das, being chased by plague officials and frightened to death, taking refuge in a neighbour's house.[115] The incident, while true, was admittedly reported with some degree of sensation, and Banerjee's intentions were further revealed when, soon after, he presented Hari Das in quite a spectacular fashion for an inspection before the municipal chairman, 'thereby attracting a large crowd outside the [municipal] office and nearly provoking a riot'.[116]

[112] 'Report on the Plague in Calcutta', Letter from the Chief Secretary to the Government of Bengal, C.W. Bolton, to Hewett of the Bengal Secretariat, dated 18 June 1898, IOR/L/PJ/6/485:1422.

[113] 'Report on the Plague in Calcutta', Letter from the Chief Secretary to the Government of Bengal, C.W. Bolton, to Hewett of the Bengal Secretariat, dated 18 June 1898, IOR/L/PJ/6/485:1422.

[114] For example, *Darussultanat and Urdu Guide*. See S. Basu, *Does Class Matter?*, p. 131.

[115] *Bengalee*, 21 May 1898. Apparently, a prostitute with a grudge against Hari Das had instigated the trouble.

[116] 'Report on the Plague in Calcutta', Letter from the Chief Secretary to the Government of Bengal, C.W. Bolton, to Hewett of the Bengal Secretariat, dated 18 June 1898, IOR/L/PJ/6/485:1422.

Briefly, the Bengali middle classes can be seen wresting the initiative and emerging as the spokespeople for larger groups of Calcutta's residents. The Municipal Ward Committees that were set up in April 1898 had leading residents in each ward overseeing the sanitation standards and tracking the disease in their areas. They established effective links with the bustee leaders to oversee the implementation of proper measures in cases of suspected plague.[117] The *Bengalee* rode the wave of anti-government sentiments. It was bold in the terms it laid down before the government:

> We have no hesitation in saying that if the Government were to force segregation, it would infallibly array popular feeling against its plague measures, and they are bound to fail if the people offer a silent but strenuous resistance We would [instead] suggest the opening of inoculation depots in different wards, and *guided by the influence and advice of their natural leaders* we have no doubt in our minds that the people will largely take to inoculation [italics mine]....[118]

The paper was consistent in its portrayal of concern for the less privileged, urging the municipality to disinfect the houses of those who could not afford it and the setting up of private ward hospitals where both middle classes and 'the poor tenants of the *bustis*' could go.[119]

The government responded by declaring that there would be no quarantine or summary segregation, and that inoculation—though desirable—would not be compulsory as well. While the police had played a major role in the discovery of cases earlier, they stopped making special inquiries following the protest in the newspapers.[120] By 1906, 8-anna rewards were being offered to individuals for getting themselves inoculated voluntarily.[121]

[117] See, for example, cases reported in *Bengalee*, 21 May and 28 May 1898.

[118] *Bengalee*, 30 April 1898.

[119] *Bengalee*, 7 May 1898.

[120] *Bengalee*, 7 May 1898. Also see *Report of the Indian Plague Commission*, vol. 1 (1898–9), Appendix XX, Report on the Plague in Calcutta, pp. 468–9.

[121] *Report on Plague in Calcutta for the Year ending June 1906*, p. 13. The report for the next year, however, complained that the reward was attracting the 'wrong' kind of people—beggars, opium addicts, drunkards, and so on.

Swadeshi Unrest and the Transformation of Urban Public Spaces

Irreverence towards the administration was steadily making itself manifest towards the end of the nineteenth century, which took a distinct 'political' turn with Swadeshi. Radicalization of community identity and anti-government feeling seems to have set the trend for street riots in Calcutta at the start of the twentieth century. It was serious enough for the Calcutta Police to include a new sub-heading in their annual reports from this period onwards: 'General occurrences during the year calling for notice'—all general disturbances and public order issues reported under it.[122] The 1905–7 Swadeshi Movement organized in defiance of Curzon's call for the partition of the Bengal province mobilized the rising waves of protest against the municipal and colonial governments to pose an unprecedented scale of agitation in the city.

Following Curzon's announcement of partition, the streets of Calcutta became animated with the first ever concentrated and sustained mass protest in the sub-continent. Curzon had anticipated, at best, 'howls' from Bengalis following his announcement.[123] Instead, he faced the most serious threat to the stability of the colonial government in Bengal. There were mass protests, boycotting of foreign goods, picketing, and a series of workers' strikes which paralyzed the city for two years. Ironically, the nationalist newspaper *Bengalee* announced: 'A new impulse has taken possession of the people—a new force has come into politics. Lord Curzon be thanked.'[124]

The protest started with a call for the boycott of foreign goods—Manchester cloth and Liverpool salt—made at a meeting in the Calcutta Town Hall on 7 August 1905. The actual day of the agitation passed off peacefully on 16 October 1905. *Rakhi*s or bracelets of coloured thread—the customary symbol avowing brotherly love—were exchanged on a mass scale among Bengalis in a gesture of fraternal unity. In a spectacular show of solidarity, a huge crowd walked barefoot through the streets of

[122] *ARPC, 1912*, p. 10.

[123] Curzon Collection, MSS Eur F. 111/210 (vol. 31).

[124] *Bengalee*, 12 September 1905.

Calcutta in a traditional sign of mourning and took a solemn dip in the water of the holy Ganges. This ritual was repeated annually until the partition was called off.[125] Shops remained closed almost all over the northern part of the city. But the general unrest that followed required considerable vigilance, for although it was 'obviously inadvisable for the police to interfere in a purely political agitation', it was necessary to intervene in the interest of 'public peace' if the agitation degenerated into acts of violence.[126]

Sudipta Kaviraj has discussed the contrasting use of public spaces in the metropolitan West and the colonial world. European urban public spaces evolved from being characterized by state pageants, royal processions, and splendour to sites of protest following the radicalization and mobilization of the urban poor. Public meetings and demonstrations used theses spaces in a gesture of gaining attention and inverting aristocratic authority. In the mythology of the French Revolution, for example, the public squares play an important role. Subsequently, public spaces symbolized national memory. Important battles and heroes were publicly commemorated by naming streets and squares after them. In that sense, stepping outside the house into the city streets, says Kaviraj, '... was instantly to step into the history of the French or the British nation'.[127]

In the colonial city, such spaces which could be called 'public', that is, meant to represent the entire people in a sense of collective ownership, did not exist. It was more a one-sided exhibition of state power. So when a political public sphere germinated in Calcutta in the late nineteenth century, the question of suitable spaces where meetings could be held arose. The earliest meetings were allowed and held in temples, library precincts, or town halls with the explicit understanding that outright political dissidence

[125] *Bengalee*, 18 October 1905; IGP Report, pp. 28–30. Also see S. Sarkar, *The Swadeshi Movement in Bengal*, p. 244.

[126] *ARPC, 1905*, p. 6.

[127] Sudipta Kaviraj, 'Filth and the Public Sphere: Concepts and Practices about space in Calcutta', *Public Culture* 10, no. 1 (1997): 83–113, at 95.

shall not be expressed at such gatherings. But with the unprecedented growth of nationalist mass politics, they moved out to public squares and parks, and spilled out onto the streets. By the end of the 1940s, audacious and astounding inversions of the colonial symbolical order were taking place—in spaces around the Ochterlony monument (dedicated to the memory of David Ochterlony, a commander of the East Indian Company forces) and the hitherto rather exclusively European space of the Maidan.[128] It altered in significant ways the relationship of the people to city spaces, especially giving a sense of 'ownership' to the poor.

Between 1905 and 1907, several protest meetings were held at the Calcutta Town Hall, starting from the first meeting on 18 March 1904.[129] At a historic meeting at the Town Hall on the 7th of August, boycott of foreign/European goods was proposed by Narendranath Sen.[130] Meetings were also held at the Star Theatre, Albert Hall, and Grand Theatre in August 1905. In addition, other symbolic locations—in private residences, temples, and community grounds—underlined the moral, communitarian, and spiritual nerve-centres of the movement. Swadeshi shops selling indigenous products—primarily cloth—sprang up in Calcutta's streets in the Bowbazar, Burrabazar, and Chitpore areas.[131]

[128] The initial significance of the Maidan as a regulatory space of control, defence (originally established to enable the firing of cannons across open space from the Fort), and segregation (exclusive leisure activities for the British and Europeans) has been highlighted. See Helen Thomas, 'Stories of Plain Territory: The Maidan, Calcutta', in *The Unknown City: Contesting Architecture and Social Space*, edited by Iain Borden, Jane Rendell, Joe Kerr, and Alicia Pivaro (Massachusetts: Massachusetts Institute of Technology Press, 2002), pp. 138–59, at pp. 144–9.

[129] IGP Report, p. 4. The Town Hall space had been claimed in the past by Indians—from the mid-nineteenth century onwards—for public meetings but these had mainly been concerned with civic and social rather than political issues. See Basudev Chattopadhyay, *The Town Hall of Calcutta: A Brief History* (Calcutta: Homage Trust, 1998), pp. 28–60.

[130] IGP Report, p. 7.

[131] S. Sarkar, *The Swadeshi Movement in Bengal*, pp. 98–9.

Homes of middle-class leaders, intellectuals, traditional aristocracy, and newspaper press offices provided critical nodes for protest meetings. The office of the radical evening daily, *Sandhya*, run by Brahmabandhab Upadhyaya at 193 Cornwallis Street became a focal point for the striking press workers and Bengali railway stationmasters.[132] On 24 September 1905, Brahmins met at the house of Pasupati Bose in Bagbazar declaring imported salt, sugar, and cloth as unfit for use in religious ceremonies.[133] *Rajbaris* or aristocratic residences in Calcutta and around, with their vast compounds and forecourts, were frequently handed over for swadeshi mass meetings.[134] Representing the bastions of Hindu aristocratic glory of a bygone era, they reminded the gathered audience of their firm purpose. When braziers whose brass trade had been affected by the import of cheap enamelled utensils met in thousands at Kansaripara (the brazier colony) in the premises of a prominent Pramanick family, the meeting was presided over by the poet Rabindranath Tagore. The *Bengalee* reported how 'every nook and corner in the balcony and terrace was filled up' and the younger braziers sang *Bande Mataram* with much patriotic fervour.[135]

Temples bestowed propitious energy to events and represented the spiritual heart of the (predominantly Hindu) protesting community. Ceremonial oath-taking and other religious rites taking place within their sanctified limits and outside of secular, civic spaces intensified bonds among participants. Two huge meetings were held at the Kalighat temple where priests presided over the administering of the swadeshi pledge between September 1905 and March 1906. The first meeting was held on the auspicious day of

[132] S. Sarkar, *The Swadeshi Movement in Bengal*, pp. 179, 185–6. A Railwaymen's Union was set up at the office on 27 July 1906, where the striking leaders were honoured.

[133] *Bengalee*, 26 September 1905.

[134] Mass meetings were, for example, organized at the Bhukailash Rajbati in Kidderpore, the golabari (granary) of Rakhal Chandra Das in Nawabganj in Malda, and Babu Rajendranath Mullick's house in Chorebagan in September 1905. See *Bengalee*, 2, 10, and 26 September 1905.

[135] *Bengalee*, 26 September 1905.

Mahalaya, preceding the Durga Puja, where an estimated 50,000 had gathered.[136] Kalighat remained a popular venue during the movement with speeches and pujas being frequently organized there.[137] Some two hundred washermen meeting at the temple thus vowed not to wash clothes of a foreign make.[138] Temples were also used as meeting places in the districts and suburbs. Their use was doubly symbolical—as mobilizing communal solidarity and as bestowing benediction to the movement.

Perhaps the most spectacular transformations took place on the city's streets, converting them from arteries of colonial authority and commerce to tributaries of mass protest, with performative posturing and ritual singing investing these everyday spaces with a rare moral authority. At a gigantic meeting held at College Square in September 1905, with 15,000 attending, many turned out dressed in the traditional style of Bengali Hindu mourners—barefooted and bare bodied, save a shawl—with 'a grim dirge-like taciturnity' hanging over the gathering. Thick crowds surrounded the Goldighi tank. Melancholy national songs were sung and speeches 'expressive of a paroxysm of grief' delivered. At the end of the meeting, processions carrying black flags and singing songs circulated in the streets of north Calcutta.[139]

Street singing and processions were regularly organized and groups went out every evening from the College Square singing patriotic songs and fund-raising in the nearby streets. Such songs were also sung at the opening and close of swadeshi meetings.[140] Following a mass meeting at the Town Hall on 22 September 1905, about 2,000 students marched in processions four deep, carrying banners and singing *Bande Mataram*.[141] In support of the press workers on strike, A.C. Banerji, one of the most active and

[136] At the second meeting, there were 20,000 present. See *Bengalee*, 29 September 1905 and 4 March 1906.

[137] *Bengalee*, 26 September 1905; 14 March 1906.

[138] *Bengalee*, 26 September 1905.

[139] *Bengalee*, 3 September 1905.

[140] Surendranath Banerji, *A Nation in the Making* (Calcutta, 1963; original edition 1925), p. 202; *Bengalee*, 3 September 1905 and 8 Nov 1906.

[141] *Bengalee*, 23 September 1905.

empathetic supporters of workers in Bengal at the time, led a fund-raising procession of Press Union members through Calcutta's streets in 1905, from Cornwallis Street to the residence of the Paikpara rajas. At specific junctures, the processionists stopped en route to be received by local notables who contributed handsomely to the fund and even offered food to the group.[142] Three years later, in 1908, he led another spectacular fund-raising procession of about seven to eight hundred dock labourers, which marched through Russa Road, Bhowanipur, Kalighat, and Hazra Road to the house of the Congress leader, Asutosh Chaudhuri at Ballygunj, where they were feted and fed royally.[143]

In addition to the streets, squares, and public halls being taken over, Sumit Sarkar has detailed the strikes of 1905–6 among tram conductors, cart-drivers, and railway and press employees that brought Calcutta to a near standstill.[144] Municipal road sweepers of districts 1 and 2 went on strike in Calcutta, resulting in rubbish to build up in roads and thoroughfares, and threatening those who continued to work.[145] Over 200 clerks of the Burn Iron Company walked out in protest over a new mechanical system being introduced to monitor attendance. There was a public campaign to raise funds for the families of the striking clerks who were hailed as 'heroes' in the vernacular press.[146] Although the excitement was short-lived and the clerks were ultimately dismissed from service, there was briefly an attempt at mobilizing them against racial harassment at work.[147] A big strike of the jetty coolies at the Kidderpore dockyard involving some two thousand coolies started

[142] Unpublished autobiographical fragment by Aswinicoomar Banerji, cited in S. Sarkar, *The Swadeshi Movement in Bengal*, p. 179.

[143] Unpublished papers of A.C. Banerji, cited in S. Sarkar, *The Swadeshi Movement in Bengal*, p. 204.

[144] S. Sarkar, *The Swadeshi Movement in Bengal*, pp. 156–214.

[145] *Bengalee*, 7 September 1905.

[146] The collection finally exceeded Rs 6,000. IGP Report, p. 34. The Star Theatre organized a Benefit Night for the clerks on the 13th of September. See this announced in *Bengalee*, 10 September 1905. *Bengalee*, 5 September 1905.

[147] *Bengalee*, 5 October 1905.

in March 1908, demanding grain allowances, paid holidays, and better pensions. Regular nightly meetings of the striking workers were held. In addition, there were several strikes in mills all over the city and the surrounding industrial areas in Howrah, Garden Reach, Budge Budge, and Hooghly. In October 1905, massive strikes and riots occurred, demanding a twelve-hour day following the introduction of extended working hours in mills that sought to take advantage of the recent introduction of electricity.[148]

School and college students emerged as important agents in the subversion of authority in public spaces in the city, including educational centres. A lot of meetings were held in College Square in the university and student quarters of the city. School and college grounds served as venues for meetings in Calcutta and around.[149] Eden Hindu Hostel, Ripon, and City Colleges were frequently used for mass meetings. Student messes served as focal points of organization. The meeting at Town Hall proclaiming boycott was preceded by a smaller meeting of students of the Eden Hindu Hostel in July, during which a similar resolution was taken up as an alternative to active action.[150] In August 1905, at a meeting held at Ripon College, the idea of a student organization was conceived with chapters in each college, actually coming into being a few months later.[151]

In an in-depth report by the Inspector-General of Police for the Lower Provinces, students were pointedly condemned. Students were apparently particularly active in picketing activities. Following a series of open-air meetings all over Calcutta, at all of which 'large crowds of students' were evident, action was started in earnest all over the city.[152] Parties of students and schoolboys circulated

[148] S. Sarkar, *The Swadeshi Movement in Bengal*, pp. 203–4, 194–206, 208.

[149] See, for example, *Bengalee* reporting a large 'monster protest meeting' on the grounds of Jagannath College, Dacca. *Bengalee*, 1 September, 1905.

[150] IGP Report, p. 10. The Eden Hindu Hostel and the Presidency College student messes served as important centres of planning all through the Swadeshi period. *Bengalee*, 5 September 1905.

[151] *Bengalee*, 1 and 8 September 1905.

[152] IGP Report, p. 34.

in bazaars, trying to persuade customers to not purchase foreign goods, with the report claiming that picketing became more aggressive from the end of August 1905 onwards and extended to even the English shops in the main thoroughfares of Calcutta.[153]

The hitherto exclusive space of the Maidan—used regularly by Europeans for the evening rambles—in particular opened up as a site for dramatic protests and demonstrations.[154] On 22 September 1905, students marched to the Town Hall by a variety of routes all over the city, with a spillover meeting being held in the Maidan. But tensions led to incidents of insults and stone-throwing at passers-by, including some European ladies in a carriage. The commissioner of police responded with disproportionate firmness, warning that in future all meetings held without permission would be dispersed by force.[155] Political meetings in the Maidan were subsequently banned by him a few months later.[156] The commencement of the building of the marble-clad and pompous Victoria Memorial in classical style the following year represented a desperate effort by the British to reassert their prominence on the Maidan grounds.

The hated Carlyle and Lyons circulars passed in November 1905 were directed against students.[157] In response, students in Calcutta formed the Anti-Circular Society, pioneering a school housing rusticated students, hawking swadeshi cloth and sarees, and training in physical fitness.[158] At a meeting of students presided over by

[153] IGP Report, p. 10. The Marwaris—the leading traders in Manchester cotton piece-goods—too temporarily lent their support to the boycott, although for reasons of economic expediency. See *Bengalee*, 29 September 1905.

[154] This is in spite of the nominal nod to wider public access by the colonial authorities by the removal of the railings surrounding the Maidan in the second half of the nineteenth century. See P.T. Nair, *A History of Calcutta's Streets* (Calcutta: Firma K.L.M., 1987), p. 918.

[155] IGP Report, p. 24.

[156] *Bengalee*, 29 September 1905.

[157] 'Order Prohibiting the Use of School Boys and Students in Connection with Political Meetings' (1905). WBSA File no. 86/1905.

[158] *Bengalee*, 28 October 1905.

Bepin Pal, a boycott of all schools and colleges and a setting up of a National University was proposed.[159] The police maintained a close watch over some student societies in particular. The Students Union was believed to be initiating members into its haloed inner circle with an oath-taking ceremony that involved holding a revolver in one hand and a *Geeta* in the other. The Brata Samiti, the Students New Society, and the Anti-Circular Society were all singled out for close attention.[160]

While the ground swell of agitation grew in the city, Curzon was critical of the Bengal administration. Referring to a note written by a senior government official in Calcutta, he wrote: 'It is no great consolation to know that while the Calcutta streets are in the hands of agitators Mr Stevenson-Moore is writing a Note.... I am not satisfied that the local government has shown either firmness or courage.' Curzon reminded the Bengal governor that it possessed the powers to deploy additional forces to maintain law and order and 'punish' the participating students.[161] The Bengal government responded accordingly. An initial ordinance regulating meetings in May 1907 was quickly succeeded by the Seditious Meetings Act a few months later. A year later, the Sunset rules decreed by magisterial order that all public meetings had to end half an hour before sunset (to allow for easy identification of speakers). Sedition cases were launched against principal leaders, journalists, and editors.[162]

The city's police were left with a dilemma. Being trained for decades in tackling riotous action by the underclasses, they were unprepared in dealing with mass protest and use of passive resistance techniques by the educated middle classes. The hesitation is seen earlier in the viceregal rebuke to Bengal. When they actually rose up to the need of the hour, the administration proved woefully inadequate in adjusting its riot-control techniques when dealing with the bhadralok swadeshis. The violence that broke out in October

[159] IGP Report, pp. 11–12.

[160] IGP Report, p. 12.

[161] Home Public Proceedings B, October 1905, n.114–15, cited in S. Sarkar, *The Swadeshi Movement in Bengal*, p. 270.

[162] *ARPC, 1912*, p. 10.

1907 after two years of non-violent opposition to the partition in the city was undoubtedly police led and took everyone by surprise.

On the evening of 2 October 1907, police broke up a peaceful meeting of swadeshis at Beadon Square, descending on those gathered with lathis. The police alleged that they had been provoked by brickbats thrown at them during the meeting, although this was disputed by those present.[163] Severe blows were delivered not only on those present at the meeting but also passers-by, mostly office workers returning home on foot. Eyewitness accounts describe people being chased into shops and bye-lanes by lathi-brandishing policemen and being robbed and stripped of clothing.[164] The mayhem extended much beyond the square itself. Shops were looted and damaged. Tramcars were stopped and Bengali passengers dragged out to be mercilessly beaten. Later on, in the night of the 3rd, roving bands of sweepers, among others, were egged on by jemadars and constables to continue the looting and assaults. Many of the shops were destroyed and individuals assaulted in the presence of senior police officers and European sergeants. This continued over three nights, from Wednesday the 2nd to Friday the 4th of October. Forty-four persons were arrested and convicted. The public squares were closed for a period to all political meetings.[165] The annual police report for that year went on to say how these incidents illustrated '... the certainty that the lower criminal classes in Calcutta will take advantage of any disturbed set of affairs to further their nefarious designs on their neighbours' property'.[166]

The Bengal government launched an eyewash of an inquiry, and commissioned two reports into the incidents. The first one, prepared by the police commissioner of the Presidency Division,

[163] Report by E.W. Collin, *Supplement to the Calcutta Gazette*, 30 October 1907, pp. 1521–22.

[164] Narendranath Sen, Rai Sreenath Pal Bahadur, and Radha Charan Pal, 'Unofficial Commission of Enquiry in to the Calcutta Disturbances, 2nd, 3rd, and 4th of October 1907'. The police statements in the Collin Report were contradicted by eyewitness accounts in this document. See pp. 18, 21, 23, 30–1.

[165] *ARPC, 1907*, p. 7.

[166] *ARPC, 1907*, p. 7.

E.W. Collin, was dismissed as 'hurried ... incomplete and perfunctory in parts' owing to its mild admission that constables might have been involved in rioting and looting. The report also appended depositions from scores of people who were either directly affected or were witness to the events.[167] The Bengal governor, Sir Andrew Fraser, made his reaction to the report felt clearly. As his Chief Secretary, E.A. Gait, wrote:

> The Lieutenant Governor is convinced that there has been gross, and in many cases deliberate, exaggeration in the charges against the Police.[168]

A second report was produced by a more compliant Donald Weston, the magistrate of Mushidabad, who was especially commissioned by the Bengal governor for the purpose of investigating the charges brought against the police. This version that was submitted two months later disproved all allegations of police complicity. Interestingly, some small-scale departmental enquiries were set up—not to enquire into cases of police brutality and raiding, but to look into inadequacies in policing, particularly where more affirmative action should have been taken.

A third parallel unofficial report was prepared voluntarily by three distinguished Bengali citizens of Calcutta who examined 173 witnesses over a period of six days. They were Narendranath Sen, erstwhile member of the Bengal Legislative Council and editor of *Indian Mirror*; Rai Sreenath Pal Bahadur, former chairman of Berhampur Municipality and manager of the estate of Maharani Swarnamoyi; and Radha Charan Pal, commissioner of the Calcutta Municipal Corporation and member of the Bengal Legislative Council. They produced a copious sixy-four page report with photographs of those wounded. Images of broken arms and legs, bandaged heads, and injured, swollen bodies bore evidence of police brutalities in the report. At least one was reported to have died

[167] Report by E.W. Collin, *Supplement to the Calcutta Gazette*, 30 October 1907, pp. 1519–27.

[168] Resolution on the Report Regarding the Recent Disturbances in Calcutta, Political Department, 18 October 1907 in *Supplement to the Calcutta Gazette*, 30 October 1907, p. 1517.

from wounds. It was clear from this report at least that Bengalis had been targeted. Swadeshi taunts and abuse had been hurled at victims by their assailants—police constables in uniforms—who had repeatedly and loudly announced how 'the Bengali Salas (bastards)' had to be taught a lesson.[169]

The police had become high-handed and unpopular, and the administration was being exposed as woefully inadequate in dealing with the upsurges. In a separate and earlier, but relevant, incident, a peaceful band of young boys singing national songs and collecting donations for the National Fund—proceeding from Entally to Beniapukur—were descended upon by police armed with lathis under the orders of Mr Hopkinson, inspector of the local thana (police station), who threatened to disband the procession.[170] Amritalal Basu, the noted contemporary playwright, summed up the average response of Calcutta's middle-class residents:

> Though respectable we hold no high official position and the ladies of our house can easily be dragged out and insulted and assaulted by these Paharawallahs [constables].... Our police have never been told that the 'citizens are ... gentlemen, they contribute to your wages and salaries, that you are to help them when wanted, that you are to trace out and detect criminals and protect and respect sober citizens.' But [instead] they are permitted to think they are Government employees and interpreting Government for Europeans and retained specially to bring every Indian high or low before a criminal court under whatever section of the Indian Penal Code they can possibly to do so.[171]

* * *

The early decades of the twentieth century revealed the 'City of Palaces' of yesteryears under siege. A series of anti-police, anti-government, and anti-colonial riots had bared the contentious nature of relationship between a mistrusted municipal

169 'Unofficial Commission of Enquiry into the Calcutta Disturbances', p. 16.

170 *Bengalee*, 25 October 1905.

171 *Bengalee*, 6 September 1905.

administration and its people. From the imposition of restrictive measures for the celebration of communal rituals and practices in public spaces and the implementation of draconian health legislation during the plague scare to the consistently high-handed nature of policing in the city, the public face of the local administration was indelibly tarnished. In addition, a hesitant and inexperienced leadership of Hindus and Muslims aligned against the colonial state was starting to forge uneven links with various layers of the city's disaffected populations.

Different constituencies of residents were galvanized into action at different points with varying intensities during this period to register their protest—often violently—on the city's streets, parks, and squares. The participation of the poor and petty urban groups in particular was spectacular and unprecedented in scale, announcing their strong presence in the political scene. More dramatically, the educated middle classes, in a marked departure from their previously formal modes of political expression, engaged in collective emotional displays of patriotic protest in urban public spaces. While on the one hand the riots and demonstrations showcased a coming together of various groups who had been frustrated by their experience of living in the city, they also allowed opportunities for the people to test Calcutta's political leadership. The tentative explorations of mutual interests and loyalties conducted and potential partnerships tried between popular energies and nationalist goals in the localized conflicts, the ground had been prepared for the massive anti-Rowlatt and non-cooperation campaigns, the earliest all-India movements that swept the country and Calcutta in 1919–20.

Conclusion

An account of Calcutta's streets in the early 1920s continues to remain as blinkered as ever before, picturizing the city as composed of its commercial quarters in Dhurumtollah with its 'shop signs tiptoe(ing) to the sky'; Clive Street busily trading in shares, where the 'young blood of England, Scotland and Ireland learns the effortless art of making money'; and the throbbing night life and entertainment at Chowringhee where 'smiling women step into the vehicles' at the end of a show at the Empire Theatre.[1] Then there were the sleepy European suburbs in western Alipore, where

> large cars roll gently by as if gliding upon cotton wool, along the red-surfaced roads that doze and stretch themselves in the fatigue of leisure beneath the heavy shade of thick mopped trees. The side walls of the houses are spotless, the edge of streets neat and drainless—the whole suburb seems as if it was unpacked out of a box from Bond Street only that morning.[2]

In this bizarre, distorted, and nostalgic mental portrait, Calcutta was visually indexed and calibrated in terms of Piccadilly and Kensington, Paris and Amsterdam. The parts of the city where the indigenous population resided were unwelcome intrusions in such imagery.

From the nineteenth century onwards, we have the educated Indians offering their own perspectives on the urban experience that was Calcutta, but even these remained largely skewed by

[1] R.J. Minney, *Round about Calcutta* (Oxford: Humphrey Milford/ Oxford University Press, 1922), pp. 30, 39, 47.

[2] Minney, *Round about Calcutta*, p. 60.

the orientalist assumptions of their British predecessors. The bhadralok, as we know, were never at home in the city. They rarely wrote about Calcutta, except by way of ridicule and despair. Despite the novelty of the metropolitan experience, the city was looked upon as a place of ruin and corruption, decay and deprivation: not surprisingly, one would think, given that the metropolis symbolized, among other things, the material and political triumph of the Raj and the concurrent enslavement of the educated Bengali, whose sole reason of existence in the city, ironically, was service to the colonial state. The city was thus not worthy of habitation because of pollution, dirt, and disease that was rampant within its limits. The countryside was fresher, purer, and idyllic in contrast.[3]

What is missing from this spectrum of representations, however, is the experience of the lower social tiers. The overwhelming centrality of the Bengali educated middle classes in studies of modern India has resulted in a lopsided narrative that ignores other less powerful, but robustly articulate groups peopling the contemporary public sphere. While, undoubtedly, some views were shared vertically across the layers—such as those on women and migrants—other more specifically socially ordered perspectives, this book has shown, were an inherent part of the city's longstanding traditions of popular street cultures. Uncovering their critical role in shaping the city—as evident in contemporary popular culture—offered a dramatic re-conceptualization of the Bengali social and cultural, and to a certain extent, political world.

The telling of popular stories on the urban experience was also inimical to the shaping of the city's social order. It helped outline a new public sphere and announce the presence of new social and political actors in Calcutta. Scandal narratives can be taken as a case in point. As cautionary tales, such narratives functioned as counterweights to the fantasies of access and movement that had propelled ambitions of social ascendancy and autonomy among the city's diverse groups, including women. The gradual

[3] Sumit Sarkar, *Writing Social History* (New Delhi: Oxford University Press, 1999), pp. 176–7.

consolidation of these communities and changes in social structures led, in turn, to the politicization of their new identities.

Street songs on the city in colonial Calcutta were also essential sites for the construction of urban discourses and the shaping of various social identities. Alongside the more elevated platforms of the press and literary and civic societies of the educated, they too presented an opportunity for public debates on the contemporary urban experience and significantly shaped the ways in which various non-elite groups made sense of themselves and their new environment. The study, thus, also traced the emergence of an urban public just under the educated layers that was visible and vocal, and quite organically located in the city's open public spaces—streets, markets, open grounds.

A principal question underpinning the book was the nature of the relationship between space and material culture, including the ways in which its constitution and usage is governed by the politics of culture. Calcutta, as a city was thus placed within its actual physical as well as imagined spaces. Accounts of monuments and prominent public spaces as self-contained facts were not the primary concern of this investigation. Rather, their embeddedness in a larger urban fabric, as symbols of social attitudes, power, and cultural preferences, was more significant.[4]

How and why urban space underwent several dramatic reorganizations during the period and its significance for social, cultural, and political life in the city of Calcutta was thus central to the study. While for the colonial government it was a carefully crafted act of civilizational dispensation, for the indigenous population it signalled disruption and turmoil. The increasing presence of marginal groups and their unavoidable access to the new urban spaces challenged the assuring spatial boundaries that had helped fix social differences in an earlier rural imaginary. Communal and indiscriminate sharing of urban transport and water from the roadside tap threatened the preservation of caste and community identity. The book showed how distinct forms of urban space were

4 For an excellent example of this approach, see Timothy Mitchell, *Colonising Egypt* (Cambridge: Cambridge University Press, 1988).

produced out of the contradictions of colonialism and the deep ambivalence about being modern.

In premising itself on not just the material ordering of Calcutta, but also its reception among the residents, the monograph addressed its second key problem: reading social meaning in cultural representations of material urban space. The study explored the rhetorical devices and imagery used in vernacular literature and popular culture to communicate ideas of the urban social order. The attempted naturalization of socio-spatial relations ensconced in the colonial idiom of liberal governance and modernization was thus consistently questioned in vernacular middle-class (often nationalist) writings, which spoke of British intervention in the lives and spaces of Indians. Literary writings on the city present alternate and contesting local experiences, not found in the colonial archive (for example, the depiction of Calcutta as a city of hapless, penniless clerks, tied in grinding service to Europeans).

The third and final aspect of the monograph saw the city as being produced out of a set of everyday practices that defined the limits of urban planning. In exploring this problem, the book considered the ordering of material things as well as people whose behaviour on the streets and in parks, for instance, rendered as much meaning to urban space as the pavements, walls, and street signs framing them. The question deliberately avoided reading power as all pervasive, and posited the everyday itself as a site of power, conflict, and resistance.[5] Within this critical framework of enquiry, agency was as, if not more, important as representation, and how things work not less valuable than what they just meant. As evident in the arduous and protracted debates on sanitation and cremation grounds, among others, the government needed to repeatedly shift priorities in accordance with the actual practices that governed the residents' experience of these spaces.

[5] Gyan Prakash and Douglas Haynes (eds), *Contesting Power: Resistance and Everyday Social Relations in South Asia* (Berkeley and Los Angeles: University of California Press, 1992); Patrick Joyce, *The Rule of Freedom: Liberalism and the Modern City* (London and New York: Verso, 2003).

The book demonstrated how Calcutta afforded the opportunity where individuals and groups could challenge, ignore, depart from, and accommodate the rhetorical to arrive at their own peculiar solutions. In a landscape that physically resisted the isolation of different groups, for instance, attempts needed to be made to reinforce social difference in newer ways; hence the housing of elite Indian women in the inner courts of family residences, and the borders between the Black and White Towns defining the limits of leisurely European excursion into the Indian quarters. The exploration of crime in the city offered valuable inroads into understanding the challenges faced by the normative urban civic, moral, and familial order. It also highlighted the low levels of social cohesion, rootless living, and permissive lifestyles that Calcutta had started to foster from the late nineteenth century onwards. Criminal acts and crime stories based on them questioned conventional hierarchies of gender and class, and helped Calcuttans to confront the changing values and morals of a busy and merciless metropolis.

Technology as a theme threads through many of the chapters and was important for exposing the contradictions of the modern civic world. From railways to bridges, steamships to motorcars, technology was spectacular and portrayed the essence of Calcutta to outsiders.[6] It also smoothed urban existence by allowing better communication, sewage disposal, water supply, and lighting of the city. But it was also injurious, as seen in the rise of traffic accidents on the streets of Calcutta, the facilitation of crime and the mismanagement of drainage systems by the municipal administration. The human cost of technological innovations and the impact on livelihoods and everyday practices offers a window into the reception of technology in colonial India.

The study was also about the spaces of protest, debate, and unrest in Calcutta in the late nineteenth and early twentieth

[6] In Calcutta's suburbs the curiosity about technological innovations in the capital was endless, and those returning to villages and towns following a visit to the city would be relentlessly pursued with questions of 'what's new'. See Beharilal Chattopadhyay, *Durgotsav* (Hooghly: Budhodoy Press, 1868), pp. 53–5.

centuries. It outlined the emergence of a multi-layered public sphere in Calcutta that seems particularly vocal and active beyond the regular fora of civic society such as the press, stage, and voluntary associations. In the study, collective forms of protest and action—often violent—related to the urban experience also formed legitimate means of understanding ways of thinking and being in the city. Thus, strikes by Calcutta's labouring population in the unorganized sectors of the city itself—rather than the much studied mill towns—anti-police and anti-administration riots, communal clashes, and prolonged and defiant unrest during the nationalist upsurge in 1905–7 period were all relevant.

Overall, this was about space and material culture of the city, but woven into it was the social history of the city's residents—their crimes and scandals, morality and culpability, aspirations and protest—highlighting their experiential frameworks in encountering urbanity and modernity. It also outlined a pre-history of explosive public action on the city streets under the sweeping waves of Gandhian mass nationalism as seem from 1919 onwards, demonstrating the ways in which the urban environment and its restrictive civic regime was already bringing together groups of protesting people in unique ways not exclusively determined by the call of nation, caste, or community.

Finally, the investigation established the extraordinary downward reach of the public sphere in the city from the late nineteenth century onwards. As the book showed, clerks and petty office workers, prostitutes and pulp writers, urban street singers, scavengers and carters were all concerned with and responded to the urban experience in ways that underlined their own investment in the city. These were not the passive consumers of urbanity and modernity as we might think, but articulate social actors who, through words and action, sought to claim the city for themselves.

Bibliography

Primary Sources

Official Sources

India Office, Asia and Pacific Collections, British Library, London, UK

Administrative Report of the Calcutta Municipality, 1869–1914.

Administrative Report of the Municipality of the Suburbs of Calcutta, 1869–80.

Annual Report of the Calcutta Improvement Trust, 1912–1925.

Annual Report on the State of Police of the Town of Calcutta, 1842–1923.

Census of the Suburbs of Calcutta, 1872.

Census of the Town and Suburbs of Calcutta, 1881–1911.

Crake, H.M. *The Calcutta Plague, 1896–1907 with Observations on the Epidemiology of Plague.* Calcutta, 1908.

Indian Newspaper Reports (*Bengal*).

O' Malley, L.S.S., and Monmohan Chakravarti. *Bengal District Gazetteer: Howrah.* Calcutta, 1909.

New Bridge between Calcutta and Howrah: Report of the Committee of Engineers, vol. 1 (1922).

Quarterly Report of the Municipality of Calcutta, 1876–1900.

Report of the Commissioners for the Improvement of the Town of Calcutta, 1848–61.

Report of the Indian Plague Commission, vol. 1 (1898–99).

Report of the Municipality of Calcutta for the Quarters Ending March 1876.

Report of the Plague Commission (Calcutta, 1896–98).

Report on Plague in Calcutta, 1905–1910.

Report of the Sanitation Commission (Calcutta, 1885).

Report of the Labour Enquiry Commission (Calcutta, 1896).

Richards, E.P. *Report by Request of the Trust on the Condition, Improvement and Town Planning of the City of Calcutta and Contiguous Areas*. Calcutta: Calcutta Improvement Trust, 1914.

Private Papers/Manuscripts

India Office, Asia and Pacific Collections, British Library

Curzon Collection (vol. 31).
Lord Ronaldshay, 'My Bengal Diary', February 1917–November 1919.
'Mr Weston's Report on the 1907 Riots' (1908).
'Papers on Chitpur Riots', Calcutta, 1897.
Report of the Inspector-General of Police, Lower Provinces, on the Agitation against the Partition of Bengal (1905).
'Report on the Plague in Calcutta', Calcutta, 1898.
Sen, Narendranath, Rai Sreenath Pal Bahadur, and Radha Charan Pal, 'Unofficial Commission of Enquiry into the Calcutta Disturbances, 2nd, 3rd and 4th of October, 1907'.

Newspapers and Periodicals (English and Bengali)

The National Library, Kolkata, India

Amrita Bazar Patrika
Bengalee
Calcutta Review
Hindoo Patriot
Sadharani
Samachar Darpan
Sangbad Prabhakar
Somprakash

Bangiya Sahitya Parishat, Kolkata, India

Sahachar

Cross-Asia Digital Collection, University of Heidelberg, Germany

Anusandhan

Unpublished Dissertations

Ray, Bidisha. 'Contesting Respectability: Sexuality, Corporeality and non-"bhadra" Cultures in Colonial Bengal'. Unpublished PhD dissertation, University of Manchester, 2008.

Bengali Printed Sources

Anon. *Bahoba Choudda Ain* (Jubilations for Act XIV). Calcutta, 1869.

Anon. *The Battle of the Markets: Bajarer Ladai*. Calcutta: Smith Co. Press, 1873.

Bandyopadhyay, Beharilal. *Asmaner Naksha: Palligramastha Babuder Durgotsav*. Calcutta: Budhodoy Press, 1868.

Bandyopadhyay, Brajendranath. *Samvadpatre Sekaler Katha*, vol. 1. Calcutta: Bangiya Sahitya Parishat, 1970.

Bandyopadhyay, Surendranath. *Great Market War Orthat Pradhan Bajarer Ladai*. Calcutta, n.d.

Basumullick, Jogendranath. *Ebar Pujor Boro Dhum*. Calcutta, 1875.

Bose, Rajnarayan. *Sekal Ar Ekal*. Calcutta, 1874.

Bose, Shib Chunder. *Hindoos As They Are*. Calcutta, 1881.

Chakrabarty, Sudhir, ed. Bangla Dehatattver Gaan. Calcutta: Pustak Bipani, 1990.

Chattopadhyay, Abinashchandra. *Pujar Utsav*. Calcutta, 1876.

Chattopadhyay, Badalbehari. *Bishom Dhnoka, Maachhe Poka*. Calcutta, 1875.

Chattopadhyay, Beharilal. *Durgotsav*. Hooghly: Budhodoy Press, 1868.

Chattopadhyay, Harimohan. *Mohanta Pakshe Bhutanandi*. Calcutta: Calcutta Press, 1873.

Das, Natabar. *Makkel Mama*. Calcutta: Kar Press, 1878.

Das, Tarinicharan. *Jongule Jhod*. Calcutta: Gyandipak Press, 1867.

Das Chaudhuri, Yogendra. *Kantalaler Kolikata Darshan*, 2 vols. Calcutta, n.d.

Das De, Maheshchandra. *Eki Asambhab Kartike Jhod*. Calcutta, 1867.

———. *Hay Ki Adbhut Jhod!* Calcutta: Harihar Press, 1864.

———. *Mama Bhaginir Natak*. Calcutta: Harihar Press, 1878.

Das Ghose, Aghorchandra. *Chai Belful*. Calcutta: Anondodoy Press, 1872.

———. *Drener Pnachali*. Calcutta, 1874.

———. *Ekei Bole Pole! Ya Bolle Tai Kolle!!!* Calcutta, 1874.

———. *Mohanter Khed*. Calcutta: Gyanollas Press, 1873.

Datta, Akhilchandra. *Sonagajir Khun*. Calcutta: Kabita Kaumudi Press, 1875.

———. *Sonagajir Khunir Fnasir Hukum*. Calcutta: Kabita Kaumudi Press, 1875.

Datta, Aminchandra. *Howrah Ghater Poler Kobi*. Calcutta: Kabita Kaumudi Press, 1874.

———. *Mechho Basante Mechhonir Darpachurna*. Calcutta: Kabita Kaumudi Press, 1875.

Dutta, Mahendranath. *Kolikatar Purano Kahini O Pratha*. Reprint edition. Calcutta: Mahendra Publishing Committee, 1975; original edition Calcutta, 1929.

Dutta, Prankrishna. *Badmaesh Jobdo*. Calcutta, n.d. Reprinted in *Dushprapya Sahitya Sangraha*, vol. 2, Calcutta, 1992.

Dutta, Prankrishna. *Kolikatar Itibritta*. Originally serialized in *Navyabharat*, 1901–3. Reprint edition, Calcutta: Pustak Bipani, 1981.

Ghose, Chandicharan. *Barangana Er Samul Ghatika Orthat Beshyai Sarbanasher Mul*. Calcutta, 1874.

Ghosh, Aghor Chandra. *Pnachali Kamalkali: Choudda Ain*. Calcutta, 1873.

Ghosh, Benoy. *Samayik Patre Banglar Samajchitra*, vols 1–3. Calcutta, 1980.

Gupta, Meghnad. *Raater Kolkata*. Calcutta, 1923.

Mitra, Rajendrakumar. *Gokulchandra Mitra O Sekaler Kolikata*, vol. 1. Calcutta, 1951.

Mukhopadhyay, Bholanath. *Mohanter Chakra Bhraman Natak*. Calcutta: Sudharnab Press, 1874.

Mukhopadhyay, Harisadhan. *Kolikata Sekaler O Ekaler*. [Original edition, Calcutta, 1915] Reprint edition, Calcutta: P. M. Bagchi, 1991.

Mukhopadhyay, Priyanath. *Darogar Daptar* (originally serialized, 1892–1904). Reprint edition, edited by Arun Mukhopadhyay, vols 1–2. Calcutta: Ananda Publishers, 2004.

———. 'Tetrish Botshorer Pulish Kahini ba Priyanath Jiboni'. In *Phire Dekha*, edited by Arindam Dasgupta, vol. 3. Calcutta: Subarnarekha, 2011.

Mullick, Pramathanath. *Sachitra Kalikatar Katha*, vols 1 and 2 Calcutta, 1935.

Nath, Babulal. *Dekhle Hashte Hobe*. Calcutta: Anondodoy Press, 1872.

Pakshiraj, Baboo Airabat [pseud.]. *Durga Puja: Ek Bitkel Mahakavya*. Calcutta: Albert Press, 1876.

Pal, Prafulla Chandra. *Prachin Kobiwalar Gaan*. Calcutta: Calcutta University Press, 1938; reprint edition, 1994.

Rajratna, Sri. *Kalighate E Ki Churi*. Calcutta, 1875.
Ray, Durgacharan. *Debganer Martye Agaman*. [Original edition, 1886] Calcutta: Deys Publishing, 2001.
Ray, Krishnaraj. *Mohanter Bilap*. Calcutta, 1878.
Ray, Nandalal. *Poler Pnachali*. Calcutta, 1874.
———. *Nabin Mohanta Elokeshi Natak*, 2nd edition. Calcutta, 1875.
———. *Nutan Poler Tappa*. Calcutta: Sudharnab Press, 1874.
Sarkar, Saralabala. *Saralabala Sarkar Rachana Sangraha*, edited by Chitra Deb, vol. 1. Calcutta: Ananda Publishers, 1989.
Sarkar, Isvarchandra. *Kartike Jhoder Pnachali*. Calcutta: Harihar Press, 1867.
Sarman, Dvijabar. *Machher Basanta*. Calcutta: Kabita Kaumudi Press, 1875.
Seth, Harihar. *Praceen Kolikata*. Calcutta, 1934.
Sharma, Devendra. *Sahar Chitra*. Calcutta, 1921.
Shil, Jaharilal. *Nutan Poler Pnachali*. Calcutta, 1874.
———. *Machher Basante Jele Mechhonir Khed*. Calcutta: Sudharnab Press, 1875.
———. *Machher Poka*. Calcutta, 1875.
———. *Mohanter Sarbanash, Nabiner Poush Mash*. Calcutta, 1876.
Shil, Nimaichand. *Tirthamahima*. Calcutta: New Sanskrit Press, 1873.
Sikdar, Chandrakanta. *Ki Mojar Shonibar*. Calcutta, 1863.
Sinha, Dineshchandra. *Purbabanger Kobigaan*, vol. 1. Calcutta: Calcutta University Press, 1993.
Sinha, Kaliprasanna. *Hutom Pnechar Naksha*. [Original edition, Calcutta, 1861] Reprint edition, edited by Arun Nag. Calcutta: Subarnarekha, 1991.
Sur, Atul. *Tinsho Bochhorer Kolkata: Patabhumi O Itikatha*. Calcutta: Ujjval Sahitya Mandir, 1988.
Tagore, Kshitindranath. *Kolikatay Chalafera: Sekale aar Ekale*. Calcutta: Adi Brahmo Samaj Press, 1930.
Tagore, Rabindranath. 'Chhelebela'. In *Rabindra Rachanabali*, Centenary Edition, vol. 10. Calcutta: West Bengal Government (Saraswati Press), 1961.

English Printed Sources

Anon. *The Confessions of Meanjahn, Darogah of Police, Dictated by him, Translated by a Mofussilite*. Calcutta, 1869.
Anon. *48 Photographs Showing the Effects of the Great Cyclone of 1864*. Calcutta, 1865.

Anderson, Herbert. *Calcutta Vice*. Calcutta, 1921.

Banerji, Surendranath. *A Nation in the Making*. Reprint edition, Calcutta, 1963 (original edition, 1925).

Basu, Prafullachandra. *The Middle Class People in Calcutta, and Their Effects upon the Health and Morals of the Rising Generation*. Calcutta: Chuckervertty, Chatterjee & Co., 1925.

Bose, Sir Bepin Krishna. *Stray Thoughts on Some Incidents in My Life*. Madras, 1923.

Chuckerbutty, Debendranath. *Life of the Late Babu Takoordas Chuckerbutty*. Calcutta, 1917.

Cox, Edmund. *Police and Crime in India*. London, 1911.

Deb, Raja Binoy Krishna. *The Early History and Growth of Calcutta*. Calcutta, 1905.

Gastrell, Lt. Col. J.E. and Henry F. Blanford. *Report on the Calcutta Cyclone of the 5th of October, 1864*. Calcutta, 1866.

Ghosh, J.N. *Social Evil in Calcutta*. Calcutta, 1923.

Gupta, Anandswarup. *The Police in British India, 1861–1947*. New Delhi: Concept Publishing 1979.

Long, James. *Selections from Unpublished Records of the Government*. Calcutta, 1869.

Macknight, W.D.K. *A Description of the Calcutta Cyclone of 5th October, 1864*. Liverpool, 1867.

Marshman, John Clark. *The History of the Serampore Mission Embracing the Life and Times of William Carey, Joshua Marshman and William Ward*, 2 vols. London, 1859.

Minney, R.J. *Nightlife of Calcutta*. Calcutta: The Muston Company, 1919.

———. *Round about Calcutta*. Oxford: Humphrey Milford/Oxford University Press, 1922.

Mitter, Kissory Chund. *Mutty Lal Seal*. Reprint edition, Calcutta: Toolat, 1993 (original edition, Calcutta, 1869).

Muddiman, A.P. 'British India: Acts of Legislative Council'. *Journal of Comparative Legislation and International Law*, Third Series, 3, no. 1 (1921): 125–35.

Mukherjee, Rai Sahib Satyendranath. *Murder of Prostitutes for Gain*. Calcutta: Jnan Printing Works, 1935.

Pal, Radhachurn. *A Rapid History of Municipal Government in Calcutta*. Calcutta, 1916.

Sarkar, Hemchandra. *Life of Anandamohan Bose*. Calcutta, 1910.

Sastri, Sivnath. *Men I Have Seen*. Calcutta: Crescent Printing Works, 1919.

Seth, Harihar. *Praceen Kolikata*. Calcutta: Prabasi Press, 1934.

Sircar, M.N. *Life of Peary Churn Sircar*. Calcutta, 1914.
Smith, D.B. *Report on the Drainage and Conservancy of Calcutta*. Calcutta, 1869.
Smith, George. *The Life of William Carey: Shoemaker and Missionary*. London: John Murray, 1885.
Wilson, C.R. *Old Fort William in Bengal*. Calcutta, 1906.

Secondary Sources (English and Bengali)

Allen, Michael T. and Gabrielle Hecht, eds. *Technologies of Power: Essays in Honor of Thomas Parke Hughes and Agatha Chipley Hughes*. Cambridge, Massachusetts: MIT Press, 2001.
Arnold, David. *Everyday Technology: Machines and the Making of India's Modernity*. Chicago: University of Chicago Press, 2013.
———. 'The Armed Police and Colonial Rule in South India, 1914–1947'. *Modern Asian Studies* 11, no. 11 (1977): 101–25.
———.'The Problem of Traffic: The Street Life of Modernity in Late Colonial India'. *Modern Asian Studies* 46, no. 1 (special issue, January 2012): 119–41.
Bailey, Peter. 'Conspiracies of Meaning: Music-hall and the Knowingness of Popular Culture'. *Past and Present*, no. 144 (August, 1994): 138–70.
———. *Popular Culture and Performance in the Victorian City*. Cambridge: Cambridge University Press, 1998.
Bakhtin, Mikhail. *Rabelais and His World*. Massachusetts: Massachusetts Institute of Technology Press, 1968.
Balachandran, A. 'Of Corporations and Caste Heads: Urban Rule in Company Madras, 1640–1720'. *Journal of Colonialism and Colonial History* 9, no. 2 (2008), at https://muse.jhu.edu/ (last accessed 11 November 2015.
Ballhatchet, Kenneth. *Race, Sex and Class under the Raj*. New York: St. Martin's Press, 1980.
Bandyopadhyay, Debjit. *Beshya Sangeet, Baiji Sangeet*. Calcutta: Subarnarekha, 1999.
Banerjee, Sumanta. *Crime and Urbanization: Calcutta in the Nineteenth Century*. New Delhi: Tulika Books, 2006.
———. *Dangerous Outcast: The Prostitute in Nineteenth Century Bengal*. Calcutta: Seagull Books, 1998.
———.'Marginalisation of Women's Popular Culture'. In *Recasting Women: Essays in Colonial History*, edited by Kumkum Sangari and Sudesh Vaid, pp. 127–77 New Delhi: Kali for Women, 1989.

Banerjee, Sumanta. *Parlour and the Streets: Elite and Popular Culture in Nineteenth Century Calcutta*. Calcutta: Seagull Books, 1989.

———. *The Wicked City: Crime and Punishment in Colonial Calcutta*. New Delhi: Orient Blackswan, 2009.

———. 'Urban Technology and the Changing Forms of Crime in Early Colonial Calcutta'. *Social Scientist*, 38, nos 3/4 (March–April 2010): 25–36.

Banerjee, Swapna. *Men, Women and Domestics: Articulating Middle-class Identity in Colonial Bengal*. New Delhi: Oxford University Press, 2004.

Barnes, David S. *The Great Stink of Paris and the Nineteenth Century Struggle against Filth and Germs*. Baltimore: Johns Hopkins University Press, 2006.

Basu, Girish Chandra. *Sekaler Darogar Kahini*. Reprint edition. Calcutta: Pustak Bipani, 1983; originally printed in Nabajivan in 1887–8.

Basu, Subho. *Does Class Matter? Colonial Capital and Workers' Resistance in Bengal, 1890–1937*. New Delhi: Oxford University Press, 2004.

Bayly, C.A. *Information and Empire: Intelligence Gathering and Social Communication in India, 1780–1870*. Cambridge: Cambridge University Press, 2000.

———. *The Local Roots of Indian Politics: Allahabad, 1870–1920*. Oxford: Oxford University Press, 1975.

———. 'Local Control in Indian Towns: The Case of Allahabad, 1880–1920'. *Modern Asian Studies* 5, no. 4 (1971): 289–311.

Beattie, Martin. 'Sir Patrick Geddes and Barra Bazaar: Competing Visions, Ambivalence and Contradiction'. *The Journal of Architecture* 9, no.2 (Summer 2004): 131–50.

Bernstein, H.T. *Steamboats on the Ganges: An Exploration in the History of India's Modernisation through Science and Technology*. Bombay: Orient Longman, 1960.

Bhattacharya, Debraj. 'Kolkata "Underworld" in the Early 20th Century'. *Economic and Political Weekly* 39, no. 38 (September 2004): 4276–82.

Bhattacharya, Tithi. 'Tracking the Goddess: Religion, Community, and Identity in the Durga Puja Ceremonies of Nineteenth-Century Calcutta'. *The Journal of Asian Studies* 66, no. 4 (November 2007): 919–62.

Bigon, Liora. 'Sanitation and Street Layout in Early Colonial Lagos: British and Indigenous Conceptions, 1851–1900'. *Planning Perspectives* 20, no. 3 (2005): 247–69.

Brand, Dana. *The Spectator and the City in Nineteenth Century American Literature*. Cambridge and New York: Cambridge University Press, 1991.

Breman, Jan. 'A Dualistic Labour System? A Critique of the "Informal Sector" Concept'. *Economic and Political Weekly*, part 1, 11, no. 48 (27 November 1976): 1870–76; part 2, 11, no. 49 (4 December 1976): 1905–8; part 3, 11, no. 50 (11 December 1976): 1933–9.

———. *Footloose Labour: Working in India's Informal Economy*. Cambridge: Cambridge University Press, 1996.

Broomfield, John. *Elite Conflict in a Plural Society: Twentieth Century Bengal*. Berkeley and Los Angeles: University of California Press, 1968.

Brown, R.M. 'The Cemeteries and the Suburbs'. *Journal of Urban History* 29, no. 2 (2003): 151–72.

Cameron, Deborah and Elizabeth Frazer. *The Lust to Kill: A Feminist Investigation of Sexual Murder*. New York: Polity Press, 1987.

Caputi, Jane. 'The Sexual Politics of Murder'. *Gender and Society* 3, no. 4 (December 1989): 437–56.

Chakrabarti, Ranjan. *Authority and Violence in Colonial Bengal: 1800–1860*. Calcutta: Bookland Private Limited, 1997.

Chakrabarty, Dipesh. 'Communal Riots and Labour: Bengal's Jute Mill-Hands in the 1890s'. *Past and Present* 91 (May 1981): 140–69.

———. 'Open Space/Public Place: Garbage, Modernity and India'. *South Asia: Journal of South Asian Studies* 14, no. 1 (1991): 15–31.

———. *Rethinking Working Class History, Bengal 1890–1940*. Princeton, NJ: Princeton University Press, 1989.

Chakravarty, Usha. *Condition of Bengali Women around the Second Half of the Nineteenth Century*. Calcutta, 1963.

Chatterjee, Partha. 'On Civil and Political Society in Post-colonial Democracies'. In *Civil Society: History and Possibilities*, edited by Sudipta Kaviraj and Sunil Khilnani, pp. 165–78 Cambridge: Cambridge University Press, 2001.

———. *The Nation and Its Fragments: Colonial and Postcolonial Histories*. Princeton, NJ: Princeton University Press, 1993.

Chatterjee, Ratnabali. 'The Indian Prostitute as a Colonial Subject: Bengal, 1864–1883'. *Canadian Women Studies* 13, no. 1 (1992): 51–55.

———. 'Prostitution in Nineteenth Century Bengal: Construction of Class and Gender'. *Social Scientist* 21, nos 9/11 (September–October 1993): 159–72.

Chatterjee, Sunil Kumar. *William Carey and Serampore*. Calcutta, 1984.

Chattopadhyay, Basudev. *Crime and Control in Early Colonial Bengal 1770–1860*. Calcutta: K.P. Bagchi and Co., 2000.

———. *The Town Hall of Calcutta: A Brief History*. Calcutta: Homage Trust 1998.

Chattopadhyay, Suchetana. 'War, Migration and Alienation in Colonial Calcutta: The Remaking of Muzaffar Ahmad'. *History Workshop Journal* 64, no. 1 (2007): 212–39.

Chattopadhyay, Swati. *Representing Calcutta: Modernity, Nationalism and the Colonial Uncanny*. London and New York: Routledge, 2005.

Cohen, Patricia Cline. 'The Helen Jewett Murder: Violence, Gender, and Sexual Licentiousness in Antebellum America'. *NWSA Journal* 2, no. 3 (Summer 1990): 374–89.

Corbin, Alain. *The Foul and the Fragrant: Odour and the French Social Imagination*. Cambridge, Massachusetts: Harvard University Press, 1986.

Crossley, Nick and John Michael Roberts, eds. *After Habermas: New Perspectives on the Public Sphere*. Oxford: Blackwell Publishing, 2004.

Das, Suranjan and Kalyan Ray. *The Goondas: Towards a Reconstruction of the Calcutta Underworld*. Calcutta: Firma K.L.M. Private Limited, 1996.

Dasgupta, Keya. 'A City Away from Home: The Mapping of Calcutta'. In *Texts of Power: Emerging Disciplines in Colonial Bengal*, edited by Partha Chatterjee, pp. 145–66 Calcutta: Samya, 1996.

Dasgupta, Ranajit. 'Factory Labour in Eastern India: Sources of Supply, 1855–1946: Some Preliminary Findings'. *Indian Economic and Social History Review* 13 (1976): 277–324.

———. *Labour and Working Class in Eastern India*. Calcutta: South Asia Books, 1994.

———. 'Material Conditions and Behavioural Aspects of Calcutta Working Class, 1875–1899'. Occasional Paper no. 22, Centre for Studies in Social Sciences, Calcutta, 1979.

———. 'Structure of the Labour Market in Colonial India'. *Economic and Political Weekly* 16, nos 44/46 (November, 1981): 1781–806.

D'Cruze, Shani, Sandra Walklate, and Samantha Pegg. *Murder: Social and Historical Approaches to Understanding Murder and Murderers*. Cullompton: Willan Publishing, 2006.

Datta, Partho. 'How Modern Planning Came to Calcutta'. *Planning Perspectives* 28, no. 1 (2013): 139–47.

———. *Planning the City: Urbanisation and Reform in Calcutta, c.1800–c. 1940*. New Delhi: Tulika Books, 2012.

Daunton, M.J. 'Public Space and Private Space: The Victorian City and the Working Class Household'. In *The Pursuit of Urban History*, edited by D. Fraser and A. Sutcliffe, pp. 212–33 London: Edward Arnold, 1983.

De Haan, Arjan. 'Unsettled Settlers: Migrant Workers and Industrial Capitalism in Calcutta'. *Modern Asian Studies* 31, no. 4 (1997): 919–49.

Desai, Renu and Romola Sanyal. *Urbanizing Citizenship: Contested Spaces in Indian Cities*. Thousand Oaks: Sage, 2011.

Dobbin, Christine. *Urban Leadership in Western India: Politics and Communities in Bombay City, 1840–85*. Oxford: Oxford University Press, 1972.

Dossal, Mariam. *Imperial Designs and Indian Realities: The Planning of Bombay City, 1845–1875*. New York: Oxford University Press, 1991.

Early, Julie English. 'A New Man for a New Century: Dr Crippen and the Principles of Masculinity'. In *Disorder in the Court: Trials and Sexual Conflict at the Turn of the Century*, edited by Nancy Erber and George Robb, pp. 209–30 New York: New York University Press, 1999.

Edgerton, David. *Shock of the Old: Technology and Global History Since 1900*. London: Profile Books Limited, 2006.

Eley, Geoff. 'Nations, Publics, and Political Cultures'. In *Habermas and the Public Sphere*, edited by Craig Calhoun, pp. 289–339 Cambridge, Massachusetts: MIT Press, 1992.

Engels, Dagmar. 'The Age of Consent Act of 1891: Colonial Ideology in Bengal'. *South Asia Research* 3, no. 2 (November 1983): 107–31.

Evenson, Norma. *The Indian Metropolis, A View Towards the West*. New Haven and London: Yale University Press, 1989.

Fernandes, Leela. *Producing Workers: The Politics of Gender, Class and Culture in the Calcutta Jute Mills*. Philadelphia: University of Pennsylvania Press, 1997.

Frasch, Tilman. 'Tracks in the City: Technology, Mobility and Society in Colonial Rangoon and Singapore'. *Modern Asian Studies* 46, no. 1 (special issue, January 2012): 97–118.

Freitag, Sandria. *Collective Action and Community: Public Arenas and the Emergence of Communalism in North India*. New Delhi: Oxford University Press, 1990.

———, ed. *Culture and Power in Banaras*. Berkeley, Los Angeles, and Oxford: University of California Press, 1989.

Gandy, Matthew. 'The Paris Sewers and the Rationalisation of Urban Space'. *Transactions of the Institute of British Geographers* 24, no. 1 (April, 1999): 23–44.

Ghosh, Anindita. *Power in Print: Popular Publishing and the Politics of Language and Culture in a Colonial Society*. New Delhi: Oxford University Press, 2006.

Ghosh, Parimal. *Colonialism, Class and a History of the Calcutta Jute Millhands, 1880–1930*. Chennai: Orient Longman, 2000.

Ghosh, Siddhartha. *Karigori Kalpana O Bangali Udyog*. Calcutta, 1983.

———. *Koler Sahar Kolkata*. Calcutta, 1991.

———.'Purono Kolkatar Kolkobja: Oupanibeshik shaharer prajukti proyash'. In *Kolkatar Purakatha*, edited by Debashis Basu, pp. 222–45 Calcutta: Pustak Bipani, 1990.

Glover, William. *Making Lahore Modern: Constructing and Imagining a Colonial City*. Minneapolis: University of Minnesota Press, 2007.

Gooptu, Nandini. *The Politics of the Urban Poor in Early Twentieth Century India*. Cambridge: Cambridge University Press, 2001.

Guha, Ranajit. 'A Colonial City and Its Time(s)'. *Indian Economic and Social History Review* 45, no. 3 (2008): 329–51.

———. *Elementary Aspects of Peasant Insurgency in Colonial India*. New Delhi: Oxford University Press, 1983.

Gupta, Anandswarup. *The Police in British India, 1861–1947*. New Delhi: Concept Publishing, 1979.

Gupta, Charu. *Sexuality, Obscenity, Community: Women, Muslims and the Hindu Public in Colonial India*. New Delhi: Permanent Black, 2001.

Gupta, Narayani. *Delhi between Two Empires, 1803–1931: Society, Government and Urban Growth*. New Delhi: Oxford University Press, 1981.

Gupta, Samita. 'Theory and Practice of Town Planning in Calcutta 1817–1912: An Appraisal'. *Indian Economic and Social History Review* 30, no. 1 (1993): 29–55.

Habermas, Jürgen. *The Structural Transformation of the Public Sphere*. Cambridge: Cambridge University Press, 1989.

Hansen, Kathryn. *Grounds for Play: The Nautanki Theatre of North India*. Berkeley and Los Angeles: University of California Press, 1992.

Hansen, Thomas Blom. *Violence in Urban India: Identity Politics, "Mumbai" and the Postcolonial City*. New Delhi: Orient Blackswan, 2001.

Hardgrove, Anne. *Community and Public Culture: The Marwaris in Calcutta*. New Delhi: Oxford University Press, 2004.

Hariss, Richard and Robert Lewis. 'Numbers Didn't Count: The Streets of Colonial Bombay and Calcutta'. *Urban History* 39, no. 2 (2012): 639–58.

Harrisson, Mark. *Public Health in British India: Anglo-Indian Preventive Medicine, 1859–1914*. Cambridge: Cambridge University Press, 1994.

Haynes, Douglas E. *Rhetoric and Ritual in Colonial India: The Shaping of a Public Culture in Surat City, 1852–1928*. Berkeley, Los Angeles, and Oxford: University of California Press, 1991.

Hazareesingh, Sandip. *The Colonial City and the Challenge of Modernity: Urban Hegemonies and Civic Contestations in Bombay City, 1900–1925*. Hyderabad: Orient Longman, 2007.

Headrick, Daniel. *Tentacles of Progress: Technology Transfer in the Age of Imperialism, 1850–1940*. New York: Oxford University Press, 1988.

Heitler, Richard. 'The Varanasi House Tax Hartal of 1810–11'. *Indian Economic and Social History Review* 9 (1972): 239–57.

Heitzman, J. *The City in South Asia*. London and New York: Routledge, 2008.

Hesse, C. 'The New Empiricism'. *Social and Cultural History* 1, no. 2 (2004): 201–7.

Holston, James and A. Appadurai. 'Cities and Citizenship'. In *Cities and Citizenship*, edited by J. Holston, pp. 1–20 Durham and London: Duke University Press, 1999.

Hornsby, Stephen J. 'Discovering the Mercantile City in South Asia: The Example of Early Nineteenth Century Calcutta'. *Journal of Historical Geography* 23, no. 2 (1997): 135–50.

Hughes, Thomas P. *Networks of Power: Electrification in Western Society, 1880–1930*. Baltimore: Johns Hopkins University Press, 1983.

Inglis, David. 'Sewers and Sensibilities: The Bourgeois Faecal Experience in the Nineteenth-century City'. In *The City and the Senses: Urban Culture Since 1500*, edited by Alexander Cowan and Jill Steward, pp. 105–30. Aldershot: Ashgate, 2007.

Jacobs, Jane. *The Death and Life of Great American Cities*. New York: Random House, 1992.

Jones, C. 'Peter Mandler's "Problem with Cultural History", or, Is Playtime Over?' *Social and Cultural History* 1, no. 2 (2004): 209–15.

Joshi, Chitra. 'Bonds of Community, Ties of Religion: Kanpur Textile Workers in the Early Twentieth Century'. *Indian Economic and Social History Review* 22, no. 3 (1985): 251–280.

———. *Lost Worlds: Indian Labour and Its Forgotten Histories*. New Delhi: Permanent Black, 2003.

Joshi, Sanjay. *Fractured Modernity: Making of a Middle Class in Colonial North India*. New Delhi: Oxford University Press, 2001.

Joshi, V.C., ed. *Rammohun Roy and the Process of Modernization in India*. Delhi: Vikas Publishing House, 1975.

Joyce, Patrick, ed. *Class: Oxford Reader*. Oxford: Oxford University Press, 1995.

———. 'The End of Social History?' *Social History* 20, no. 1 (1995): 73–91.

———. *The Rule of Freedom: Liberalism and the Modern City*. London and New York: Verso, 2003.

———. 'What is the Social in Social History?' *Past and Present* 206 (February 2010): 213–48.

Kaviraj, Sudipta. 'Filth and the Public Sphere: Concepts and Practices about Space in Calcutta'. *Public Culture* 10, no. 1 (1997): 83–113.

Kaur, Raminder. *Performative Politics and the Cultures of Hinduism: Public Uses of Religion in Western India*. London: Anthem Press, 2005.

Kerr, Ian J. 'Working Class Protest in 19th Century India: Example of Railway'. *Economic and Political Weekly* 20, no. 4 (26 January 1985): PE 34–PE 40.

Kidambi, Prashant. *The Making of an Indian Metropolis: Colonial Governance and Public Culture in Bombay, 1890–1920*. Aldershot: Ashgate, 2007.

King, P. *Crime, Justice and Discretion in England, 1740–1820*. Oxford: Oxford University Press, 2000.

Knight, Stephen. *Form and Ideology of Crime Fiction*. London: Macmillan, 1980.

Kopf, David. *British Orientalism and the Bengal Renaissance*. Berkeley and Los Angeles: University of California Press, 1969.

Kosambi, Meera. *Bombay in Transition: The Growth and Social Ecology of a Colonial City, 1880–1980*. Stockholm: Almqvist & Wiksell International, 1986.

Kumar, M. Satish. 'The Evolution of Spatial Ordering in Colonial Madras'. In *Postcolonial Geographies*, edited by Cheryl McEwan and Alison Blunt, pp. 85–98. London and New York: Continuum, 2002.

Kumar, Nita. *Artisans of Benares: Popular Culture and Identity, 1880–1986*. Princeton: Princeton University Press, 1989.

Lahiri-Choudhury, Deep Kanta. *Telegraphic Imperialism: Crisis and Panic in the Indian Empire, c. 1830–1920*. Basingstoke: Palgrave Macmillan, 2010.

Landes, Joan. *Women and the Public Sphere on the Age of the French Revolution*. Ithaca: Cornell University Press, 1988.

Lefebvre, Henri. *The Production of Space*, translated by Donald Nicholson Smith. Oxford: Blackwell Publishing, 1991.

Lefebvre, Henri. *Writings on Cities*, selected, translated, and introduced by E. Kofman and E. Lebas. Oxford: Blackwell Publishing, 1996.

Legg, Stephen. *Spaces of Colonialism: Delhi's Urban Governmentalities*. Oxford: Blackwell Publishing, 2004.

Lenin, V.I. 'Inflammable Material in World Politics' (speech given on 5 August 1908). *Collected Works*, vol. XV. Moscow, 1963.

Levine, Philippa. 'Venereal Disease, Prostitution and the Politics of Empire: The Case of British India'. *Journal of the History of Sexuality* 4, no. 4 (1994): 579–602.

Lutgendorf, Philip. *The Life of a Text: Performing the Ramcaritmanas of Tulsidas*. Berkeley and Los Angeles: University of California Press, 1991.

Major, Andrea. 'State and Criminal Tribes in Colonial Punjab: Surveillance, Control and the Reclamation of the Dangerous Classes'. *Modern Asian Studies* 33, no. 3 (1999): 657–88.

Majumdar, Rochona. *Marriage and Modernity: Family Values in Colonial Bengal*. Durham and London: Duke University Press, 2009.

Mandler, Peter. 'The Problem with Cultural History'. *Social and Cultural History* 1, no. 1 (2004): 94–117.

Marshall, Peter. 'The White Town of Calcutta Under the Rule of the East India Company'. *Modern Asian Studies* 34, no. 2 (2000): 307–31.

Martin, Alexander M. 'Sewage and the City: Filth, Smell and Representations of Urban Life in Moscow, 1770–1880'. *The Russian Review* 67, no. 2 (2008): 243–74.

Masselos, Jim. 'Audiences, Actors and Congress Dramas: Crowd Events in Bombay City in 1930'. *South Asia: Journal of South Asian Studies* 8, nos 1–2 (1985): 71–86.

McPherson, Kenneth. *The Muslim Microcosm: Calcutta, 1918 to 1935*. Weisbaden: Steiner, 1974.

Meller, Helen. *Patrick Geddes: Social Evolutionist and City Planner*. London: Routledge, 1990.

Messent, Peter. *The Crime Fiction Handbook*. Chichester: Wiley-Blackwell, 2013.

Metcalf, Thomas. *An Imperial Vision: Indian Architecture and Britain's Raj*. Berkeley and Los Angeles: University of California Press, 1989.

Mitchell, Timothy. *Colonising Egypt*. Cambridge: Cambridge University Press, 1988.

Morris, Morris D. *The Emergence of an Indian Labour Force: A Study of the Bombay Cotton Mills, 1854–1947*. Berkeley: University of California Press, 1965.

Mort, Frank. 'Scandalous Events: Metropolitan Culture and Moral Change in Post-Second World War London'. *Representations* 93, no. 1 (Winter 2006): 106–37.

Mitra, Radharaman. *Kolikata Darpan*. Calcutta: Subarnarekha, 1988.

Mrázek, Rudolf. *Engineers of Happy Land: Technology and Nationalism in a Colony*. Princeton, NJ: Princeton University Press, 2002.

Mukherjee, S.N. 'Bhadralok and Their Dals—Politics of Social Factions in Calcutta, c. 1820–1856'. In *The Urban Experience: Calcutta*, edited by Pradip Sinha, pp. 192–212 Calcutta: Riddhi-India, 1987.

———. *Calcutta: Essays in Urban History*. Calcutta: Subarnarekha, 1993.

———. 'Class, Caste and Politics in Calcutta, 1815–1838'. In *Elites in South Asia*, edited by Edmund Leach and S.N. Mukherjee, pp. 33–78 Cambridge: Cambridge University Press, 1970.

———. 'Daladali in Calcutta in the Nineteenth Century'. In *Calcutta: Myth and History*. Calcutta, 1976.

———. *Images and Realities: Nineteenth Century Calcutta in Bengali Literature, c. 1818–1910*. Kuruvila Zachariah Memorial Lecture 2004. Calcutta, 2005.

Nair, Janaki. *The Promise of the Metropolis: Bangalore's Twentieth Century*. New Delhi: Oxford University Press, 2005.

Nair, P.T. *A History of Calcutta's Streets*. Calcutta: Firma K.L.M., 1987.

Nandi, Sugata. 'Constructing the Criminal: Politics of the Social Imaginary of the Goonda'. *Social Scientist* 38, nos 3/4 (March–April 2010): 37–54.

Nield, Susan. 'Colonial Urbanism: The Development of Madras City in the Eighteenth and Nineteenth Centuries'. *Modern Asian Studies* 13 (1979): 217–46.

O'Hanlon, Rosalind. *Caste, Conflict and Ideology: Mahatma Jotirao Phule and Low Caste Protest in Nineteenth-Century Western India*. Cambridge: Cambridge University Press, 1985.

Oldenburg, Veena Talwar. *The Making of Colonial Lucknow, 1857–1877*. Princeton, NJ: Princeton University Press, 1984.

Orsini, Francesca. *The Hindi Public Sphere, 1920–1940*. New Delhi: Oxford University Press, 2006.

Pandey, Gyanendra. *The Construction of Communalism in Colonial North India*. New Delhi: Oxford University Press, 1990.

Paul, Ashit, ed. *Woodcut Prints of Nineteenth Century Calcutta*. Calcutta: Seagull Books, 1983.

Pleck, Elizabeth. *Domestic Tyranny: The Making of Social Policy Against Family Violence from Colonial Times to the Present*. Oxford: Oxford University Press, 1987.

Polk, K. *When Men Kill: Scenarios of Masculine Violence*. Cambridge: Cambridge University Press, 1994.

Prakash, Gyan. *Another Reason: Science and the Imagination of Modern India*. Princeton, NJ: Princeton University Press, 1999.

Prakash, Gyan and Douglas Haynes, eds. *Contesting Power: Resistance and Everyday Social Relations in South Asia*. Berkeley and Los Angeles: University of California Press, 1992.

Prashad, Vijay. 'The Technology of Sanitation in Colonial Delhi'. *Modern Asian Studies* 35, no. 1 (2001): 113–55.

Purcell, M. 'Citizenship and the Right to the Global City: Reimagining the Capitalist World Order'. *International Journal of Urban and Regional Research* 27, no. 3 (2003): 564–90.

Radhakrishna, M. *Dishonoured by History: "Criminal Tribes" and British Colonial Policy*. New Delhi: Orient Longman, 2001.

Raha, Kironmoy. 'Calcutta Theatre: 1835–1944'. In *Calcutta: The Living City*, edited by Sukanta Chaudhuri, vol. 1, pp. 186–94. Calcutta: Oxford University Press, 1990.

Raj, Kapil. 'The Historical Anatomy of a Contact Zone: Calcutta in the Eighteenth Century'. *Indian Economic and Social History Review* 48, no. 1 (2011): 55–82.

Ramanathan, U. 'Illegality and the Urban Poor'. *Economic and Political Weekly* 41, no. 29 (2006): 3193–7.

Rao, Anupama. 'Violence and Humanity: Or, Vulnerability as Political Subjectivity'. *Social Research* 78, no. 2 (2011): 607–32.

Ray, Alok, ed. *Nineteenth Century Studies*. Calcutta, 1974.

Ray, Nisith Ranjan. *Calcutta: The Profile of a City*. Calcutta: K.P. Bagchi, 1986.

Ray, Rajat K. *Social Conflict and Political Unrest in Bengal, 1875–1927*. New Delhi: Oxford University Press, 1984.

———. *Urban Roots of Indian Nationalism: Pressure Groups and Conflict of Interests in Calcutta City Politics, 1875–1939*. New Delhi: Vikas Publishing House, 1979.

Raychaudhuri, Tapan. 'Love in a Colonial Climate: Marriage, Sex and Romance in Nineteenth-century Bengal'. *Modern Asian Studies* 34, no. 2 (2000): 349–78.

———. 'Norms of Family Life and Personal Morality among the Bengali Hindu Elite, 1600–1850'. In *Aspects of Bengali History and Society*, edited by R. Van M. Baumer. Asian Studies at Hawaii, no. 12. Hawaii, 1975.

Rieger, Bernhard. '"Modern Wonders": Technological Innovation and Public Ambivalence in Britain and Germany, 1890s to 1933'. *History Workshop Journal* 55, no. 1 (Spring 2003): 152–76.

Rose, Mark. *Cities of Light and Heat*. University Park, PA: Penn State University Press, 1995.

Roy, Ananya. 'Slumdog Cities: Rethinking Subaltern Urbanism'. *International Journal of Urban and Regional Research* 35, no. 2 (2011): 223–38.

Roy, Pulakesh. 'The Story of the Mehter Strike in Calcutta in 1877'. *Revolt Studies* 1, no. 1 (1985).

Sanyal, Rajat. *Voluntary Associations and the Urban Public Life in Bengal (1815–1876): An Aspect of Social History*. Calcutta: Riddhi-India, 1980.

Sarkar, Sumit. '"Kaliyuga", "Chakri" and "Bhakti": Ramakrishna and His Times'. In *Writing Social History*. New Delhi: Oxford University Press, 1999.

———. 'The City Imagined: Calcutta of the Nineteenth and the Early Twentieth Centuries'. In *Writing Social History*. New Delhi: Oxford University Press, 1999.

———. 'The Conditions and Nature of Subaltern Militancy: Bengal from Swadeshi to Non-Cooperation, c. 1905–22'. In *Subaltern Studies III: Writings on South Asian History and Society*, edited by Ranajit Guha, pp. 271–320 New Delhi: Oxford University Press, 1984.

———. *The Swadeshi Movement in Bengal*. New Delhi: Oxford University Press, 2011 (original edition 1973).

Sarkar, Tanika. *Hindu Wife, Hindu Nation: Community, Religion and Cultural Nationalism*. Bloomington: Indiana University Press, 2001.

———.'Rhetoric against Age of Consent: Resisting Colonial Reason and Death of a Child Wife'. *Economic and Political Weekly* 28, no. 36 (4 September 1993): 1869–78.

———. 'Talking about Scandals: Religion, Law and Love in Late Nineteenth Century Bengal'. *Studies in History* 13, no. 1 (1997): 63–95.

Schatzberg, Eric. 'Culture and Technology in the City: Opposition to Mechanised Street Transportation in Late-nineteenth-Century America'. In *Technologies of Power: Essays in Honor of Thomas Parke Hughes and Agatha Chipley Hughes*, edited by Michael T. Allen and Gabrielle Hecht, pp. 57–94. Cambridge, Massachusetts: MIT Press, 2001.

Schmid, David. 'Imagining Safe Urban Space: the Contribution of Detective Fiction to Radical Geography'. *Antipode* 27, no. 3 (1995): 242–69.

Sen, Atreyee. *Shiv Sena Women: Violence and Communalism in a Bombay Slum*. London: C. Hurst & Co., 2007.

Sen, Ranjit. *A Stagnating City: Calcutta in the Eighteenth Century*. Calcutta: Institute of Historical Studies, 2000.

Sen, Samita. '"Without His Consent?": Marriage and Women's Migration in Colonial India'. *International Labour and Working-Class History* 65 (Spring, 2004): 77–104.

———. *Women and Labour in Late Colonial India: The Bengal Jute Industry*. Cambridge: Cambridge University Press, 1999.

Sen, Sukumar. *Crime Kahinir Kalkranti*. Calcutta: Ananda Publishers, 1988.

Sengoopta, Chandak. *Imprint of the Raj: How Fingerprinting Was Born in Colonial India*. London: Macmillan, 2003.

Sengupta, Tania. 'Between Country and City: Fluid Spaces of Provincial Administrative Towns in Nineteenth-century Bengal'. *Urban History* 39, no. 1 (February 2012): 56–82.

Shoemaker, R. 'Male Honour and the Decline of Public Violence in 18th-century London'. *Social History* 26 (2001): 190–208.

Siddiqui, Majid Hayat. 'History and Society in a Popular Rebellion: Mewat, 1920–33'. *Comparative Studies in Society and History* 28 (1986): 442–67.

Sinha, Pradip. *Calcutta in Urban History*. (Calcutta: Firma K.L.M. Private Limited, 1978.

———, ed. *The Urban Experience: Calcutta*. Calcutta: Riddhi-India, 1987.

Sircar, Sanjay. 'Mou-rani: A Lost 1940s Bengali Pornographic Street Text'. *South Asian Popular Culture* 4, no. 1 (2006): 87–90.

Sripantha. *Mohanto Elokeshi Sambad*. Calcutta: Ananda Publishers, 1984.

Stewart, David M. 'Cultural Work, City Crime, Reading Pleasure'. *American Literary History* 9, no. 4 (1997): 676–701.

Stewart, Gordon T. *Jute and Empire: The Calcutta Jute Wallahs and the Landscapes of Empire*. Manchester: Manchester University Press, 1998.

Strange, C. 'Masculinities, Intimate Femicide and the Death Penalty in Australia, 1890–1920'. *British Journal of Criminology* 43, no. 2 (2003): 310–39.

Tambe, Ashwini. *Codes of Misconduct: Regulating Prostitution in Late Colonial Bombay*. Minneapolis: University of Minnesota Press, 2009.

Thomas, Helen. 'Stories of Plain Territory: The Maidan, Calcutta'. In *The Unknown City: Contesting Architecture and Social Space*, edited by Iain Borden, Joe Kerr, Jane Rendell, and Alice Pivarro, pp. 138–59 Cambridge, Massachusetts: MIT Press, 2002.

Tyrwhitt, Jaqueline, ed. *Patrick Geddes in India*. London: Lund Humphries, 1947.

Urban, Hugh. 'The Marketplace and the Temple: Economic Metaphors and Religious Meanings in the Folk Songs of Colonial Bengal'. *Journal of Asian Studies* 60, no. 4 (November 2001): 1085–114.

Walkowitz, Judith. *City of Dreadful Delight: Narratives of Sexual Danger in Late-Victorian London*. Chicago: University of Chicago Press, 1992.

———. 'Jack the Ripper and the Myth of Male Violence'. *Feminist Studies* 8, no. 3 (Fall 1982): 543–74.

———. *Prostitution and Victorian Society: Women, Class and the State*. Cambridge: Cambridge University Press, 1980.

Warren, James F. *Rickshaw Coolie: A People's History of Singapore, 1880–1940*. Singapore: Singapore University Press, 2003.

Watts, C. 'Thinking about the X Factor, or, What's the Cultural History of Cultural History?' *Social and Cultural History* 1, no. 2 (2004): 217–24.

White, Luise. *The Comforts of Home: Prostitution in Colonial Nairobi*. Chicago: University of Chicago Press, 1990.

———.'Women's Domestic Labour in a Colonial City: Prostitution in Colonial Nairobi, 1900–1950'. In *Patriarchy and Class: African Women at Home and in the Workplace*, edited by Jane Parpart and Sharon Stichter, pp. 139–60. Boulder, CO: Westview Press, 1988.

Wiener, Martin. *Men of Blood: Violence, Manliness and Criminal Justice in Victorian England*. Cambridge: Cambridge University Press, 2004.

Yang, Anand A. *Crime and Criminality in British India*. Tucson: University of Arizona Press, 1985.

Yeoh, Brenda. *Contesting Space: Power Relations and the Urban Built Environment in Colonial Singapore*. Singapore: Singapore University Press, 2003.

Index

aaguner kol (fire machine) 65
adulteration of food 68
adultery 6, 126, 128, 130, 139
Amrita Bazar Patrika 277
Andamans 128, 213
anonymity 17, 207–8, 227, 231, 244, 245, 246
Anti-Circular Society 286
anti-cow-killing agitation (1895) 261, 266, 269
anti-government sentiments 6, 273–8
anti-Marwari riots (1918) 17, 249
anti-police riots (1891–1918) 30, 35, 254–63
aqueducts 74, 173, 191
assaults 84, 103, 175, 199, 237, 250, 253, 266, 271, 288

baganbaris (recreational houses) 243
Bahoba Choudda Ain (Jubilations for Act XIV) 154, 154n110
Bailey, Peter 100, 104
Bakr Id 249, 266–7; anti-cow-killing agitation during 266, 269; *qurbani* (sacrifice) of cows 267; riots (1910) 269
Banerjee, Sumanta 5–6, 91, 124, 149
Banerjee, Surendranath 192, 205, 277
Banerji, A.C. 284
Basu, Amritalal 63, 254, 290
Basu, Subho 262
bazaar rivalries 203
Beadon Square 288
Beliaghata 47, 231, 256, 271
belonging and unbelonging, experiences of 79–85
Bengalee (newspaper) 191, 203, 250, 254, 262–3, 276–7, 279, 282
Bengali Commissioners of the Municipality 71
Bengali society, *bhadra*-fication (gentrification) of 150
bhaaries (human water-carriers) 73
bhadralok 37–8, 67, 79–80, 95, 120, 123
bhadramahila (genteel woman) 151
Bhawanipore 48, 82, 144, 153
bheesties (water-carriers) 75, 199
bidesh (foreign land) 132
black sailors 219
Black Town 7, 10, 12, 53, 62, 73, 169, 180, 241

boarding houses 243n123
Bolton, C.W. 261, 269
borolok (high in wealth and status) 126
Bose, Upendranath 126–7
Bowbazar 39, 61, 92, 94, 144, 180, 219, 232, 281
Brata Samiti 287
brothels in Calcutta 146; *See also* Sonagatchi, red-light area of
budmashes 216, 260; characterization of 251
building and street bye-laws 46
burglary 235, 239, 246
Burn Iron Company 284
Burrabazar 8, 18, 49, 61, 80–1, 213, 219, 243, 270n82, 281; business area 48; Marwaris of 84; traders and moneylenders of 170
bustees (ill-ventilated huts) 40, 45, 49–51, 57, 188, 269, 274
butchers 23, 64, 201, 204

Calcutta: cartographies of crime and safety 241–7; caste-ordered layouts 51; as 'City of Palaces' 7, 12, 38, 290; civic infrastructure of 39; as colonial metropolis 6; colonial spaces 41–52; cultural and social history of 4–12; as dangerous city 225–40; everyday spaces 26–32; importance for British India 7; insanitary condition in 183; in its early days 38–41; layout of 58; lived experience 41–52; locality, community, and vernacular spaces 52–64; map of 11; metropolitan visions 41–52; migration, issue of 18; plan for turning into the model of London 49; residential settlement pattern 7; 'safe' and 'unsafe' zones in 247; sanitary condition of 183; social order 22, 33; steps for improvement of 41–2; subaltern cultures 26–32; urban culture 22; urban population in 19; urban public sphere 26–32; women in 19–20
Calcutta Improvement Trust (CIT) 42–3, 47, 50, 181; rebuilding programme 48
Calcutta Tramway Company (CTC) 70, 78
caste: hierarchies 74, 84, 91; privileges 76; (occupational) settlements 40
caste-panchayats 266
Chadak festival 166, 168–9
Chakrabarty, Dipesh 15, 261, 264–6
chhotolok (lower classes) 120
Chitpore 39, 57, 63, 74, 144, 153, 167; riots (1897) 255–6
citizenship, concept of 25
cityscape of Calcutta 48
civic amenities, modernization of 78
civic public spaces 25
'civil society' in colonial India 31
clean water: shortage of 75; supply of 75
cohabitation, practice of 99
coin-forging trade 222–3
Colinga Bazar Street 153
College Square 35, 283, 285
Collin, E.W. 289
colonial technology 66, 113–19, 224

communal riots 16–18, 34
community identity, radicalization of 279
conjugality and sexuality, cultural constructions of 124
Conservancy Act VI of 1863 183
Contagious Diseases Acts (CDA) 145, 153, 219
coolies and the poorer classes 46–7
corporeal chastisement 125
counterfeiting coins and trademarks, cases of 222–3
'court fees' stamps, counterfeiting of 222–3
Cow Protection Societies 272
cows, sacrificial slaughter of. See *qurbani* (sacrifice) of cows
criminal activity in Calcutta 207; Annual Police Reports on 217; anthropometry and fingerprinting 216–17; 'bad characters' and thieves, influx of 215; break-ins and burglaries 209, 215; caste- and region-based identification of criminal 'gangs' 218; constructing the 'criminal' 215–21; counterfeiting coins and trademarks, cases of 222; 'court fees' stamps, counterfeiting of 225; under the cover of respectability and ostentation 212; ethnographic taxonomies of crime 218; false mercantile establishments 212; fraud and forgery, cases of 235; fraudulent firms, operation of 222; *ghat marra* (those who stole people's clothes) 211; homicides 210; Indian Penal Code and 236; known offenders, records of 216; middle-class criminals 221–5; murders and robbery of prostitutes 155–62; pests of the society 216; printing of false currency notes 224; professional criminal class 216; public hangings and brandings 209; 'regular' urban spaces, use of 246; religious communities in their role as criminals 217
Criminal Investigation Department (CID) 222
criminal tribes 232
Curzon, Lord 30, 202, 279, 287
cyclones, disaster due to 89, 110–11

dalapatis (group leaders) 77, 92n13
Dalhousie, Lord 49
Dalhousie Square 43, 49
Darogar Daptar (Priyanath Mukhopadhyay) 208, 226–8, 234. *See also* Mukhopadhyay, Priyanath
Das, Ramanath 60, 62
death rituals, performance of 74
Deb, Binoykrishna 52
Debganer Martye Agaman (Durgacharan Ray) 54, 62, 66, 82
decadence and disasters, issue of 110–13
dengue fever, spread of (1872 and 1874) 89
Dharamtala market 203–5
Dharma Sabha 75
displacement and competition, among Bengalis and non-Bengalis 84

doggerels and street humour 91–5
domestic violence 135, 139
domesticity and family, cultural constructions of 124
Doyle, Conan 226
drinking water, supply of 73
Dupont 245
Durga Puja 119, 166–7, 283
Dutta, Mahendranath 73
Dutta, Prankrishna 67–9, 154

East India Company 7, 41, 57–8, 92–3, 209, 281
East Indian Railway 19, 253
Elokeshi–Mohunta case of 1874 4, 6, 124, 127–33; courtroom scene of 129
erotic violence. *See* sexual violence
European Justices of Peace 12
exodus 265, 274

false currency notes, printing of 224
family hospitals 274
famine of 1865–6 55
female sexuality, in bhadralok writings 121
fines 72, 181, 185, 188, 190, 200
fingerprinting 216–17
filtered water supply 192n119
folk artists and street performers 87
folk theatre 109, 167
foreign goods, boycott of 280
forgeries 92, 207, 219, 221, 223–5, 235
Fort William 38–9, 193, 242
Fraser, Andrew 289
fraudulent firms 222
Freitag, Sandria 28

Gajan festival 93, 168
Ganges River 66, 69, 73, 118
gas lights, for public lighting 71
Geddes, Patrick 47–8, 181
gender and class, cultural constructions of 124
gender hierarchies 135, 145
ghats 25, 39, 53, 55, 58–61, 63, 74, 176, 211
ghee 68, 83, 84, 148; contamination of 272
Ghosh, Girish 63
Ghous, Mullah Gholam 205
global capitalism 2
goalas (milkmen) 78, 200
gomasta (commercial bill-collector) 213
Goonda Act of 1923 251
Gooptu, Nandini 14, 249
Government of India Acts 20
groundwater contamination 73
Guha, Ranajit 87–8, 95, 104–5, 164

Habermas, Jürgen 27, 126
Hackney Carriage Act (1864 and 1866) 175, 194
hackney carriages 23, 34, 78, 83, 158, 163, 175, 178, 194–5, 206, 235, 254
halalcore system 198
Hansen, Thomas Blom 31
Harrison, Mark 190n112, 192
Harrison Road 203, 258, 261, 269
Hendua Tank 73
Hewett, J.P. 269
Hindoo Patriot 72, 200, 252

Hindu conjugal norms 130
Hindu patriarchy 130
Hindu residence, idea of 192
Hogg Market 76, 204
Hogg, Stuart 204–5
holdey bhatar (yellow husband) 148
Holmes 228, 245
Hooghly, River 9, 19, 38, 59
horse-driven carriages 194
hotels 20, 40, 43, 110, 233, 243, 244
house tax: assessment of 71; imposition of 197
house-letting 40
Howrah bridge 9, 43, 45, 48, 69, 89, 114, 195; portrayal of 116
hutments, breaking up of 51
Hutom, *See* Tagore, Kshitindranath

Indian Daily News 270, 272
Indian Justices of Peace 206
Indian Mirror 289
Indian nationalism 13, 31
Indian Penal Code 236, 290
Insolvency Act (1830) 93
intimate violence 125, 135–41, 143

jatra (Bengali indigenous theatre) 94, 109
*jemadar*s (intermediary sanitary officers) 198, 242, 288
jihad, declaration of 270
jolahas 255
Jorasanko 40n5, 41, 70–1, 73, 145–6, 219
Justices of Peace Committee 74
jute mills in Bengal: closure of 215–16; demand for labour 265; labour recruitment patterns 265; migrant workers in 265; scramble for jobs in 266

Kalami, Jaffar 270
Kali Age 119
Kalighat, temple of 64, 283–4
Kalikata Kamalalaya 90
kaviraj (physician) 76
Kaviraj, Sudipta 24, 35, 66, 67n87, 182, 191, 280
kerani 165
Kerr, Ian 202
kheud (part of a song that is sung extempore) 96–7, 102
*khotta*s (offensive term for Hindi-speaking migrants) 112
kobi-songs (poet-songs) 88, 95–104; compositions of 102; dig-and-retort format of 97; exchange of ideas and sentiments 101; historical evolution of 96n23; kheud element of 102; lack of classical restraint in 102; messages to the audience 100; metalanguage underlying 104; pleasure and bodily excitement in 98; rhythmic dance routines 101; role-playing 101; social and caste rivalries and aspirations 103; social vulnerability of poets 103; themes of 98

Lambert 174, 255
land acquisition, patterns of 5
Lefebvre, Henri 21; city, concept of 21; urban planning model 22

lodges 243
Lottery Committee 41–2
Maidan 7, 35, 43, 48, 73, 193, 246, 281, 286
male 'proprietary rights,' assertion of 135
Manicktala market 271, 275
manual labour, unorganized sector of 202
mapping of the city 241–7
marginalization of the trade, process of 142
Marwari tradesmen 48, 80, 83–4, 153, 203, 260, 269–72
masonry (*pucca*) houses 40
Meanjahn Darogar Ekrarnama (The Confessions of Meanjahn, Darogah of Police) 227
Mechhuabazar (fishmarket) 51, 63, 219, 243, 256
methars (scavengers) 23, 78, 197
migrants: alienation of 82; women migrants 144, 147
migration, social costs of 80
Millat (Muhammadan paper) 272
Mitra, Rajendralal 54–5, 206
'mob' action, idea of 251
modernity, idea of 14
morality and purity, cultural constructions of 124
mosques, demolition of 269
motor cars 9, 171, 177, 179–80, 271
Mukhopadhyay, Priyanath 161, 208, 226–30, 236, 239, 243–7; crime stories 218, 230; *Darogar Daptar* 226–8
Mullick, Rajendra 77
municipal administration and police, in Calcutta 215
municipal bodies, politics of 5
Municipal Corporation 9, 11, 57, 152, 189
municipal drains, in Calcutta 89
municipal police constabulary 18
Municipal Ward Committees 278
murder 6, 12, 157, 160–1, 207, 225, 231, 232, 234; Elokeshi murder case 4, 6, 124, 127–138; Sonagatchi murder case 135–141

Nabakrishna Deb, Raja 57, 93
Nakhoda mosque 260, 262–3, 273
Naqqash (Muhammadan paper) 271n85, 272
native urban criminals, classification of 216
Nawab of Oudh 105
night-soil service 183, 197
Nimtala Burning Ghat controversy 74
nuisances, in the public streets 173
Nutan Bazar 76

obscenity, campaign against 95n20
occupational and caste habitation, patterns of 52
Ochterlony monument 281
oil lamps, used in public spaces 42, 71, 72
Old Delhi Municipal Corporation (DMC) 21n54
omnibuses 9, 78, 139, 171
Oriental Gas Company 71, 72
Oriya 40, 83, 103, 196, 196n31, 227

paanwallahs 158
Pakshi, Rupchand 64
Pal, Bepin 287
Pal, Krishnadas 206
Pal, Radha Charan 288n164, 289
palki (palanquin) 193–4
Palmer's Bridge 187
panic 257, 273–4
pan-Islamism, rise of 270
paras 51, 58, 61, 80
Paris sewers, reconstruction of 188
Park Street 43–4, 48
partition of Bengal 279
pavements, for Indian pedestrians 115, 180–1
pedestrians 34, 71, 72, 115, 163, 172, 175, 177, 179, 180
phooka (injecting salt into cows) 200
physical violation, of neatly ordered spaces 34, 124, 248
picketing 12, 279, 286
plague riots (1898) 273–8
poddars (pawnbrokers) 158, 210
Police Acts of the 1830s and 1867 172
police commissioner 174, 181, 217, 219, 228, 241, 249, 254–6, 258, 289
police repression 249–54
political leadership, in Calcutta 291
politics of the poor 14–15
population of Calcutta 41
Prachya Sukh (Happiness in the East) 76
printed street songs 104–9
private privies, construction of 184
prostitutes 230, 233, 235, 243; access to money and social independence 149; collusion with thieves 219; in colonial India 142; female subculture 149; *holdey bhatar* (yellow husband) 148; illegal marriage and 142; medical examination for checking venereal diseases 154; middle-class perceptions 152; murders and robbery of 155–62; as proxy wives to harlots 141–55; public decorum on 219; reformist campaigns 150; serial killing of 124; sexual abuse and physical violence 149; sexual economies of 143; sexual relations, commoditization of 153; Sonagatchi, red-light area of 124; in urban culture 141–55; venereal diseases scare 148, 154; vilification of 142, 148, 150
Protective Agency for Women and Children 134n33
public culture, of Indian cities 13
public entertainment 169
public sphere, politicization of 20

qurbani (sacrifice) of cows 266–7; Marwari community's objection to 269–70

race course 160, 246
racial violence 249–54
racing grounds 234
rain-gambling 260n47
rajbaris (aristocratic residences in Calcutta) 282
rakhis 279
Ramlila celebrations 170

ranger kaj (colourful crime) 157
Ratha Yatra festivals 167–8
Ras Mela 166–7, 169
Registrar of Hackney Carriages 195
religious fundamentalism 31
religious rituals 77
residence and sociability, Bengali notions of 37
residential areas, formation of 40
Reynold's Mysteries 226
Richards, E.P. 43–6, 179; report on Calcutta's 'street-less state' 179; report on sociological map of Calcutta 46–7
Riponian reforms (1882) 20
Ronaldshay, Lord 260n45
rubbish, collection of 183
rumour 12, 105, 128, 237, 255, 256, 274, 276
rural–urban divide 90

Sahar Chitra (Picture of the City) 76, 84
sahib company (white man's company) 70, 115
sailors 217, 219, 242–3, 245
salt water lakes 186
Samachar Darpan 52, 65
Samay (newspaper) 262
Sandhya (evening daily) 282
Sangbad Prabhakar 195
sardars 196, 266
Sarkar, Sumit 6, 284
Sarkar, Tanika 6, 128
Sastri, Shivnath 55
sawng performances 93, 166, 169
scandals, debates on 126–35
scavengers 23, 34, 57, 78, 80, 163, 183, 197, 202, 206, 274, 297
Seditious Meetings Act (1907) 287
Sekaler Darogar Kahini (Daroga Tales from the Past) 227
semi-public latrines 188
settlements and layout, of Calcutta 38–41
sewage and drainage systems 184; campaign against sanitary regimes 192; Conservancy Committee on 187; and insanitary condition in Calcutta 183; management of 189; Municipal Conservancy Offences 185; privies connected to public sewers 185; semi-public latrines 188; sewers, building of 74; underground drainage scheme 186; water supply 186
sex industry 119, 125
sex ratios 19, 135
sexual freedom for women 131, 138
sexual liberty 138
sexual relations, commoditization of 153
sexual sin, male and female complicity in 138
sexual transgression 124
sexual violation of wives 134
sexual violence 124, 135, 155–62
Shambazar riots (1891) 255, 258, 261, 269
Shil, Hiralal 204, 205
shop looting 271, 288
Sinha, Kaliprasanna 68, 95, 119, 166
Sinha, Pradip 8, 51
sircars (middling-level clerks) 158
Sketches of the Night-Owl 105
slaughterhouses 42, 201
snidhel churi (housebreaking) 232

snidh-kathi (iron crowbar) 236
social anarchy 120
social imaginary, in nineteenth-century Calcutta 64–79
social justice 229, 231, 240
social marginalization 273
social order 22, 33, 77, 86–7, 91, 104, 123, 226, 293, 295
social organization, ideological constructs of 263
social prestige 67, 230
social purity reformers 134
Somprakash 55, 75, 127
Sonagatchi, red-light area of 124; intimate violence, case of 135–41
songs on Calcutta 87–9
Souttar, W.M. 219, 251
Star Theatre 254
stories of sexual intrigue 122
Strand Bank 9, 50
street brawls and rioting 203
street culture, of Calcutta 91–5; kobi-songs 88, 95–104; printed street songs 104–9
street entertainment, based on religious and sensual themes 88
street lighting: electric lights 71; gas lights 71, 72; oil lamps 71; protest against taxation for 71–2; rent for 71
street musicians and singers 92
street offences 172
street singing and processions 166, 283–4, 294
street songs, printed 104–9; *hujuk* (temporary excitement) 105; importance of 109; patronage of 114; *pnachali* 106; role of 'immediacy' 105; Sketches of the Night-Owl 105
streets of Calcutta: accidents on 176, 177; casualties caused by careless driving 175; conflicts and its resolutions 164–82; festivals and entertainment dominating 165; forms of transport 171; mechanized vehicles 176; meshes 47; privy wars 183–92; public lighting 71; regulation of traffic and street activity 172; renaming of 57; sanitary rules 172; street offences 172; trams running on 177
strikes and trade disputes 192–206
student messes 285
students 7, 17, 55, 83, 160, 244, 253, 283–7
Students New Society 287
Suburban Slaughter House Act 201
Sulabh Patrika 67
Swadeshi agitation (1905–7) 6, 24, 83, 253; and transformation of urban public spaces 279–91

Tagore, Dwarkanath 196
Tagore, Kshitindranath 50, 70, 73, 84, 219; portrayal of the festivals 168
Tagore, Rabindranath 71, 73n109, 282
Talla 255, 261–2, 268–9
taxes: for civic amenities 71; house tax 71, 197; income tax 72; municipal 72, 182, 206; repeal of 197
technological innovations, in nineteenth-century Calcutta 65, 79
thanas (police stations) 58, 290

theatres 28, 60, 63, 78, 94, 104, 109, 128, 160, 174, 254, 281, 292
tolah methars 183, 184, 197–8
Town Hall 7, 10, 35, 39, 54, 60, 280, 281, 285–6
Town Improvement Committee 41–2
town-planning, European concept of 180
trade union 15, 202
traffic: accidents, injury and death rates in 176, 177; management of 179
trams 9, 69–70, 78, 171, 178
tramways 1, 32, 33, 37, 78, 114, 206

uniform civic code, standards of 264
Upadhyaya, Brahmabandhab 282
Upper Circular Road 57, 258
urban communities 14, 17, 79–84
urban dislocation, civic markers of 111
urban employment 151
urban order and disorder: anonymity, opportunity, and crime in 208–15; phenomenon of 182, 192–206
urban planning: in Calcutta 12n29, 84; Lefebvrian model of 22; Western conceptions of 37
urban policing 248
urban poor: in north India 14; politics of 254–63
urban public: emergence of 87; mosques, festivals, and community 263–73; in nineteenth-century Calcutta 105, 119–22; spatial and customary tensions 263–73; swadeshi unrest and transformation of 279–90; urban public sphere 6, 40
urban rentiership, growth of 40
urban social space, in Calcutta 86, 119–21
urban socialities 17
urban street cultures 87
urban transport 174, 294
urbanization 1, 3, 59, 67
Ure (Bengali distortion of Oriya) 40

vernacular print culture 109
vernacular spaces 52–64
Victoria Memorial 286
Vidyabhushan, Dwarkanath 55, 75
vigilance committees 274

wage labour 16, 142
waste-disposal services 73
water supply 9, 66, 74–5, 90, 186–8, 296
Wauchope, S. 211, 241, 249
Wellesley, Lord 9, 25, 41–2
widows 99n35, 112n80, 144, 238, 240
Wiener, Martin 135, 136n38, 160n129
women in Calcutta 19–20; marginalization of sexuality of 160; as migrants 144, 147
working classes 104, 136
World War: First 15n38, 21, 48, 69n95, 161, 264, 270; Second 69n95

Yeoh, Brenda 174

zamindari privies 188

About the Author

Anindita Ghosh is Senior Lecturer in Modern Indian History at the University of Manchester. She is the author of *Power in Print: Popular Publishing and the Politics of Language and Culture in a Colonial Society* (Oxford University Press, 2006), and has published widely on popular culture, print, women, and the city. Ghosh has featured on interviews and programmes on BBC Radio 3 and Radio 4 and is also a Fellow of the Royal Historical Society, London, UK.